KICK-ASS

KICK-ASS. ISBN: 9781848565340. Published by Titan Books, a division of Titan Publishing Group Ltd., 144 Southwark St, London, SE1 0UP. © 2008, 2009 and 2010 Mark Millar and John S. Romita. All Rights Reserved.
KICK-ASS, the Kick-Ass logo and all characters and content herein and the likenesses thereof are trademarks of Mark Millar and John S. Romita, unless otherwise expressly noted. No part of this book may be
reproduced or transmitted in any form or by any means, without the express written permission of the publisher. Names, characters, places and incidents featured in this publication are either the product of the
author's imagination or used fictitiously. Any resemblance to actual persons, living or dead (except for satirical purposes), is entirely coincidental. A CIP catalogue record for this title is available from the British Library.
First edition: February 2010. Printed in Spain. Please visit our website: www.titanbooks.com or email us at: readerfeedback@titanemail.com.

10 9 8 7 6 5 4 3 2 1

KICK-ASS

Writer & Co-Creator
MARK MILLAR

Penciller & Co-Creator
JOHN ROMITA JR.

Inker
TOM PALMER

Colourist
DEAN WHITE

Letterer
CHRIS ELIOPOULOS

Assistant Editor
MICHAEL HORWITZ

Editor
JOHN BARBER

Collection Editor: **JENNIFER GRÜNWALD**
Assistant Editors: **ALEX STARBUCK & JOHN DENNING**
Editor, Special Projects: **MARK D. BEAZLEY**
Senior Editor, Special Projects: **JEFF YOUNGQUIST**
Senior Vice President of Sales: **DAVID GABRIEL**
Book Designer: **SPRING HOTELING**
SVP of Business Affairs & Talent Management: **DAVID BOGART**

Editor in Chief: **JOE QUESADA**
Publisher: **DAN BUCKLEY**
Executive Producer: **ALAN FINE**

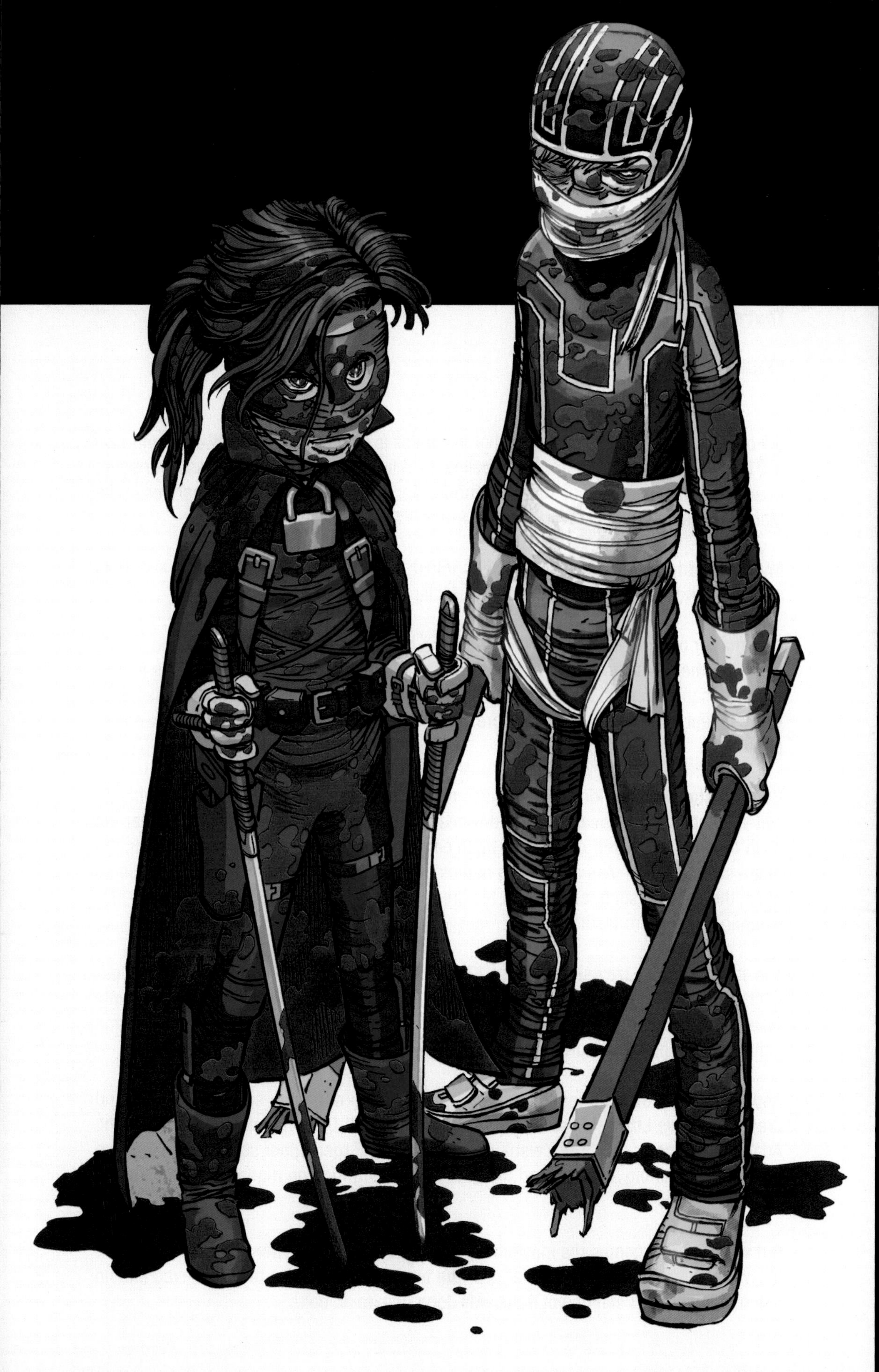

"KICK-ASS?"

Yup.

"KICK-ASS??"

That's it.

"KICK-ASS????"

So this is how the best-selling author in comics is going to follow up *Wanted* and *Civil War*? The guy that brought us Angelina Jolie as a naked, ruthless assassin dripping in wax, the guy who gave us Captain America versus Iron Man for all the marbles in the Marvel Universe? His next work was *Kick-Ass*???

My reaction to the title of Mark Millar's latest, greatest magnum opus was less than stellar. But he just smiled. Because Mark Millar gets it.

As a matter of fact, Mark got it way before the rest of us. See, If you're gonna do a book featuring the most Kick-Ass writing, the most Kick-Ass art, the most Kick-Ass action, then you can't afford to be shy, you just call it the way you see it. And in this case, with this concept and these creators, there was no doubt this comic would be Kick-Ass in every way.

Here's a story about a kid who imagines himself as a real life crime-fighter, combating evil with homemade weapons and devices available at your local Wal-Mart. What kid hasn't imagined himself grabbing a trash can lid and a baseball bat and wandering the mean streets Kickin' Ass and taking names? Dave Lizewski IS THAT KID! That kid in all of us, the kid who sought to live out his dreams and bust some bad guy ass in real-life-wannabe-superhero fashion.

The minute Dave Lizewski becomes Kick-Ass and steps into the neighborhood, your heart leaps with hope as he confronts local gang members. Your heart subsequently falls and is crushed as Dave receives his first serious beat down at the hands of same gangstas. The blood, the grit, the bloody failure. It drew us in, we couldn't look away.

And as Dave Lizewski rises again with renewed determination, so do our hopes and dreams. If Dave Lizewski can overcome, than so can I! Dave has no super powers, no Adamantium claws, no spider webbing, no gamma charged super strength. He just has a heart twice as big as yours and the guts to see it through no matter what. This is the heart of Kick-Ass!

But with courage comes the inevitable Mark Millar-imagined hyper-real super-violence. It's brutal, it's messy and it's so far over the top it has to be seen to be believed and no one on planet earth can depict it the way John Romita Jr. can.

John Romita Jr. has drawn every Marvel character imaginable. He's the ace, the closer, the go-to guy. He's the closest thing to clutch that exists in the comics biz. A few years back, he and Millar combined for the first time to bring us the super-charged epic *Wolverine: Enemy of the State*. Sales soared and fans demanded that these two team up again as often as possible. When they answered the call, was there any doubt it would be as Kick-Ass as possible?

Romita Jr's. storytelling in *Kick-Ass* is the most cinematic, widescreen, high-def he's ever attempted. The pacing, the drama, the violence in these pages is as brutal as any you will ever find. It makes you cringe and wince and ultimately leaves you with your slack-jawed mouth scraping the bottom of the floor. John Romita Jr. leaves it all on the page, he holds nothing back here and in doing so produces the seminal work of his career. Millar and Romita Jr. are peas and carrots, bees and honey, cookies and cream. Simply put, they are irresistible.

HIT-GIRL! RED MIST! BIG DADDY! It's all KICK-ASS, all the time, as only two of the brightest stars in the history of graphic novels could depict it.

When *Kick-Ass* hit the stands, fans hit the streets talking about the best damn comic to come down the pike in a long damn time. *Kick-Ass* is courageous. *Kick-Ass* is contagious. You had to get *Kick-Ass*!

It used to be that you had to be grim and gritty in order to grab everyone's attention. Now you most definitely have to Kick-Ass.

So what the hell are you waiting for? Turn the page and prepare to go KICK some ASS!

Rob Liefeld
January 2010

Rob Liefeld was one of the forefathers of the 1990s comics revolution — co-creating Cable *and* Deadpool, *and transforming* New Mutants *into* X-Force *before helping found Image Comics with his original property* Youngblood. *In 2007, Liefeld returned to Marvel to pencil the* Onslaught Reborn *miniseries.*

ONE

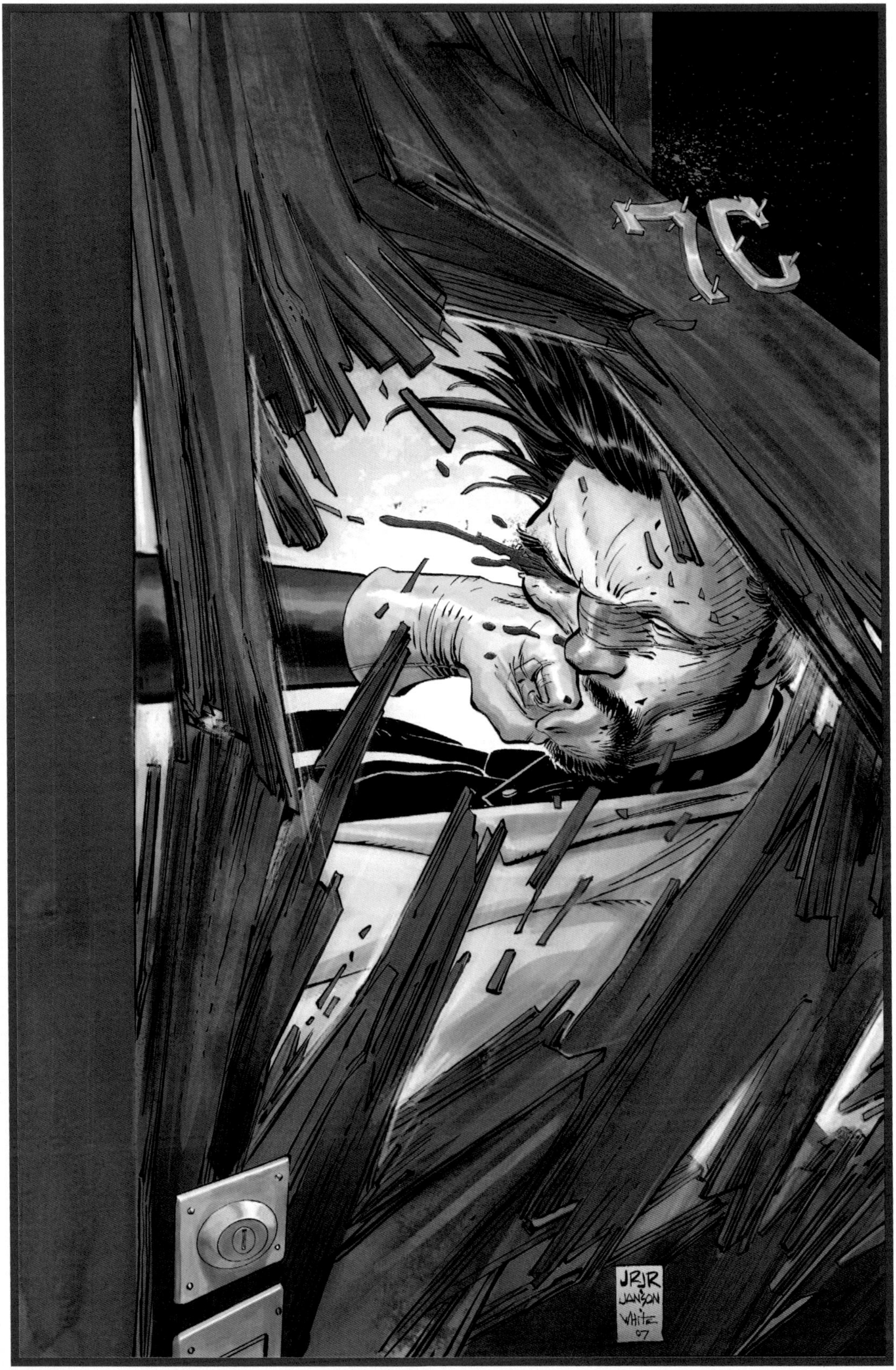
7C
JRJR
JANSON
WHITE
07

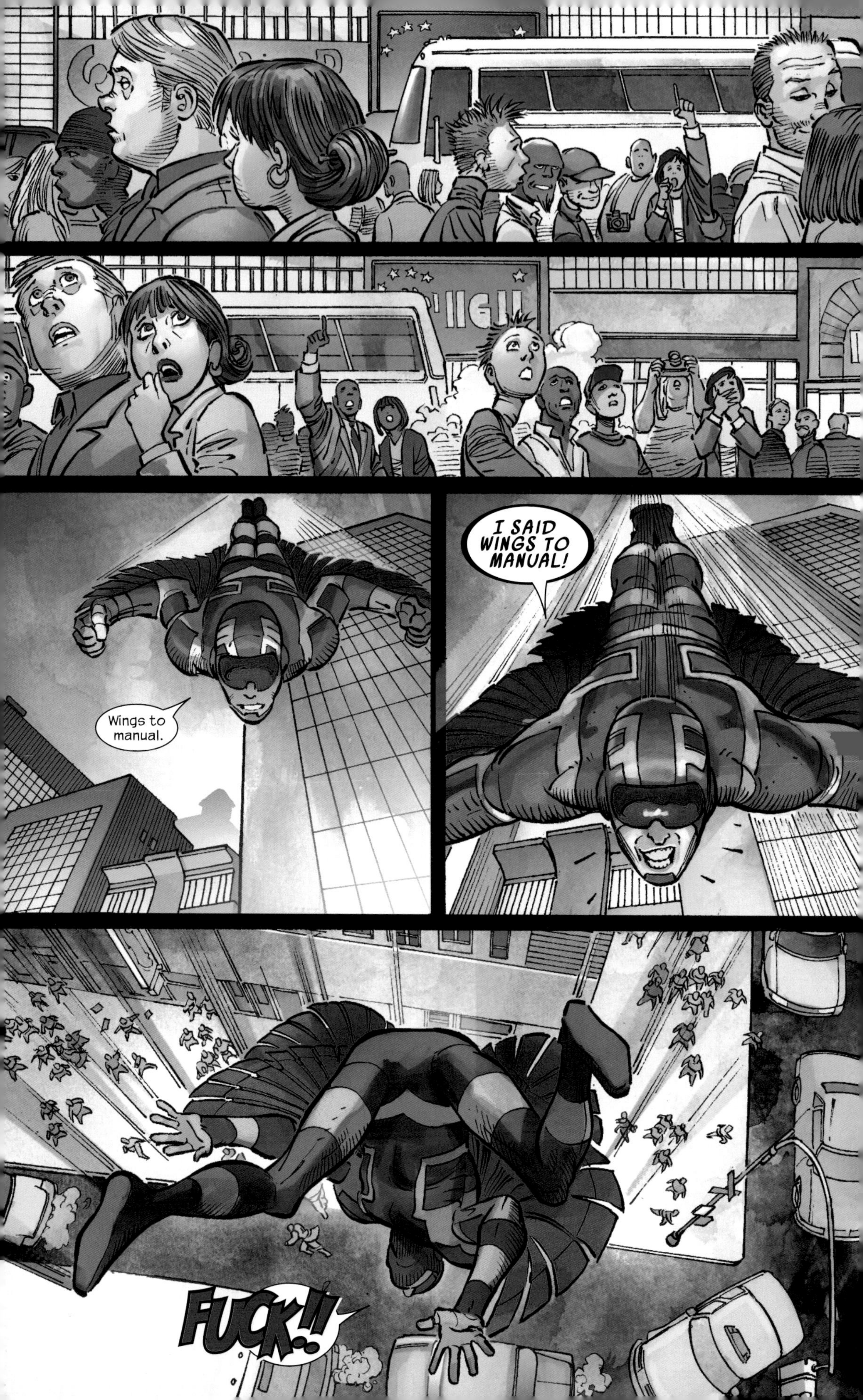
Wings to manual.
I SAID WINGS TO MANUAL!
FUCK!!

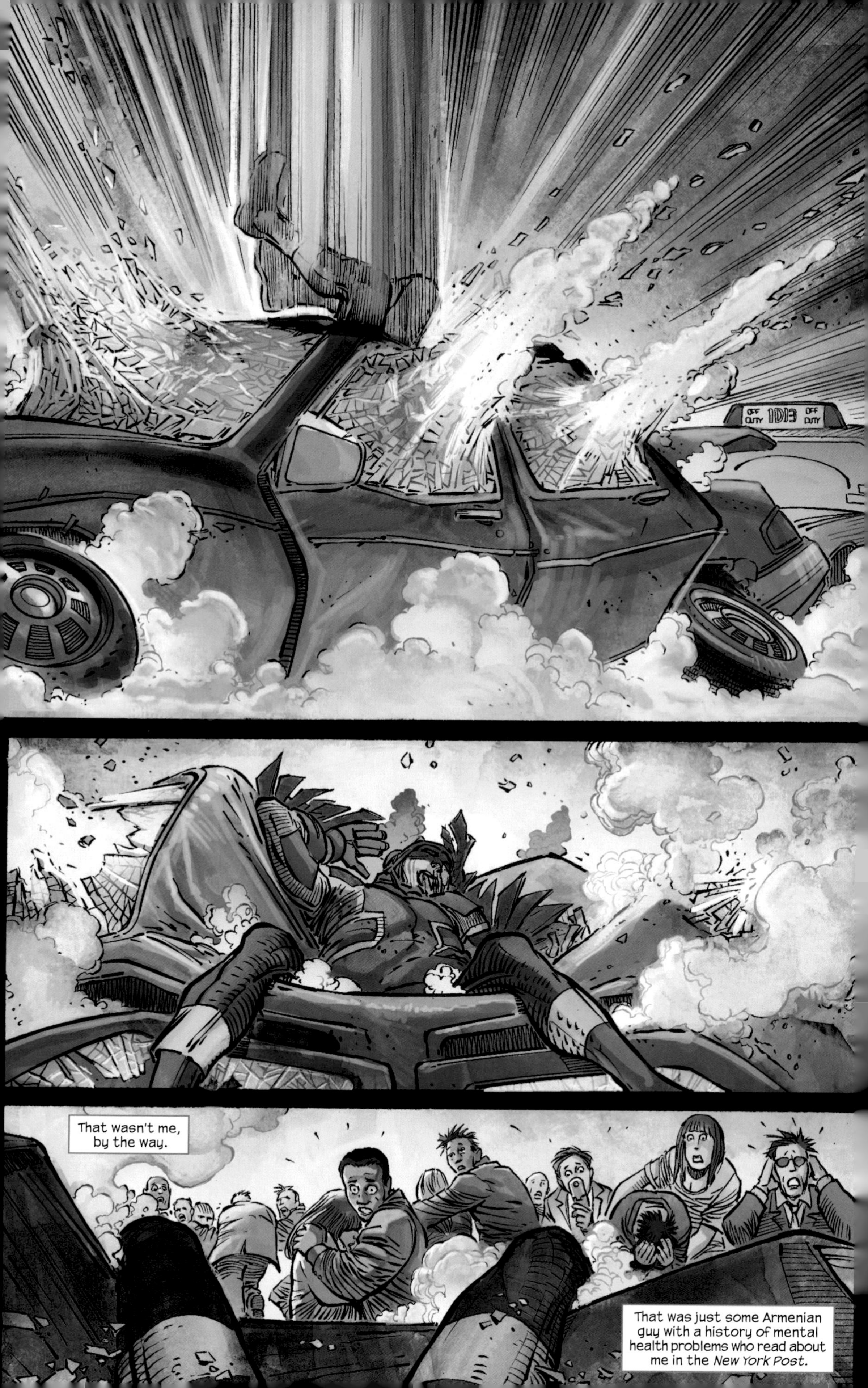
OFF DUTY 1D13 OFF DUTY
That wasn't me, by the way.
That was just some Armenian guy with a history of mental health problems who read about me in the *New York Post*.

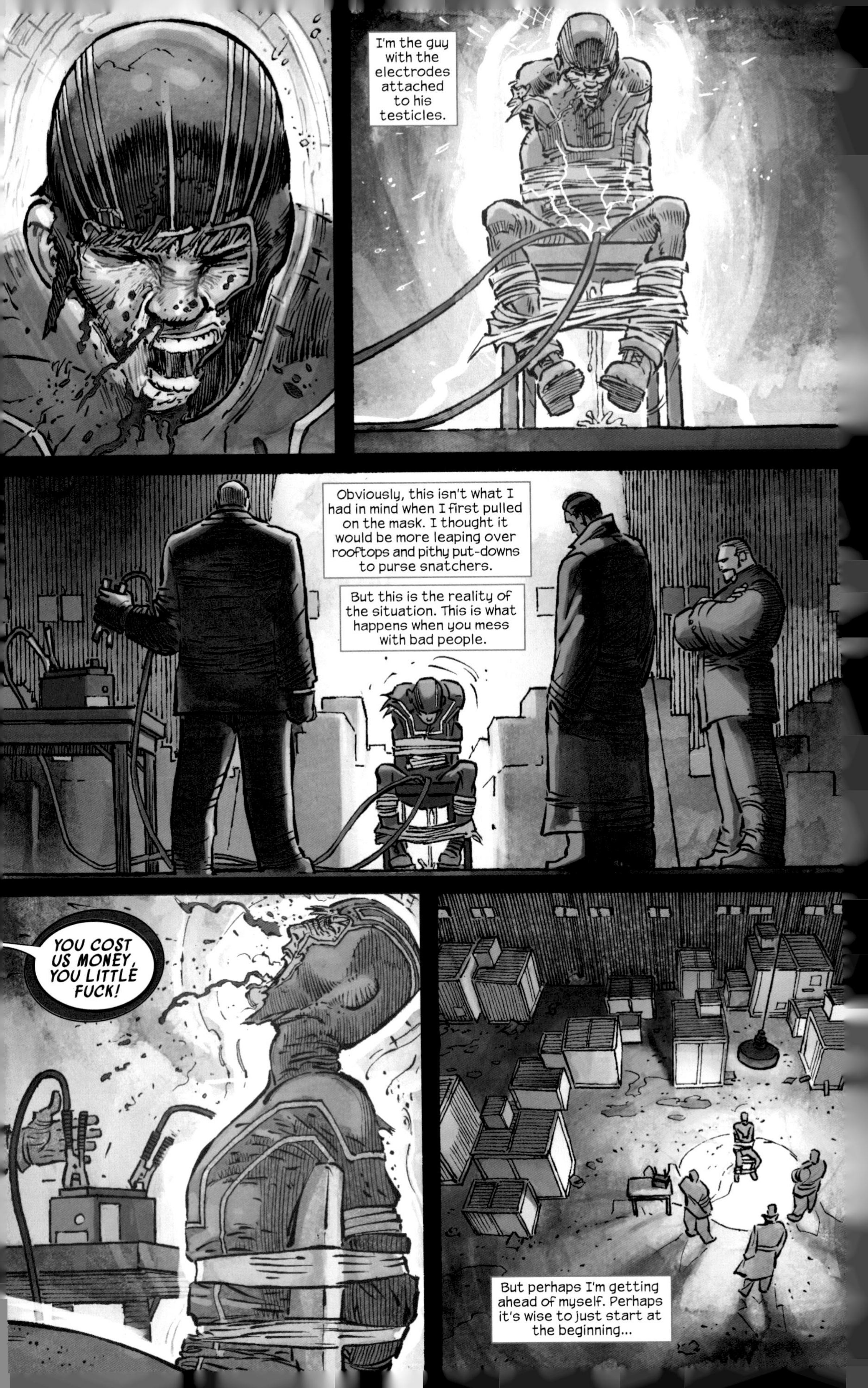

I'm the guy with the electrodes attached to his testicles.
Obviously, this isn't what I had in mind when I first pulled on the mask. I thought it would be more leaping over rooftops and pithy put-downs to purse snatchers.
But this is the reality of the situation. This is what happens when you mess with bad people.
YOU COST US MONEY, YOU LITTLE FUCK!
But perhaps I'm getting ahead of myself. Perhaps it's wise to just start at the beginning...

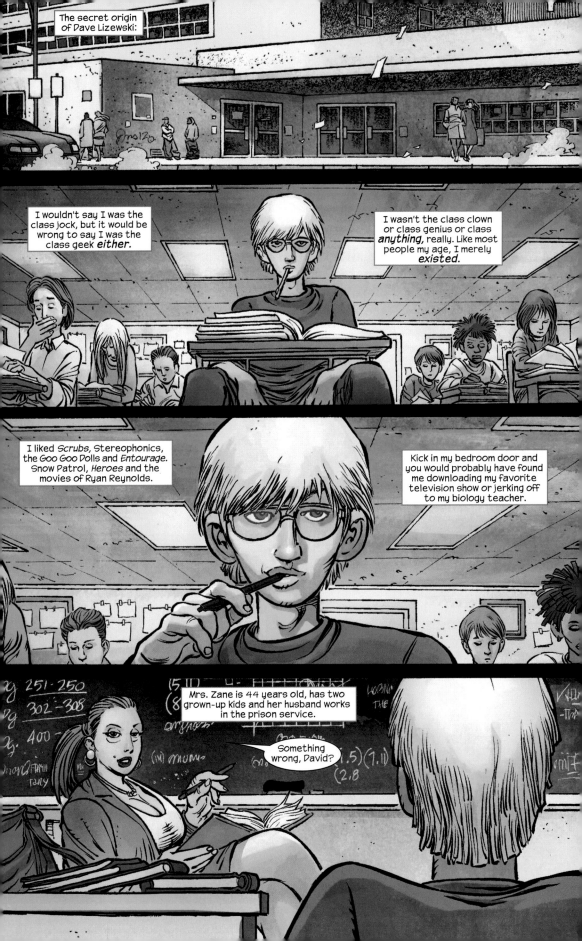

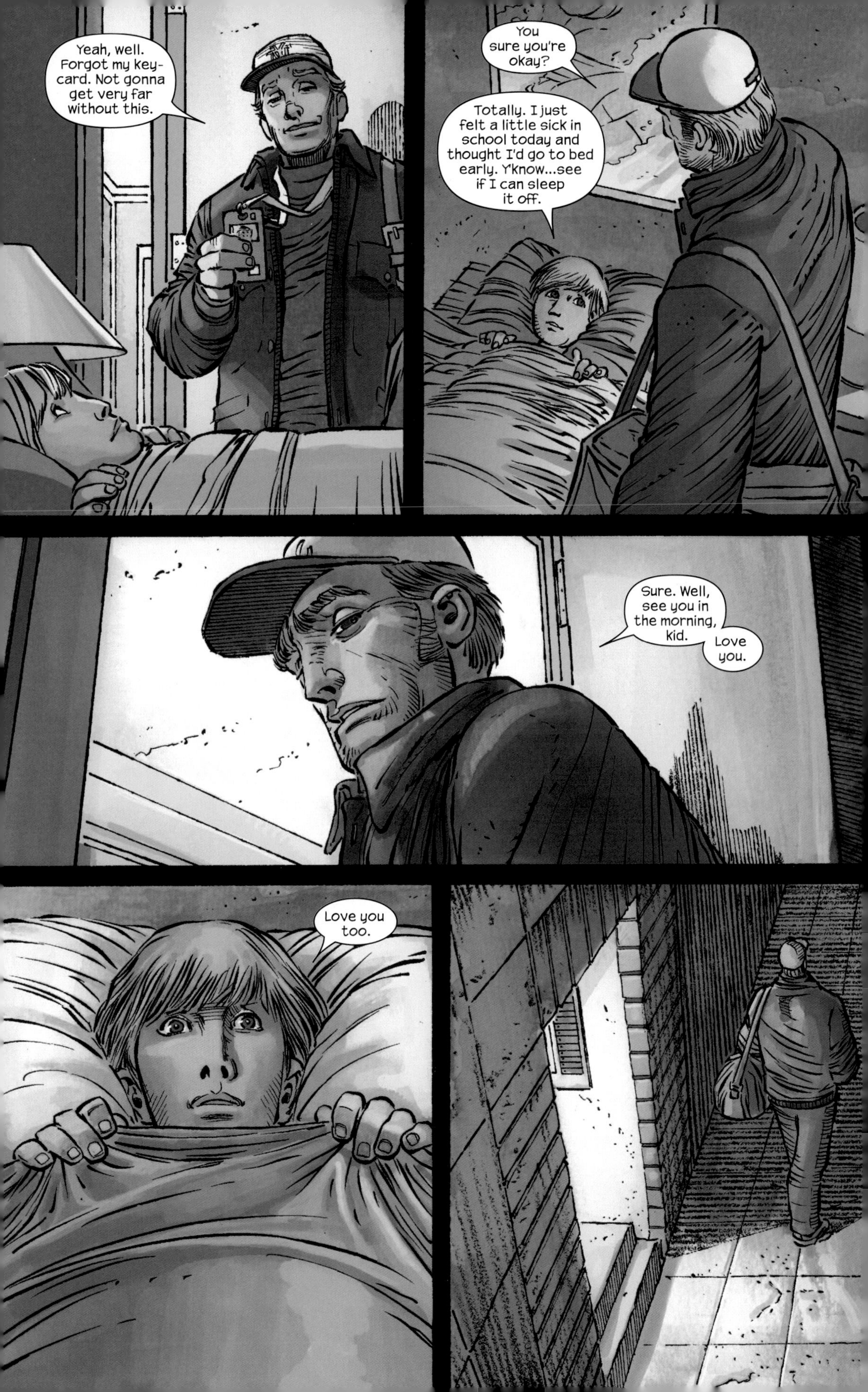
Yeah, well. Forgot my key-card. Not gonna get very far without this.
You sure you're okay?
Totally. I just felt a little sick in school today and thought I'd go to bed early. Y'know...see if I can sleep it off.
Sure. Well, see you in the morning, kid.
Love you.
Love you too.

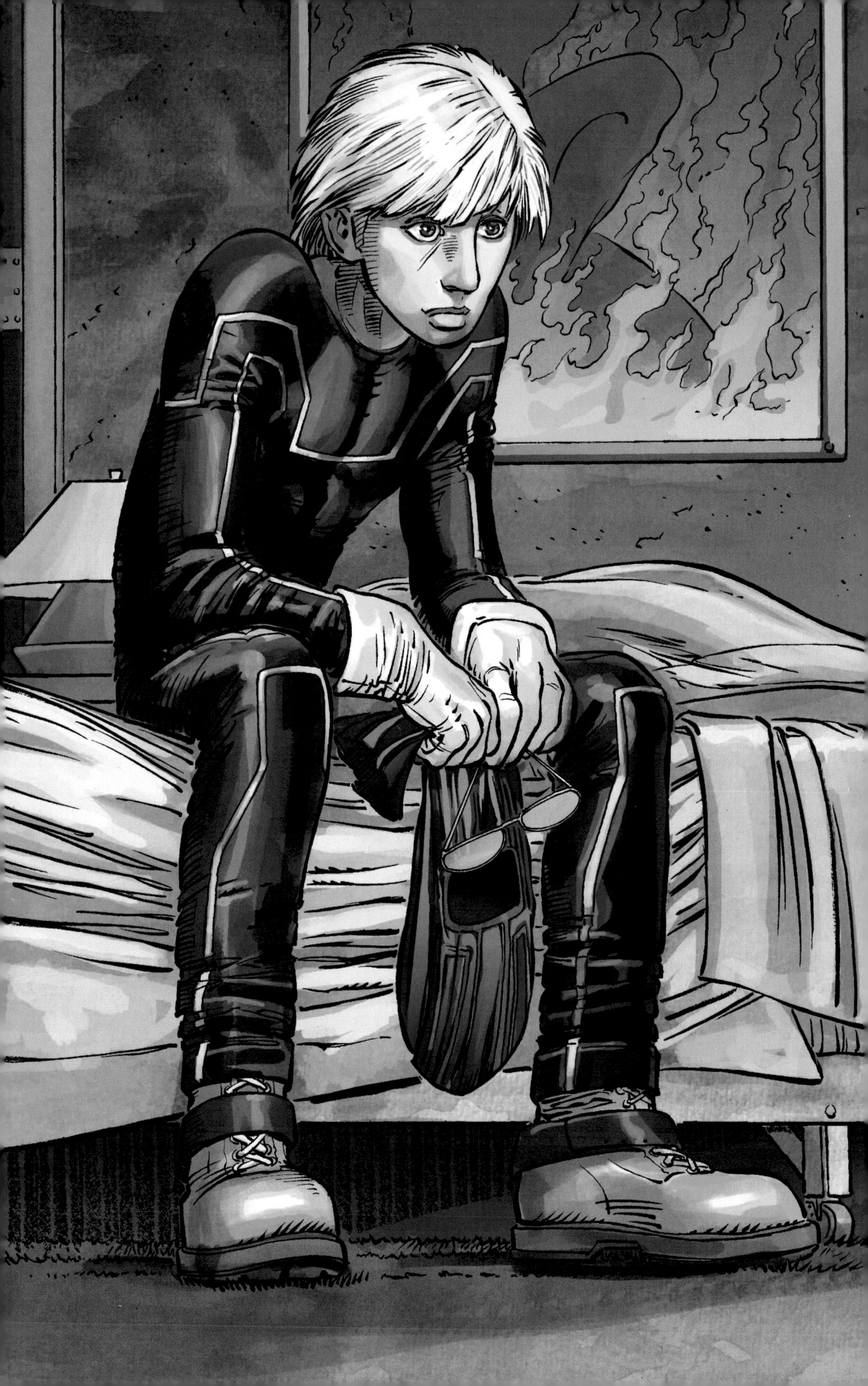

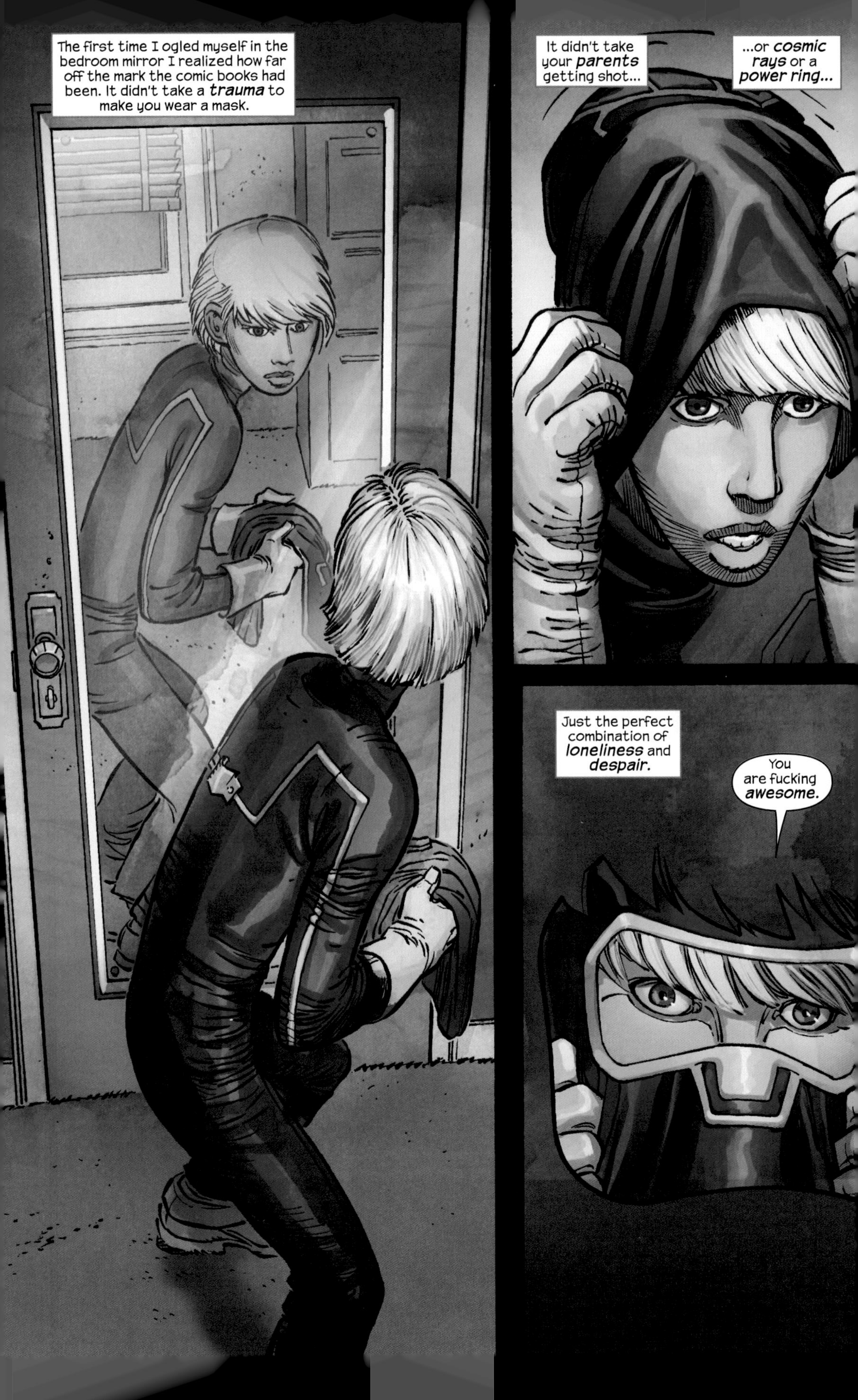
The first time I ogled myself in the bedroom mirror I realized how far off the mark the comic books had been. It didn't take a *trauma* to make you wear a mask.
It didn't take your *parents* getting shot...
...or *cosmic rays* or a *power ring...*
Just the perfect combination of *loneliness* and *despair.*
You are fucking *awesome.*

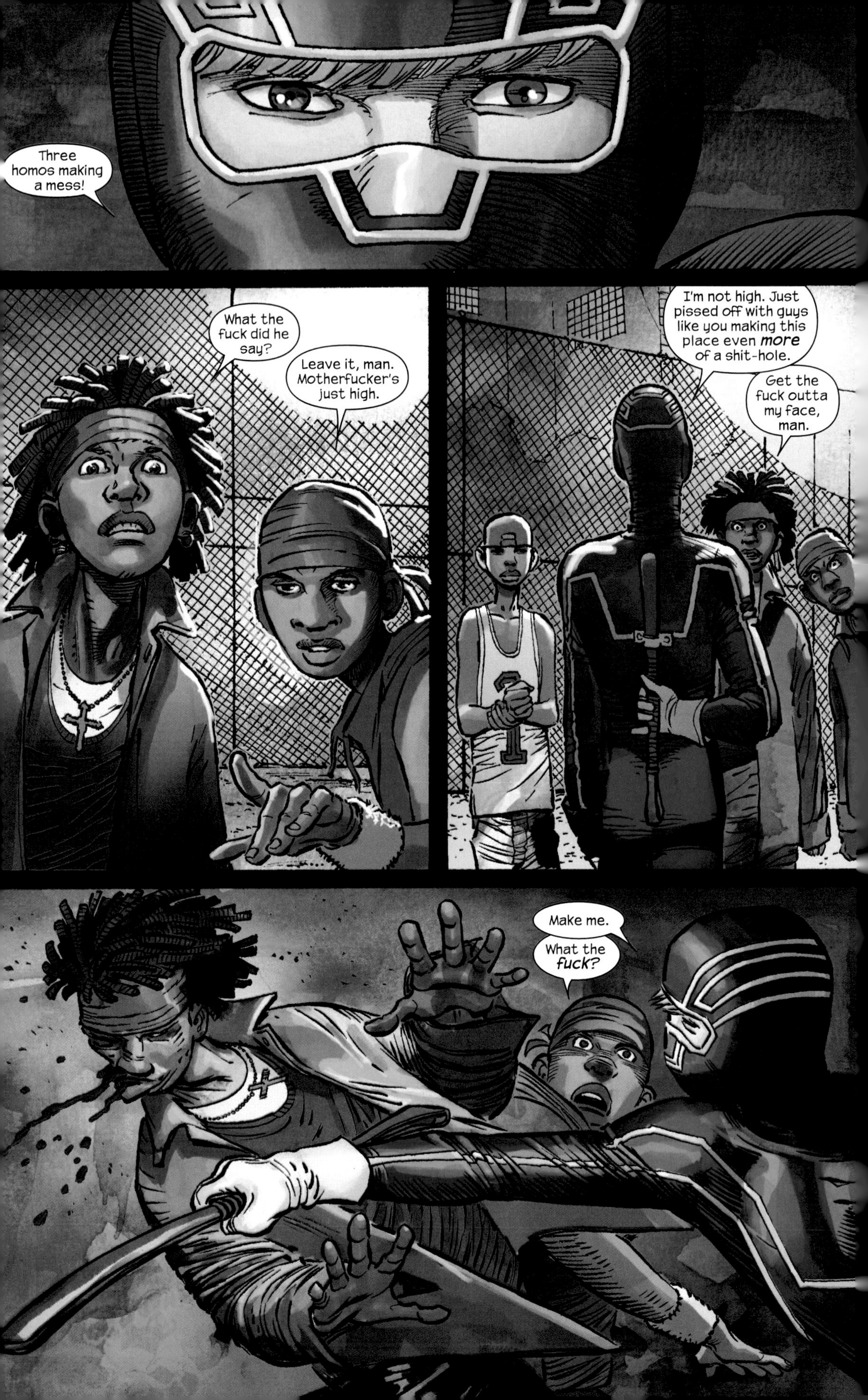
Three homos making a mess!
What the fuck did he say?
Leave it, man. Motherfucker's just high.
I'm not high. Just pissed off with guys like you making this place even *more* of a shit-hole.
Get the fuck outta my face, man.
Make me.
What the *fuck*?

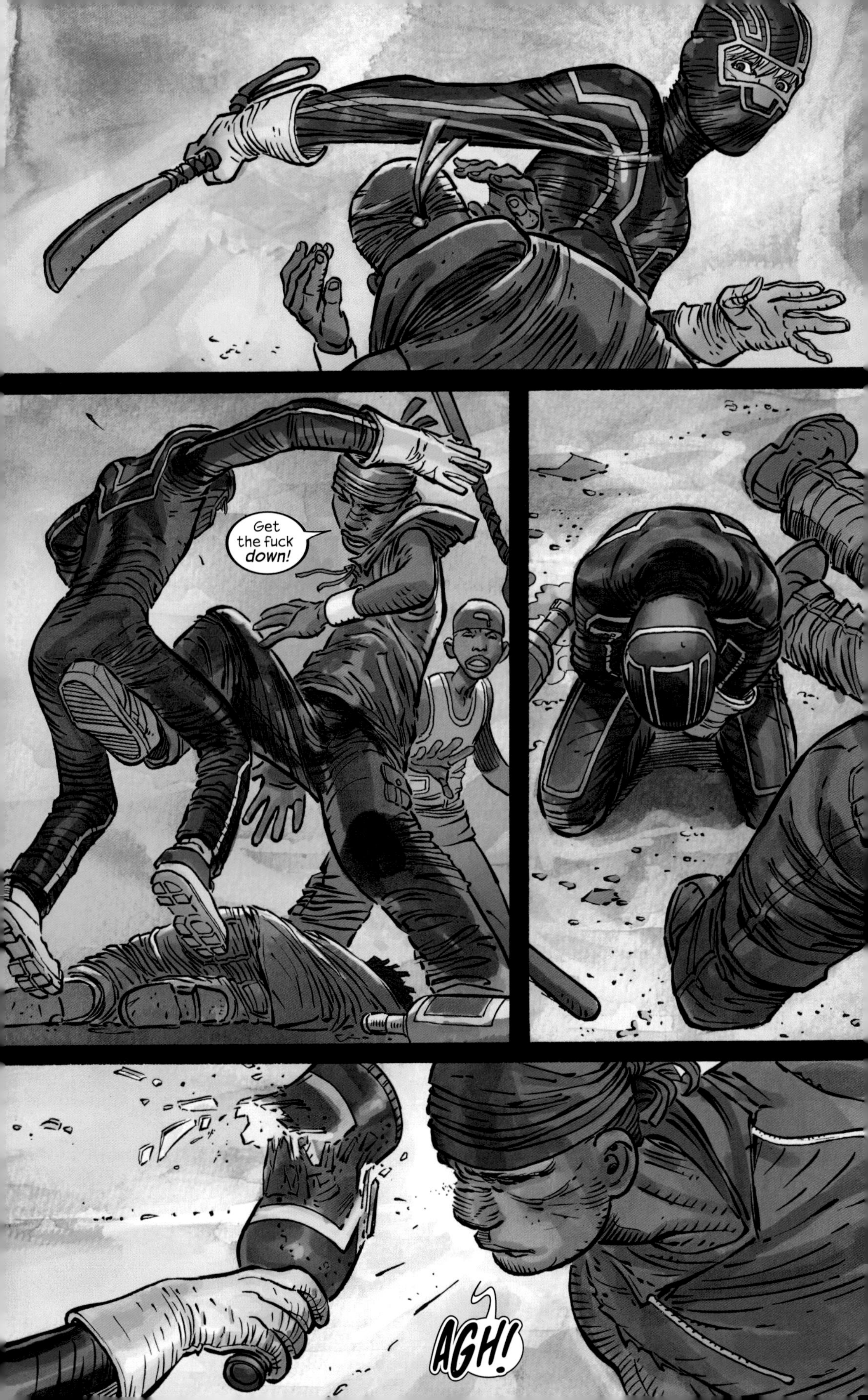
Get the fuck *down!*
AGH!

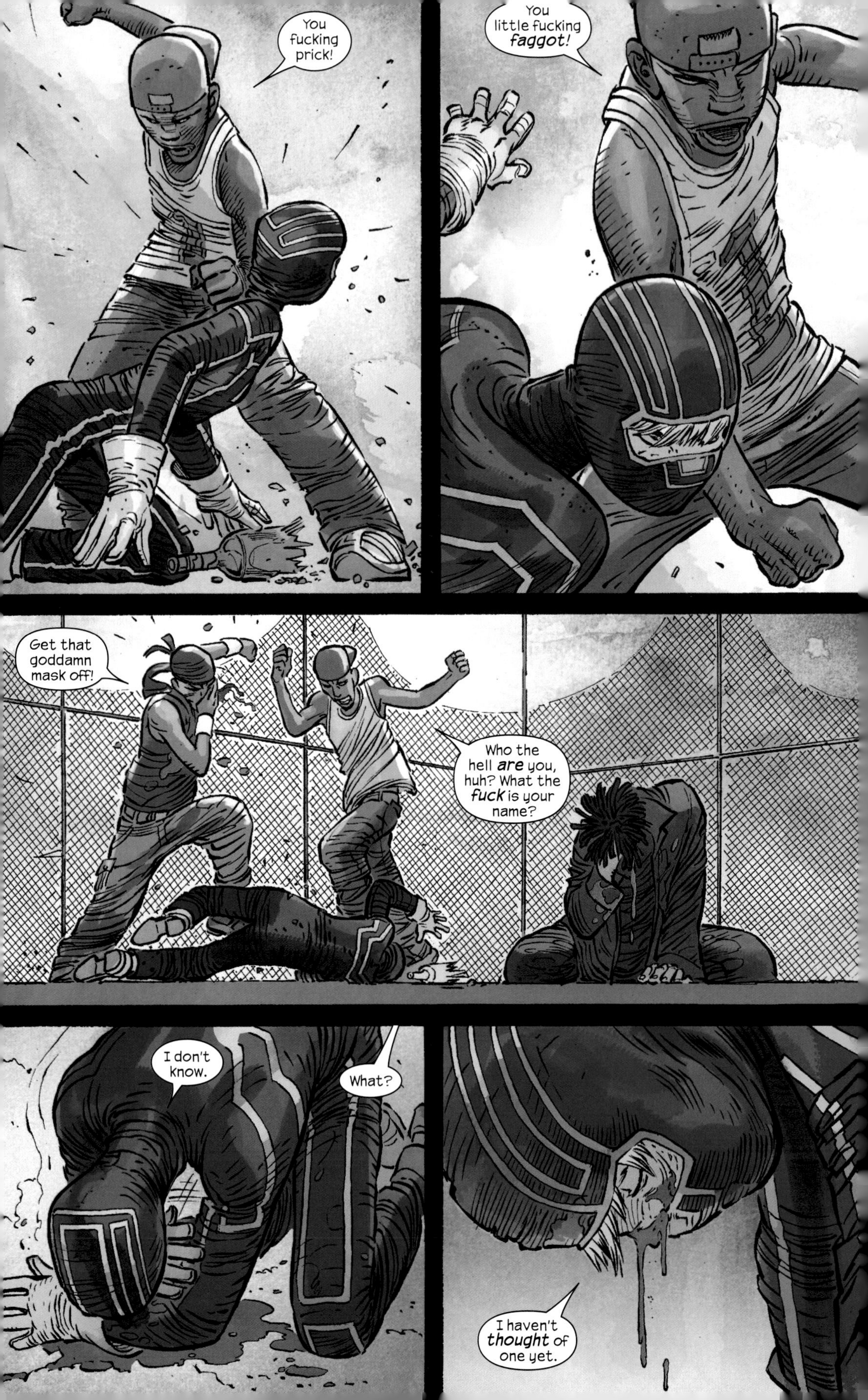
You fucking prick!
You little fucking *faggot!*
Get that goddamn mask off!
Who the hell *are* you, huh? What the *fuck* is your name?
I don't know.
What?
I haven't *thought* of one yet.

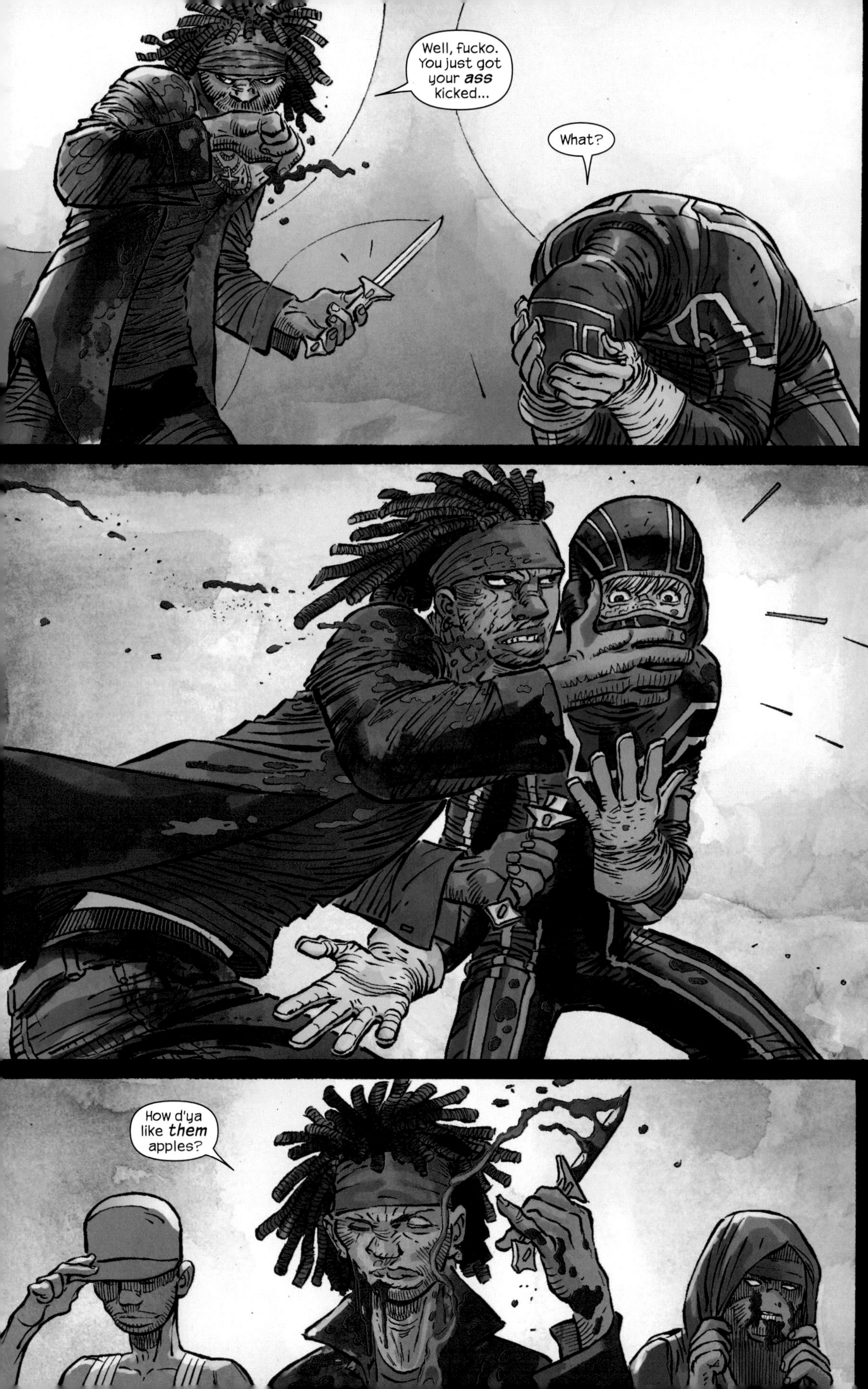
Well, fucko. You just got your *ass* kicked...
What?
How d'ya like *them* apples?

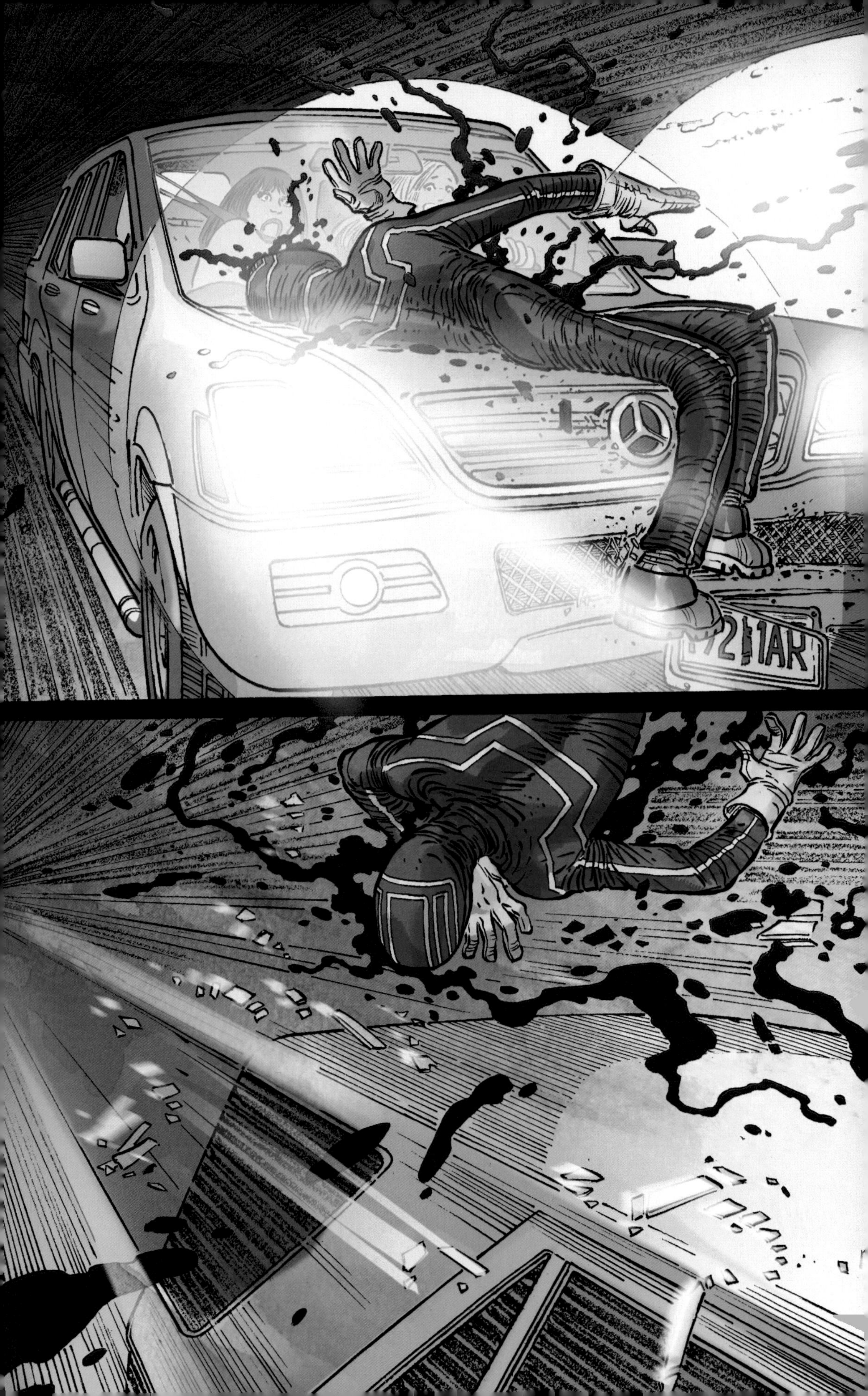

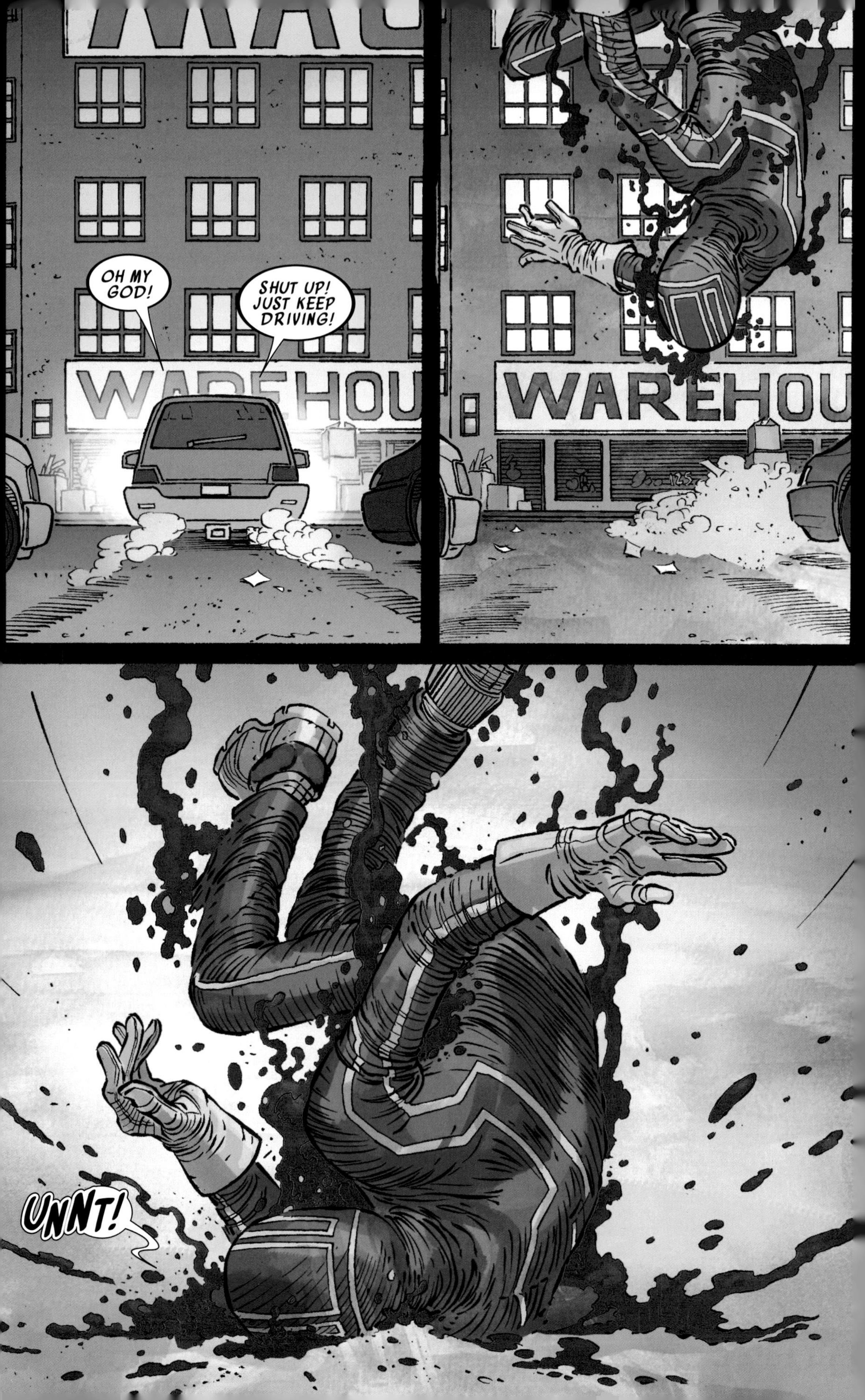
OH MY GOD!
SHUT UP! JUST KEEP DRIVING!
WAREHOU
WAREHOU
UNNT!

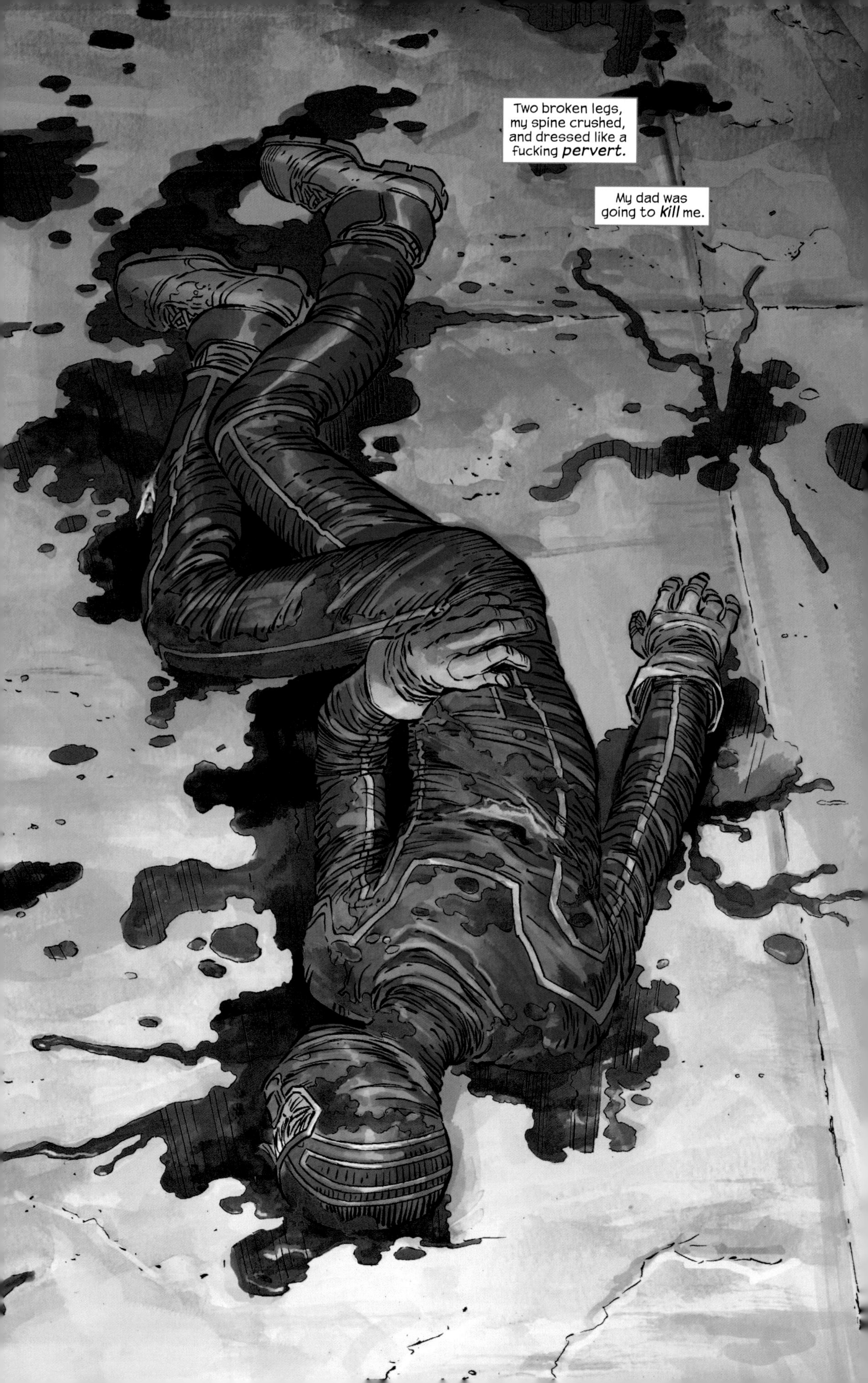
Two broken legs, my spine crushed, and dressed like a fucking *pervert*.
My dad was going to *kill* me.

TWO

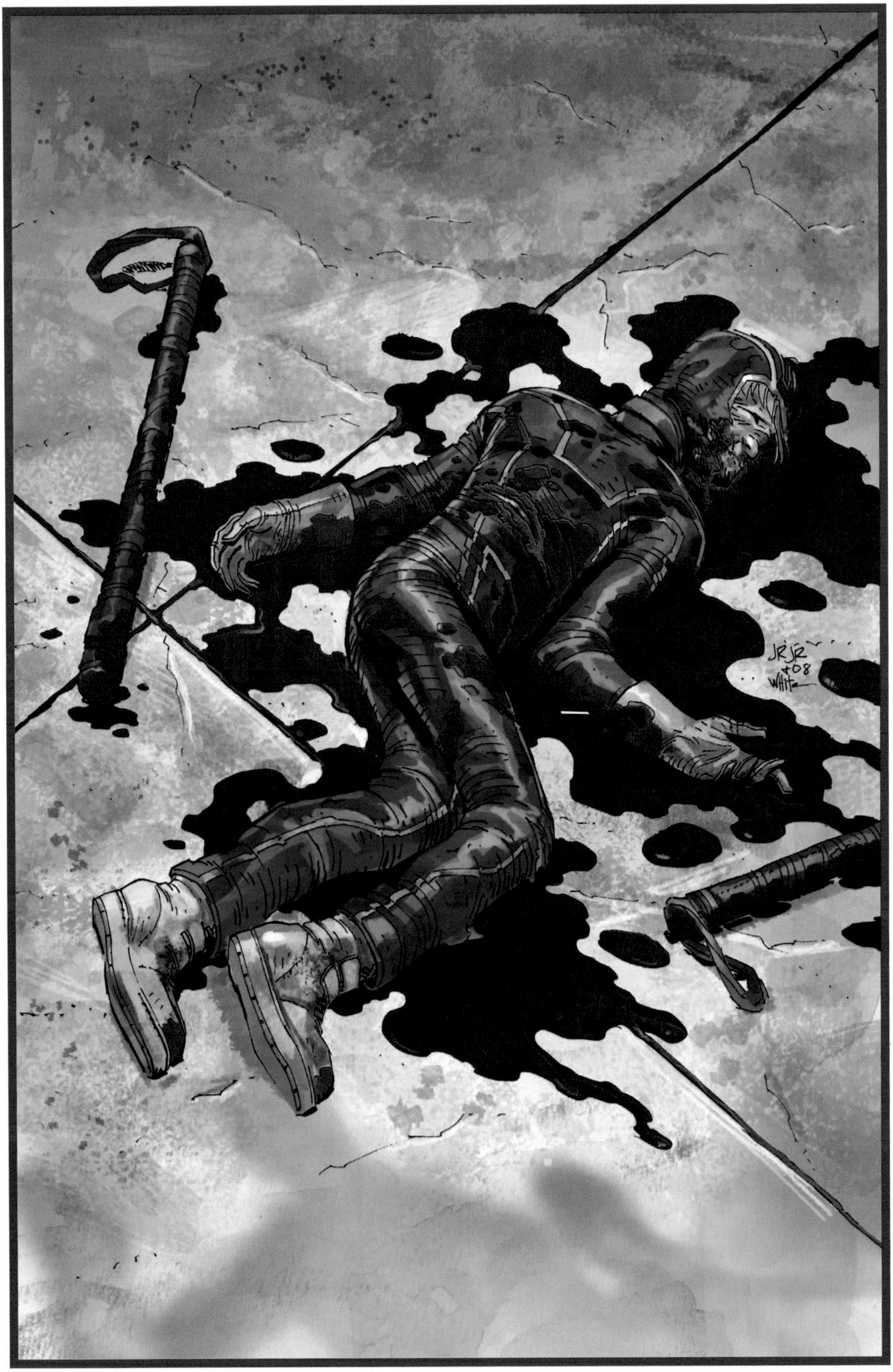
JRJR
'08
WHITE

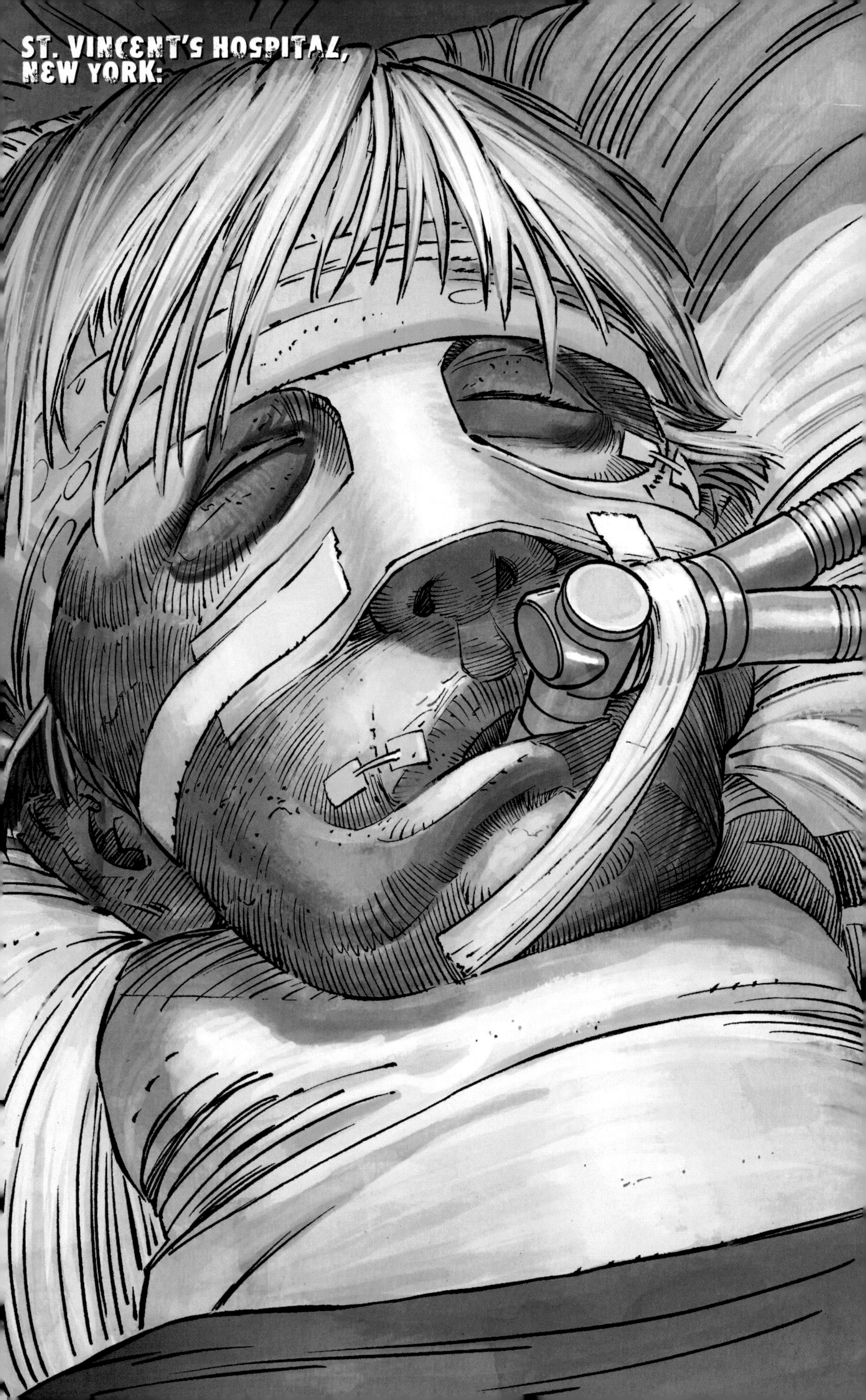
ST. VINCENT'S HOSPITAL, NEW YORK:

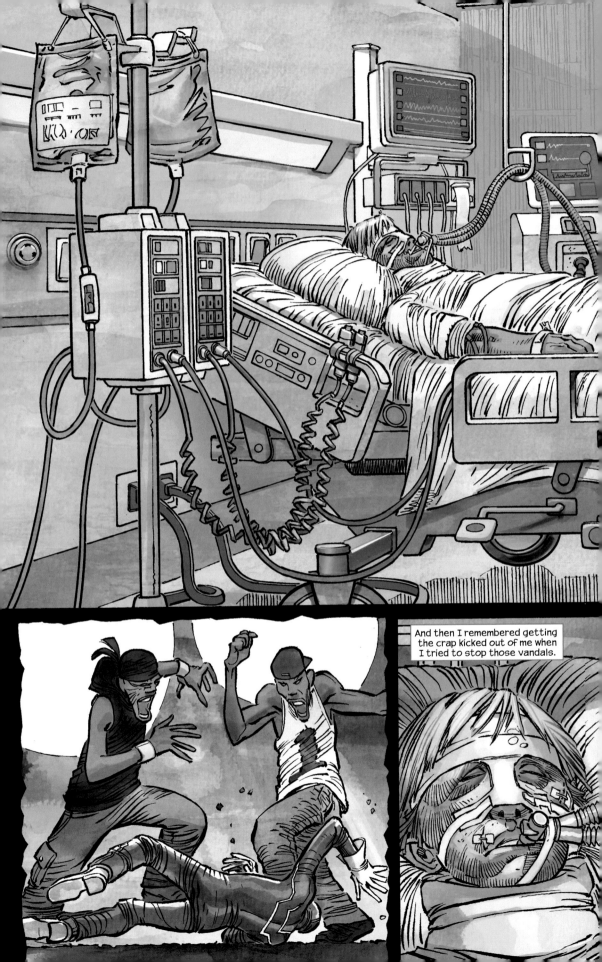

And then I remembered getting the crap kicked out of me when I tried to stop those vandals.

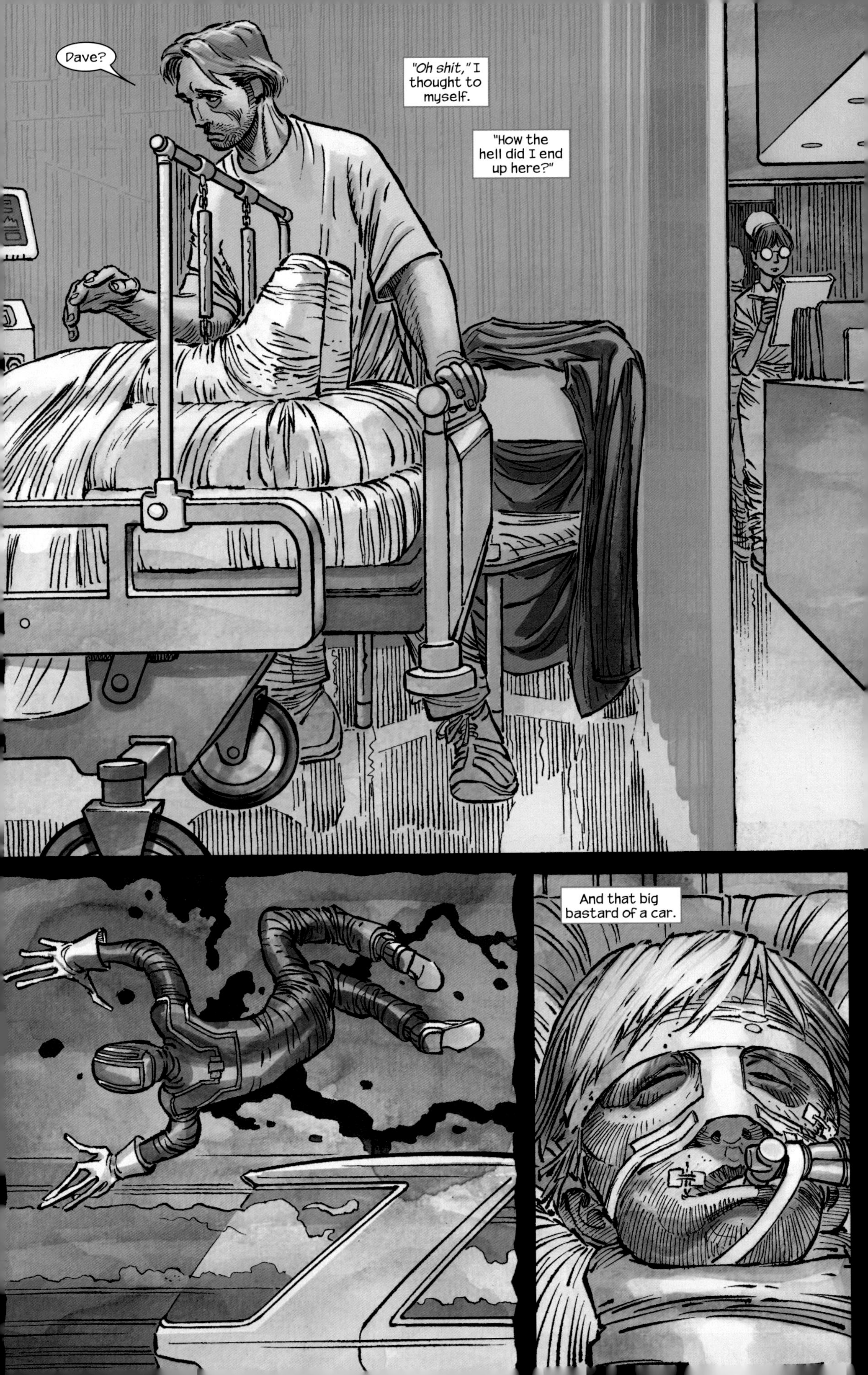
Dave?
"Oh shit," I thought to myself.
"How the hell did I end up here?"
And that big bastard of a car.

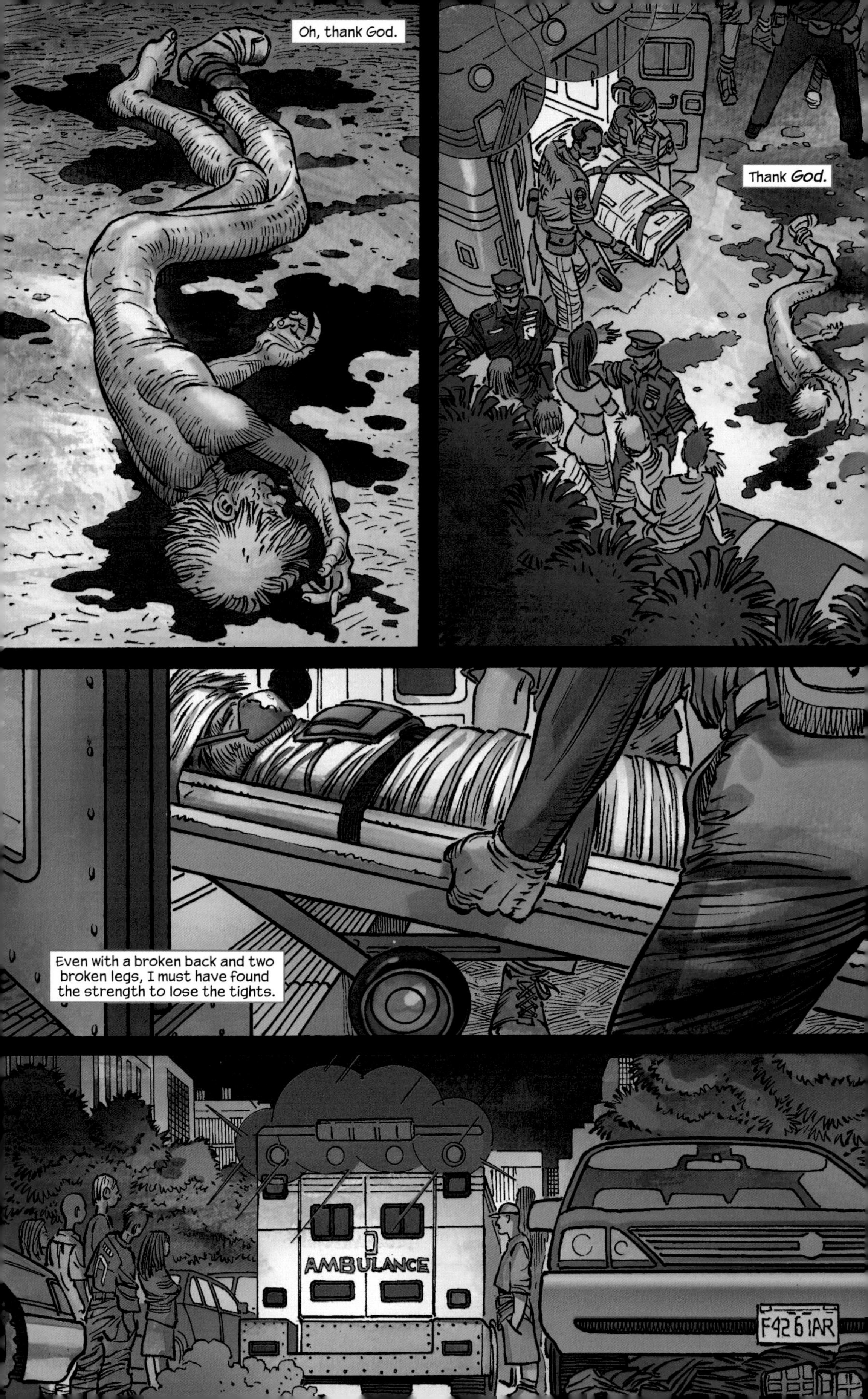
Oh, thank God.
Thank God.
Even with a broken back and two broken legs, I must have found the strength to lose the tights.
AMBULANCE

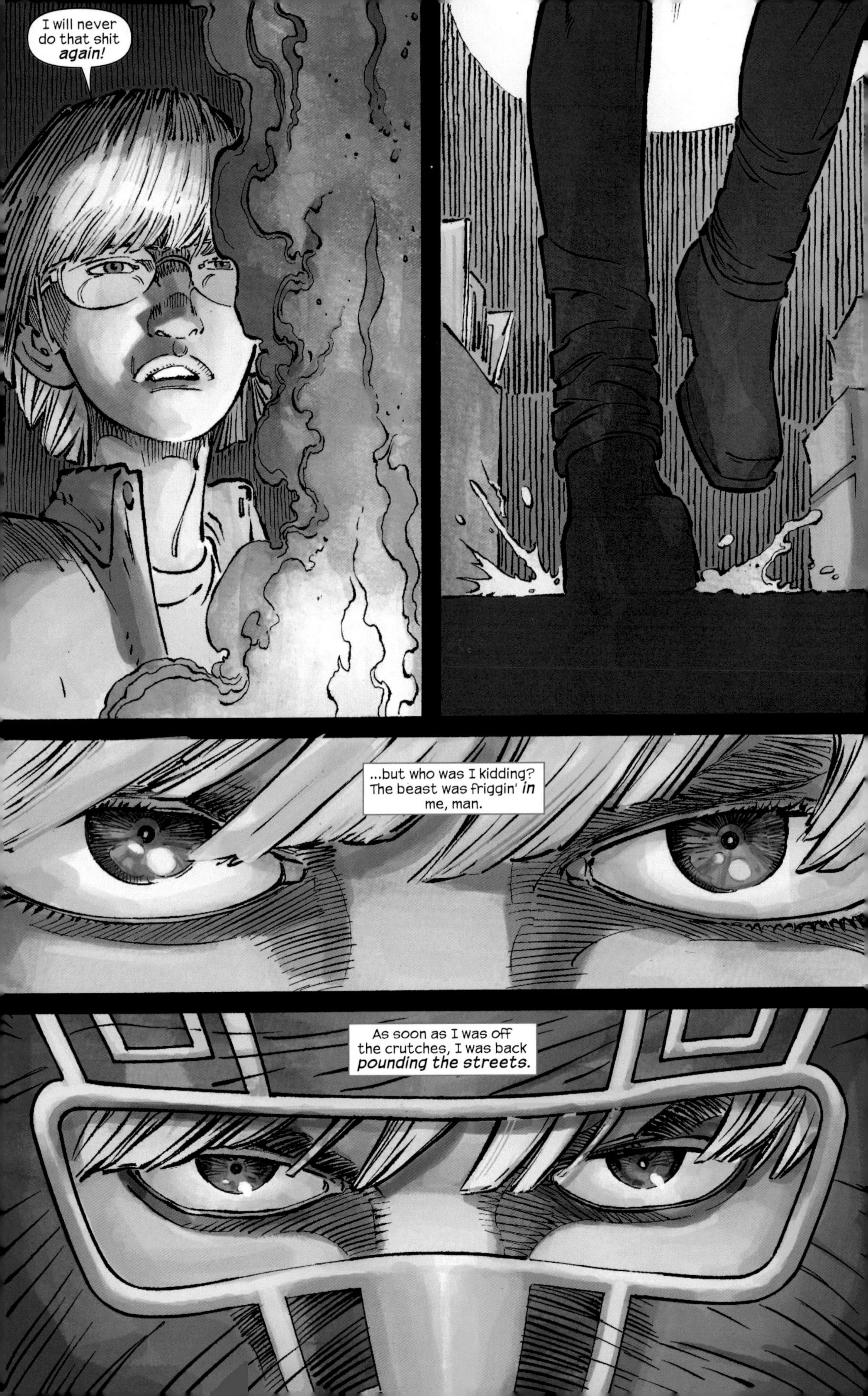
I will never do that shit *again!*
...but who was I kidding? The beast was friggin' *in* me, man.
As soon as I was off the crutches, I was back *pounding the streets.*

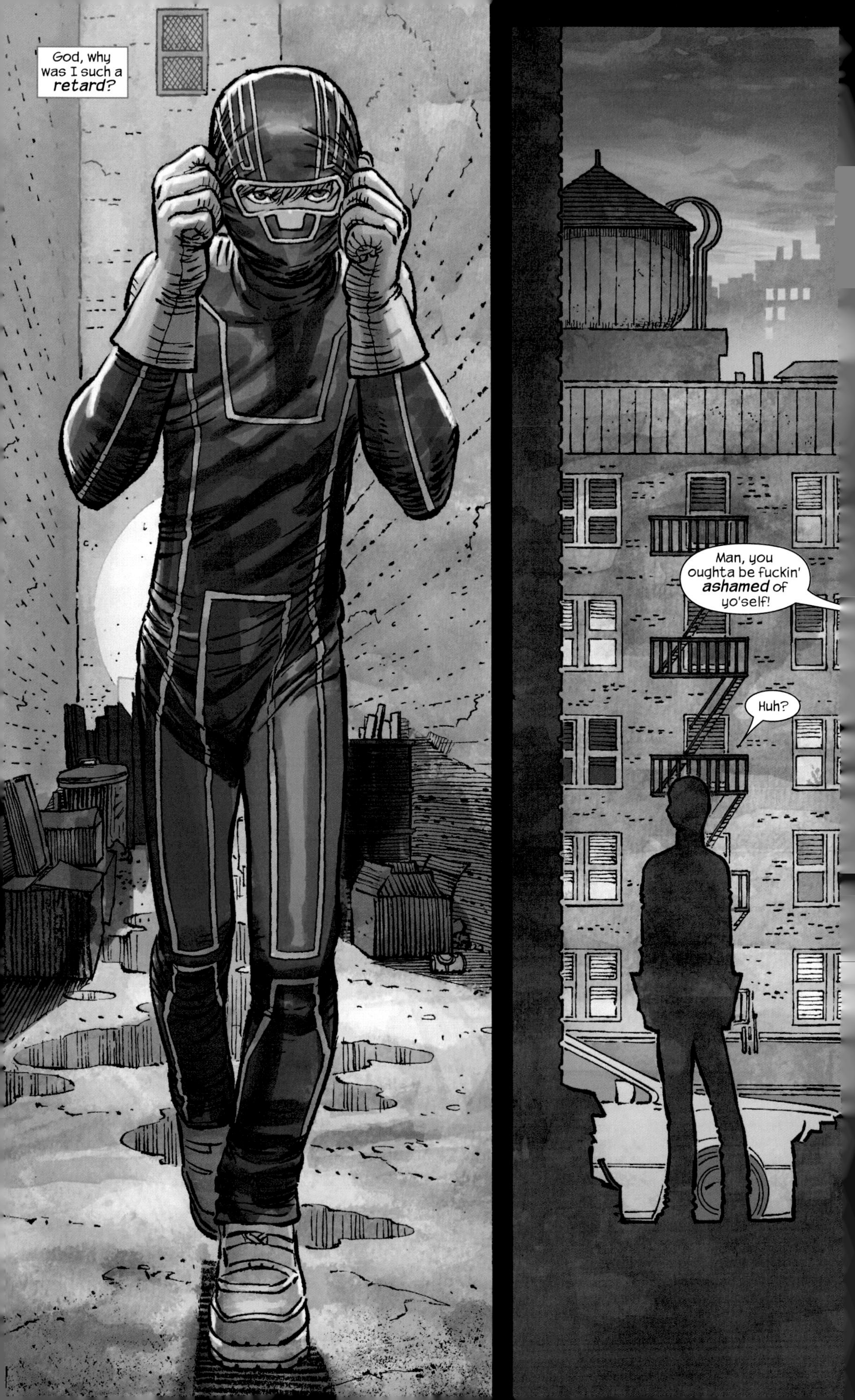
God, why was I such a *retard*?
Man, you oughta be fuckin' *ashamed* of yo'self!
Huh?

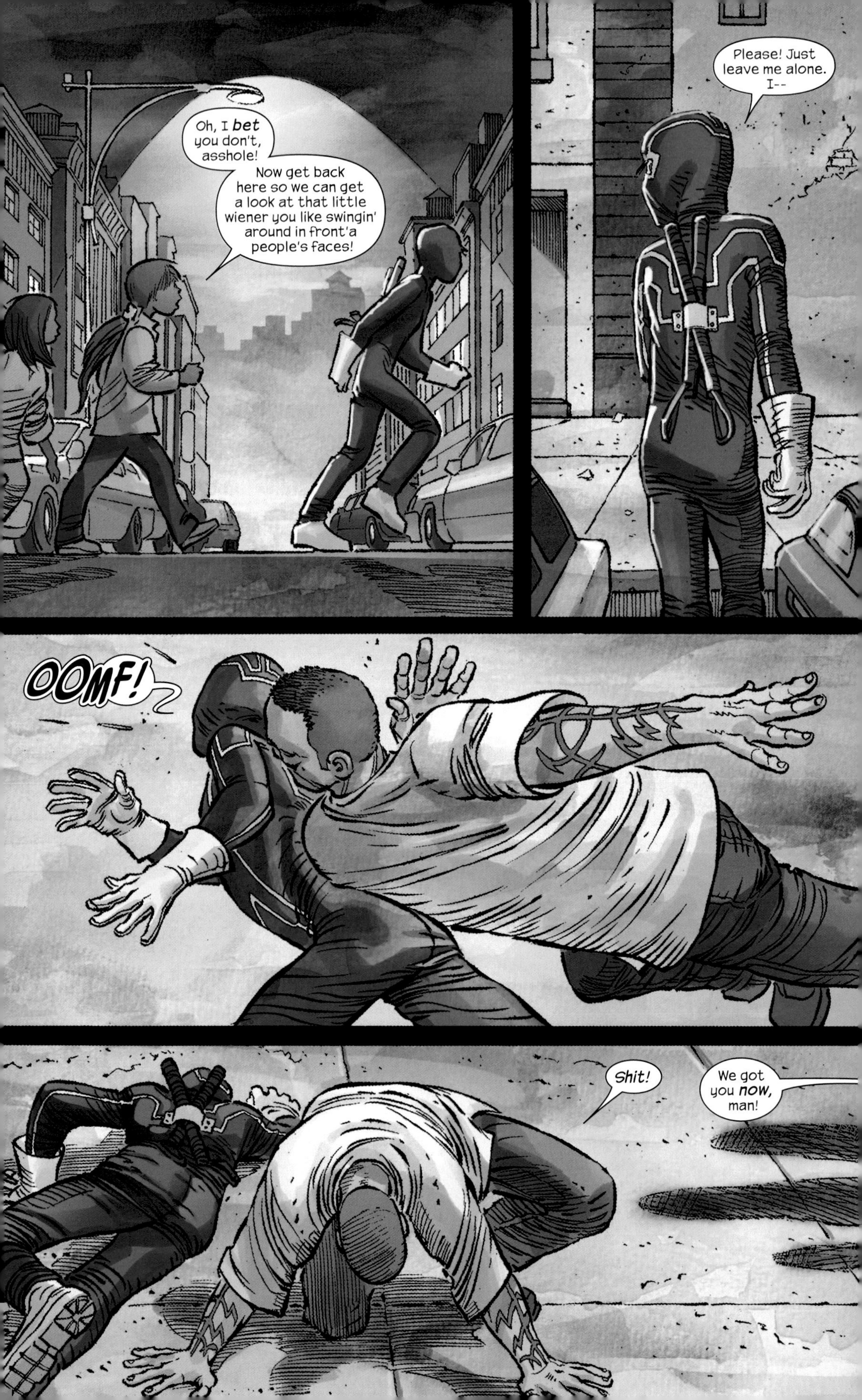
Oh, I *bet* you don't, asshole!
Now get back here so we can get a look at that little wiener you like swingin' around in front'a people's faces!
Please! Just leave me alone. I--
OOMF!
Shit!
We got you *NOW,* man!

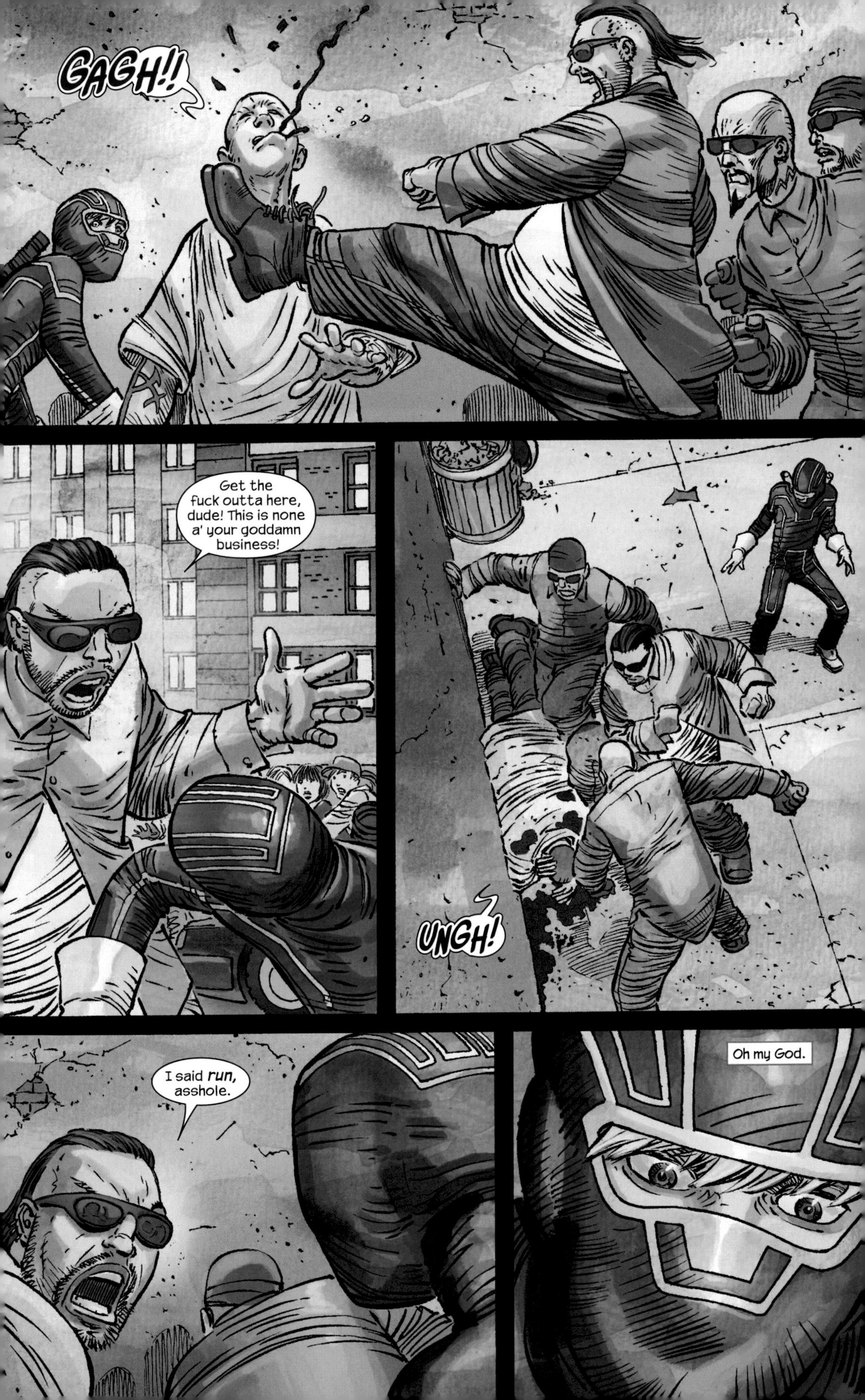
GAGH!!
Get the fuck outta here, dude! This is none a' your goddamn business!
UNGH!
I said *run,* asshole.
Oh my God.

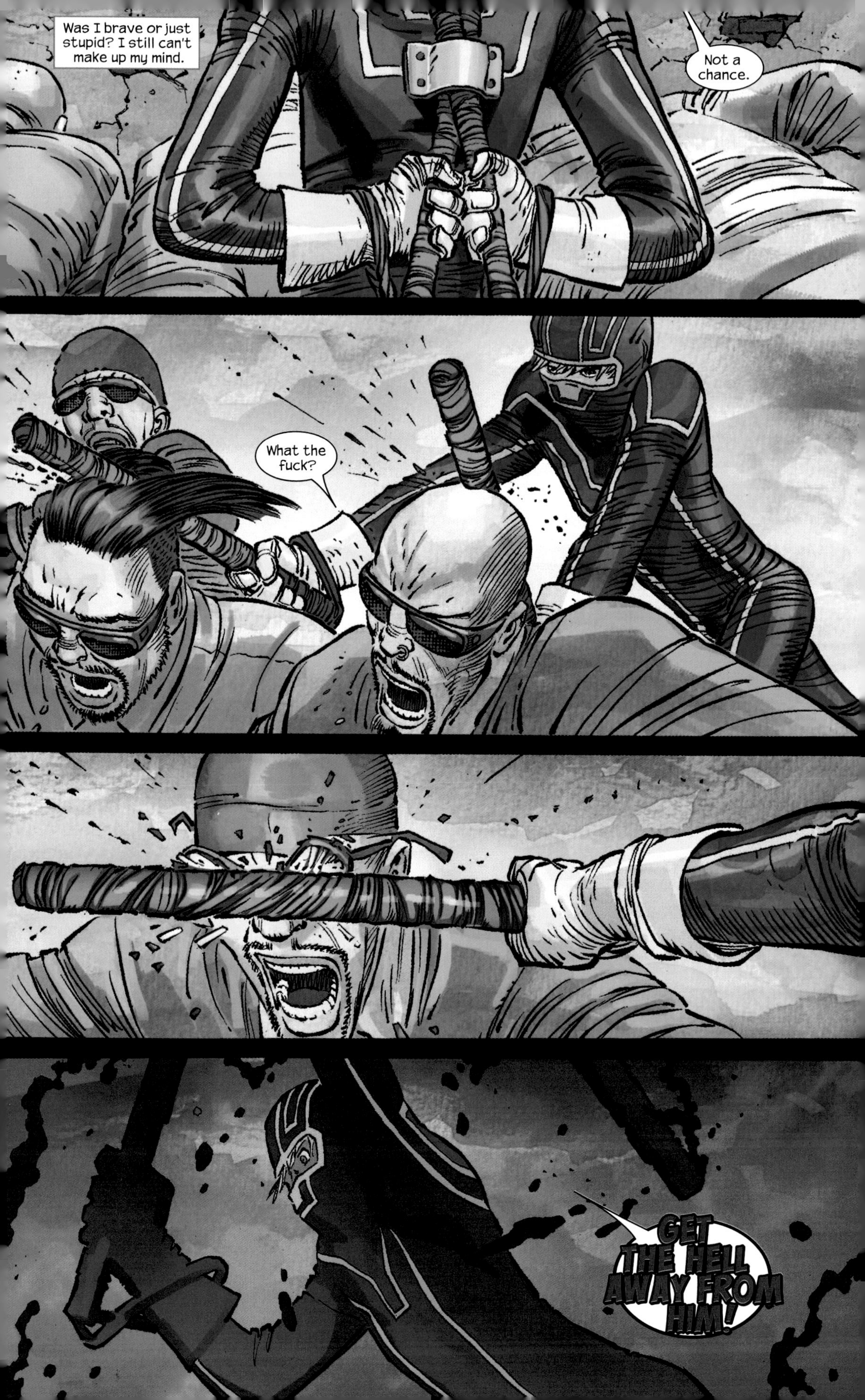
Was I brave or just stupid? I still can't make up my mind.
Not a chance.
What the fuck?
GET THE HELL AWAY FROM HIM!

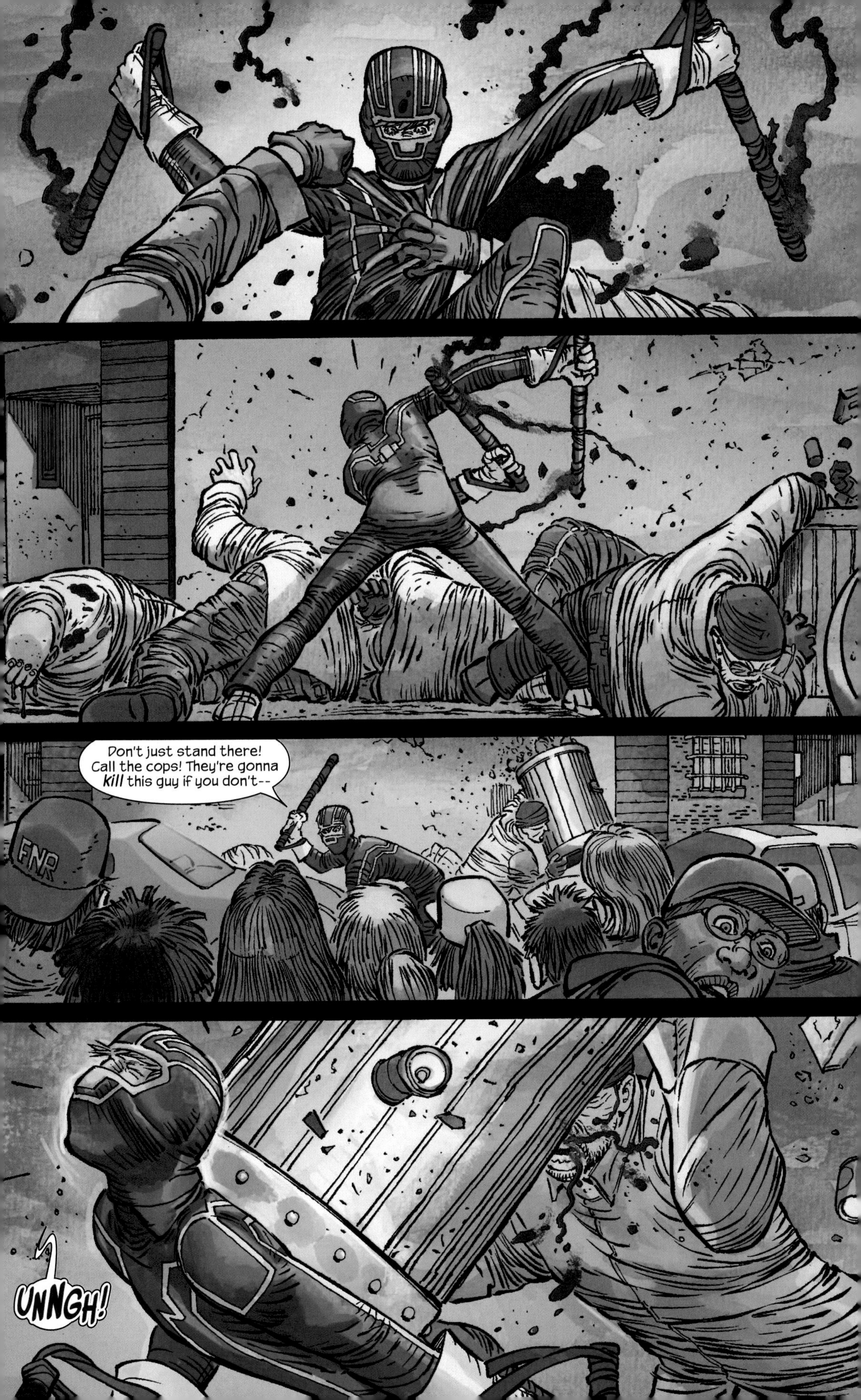
Don't just stand there! Call the cops! They're gonna *kill* this guy if you don't--
FNR
UNNGH!

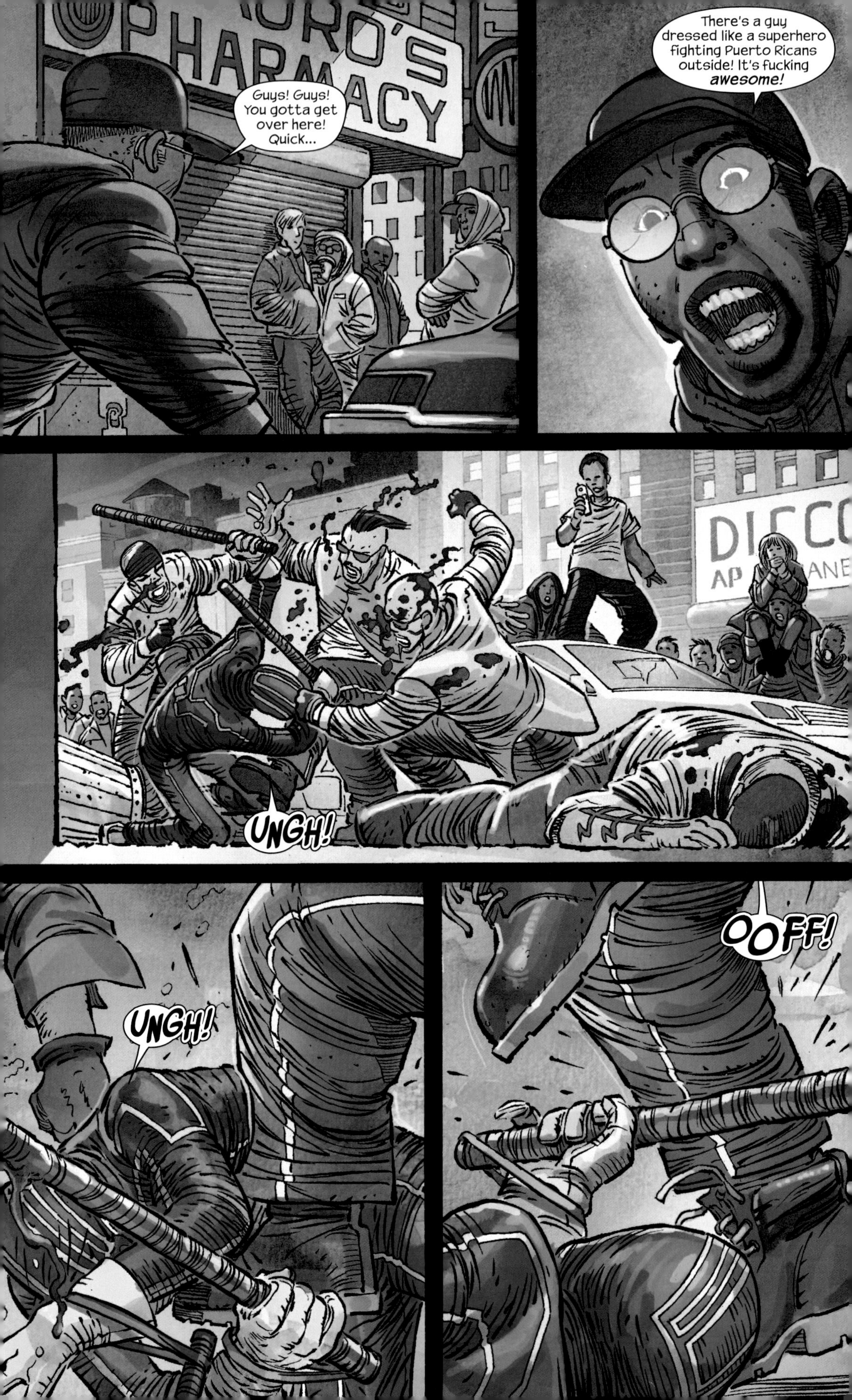
PHARMACY
Guys! Guys! You gotta get over here! Quick...
There's a guy dressed like a superhero fighting Puerto Ricans outside! It's fucking *awesome!*
UNGH!
UNGH!
OOFF!

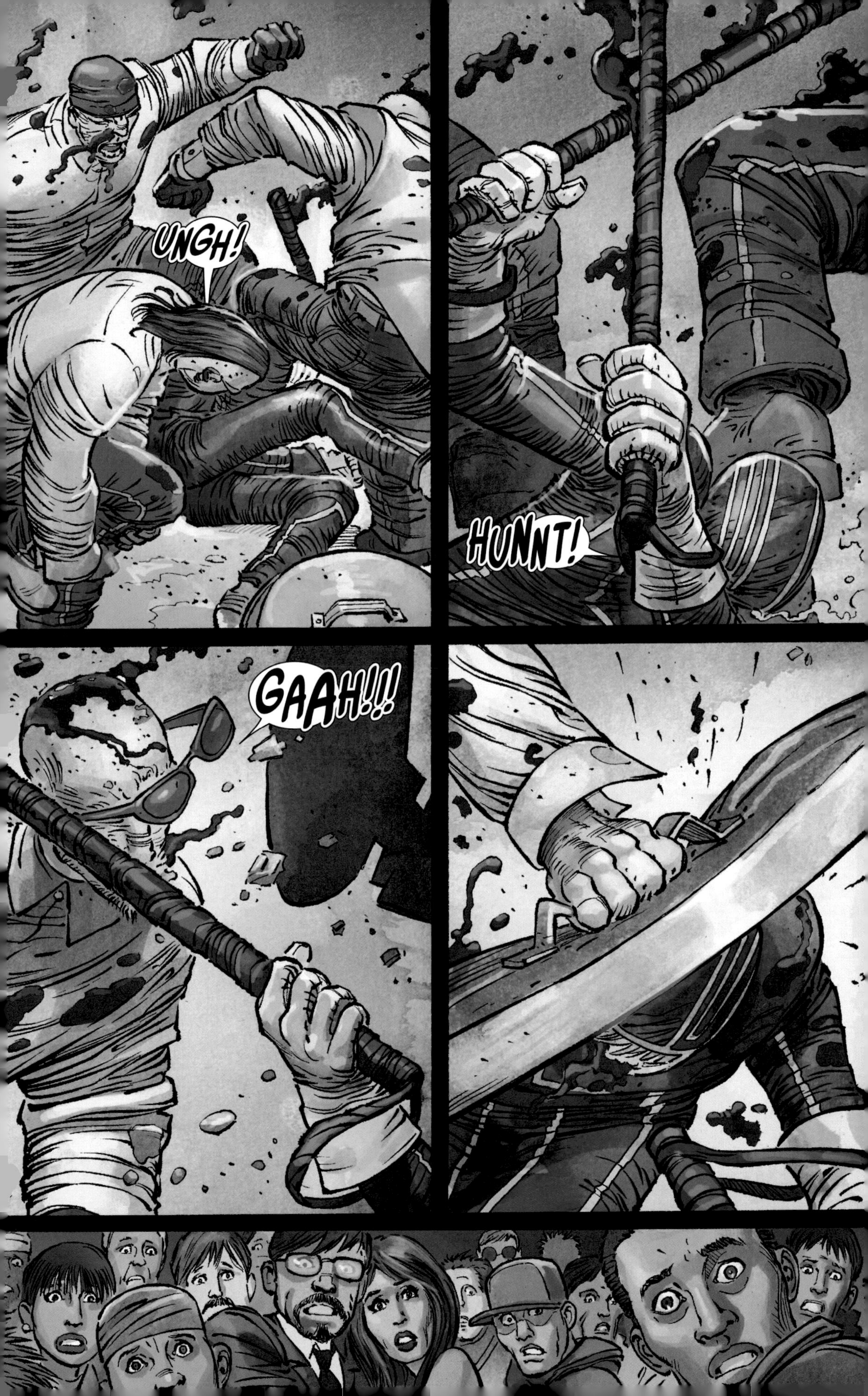
UNGH!
HUNNT!
GAAH!!!

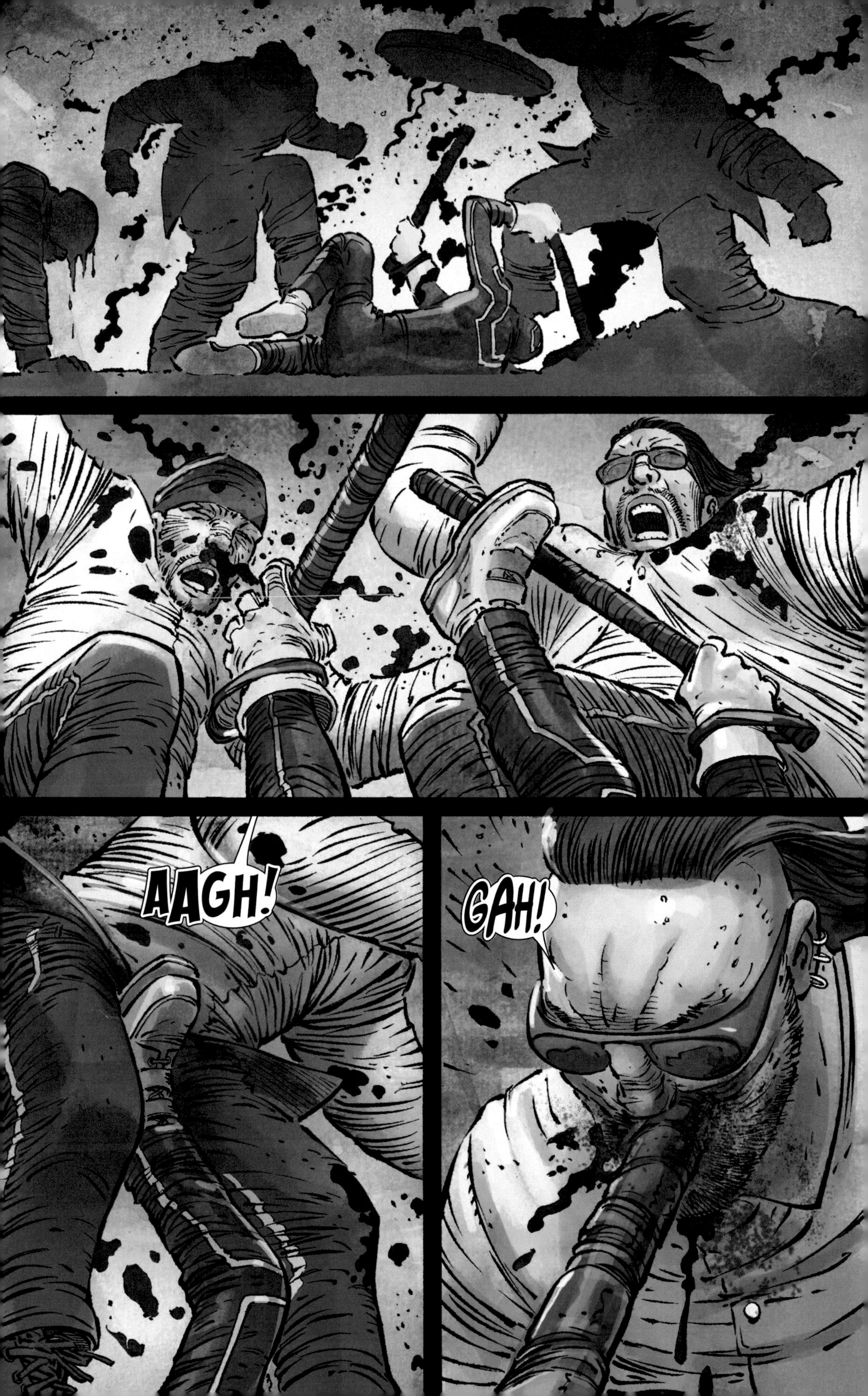
AAGH!
GAH!

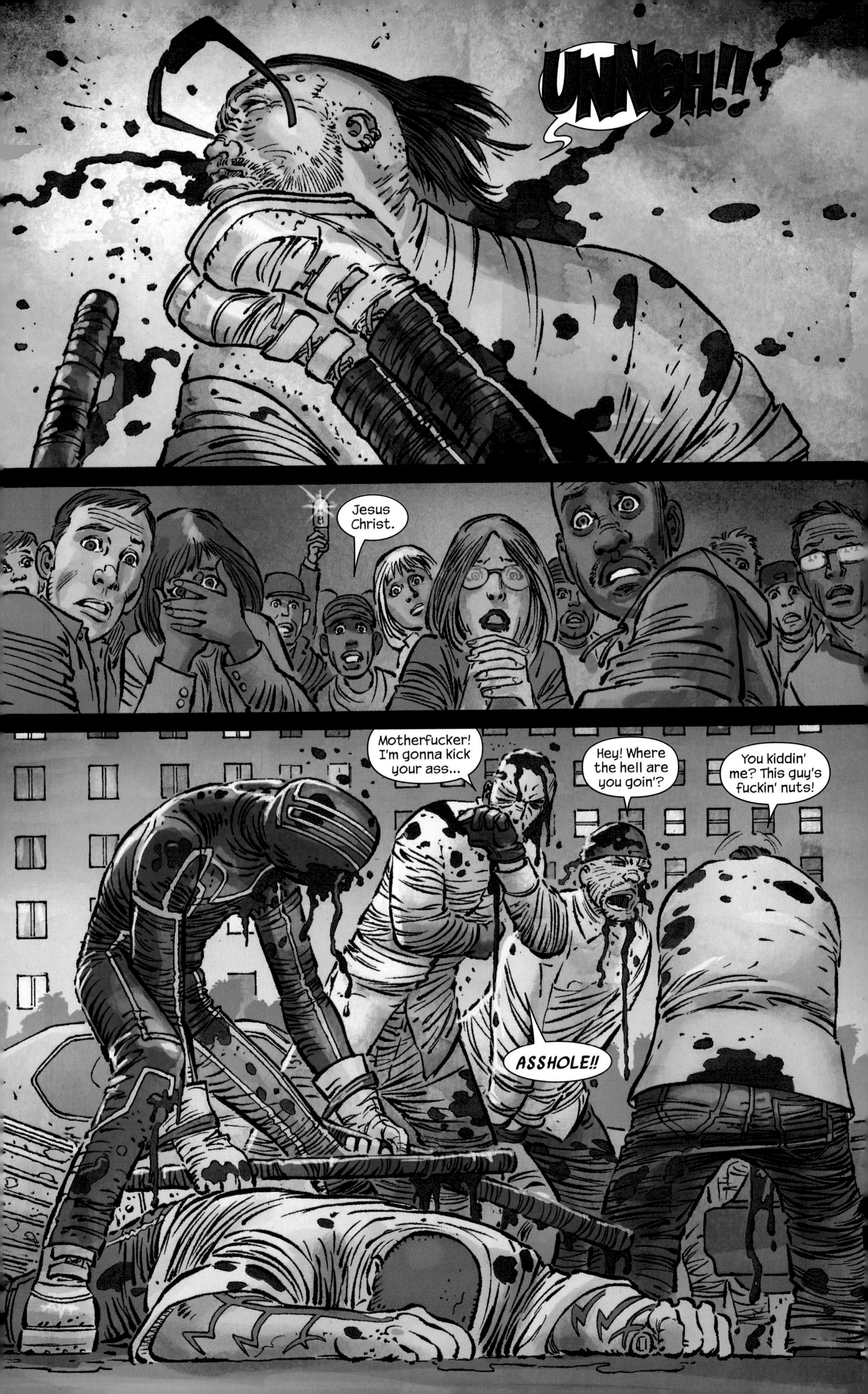
UNNGH!!
Jesus Christ.
Motherfucker! I'm gonna kick your ass...
Hey! Where the hell are you goin'?
You kiddin' me? This guy's fuckin' nuts!
ASSHOLE!!

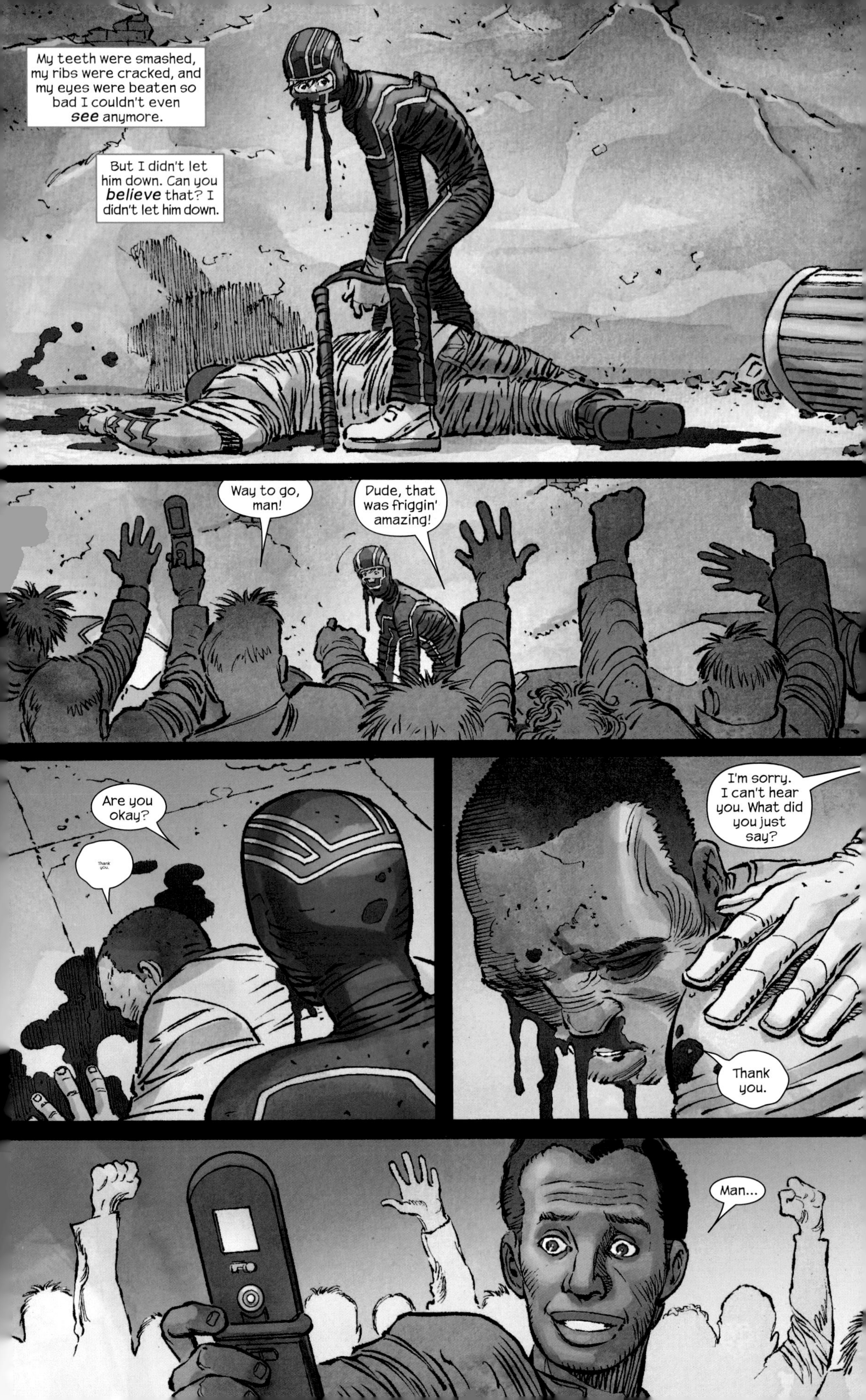

My teeth were smashed, my ribs were cracked, and my eyes were beaten so bad I couldn't even *see* anymore.
But I didn't let him down. Can you *believe* that? I didn't let him down.
Way to go, man!
Dude, that was friggin' amazing!
Are you okay?
Thank you.
I'm sorry. I can't hear you. What did you just say?
Thank you.
Man...

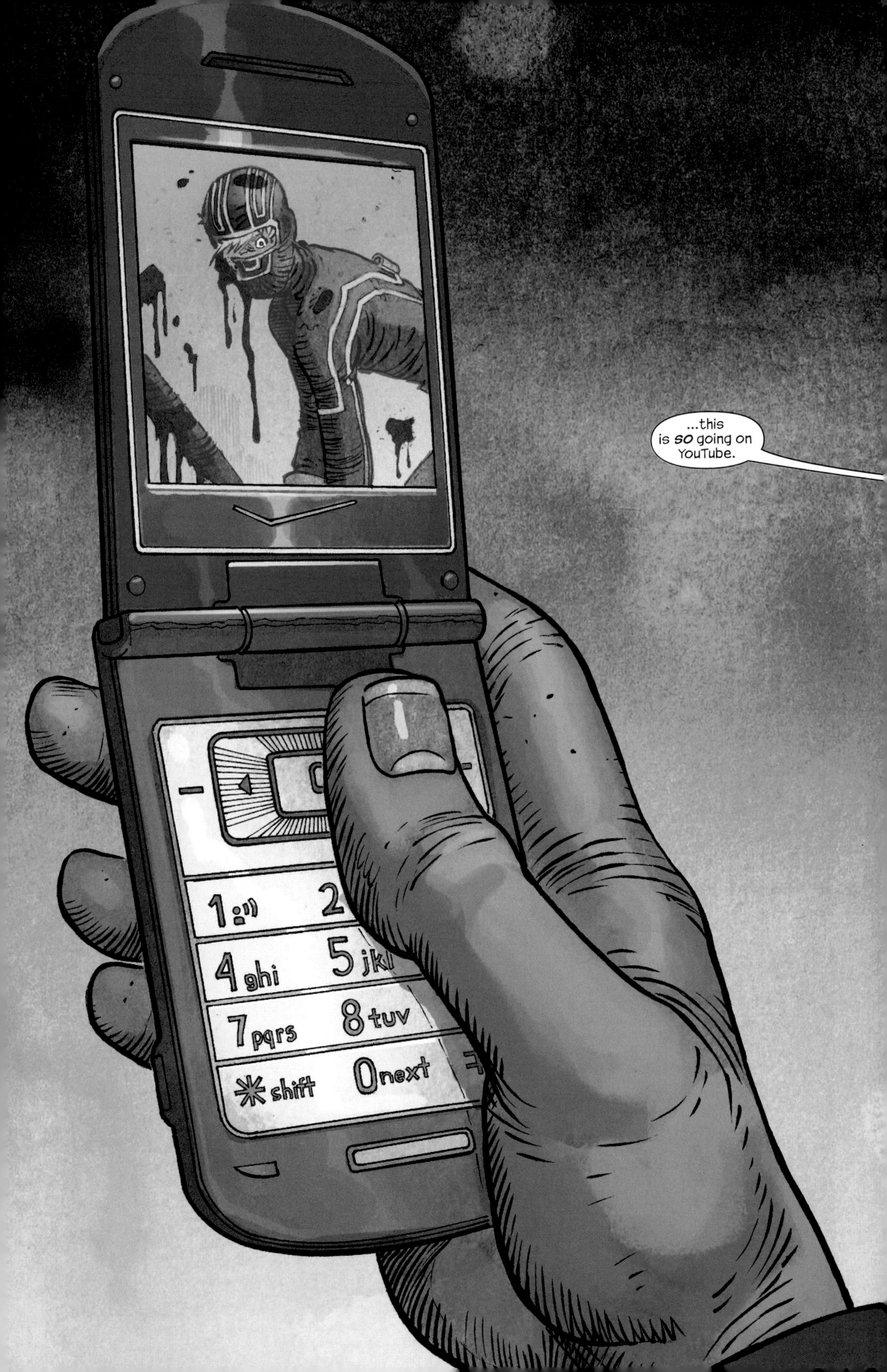
...this is **SO** going on YouTube.

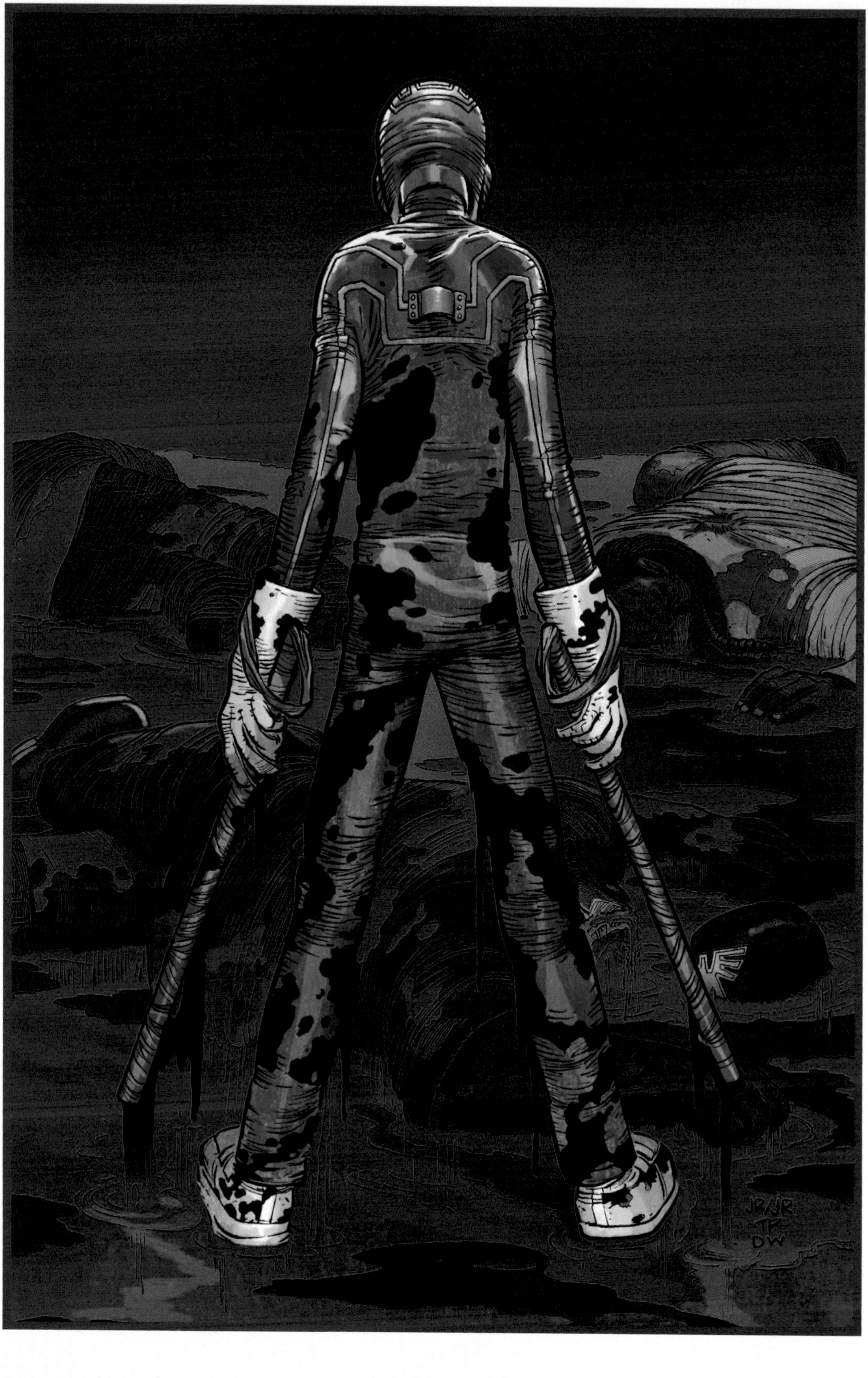
JR/JR
TF
DW

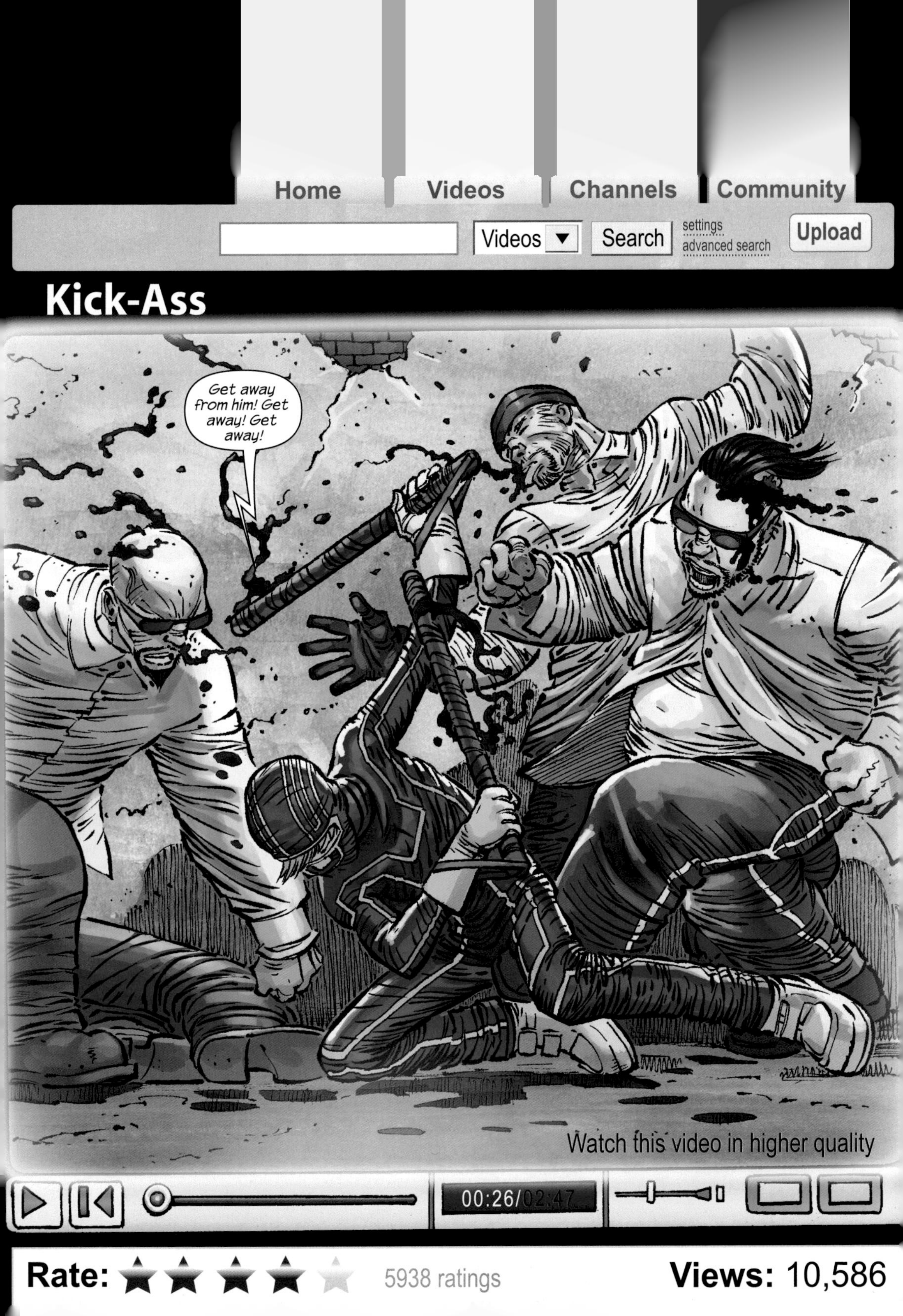
Home
Videos
Channels
Community
Videos
Search
settings
advanced search
Upload
Kick-Ass
Get away from him! Get away! Get away!
Watch this video in higher quality
00:26/02:47
Rate:
5938 ratings
Views: 10,586

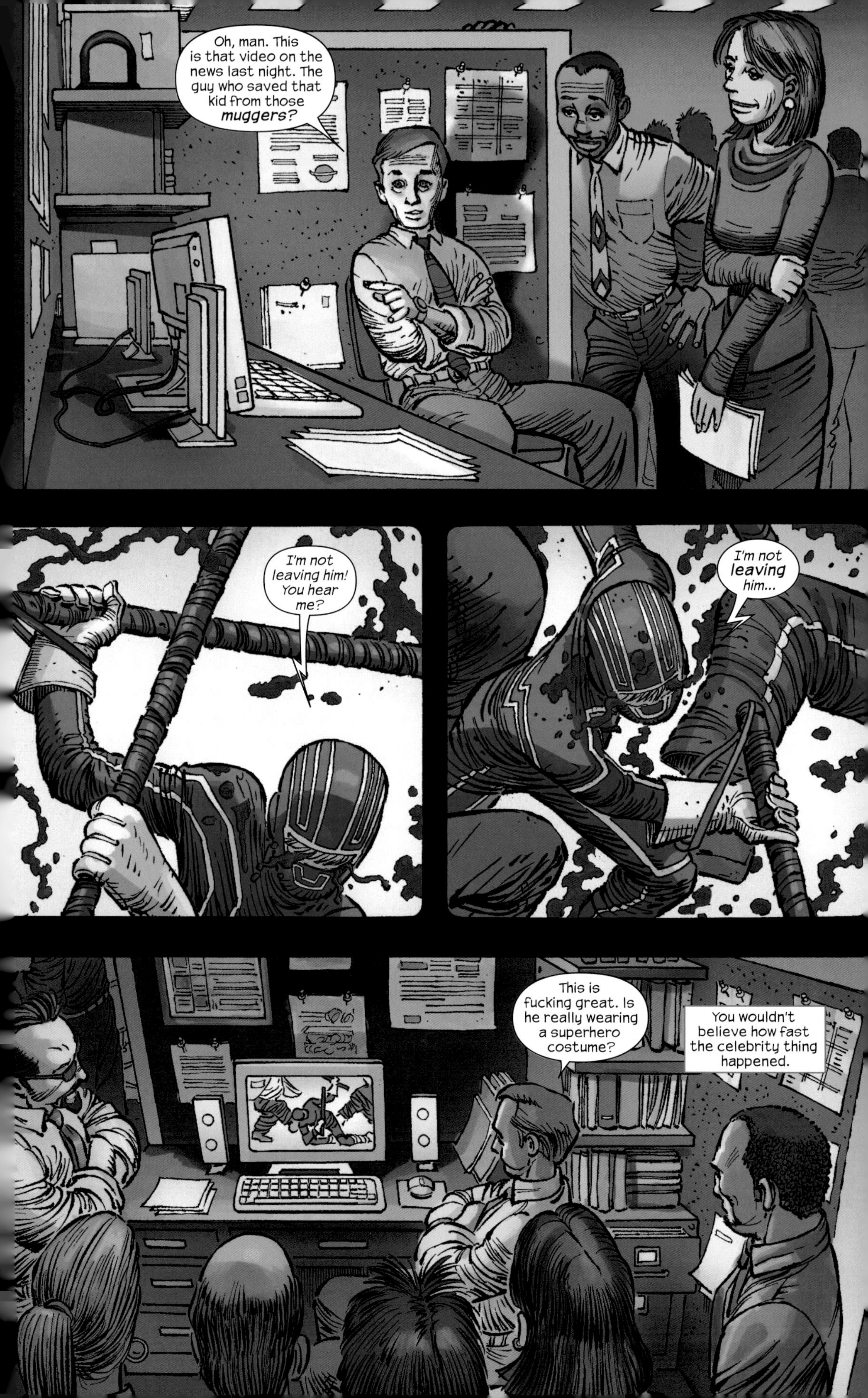
Oh, man. This is that video on the news last night. The guy who saved that kid from those *muggers?*
I'm not leaving him! You hear me?
I'm not ***leaving*** *him...*
This is fucking great. Is he really wearing a superhero costume?
You wouldn't believe how fast the celebrity thing happened.

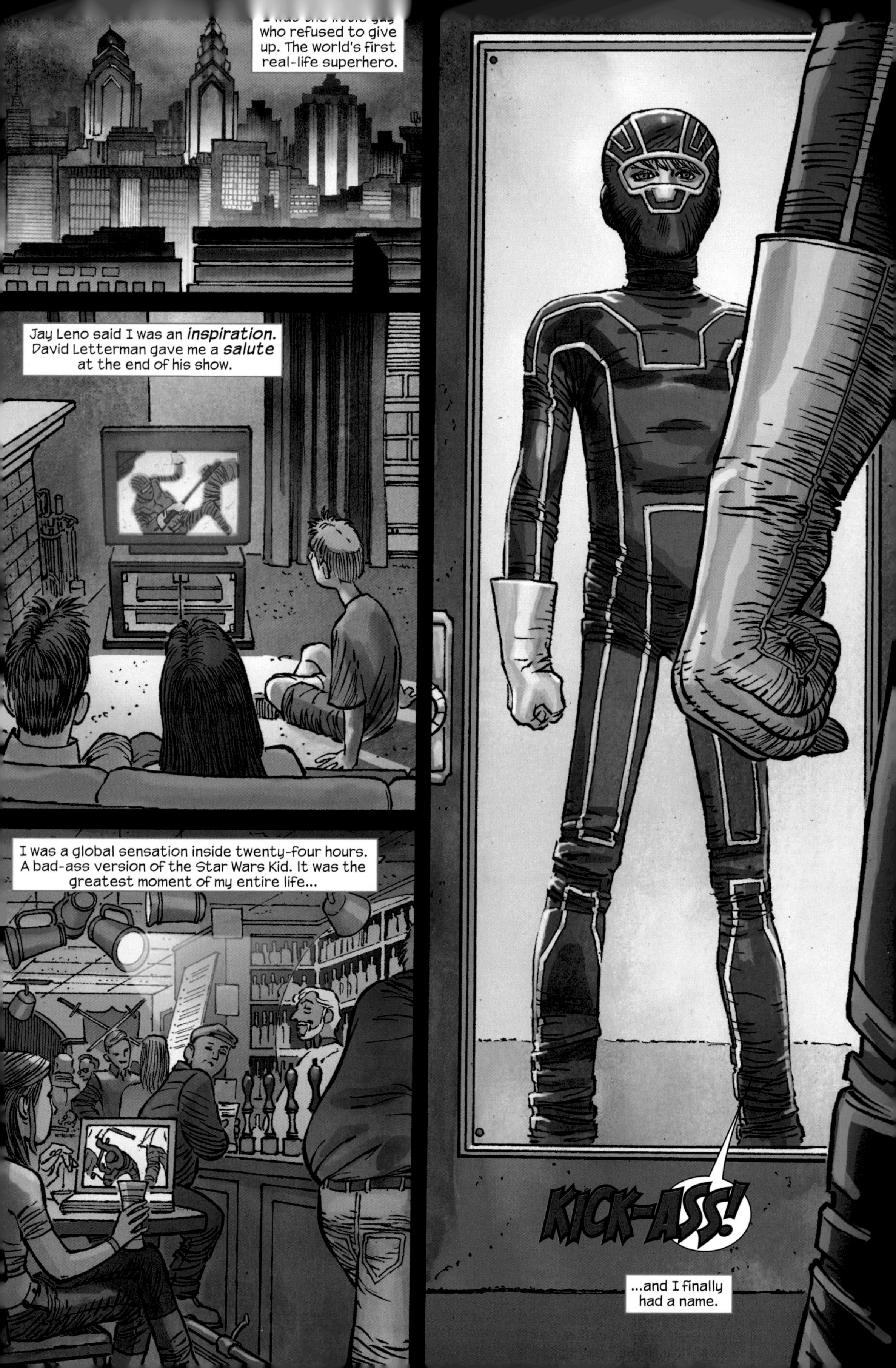
who refused to give up. The world's first real-life superhero.
Jay Leno said I was an *inspiration.* David Letterman gave me a *salute* at the end of his show.
I was a global sensation inside twenty-four hours. A bad-ass version of the Star Wars Kid. It was the greatest moment of my entire life...
KICK-ASS!
...and I finally had a name.

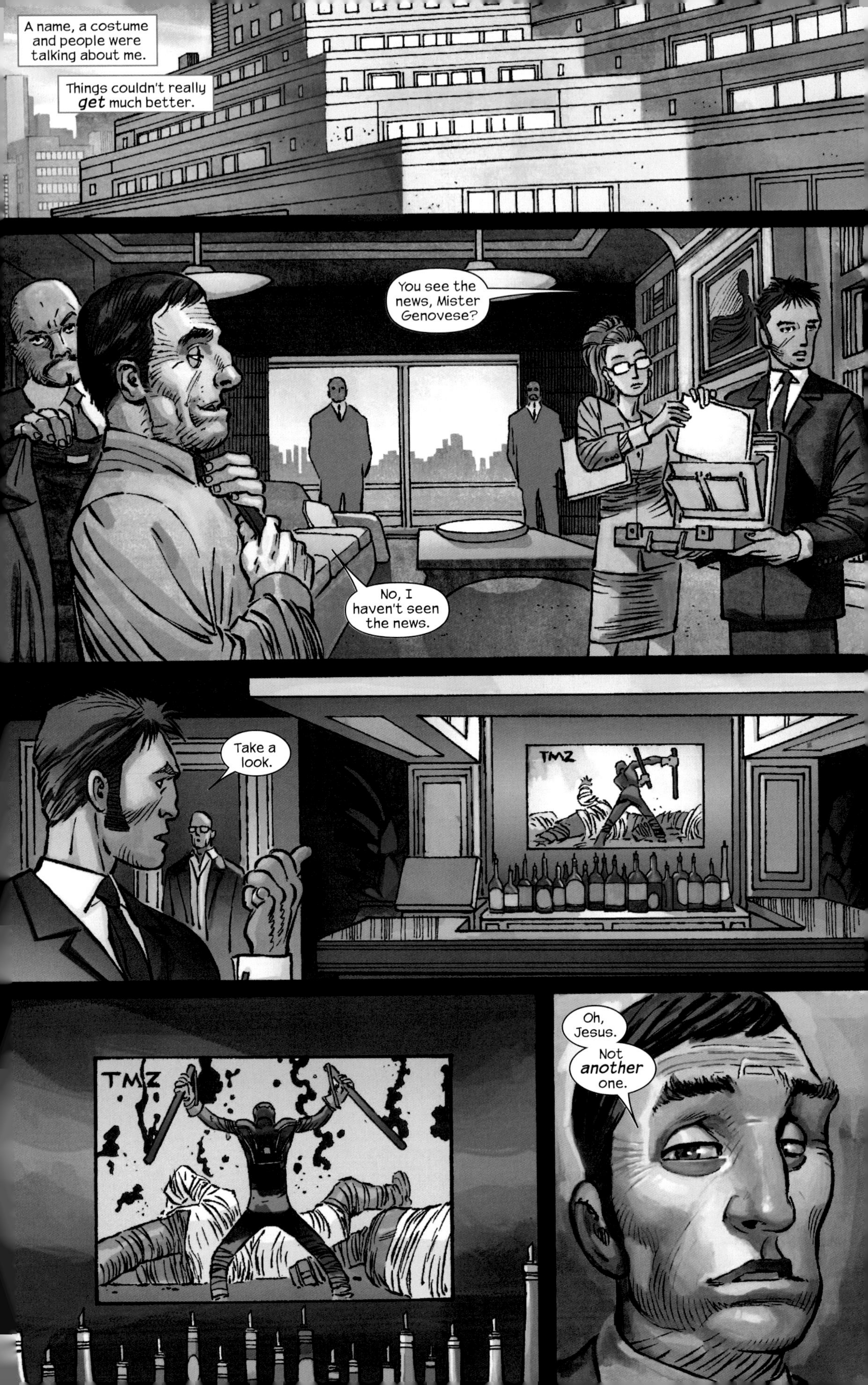
A name, a costume and people were talking about me.
Things couldn't really *get* much better.
You see the news, Mister Genovese?
No, I haven't seen the news.
Take a look.
TMZ
TMZ
Oh, Jesus.
Not *another* one.

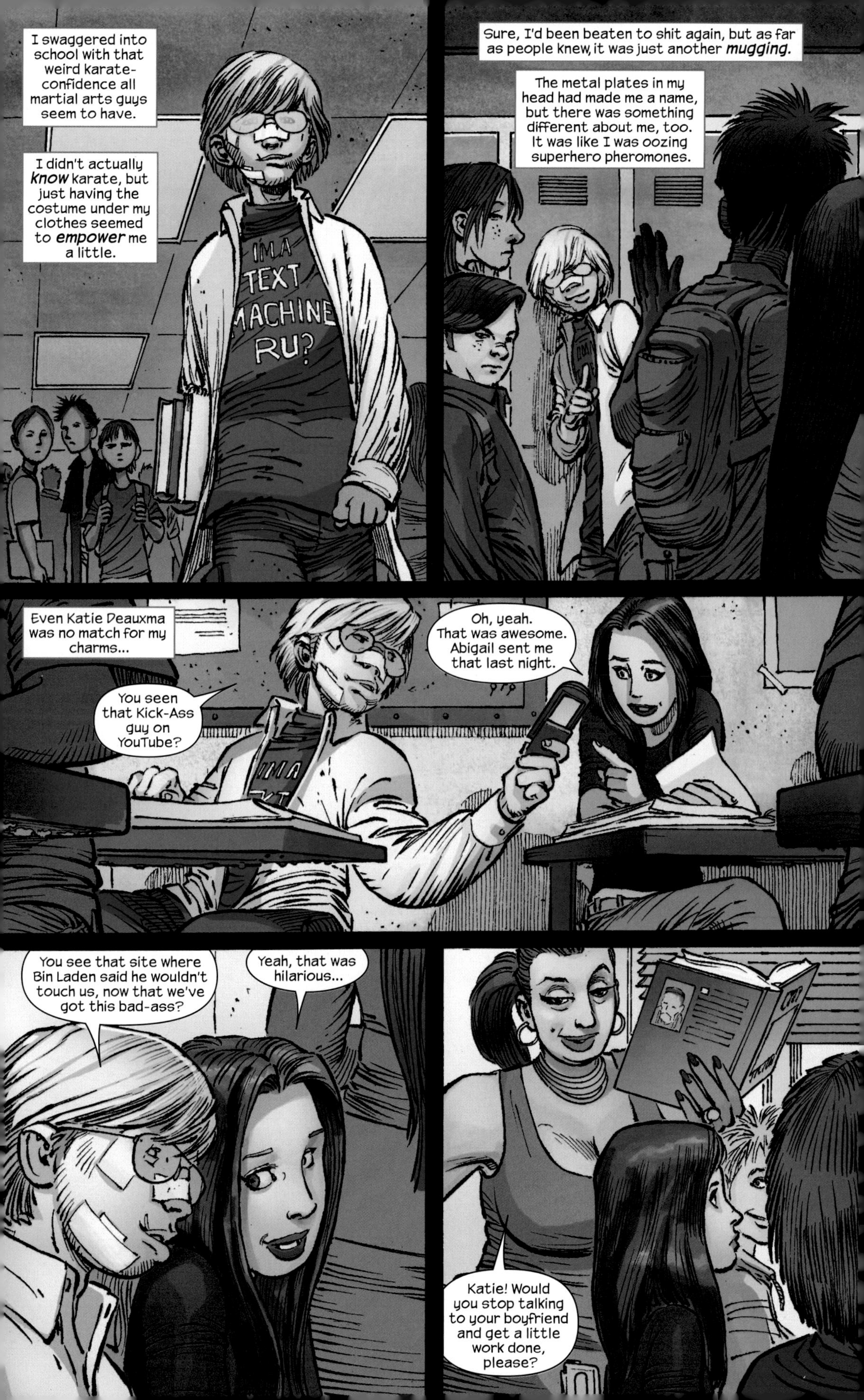

I swaggered into school with that weird karate-confidence all martial arts guys seem to have.
I didn't actually *know* karate, but just having the costume under my clothes seemed to *empower* me a little.
I'M A TEXT MACHINE RU?
Sure, I'd been beaten to shit again, but as far as people knew, it was just another *mugging.*
The metal plates in my head had made me a name, but there was something different about me, too. It was like I was oozing superhero pheromones.
Even Katie Deauxma was no match for my charms...
You seen that Kick-Ass guy on YouTube?
Oh, yeah. That was awesome. Abigail sent me that last night.
You see that site where Bin Laden said he wouldn't touch us, now that we've got this bad-ass?
Yeah, that was hilarious...
Katie! Would you stop talking to your boyfriend and get a little work done, please?

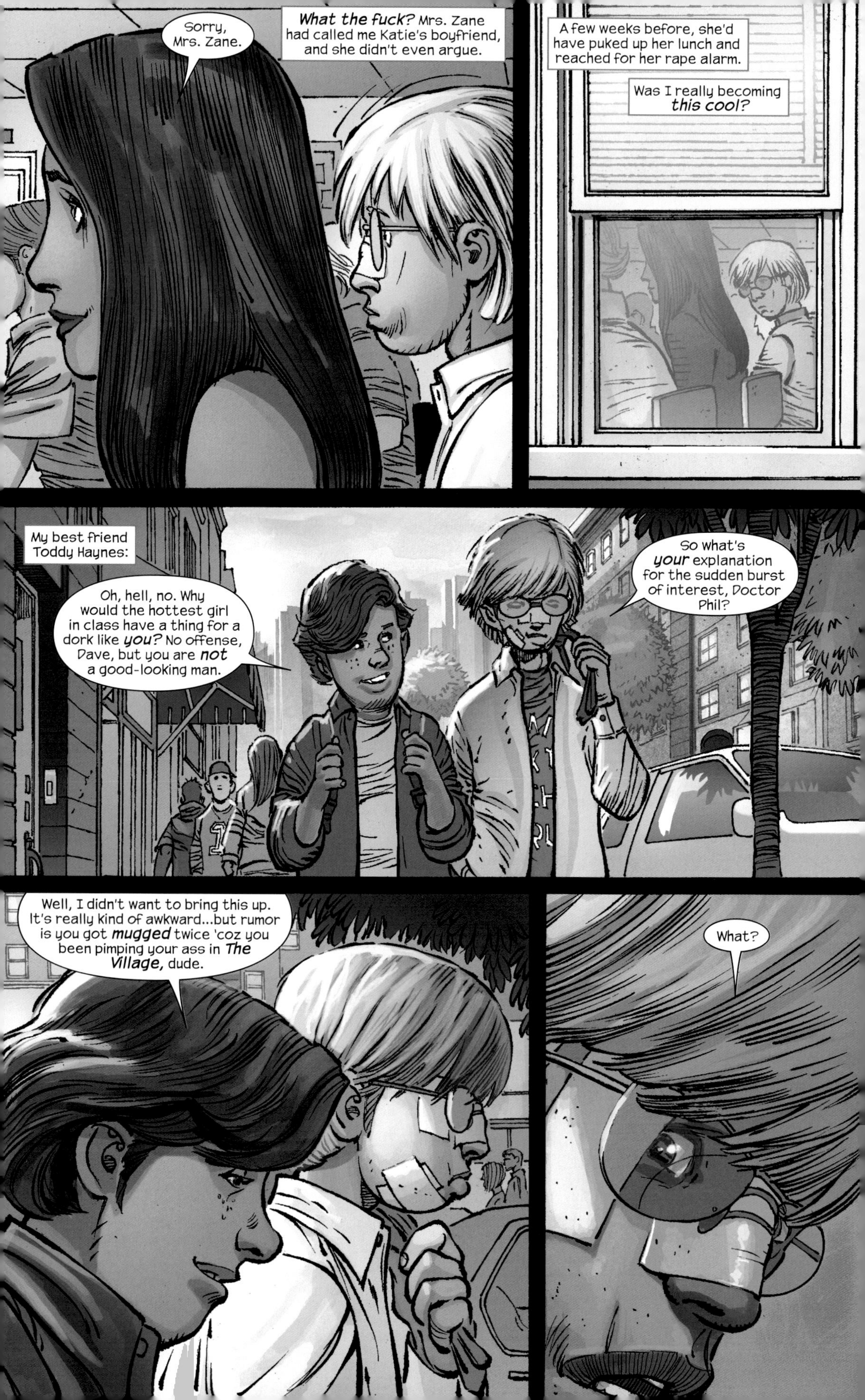
Sorry, Mrs. Zane.
What the fuck? Mrs. Zane had called me Katie's boyfriend, and she didn't even argue.
A few weeks before, she'd have puked up her lunch and reached for her rape alarm.
Was I really becoming this cool?
My best friend Toddy Haynes:
Oh, hell, no. Why would the hottest girl in class have a thing for a dork like you? No offense, Dave, but you are not a good-looking man.
So what's your explanation for the sudden burst of interest, Doctor Phil?
Well, I didn't want to bring this up. It's really kind of awkward...but rumor is you got mugged twice 'coz you been pimping your ass in The Village, dude.
What?

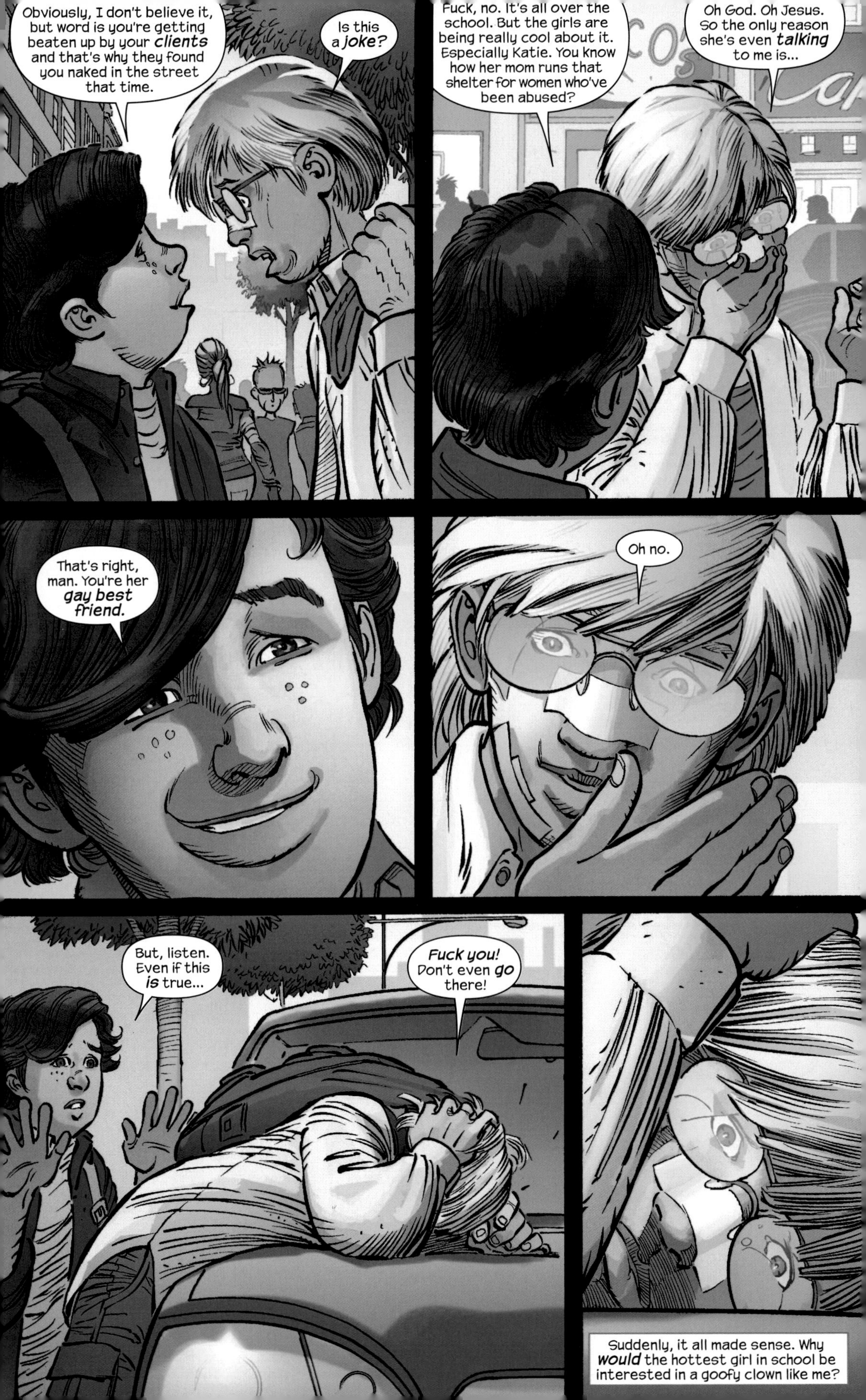
Obviously, I don't believe it, but word is you're getting beaten up by your *clients* and that's why they found you naked in the street that time.
Is this a *joke?*
Fuck, no. It's all over the school. But the girls are being really cool about it. Especially Katie. You know how her mom runs that shelter for women who've been abused?
Oh God. Oh Jesus. So the only reason she's even *talking* to me is...
That's right, man. You're her *gay best friend.*
Oh no.
But, listen. Even if this *is* true...
Fuck you! Don't even *go* there!
Suddenly, it all made sense. Why *would* the hottest girl in school be interested in a goofy clown like me?

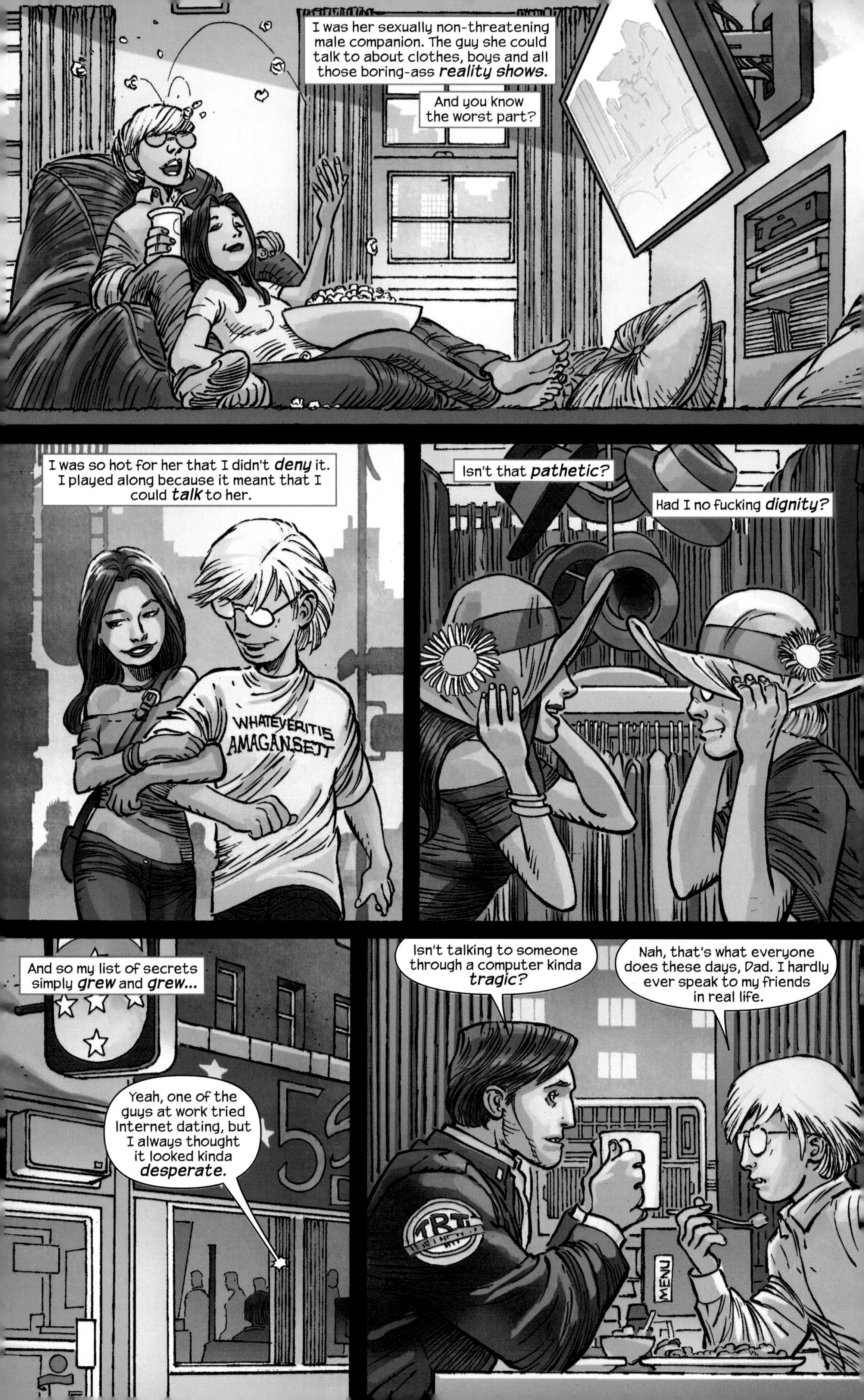
I was her sexually non-threatening male companion. The guy she could talk to about clothes, boys and all those boring-ass *reality shows.*
And you know the worst part?
I was so hot for her that I didn't *deny* it. I played along because it meant that I could *talk* to her.
WHATEVER IT IS AMAGANSETT
Isn't that *pathetic?*
Had I no fucking *dignity?*
And so my list of secrets simply *grew* and *grew...*
Yeah, one of the guys at work tried Internet dating, but I always thought it looked kinda *desperate.*
Isn't talking to someone through a computer kinda *tragic?*
Nah, that's what everyone does these days, Dad. I hardly ever speak to my friends in real life.
MENU

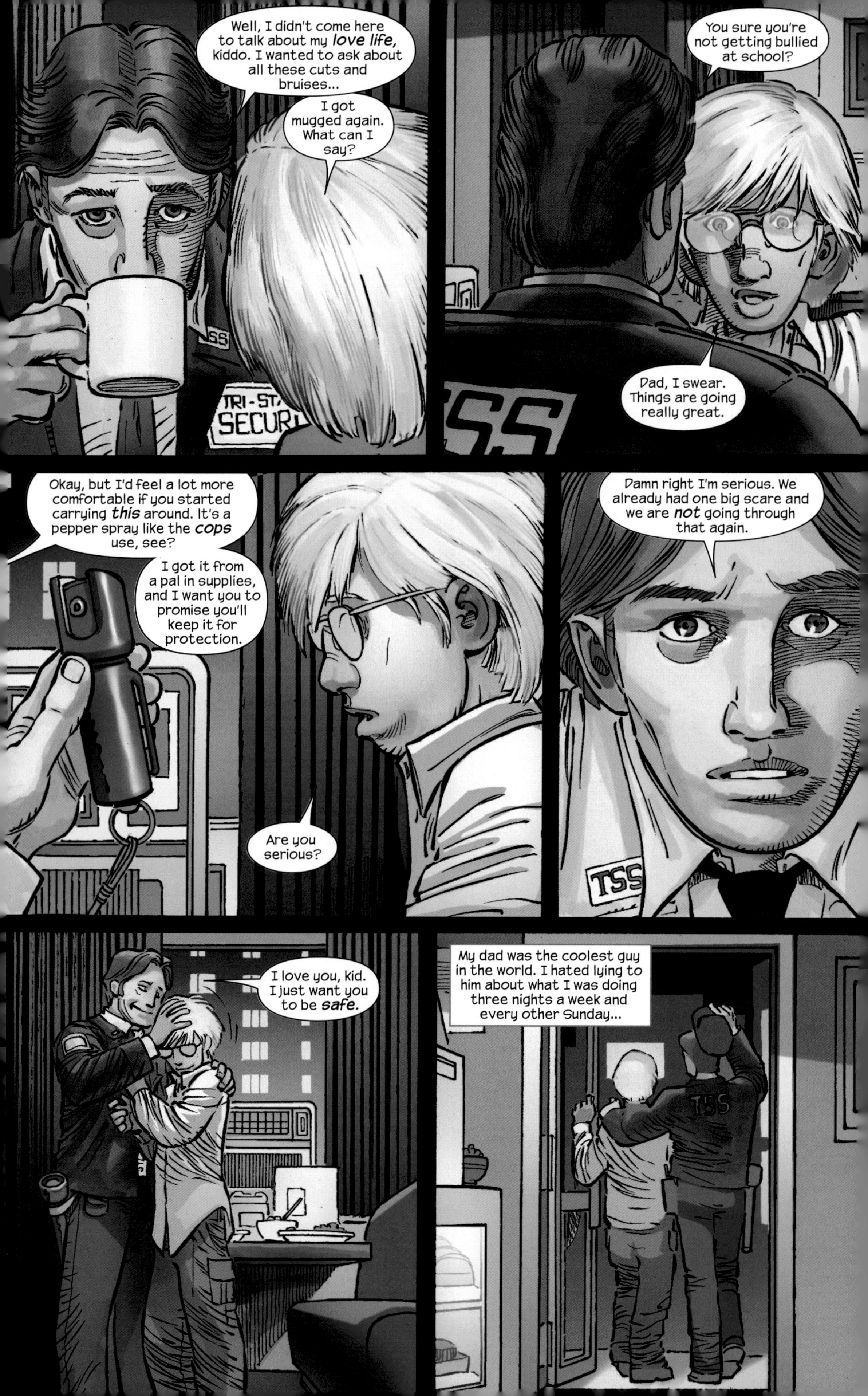
Well, I didn't come here to talk about my *love life,* kiddo. I wanted to ask about all these cuts and bruises...
I got mugged again. What can I say?
TRI-STA
SECURI
You sure you're not getting bullied at school?
Dad, I swear. Things are going really great.
TSS
Okay, but I'd feel a lot more comfortable if you started carrying ***this*** around. It's a pepper spray like the ***cops*** use, see?
I got it from a pal in supplies, and I want you to promise you'll keep it for protection.
Are you serious?
Damn right I'm serious. We already had one big scare and we are ***not*** going through that again.
TSS
I love you, kid. I just want you to be ***safe.***
My dad was the coolest guy in the world. I hated lying to him about what I was doing three nights a week and every other Sunday...
TSS

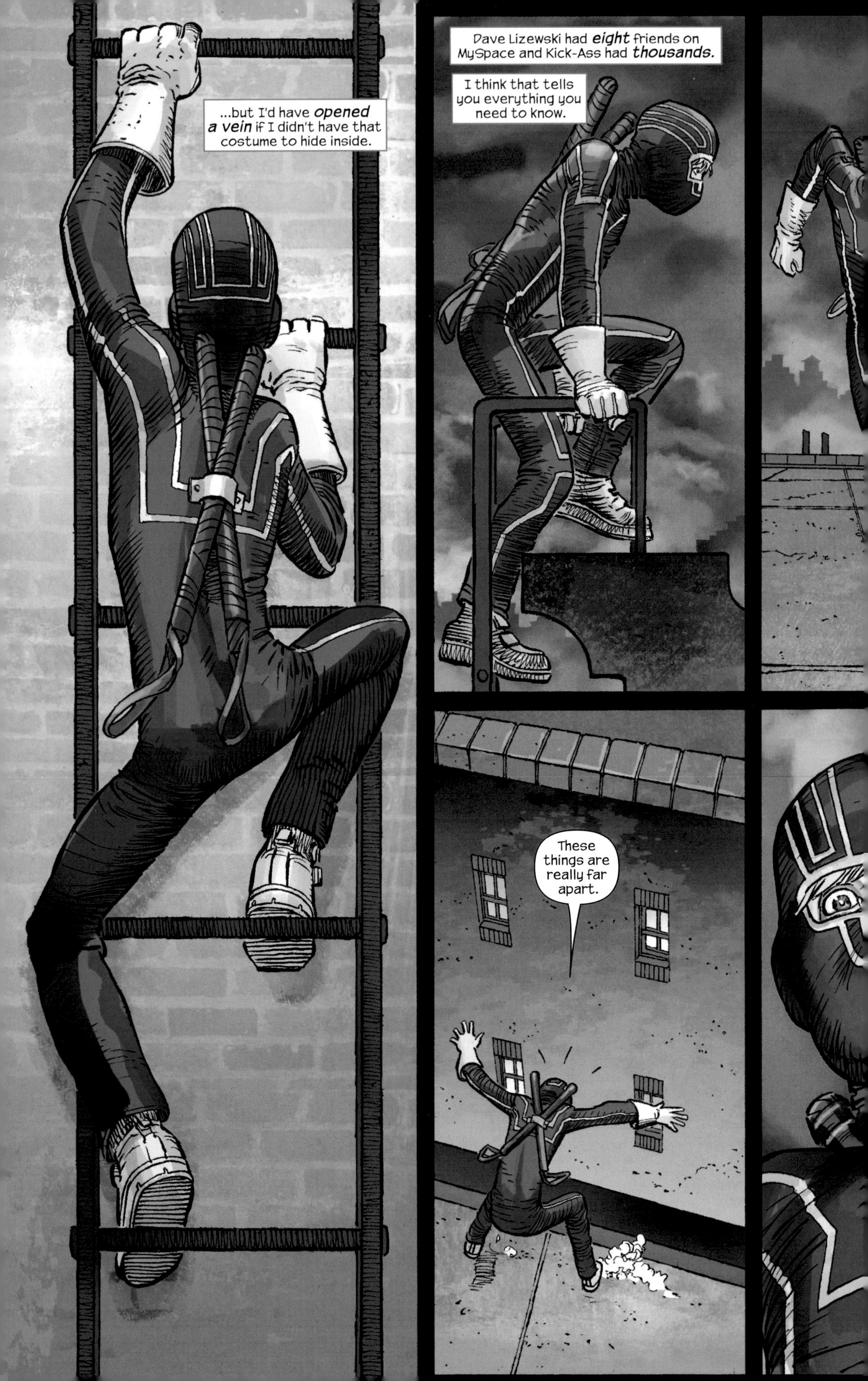
...but I'd have opened a vein if I didn't have that costume to hide inside.
Dave Lizewski had eight friends on MySpace and Kick-Ass had thousands.
I think that tells you everything you need to know.
These things are really far apart.

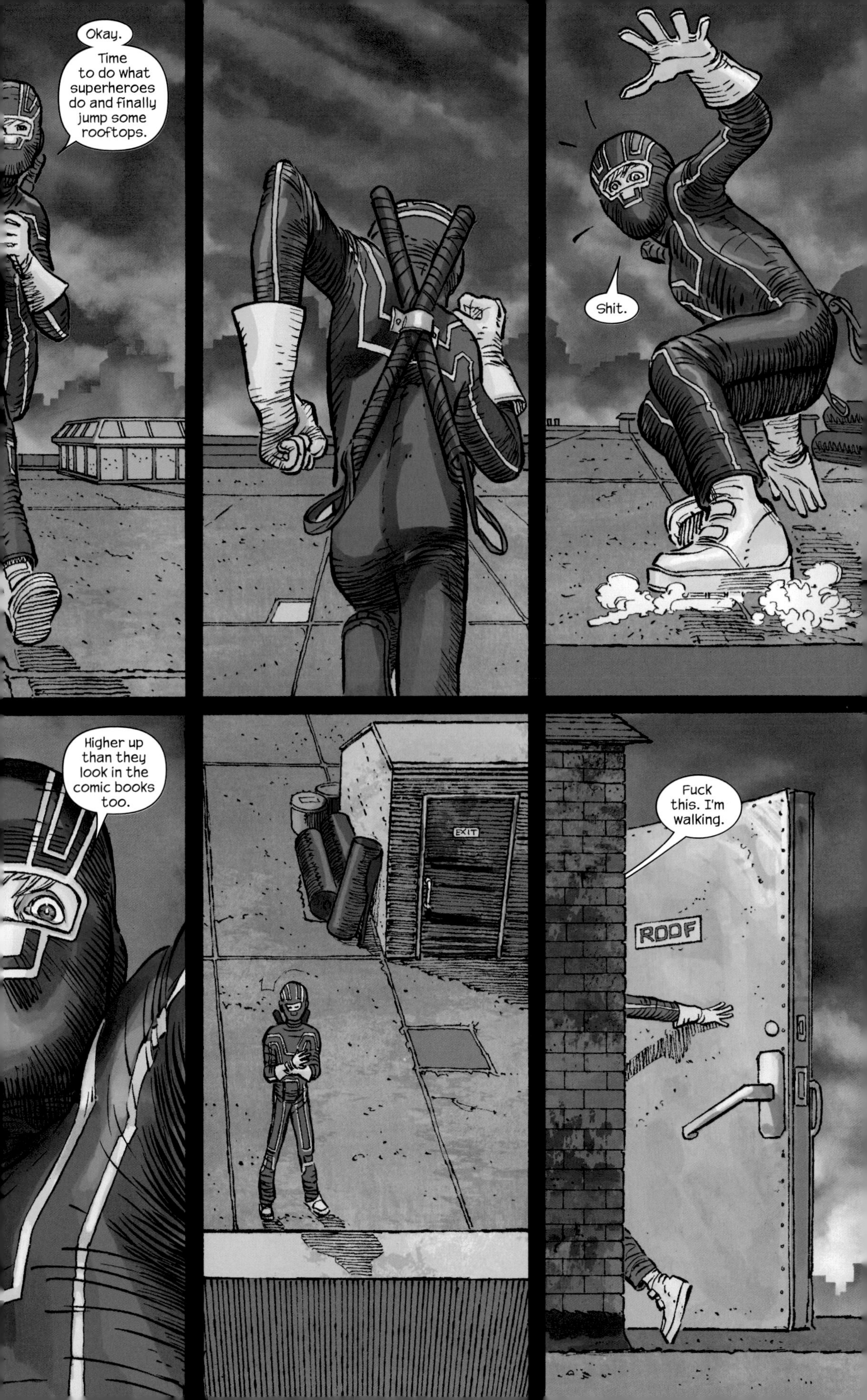
Okay.
Time to do what superheroes do and finally jump some rooftops.
Shit.
Higher up than they look in the comic books too.
EXIT
Fuck this. I'm walking.
ROOF

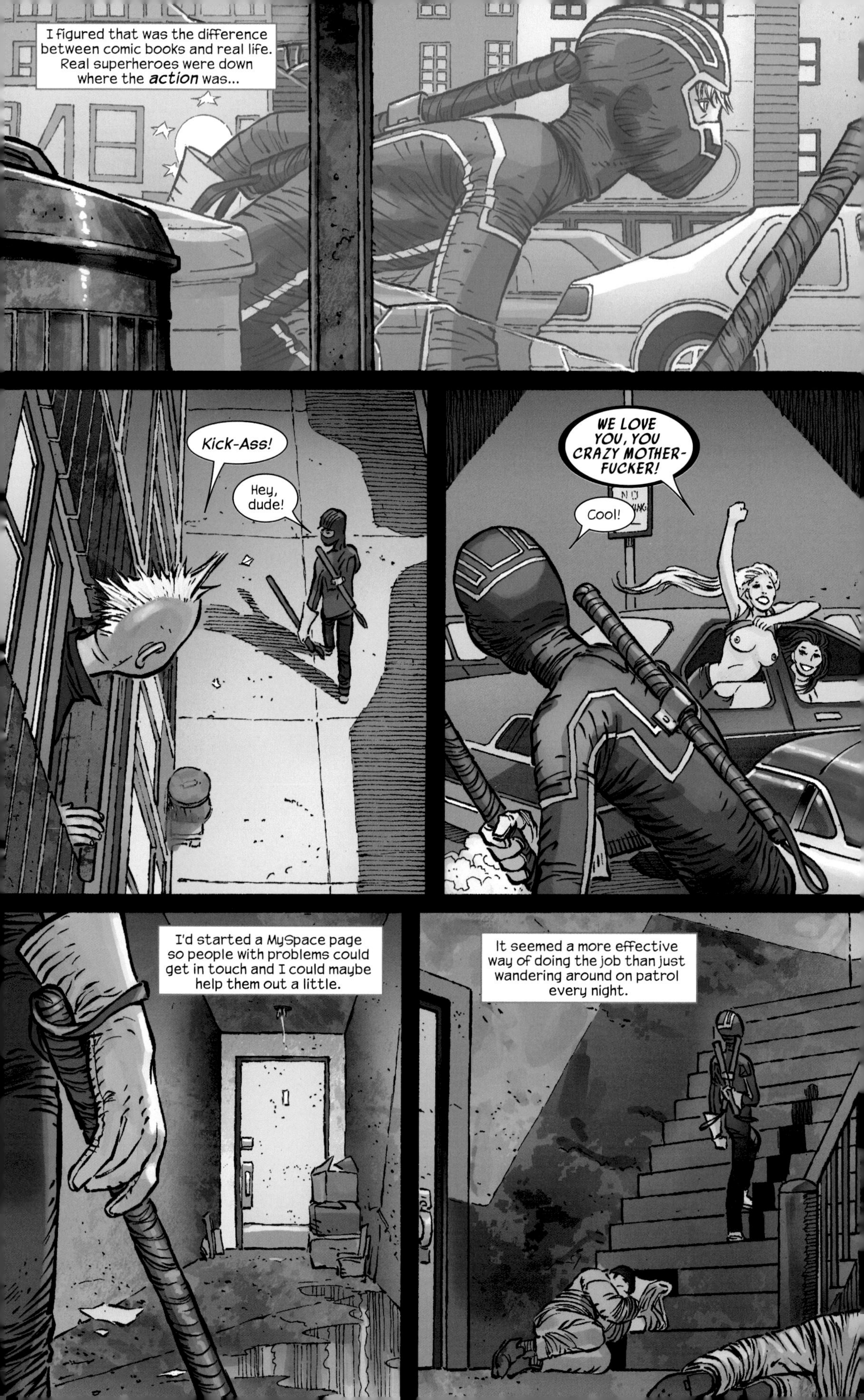
I figured that was the difference between comic books and real life. Real superheroes were down where the *action* was...
Kick-Ass!
Hey, dude!
WE LOVE YOU, YOU CRAZY MOTHER-FUCKER!
Cool!
I'd started a MySpace page so people with problems could get in touch and I could maybe help them out a little.
It seemed a more effective way of doing the job than just wandering around on patrol every night.

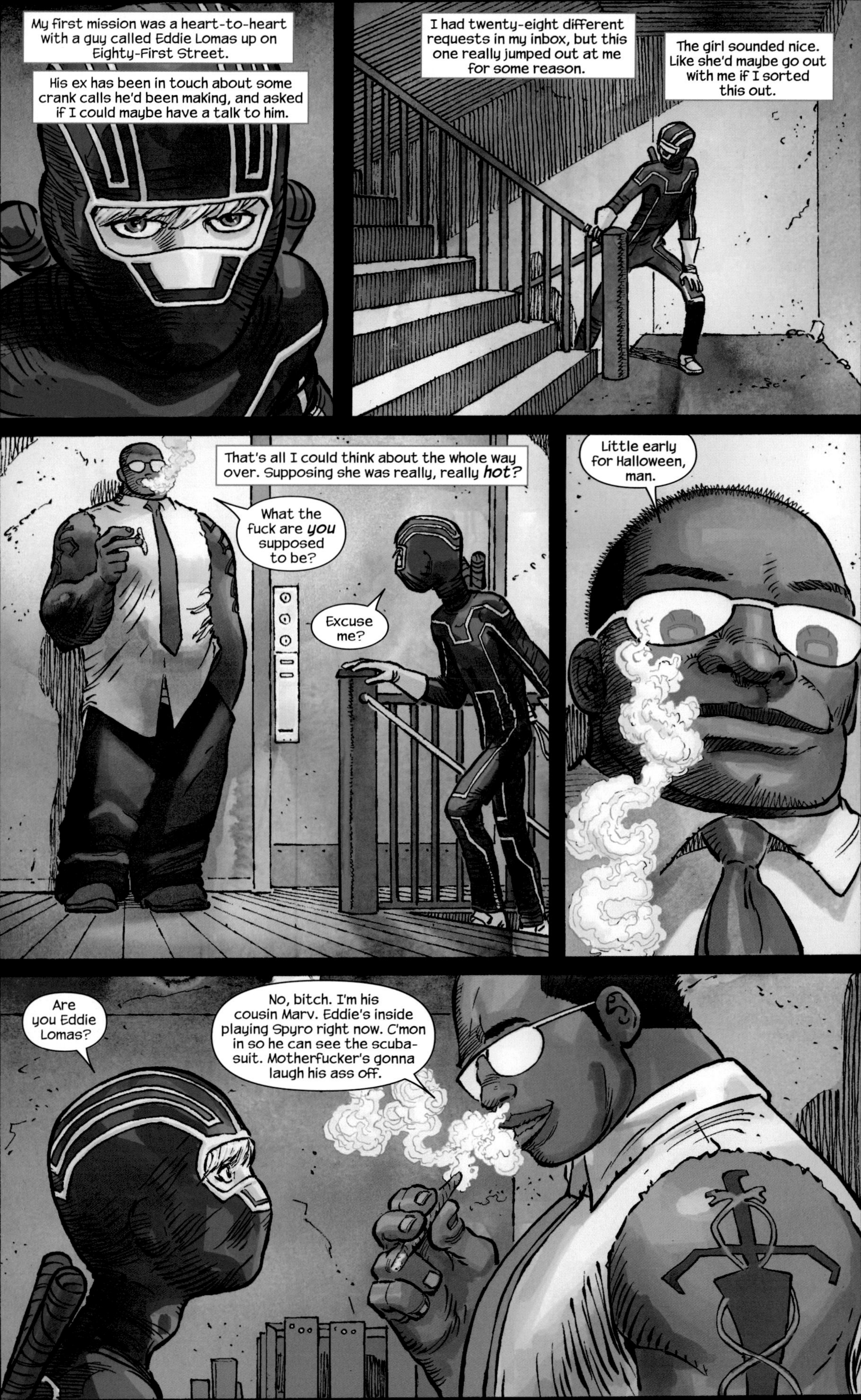
My first mission was a heart-to-heart with a guy called Eddie Lomas up on Eighty-First Street.
His ex has been in touch about some crank calls he'd been making, and asked if I could maybe have a talk to him.
I had twenty-eight different requests in my inbox, but this one really jumped out at me for some reason.
The girl sounded nice. Like she'd maybe go out with me if I sorted this out.
That's all I could think about the whole way over. Supposing she was really, really hot?
What the fuck are you supposed to be?
Excuse me?
Little early for Halloween, man.
Are you Eddie Lomas?
No, bitch. I'm his cousin Marv. Eddie's inside playing Spyro right now. C'mon in so he can see the scuba-suit. Motherfucker's gonna laugh his ass off.

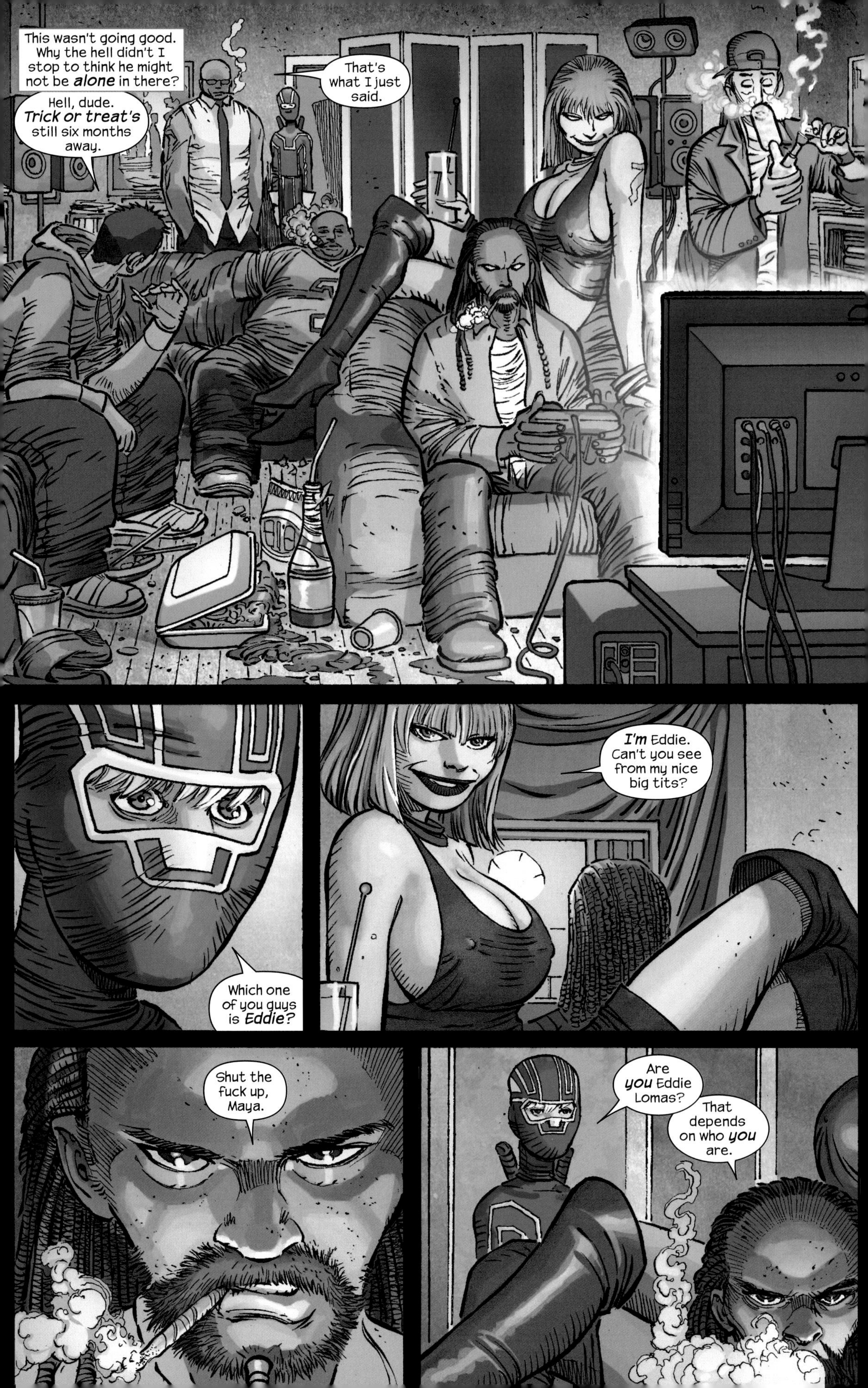
This wasn't going good. Why the hell didn't I stop to think he might not be *alone* in there?
Hell, dude. *Trick or treat's* still six months away.
That's what I just said.
Which one of you guys is *Eddie?*
I'm Eddie. Can't you see from my nice big tits?
Shut the fuck up, Maya.
Are *you* Eddie Lomas?
That depends on who *you* are.

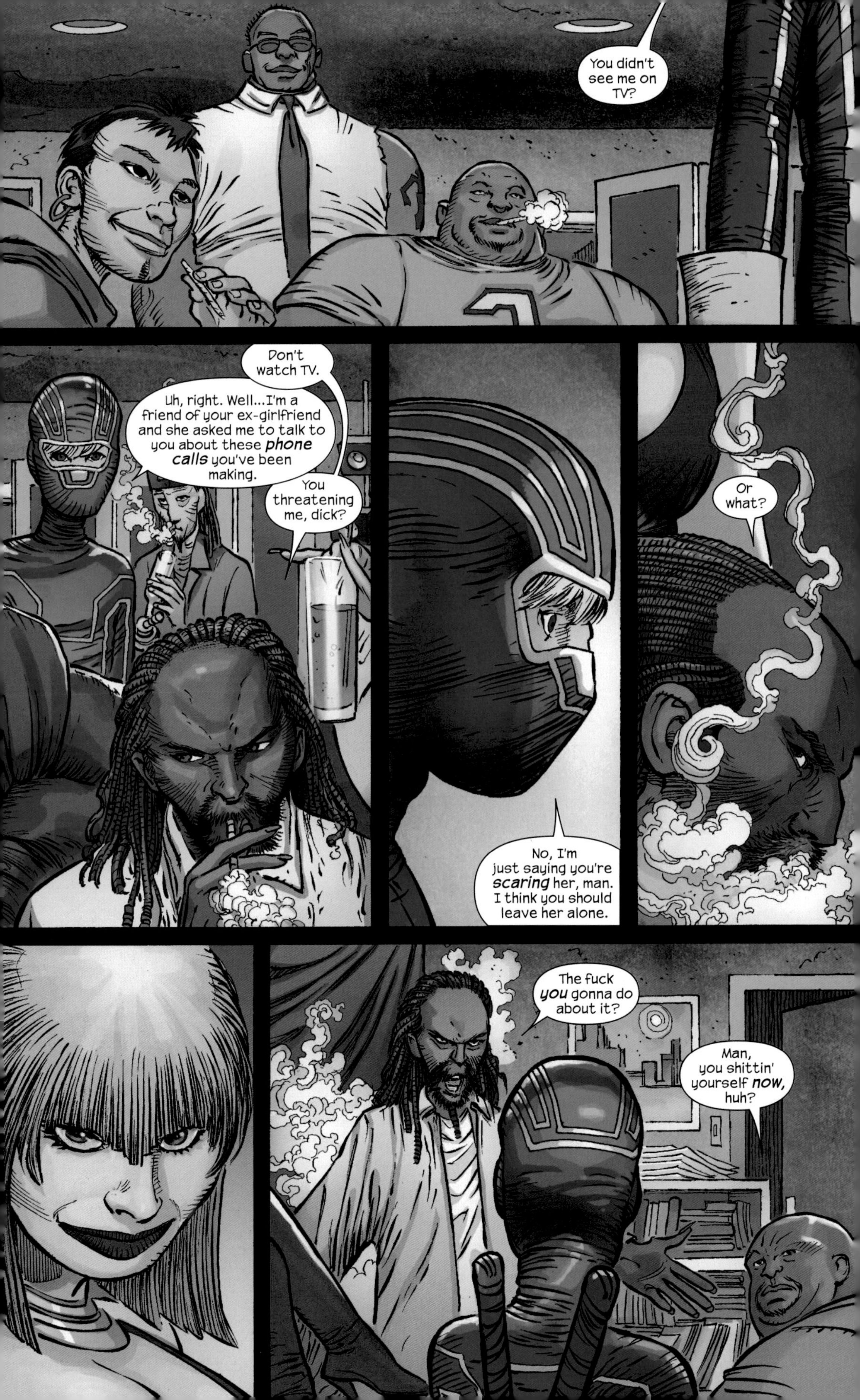

You didn't see me on TV?
Don't watch TV.
Uh, right. Well...I'm a friend of your ex-girlfriend and she asked me to talk to you about these *phone calls* you've been making.
You threatening me, dick?
No, I'm just saying you're *scaring* her, man. I think you should leave her alone.
Or what?
The fuck *you* gonna do about it?
Man, you shittin' yourself *now,* huh?

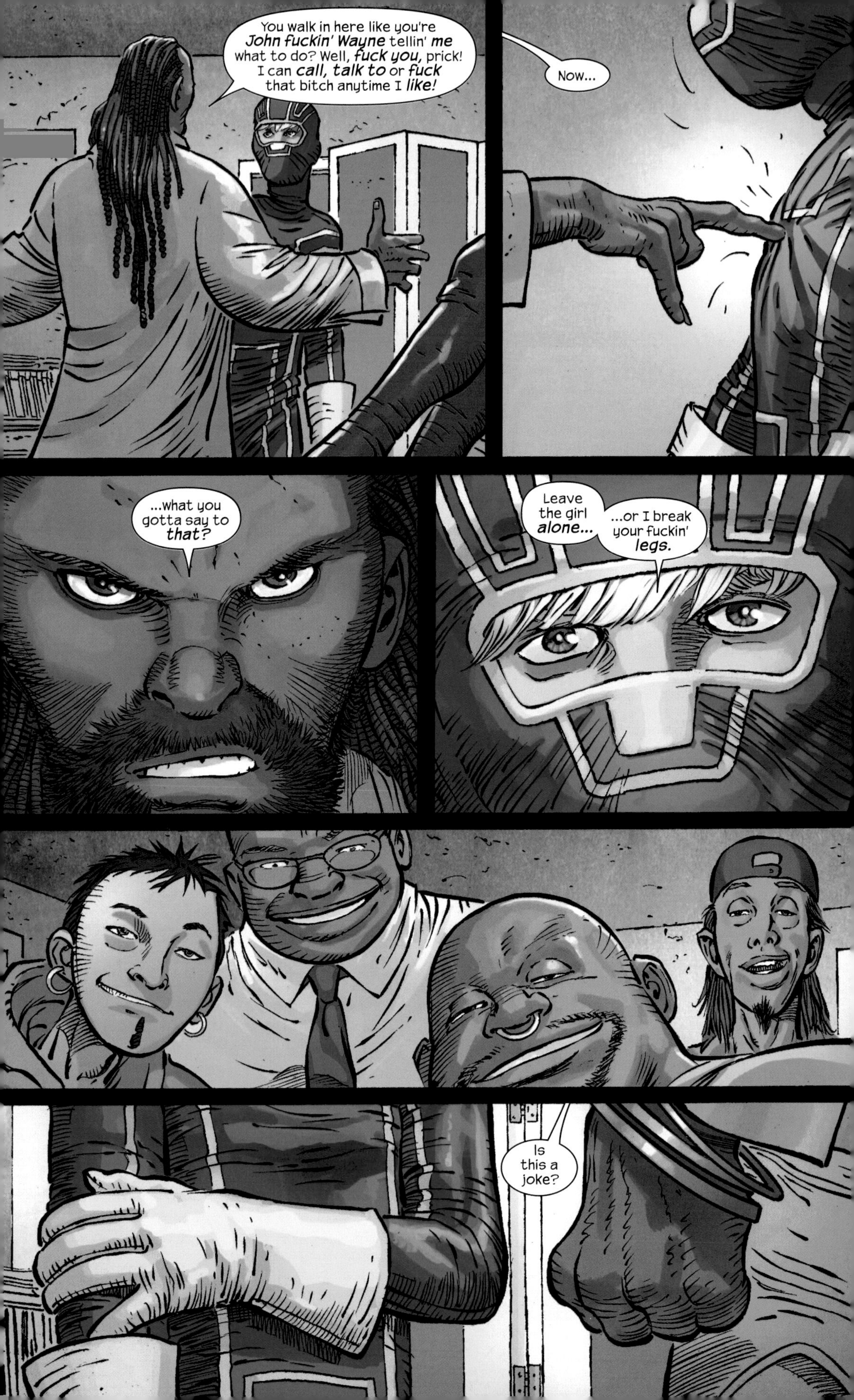
You walk in here like you're *John fuckin' Wayne* tellin' *me* what to do? Well, *fuck you,* prick! I can *call, talk to* or *fuck* that bitch anytime I *like!*
Now...
...what you gotta say to *that?*
Leave the girl *alone...*
...or I break your fuckin' *legs.*
Is this a joke?

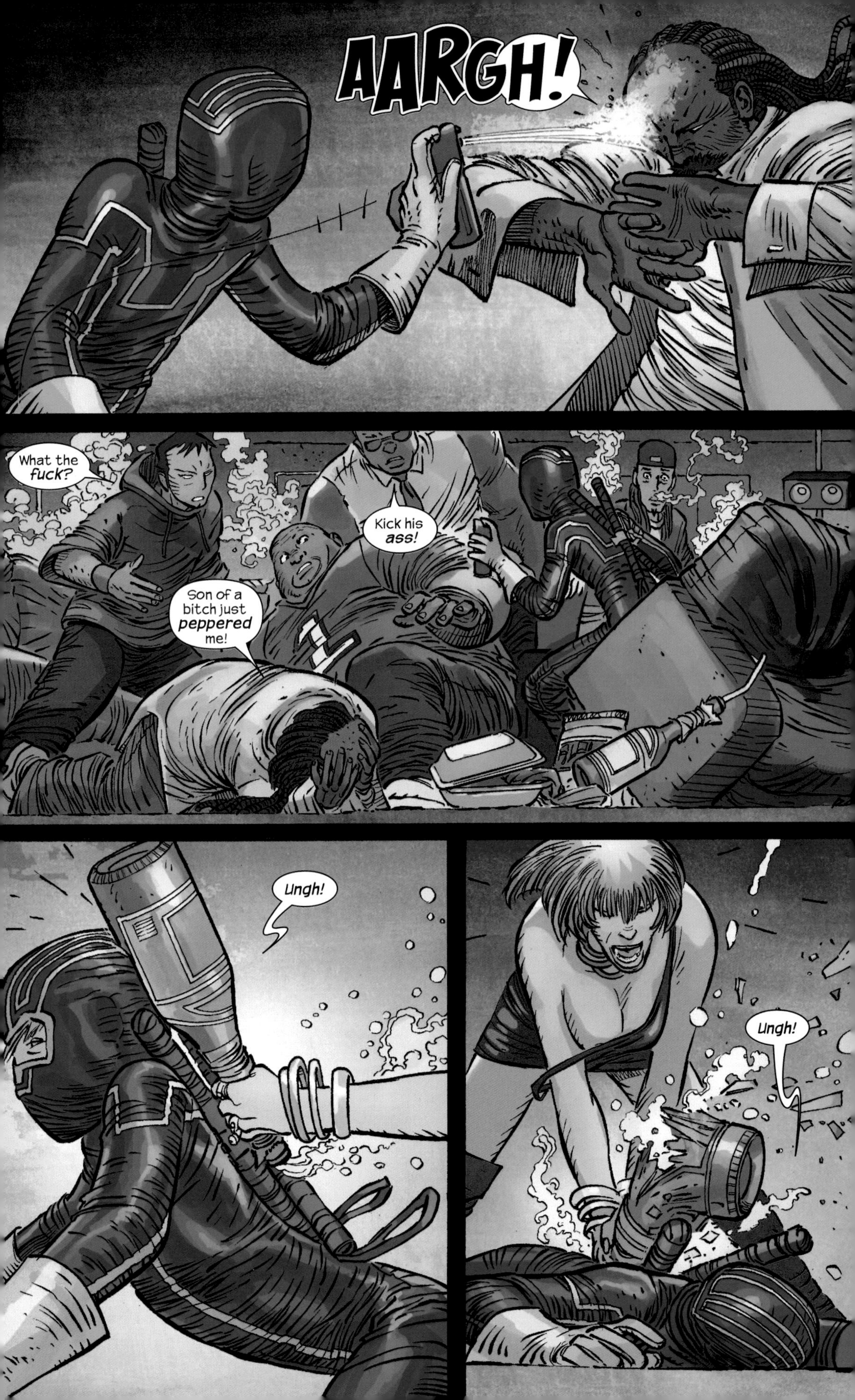
AARGH!
What the fuck?
Kick his ass!
Son of a bitch just peppered me!
Ungh!
Ungh!

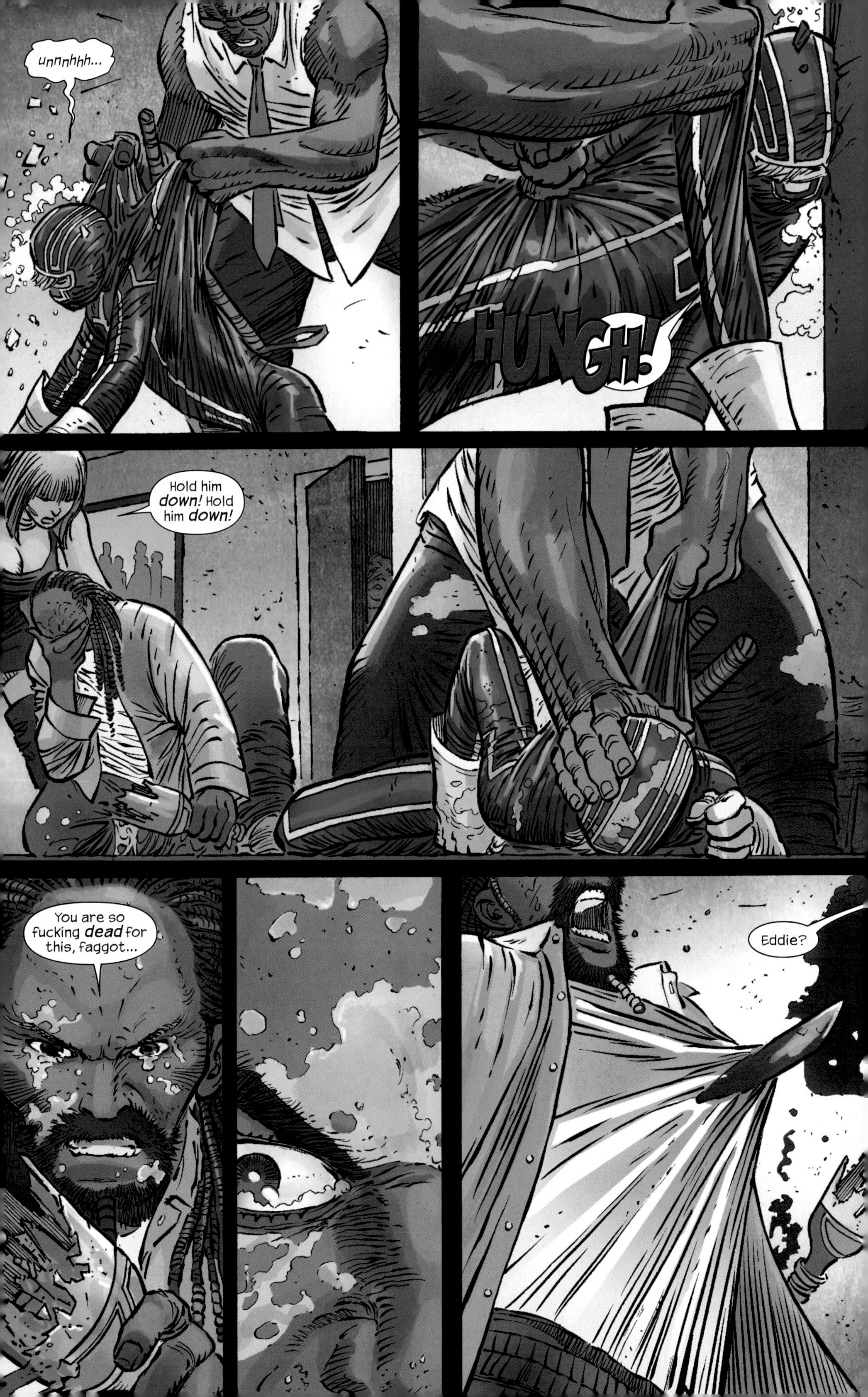
unnnhhh...
HUNGH!
Hold him down! Hold him down!
You are so fucking dead for this, faggot...
Eddie?

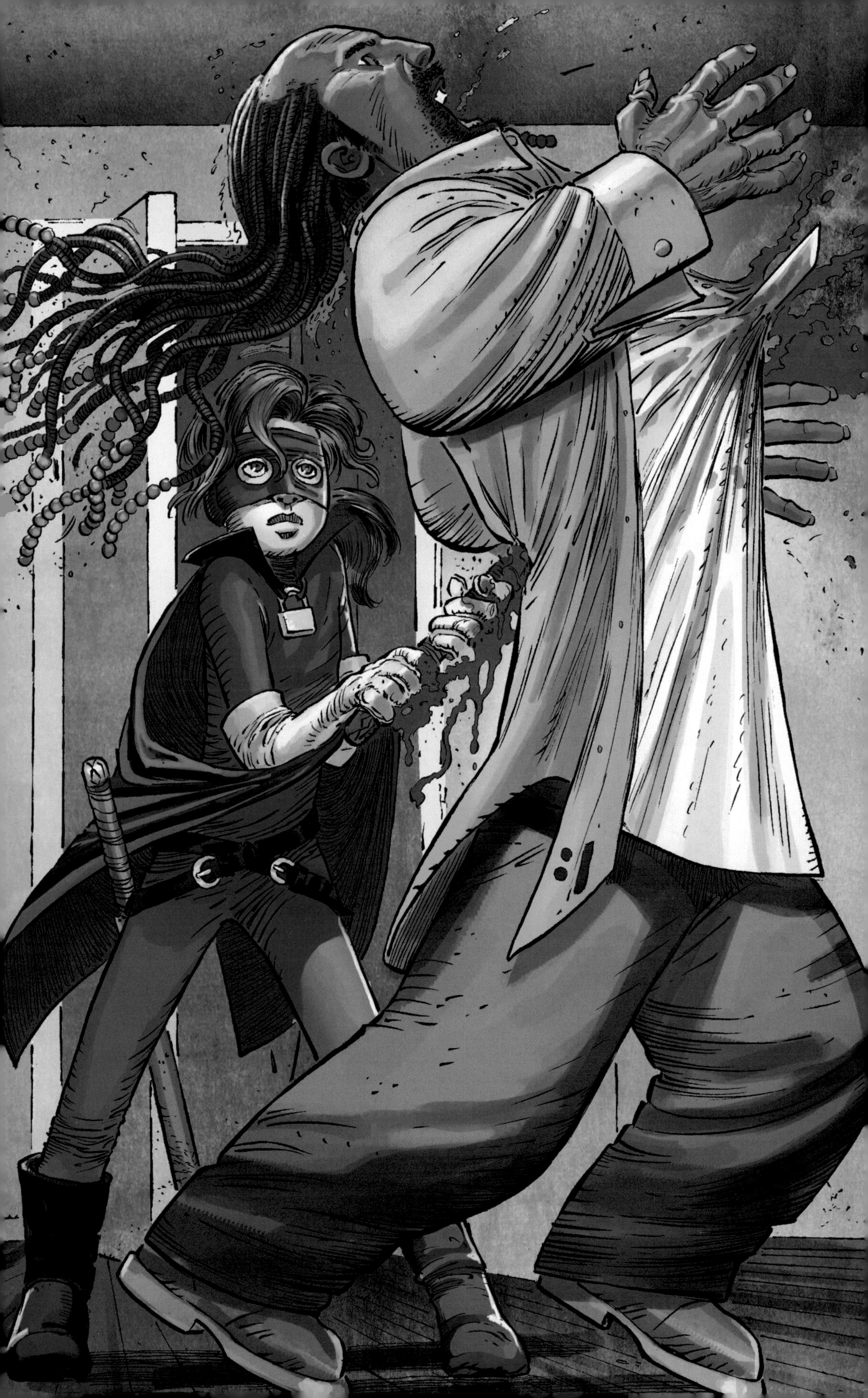

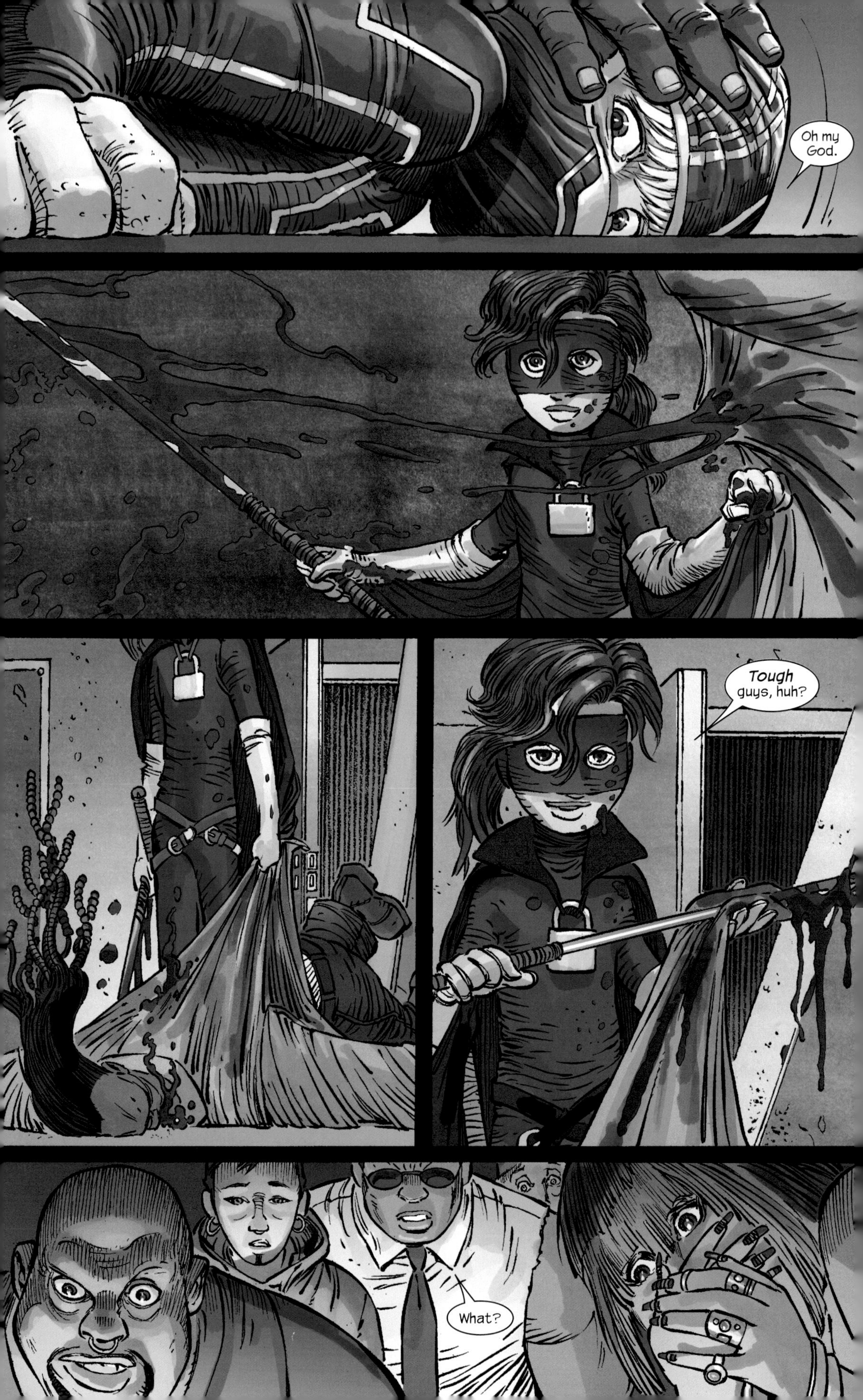
Oh my God.
Tough guys, huh?
What?

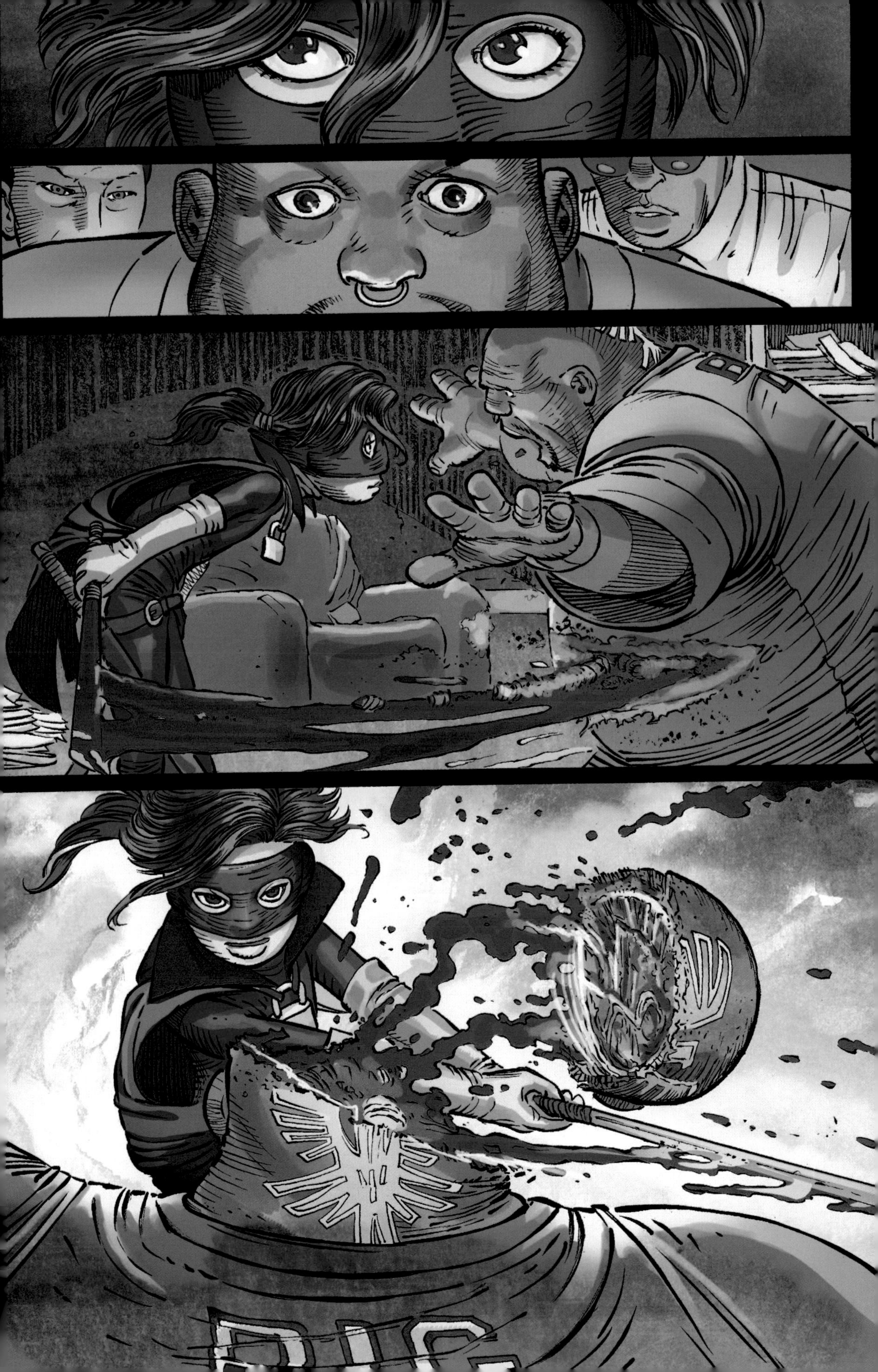

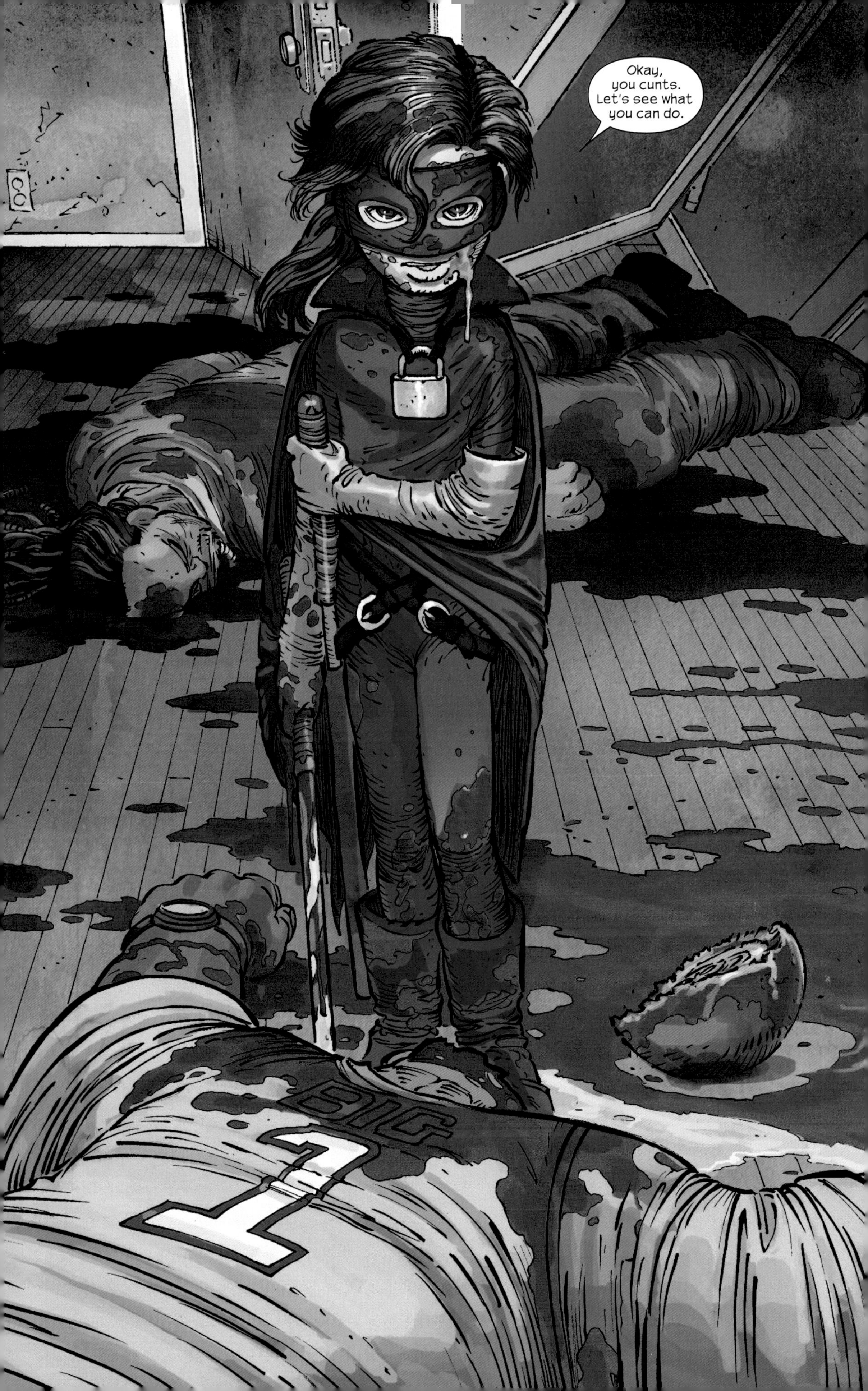
Okay, you cunts. Let's see what you can do.

FOUR

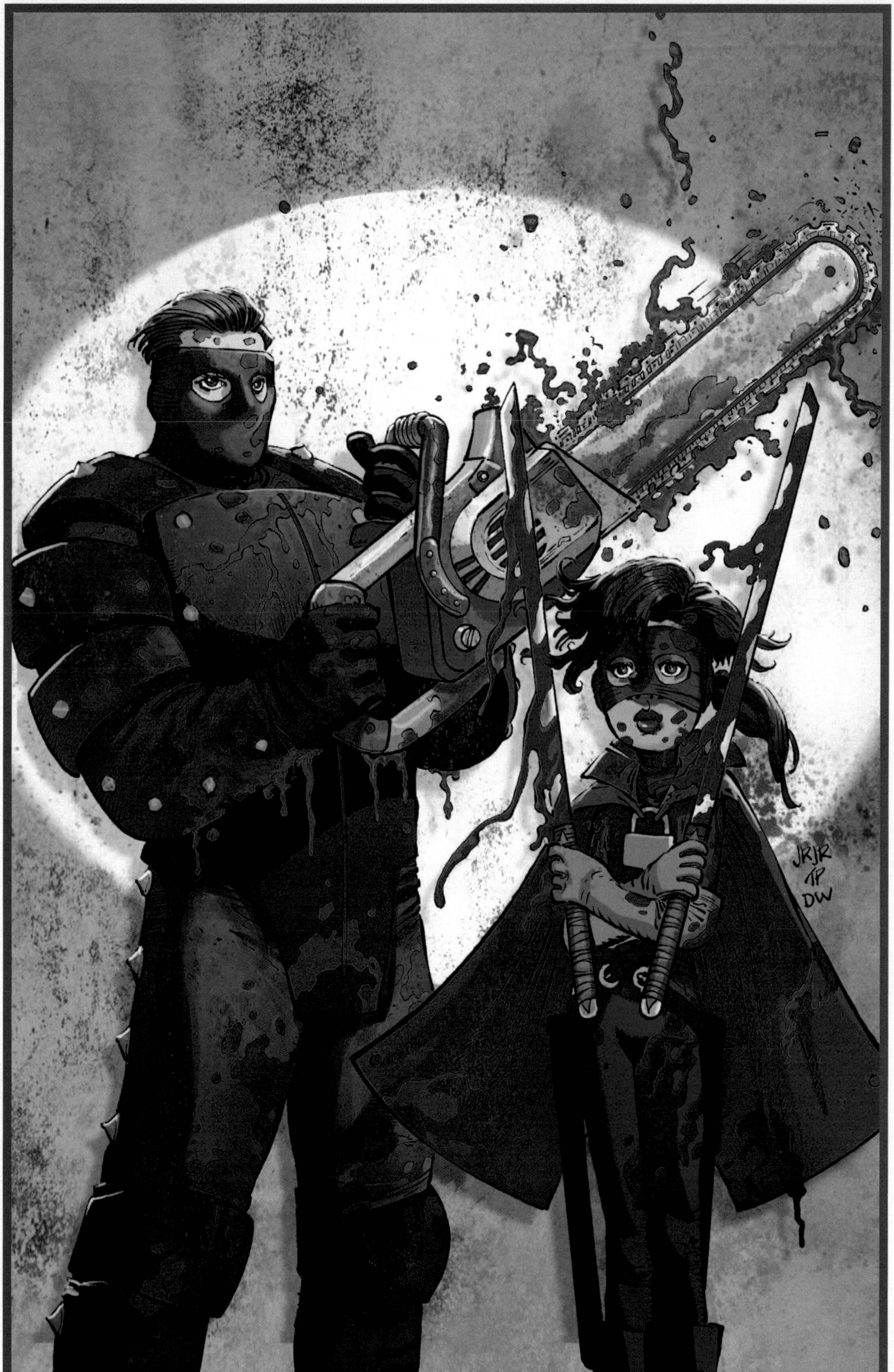
JRJR
TP
DW

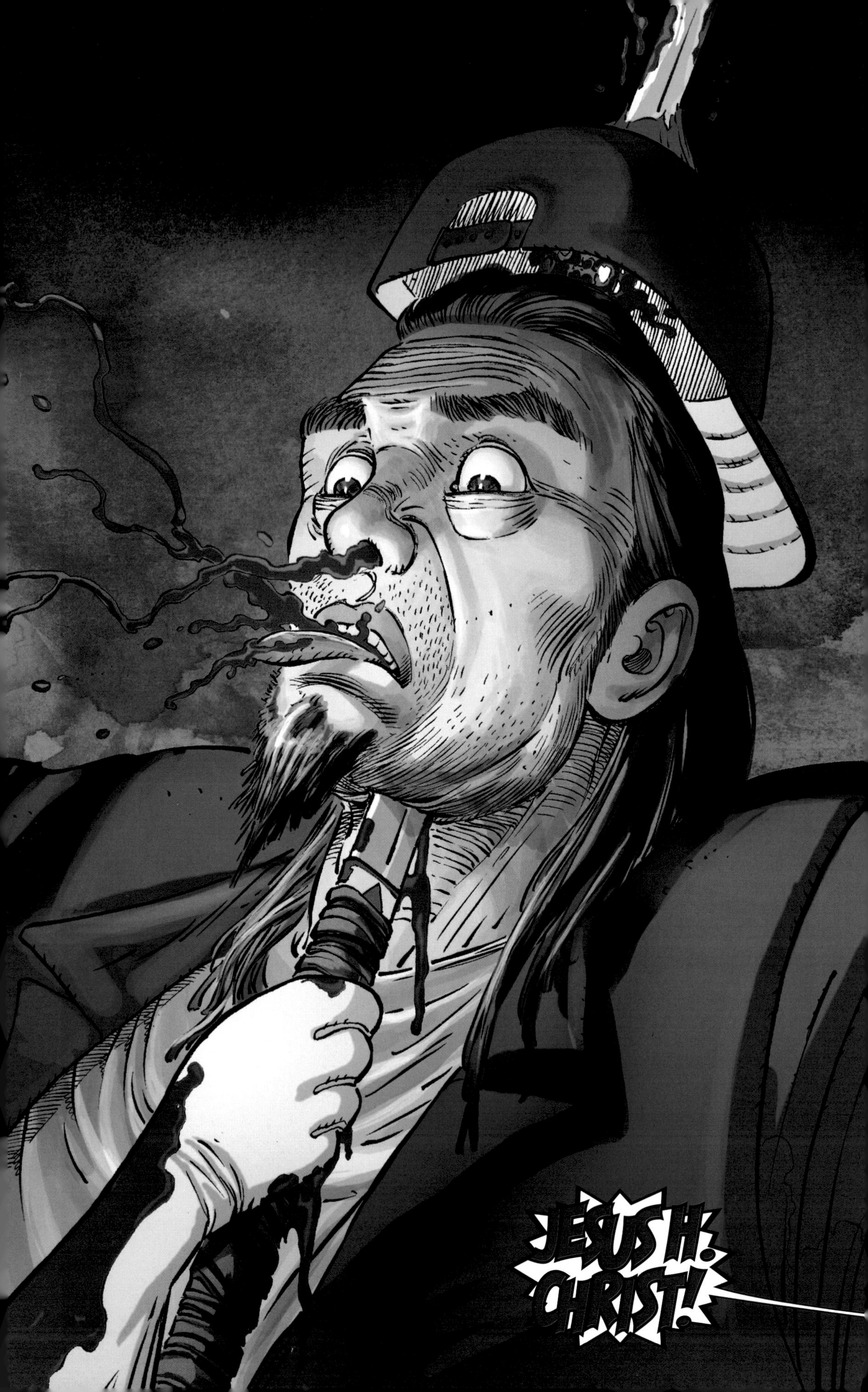
JESUS H. CHRIST!

She was like John Rambo meets Polly Pocket.

Dakota Fanning crossed with Death Wish 4.

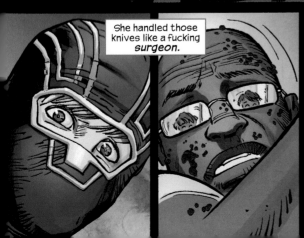

She handled those knives like a fucking *surgeon*.

I still can't believe she was only *ten...*

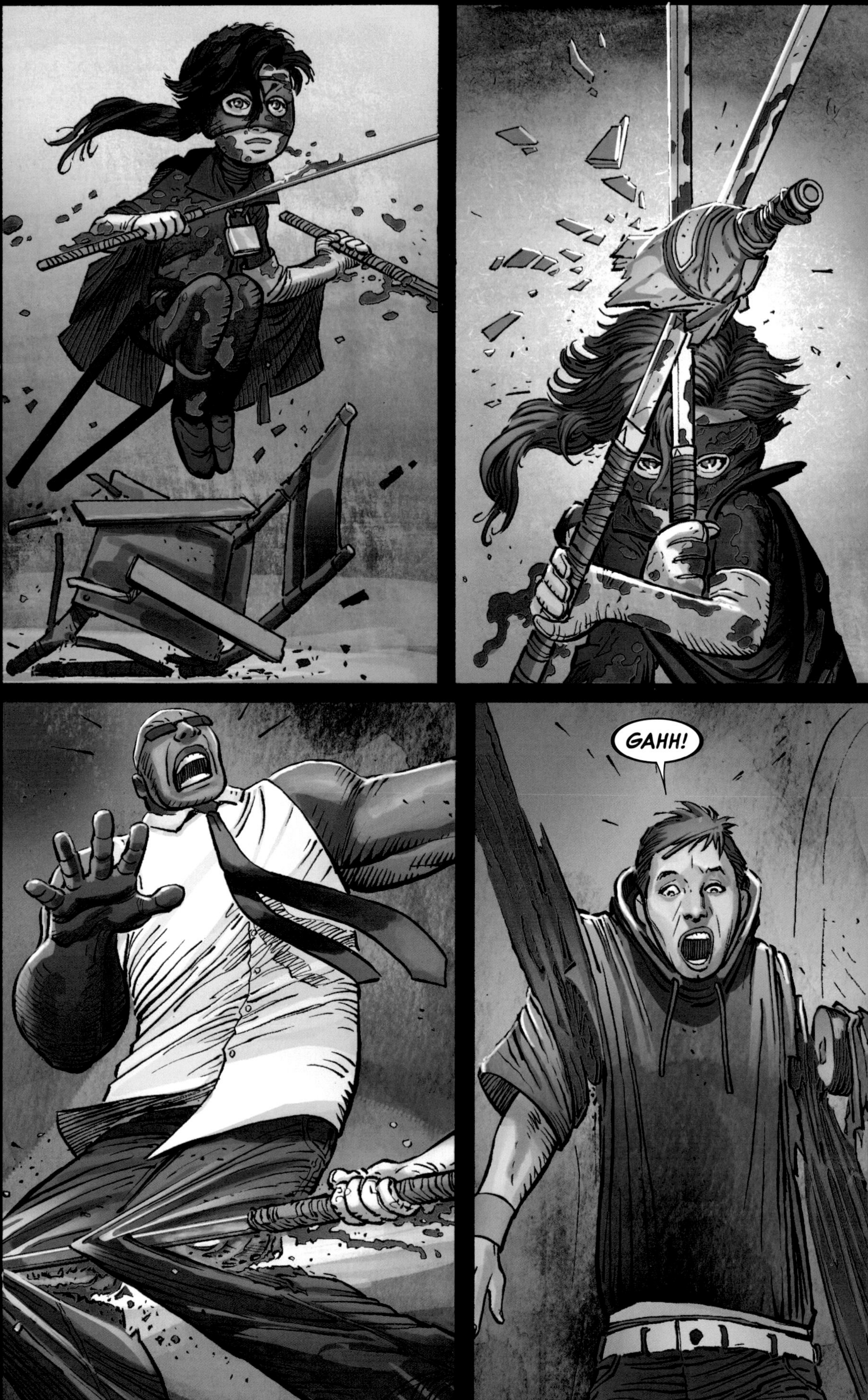
GAHH!

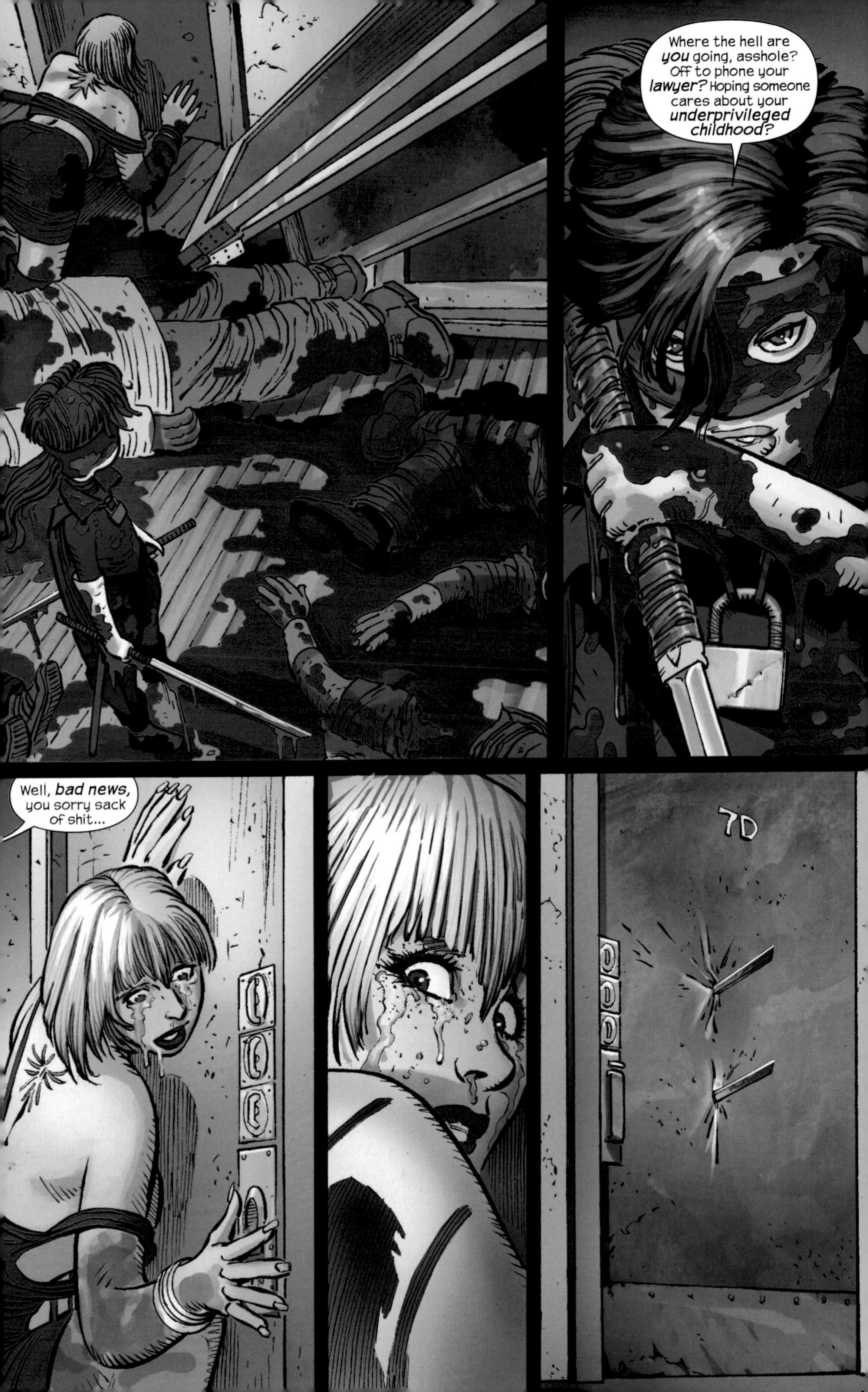
Where the hell are *you* going, asshole? Off to phone your *lawyer?* Hoping someone cares about your *underprivileged childhood?*
Well, *bad news,* you sorry sack of shit...
7D

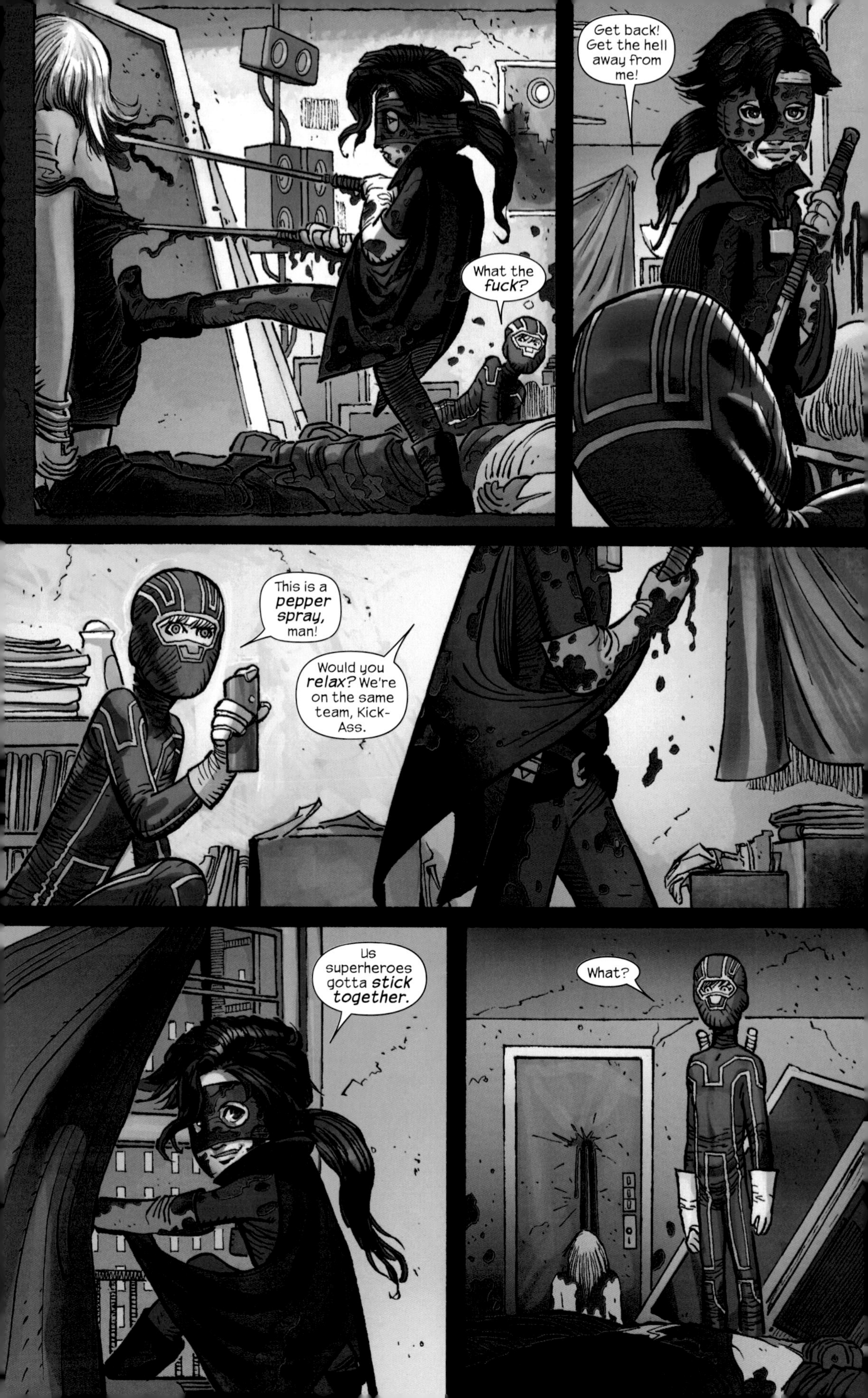
What the fuck?
Get back! Get the hell away from me!
This is a pepper spray, man!
Would you relax? We're on the same team, Kick-Ass.
Us superheroes gotta stick together.
What?

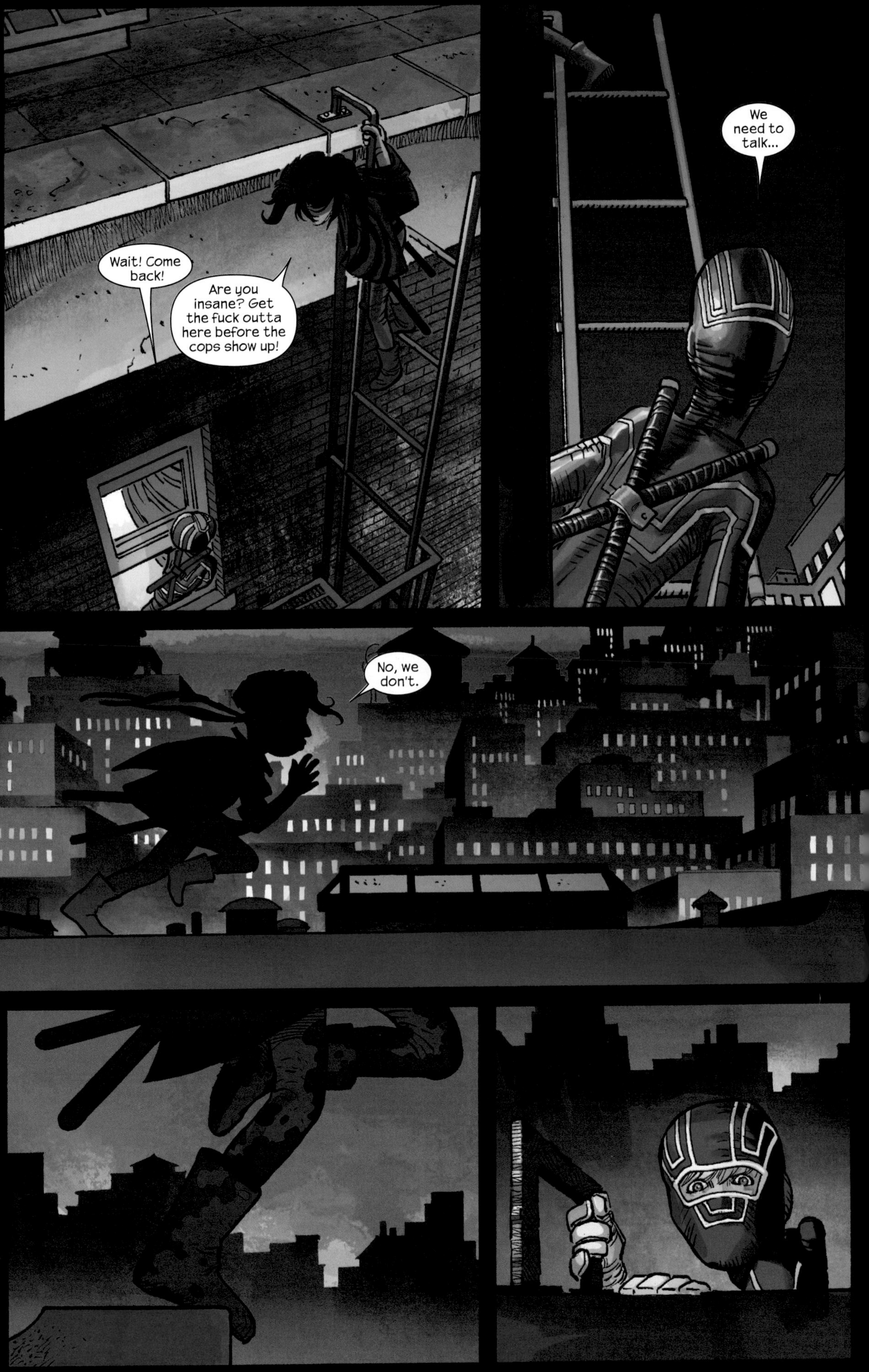
Wait! Come back!
Are you insane? Get the fuck outta here before the cops show up!
We need to talk...
No, we don't.

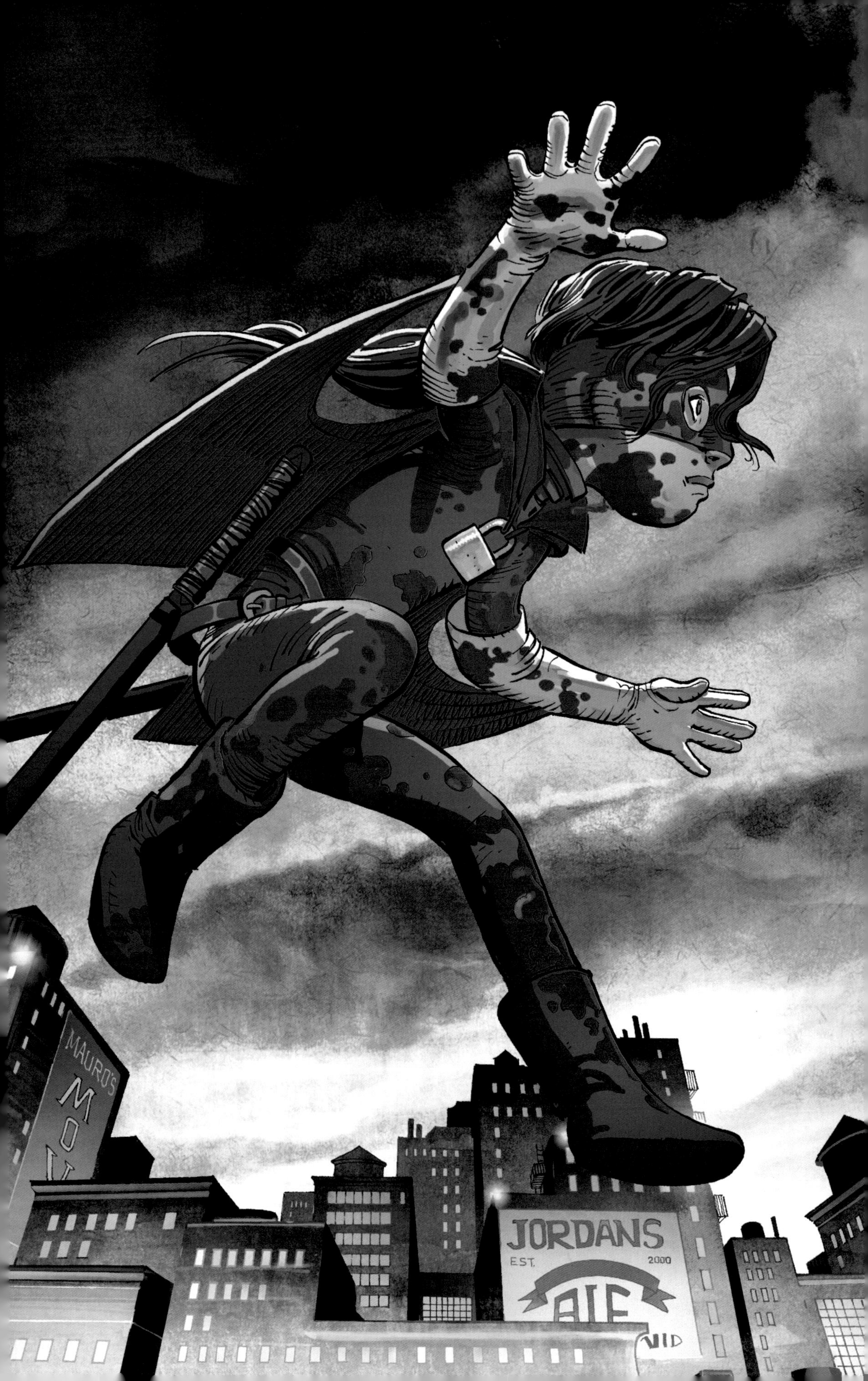
MAURO'S
JORDANS
EST.
2000

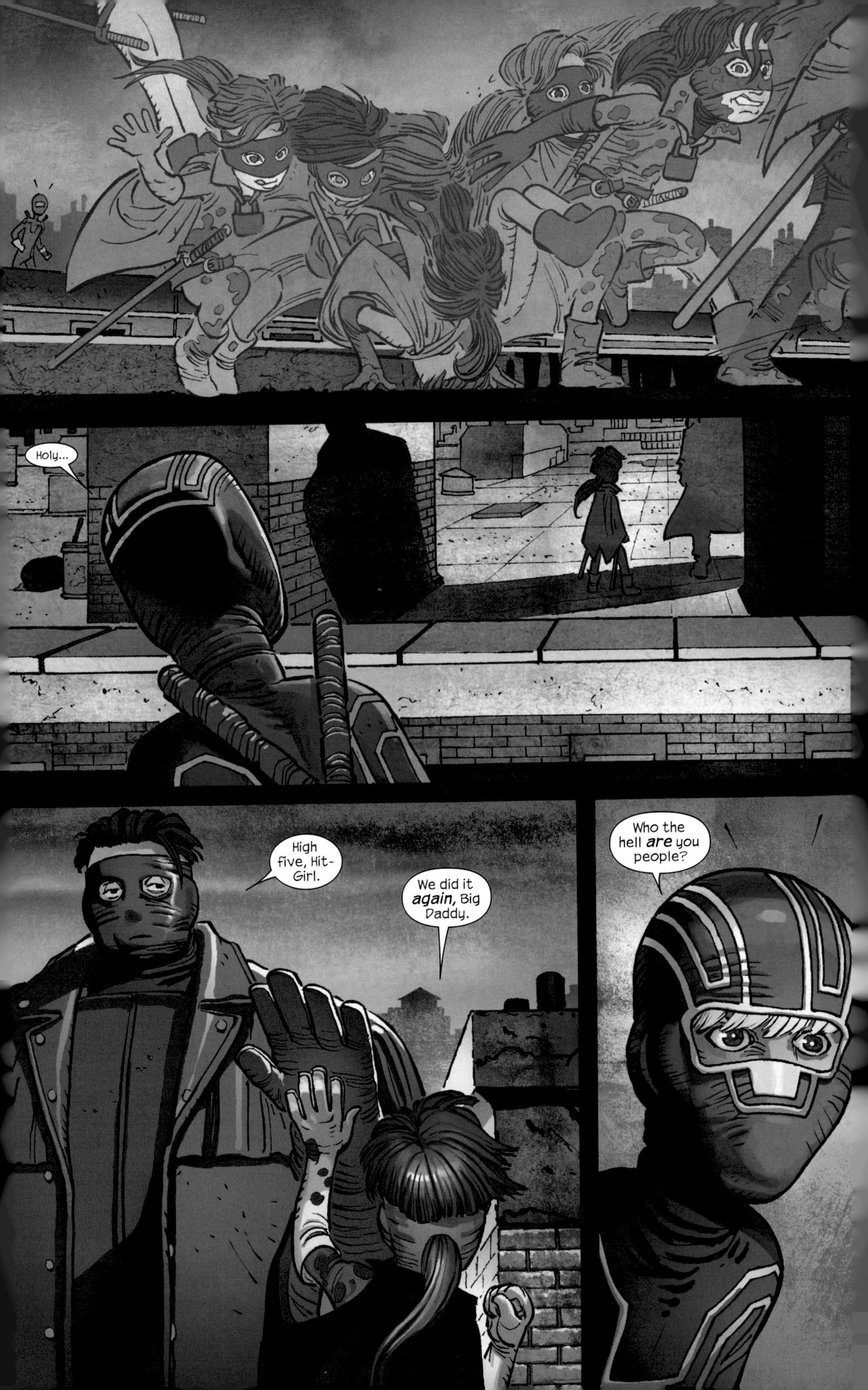
Holy...
High five, Hit-Girl.
We did it again, Big Daddy.
Who the hell are you people?

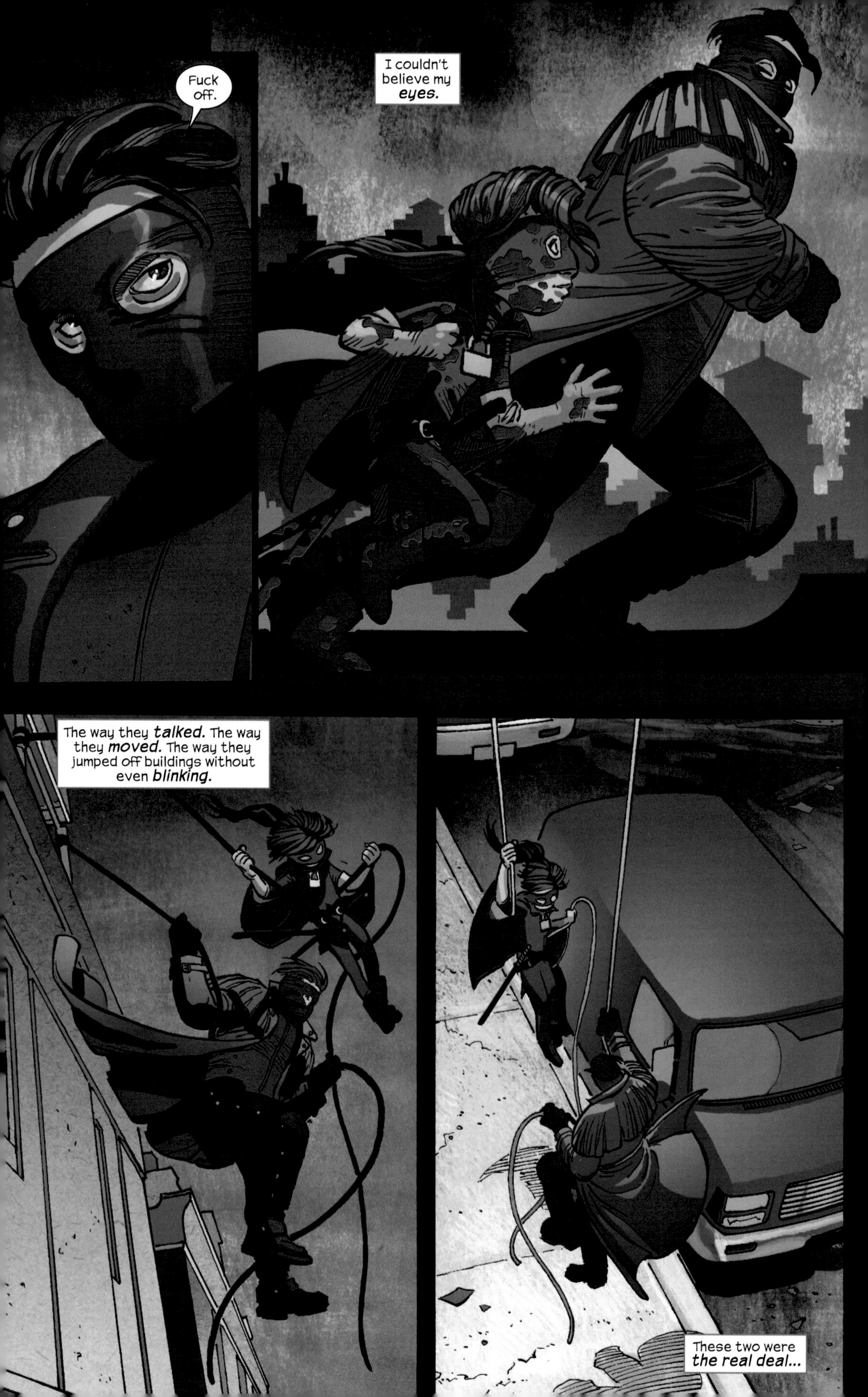
Fuck off.
I couldn't believe my eyes.
The way they talked. The way they moved. The way they jumped off buildings without even blinking.
These two were the real deal...

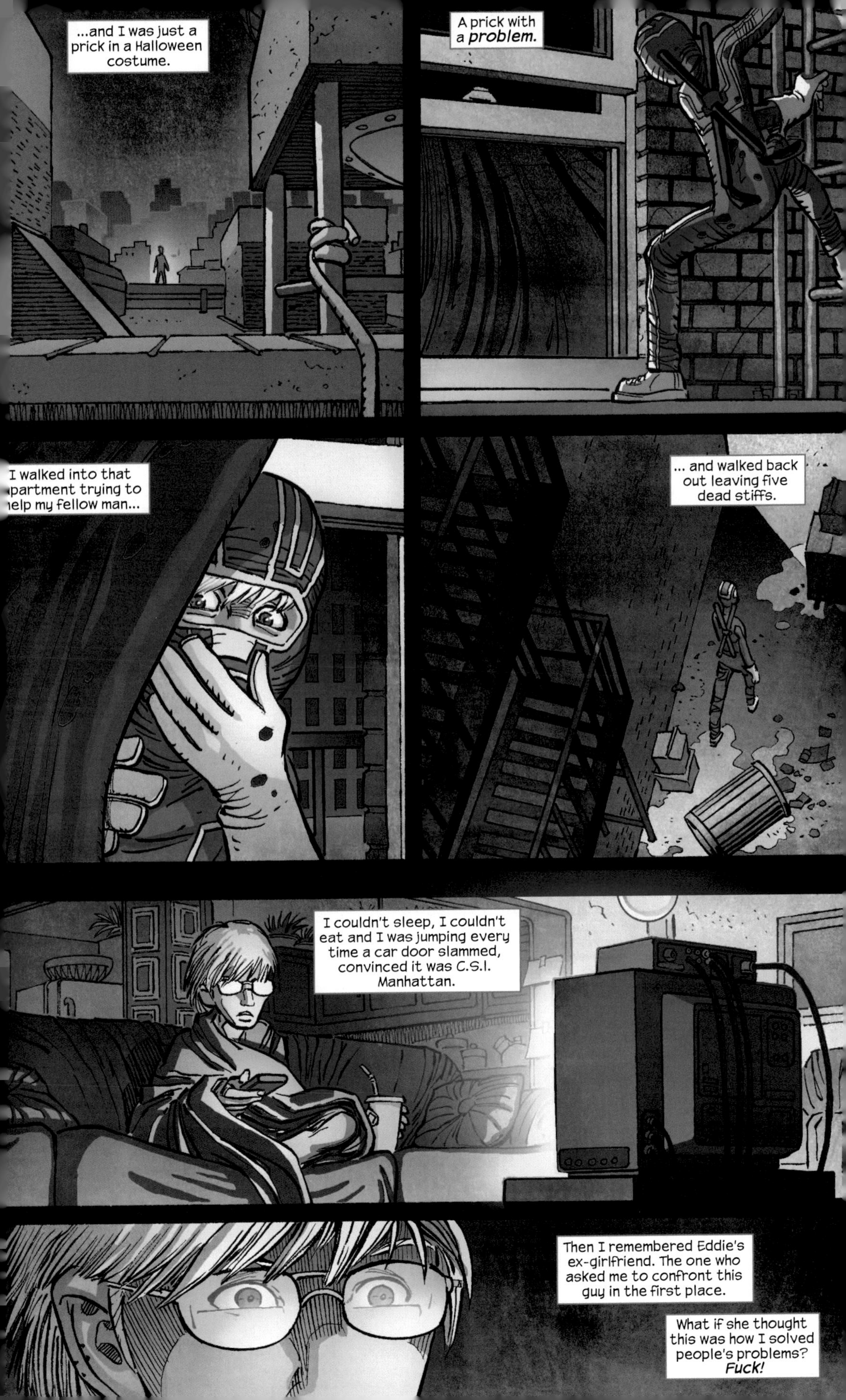
...and I was just a prick in a Halloween costume.
A prick with a problem.
I walked into that partment trying to elp my fellow man...
... and walked back out leaving five dead stiffs.
I couldn't sleep, I couldn't eat and I was jumping every time a car door slammed, convinced it was C.S.I. Manhattan.
Then I remembered Eddie's ex-girlfriend. The one who asked me to confront this guy in the first place.
What if she thought this was how I solved people's problems? Fuck!

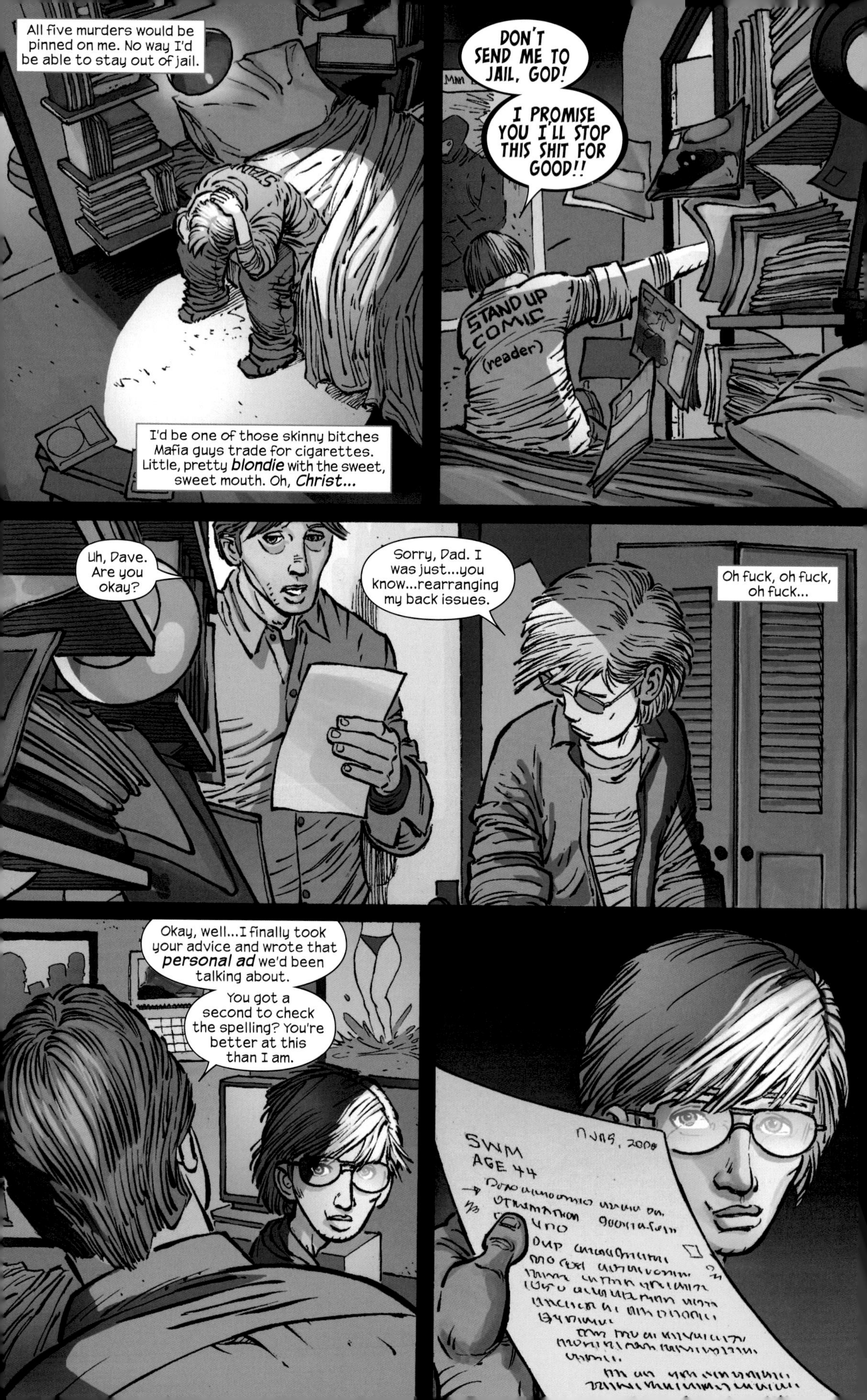
All five murders would be pinned on me. No way I'd be able to stay out of jail.
I'd be one of those skinny bitches Mafia guys trade for cigarettes. Little, pretty *blondie* with the sweet, sweet mouth. Oh, *Christ...*
DON'T SEND ME TO JAIL, GOD!
I PROMISE YOU I'LL STOP THIS SHIT FOR GOOD!!
STAND UP COMIC (reader)
Uh, Dave. Are you okay?
Sorry, Dad. I was just...you know...rearranging my back issues.
Oh fuck, oh fuck, oh fuck...
Okay, well...I finally took your advice and wrote that *personal ad* we'd been talking about.
You got a second to check the spelling? You're better at this than I am.
SWM
AGE 44

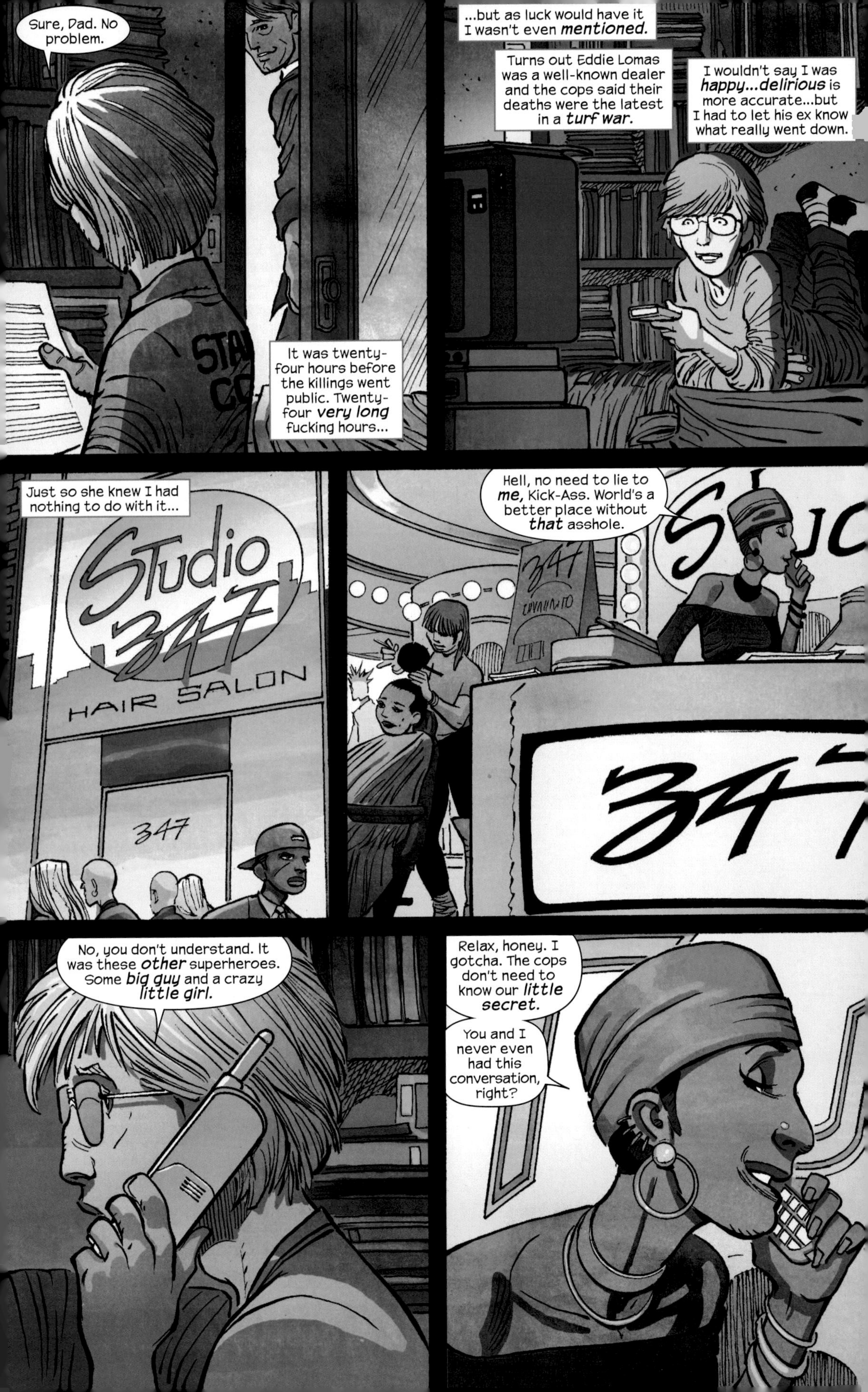
Sure, Dad. No problem.
It was twenty-four hours before the killings went public. Twenty-four very long fucking hours...
...but as luck would have it I wasn't even mentioned.
Turns out Eddie Lomas was a well-known dealer and the cops said their deaths were the latest in a turf war.
I wouldn't say I was happy...delirious is more accurate...but I had to let his ex know what really went down.
Just so she knew I had nothing to do with it...
Studio 347
HAIR SALON
347
Hell, no need to lie to me, Kick-Ass. World's a better place without that asshole.
No, you don't understand. It was these other superheroes. Some big guy and a crazy little girl.
Relax, honey. I gotcha. The cops don't need to know our little secret.
You and I never even had this conversation, right?

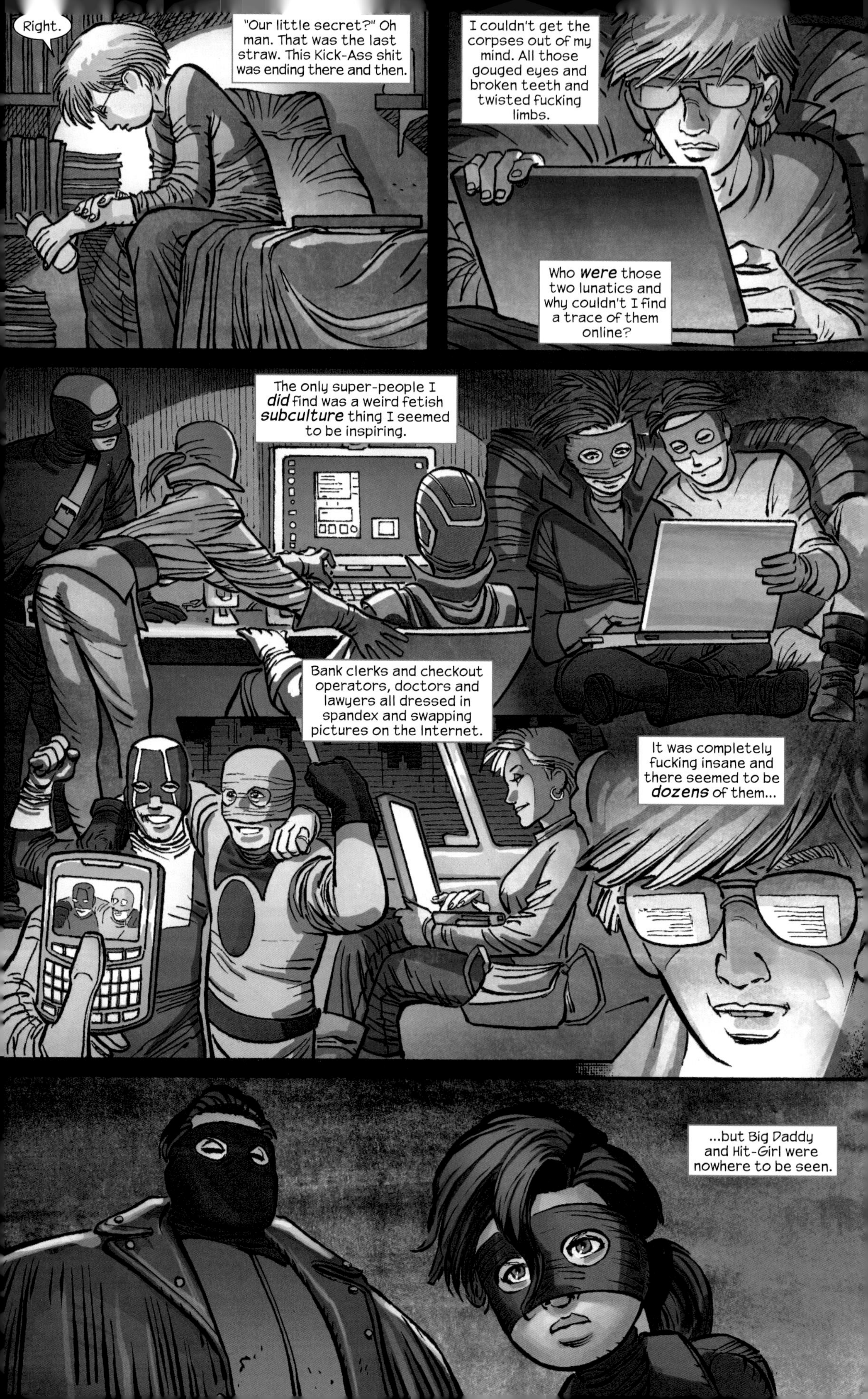
Right.
"Our little secret?" Oh man. That was the last straw. This Kick-Ass shit was ending there and then.
I couldn't get the corpses out of my mind. All those gouged eyes and broken teeth and twisted fucking limbs.
Who *were* those two lunatics and why couldn't I find a trace of them online?
The only super-people I *did* find was a weird fetish *subculture* thing I seemed to be inspiring.
Bank clerks and checkout operators, doctors and lawyers all dressed in spandex and swapping pictures on the Internet.
It was completely fucking insane and there seemed to be *dozens* of them...
...but Big Daddy and Hit-Girl were nowhere to be seen.

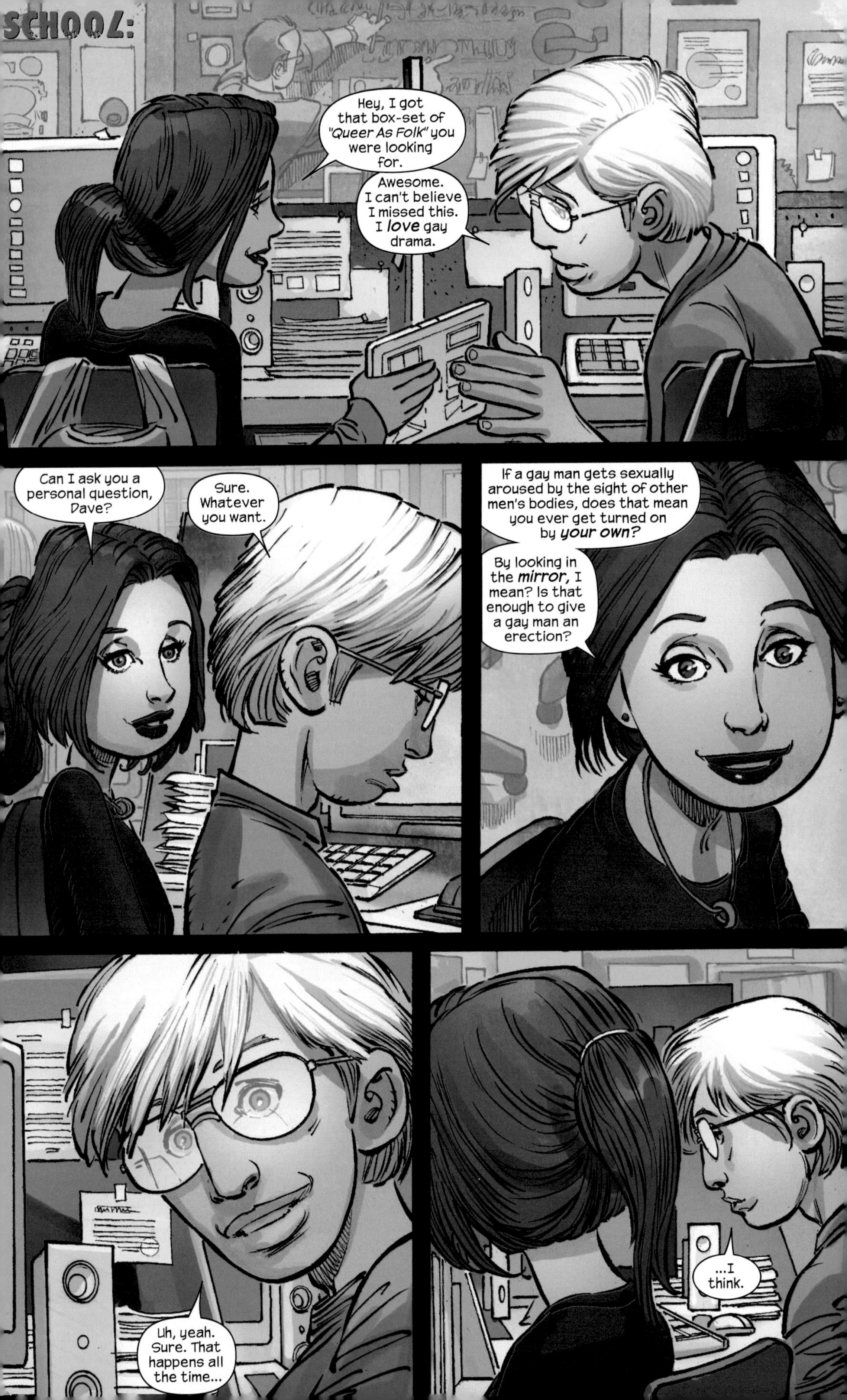
SCHOOL:
Hey, I got that box-set of "Queer As Folk" you were looking for.
Awesome. I can't believe I missed this. I *love* gay drama.
Can I ask you a personal question, Dave?
Sure. Whatever you want.
If a gay man gets sexually aroused by the sight of other men's bodies, does that mean you ever get turned on by *your own?*
By looking in the *mirror,* I mean? Is that enough to give a gay man an erection?
Uh, yeah. Sure. That happens all the time...
...I think.

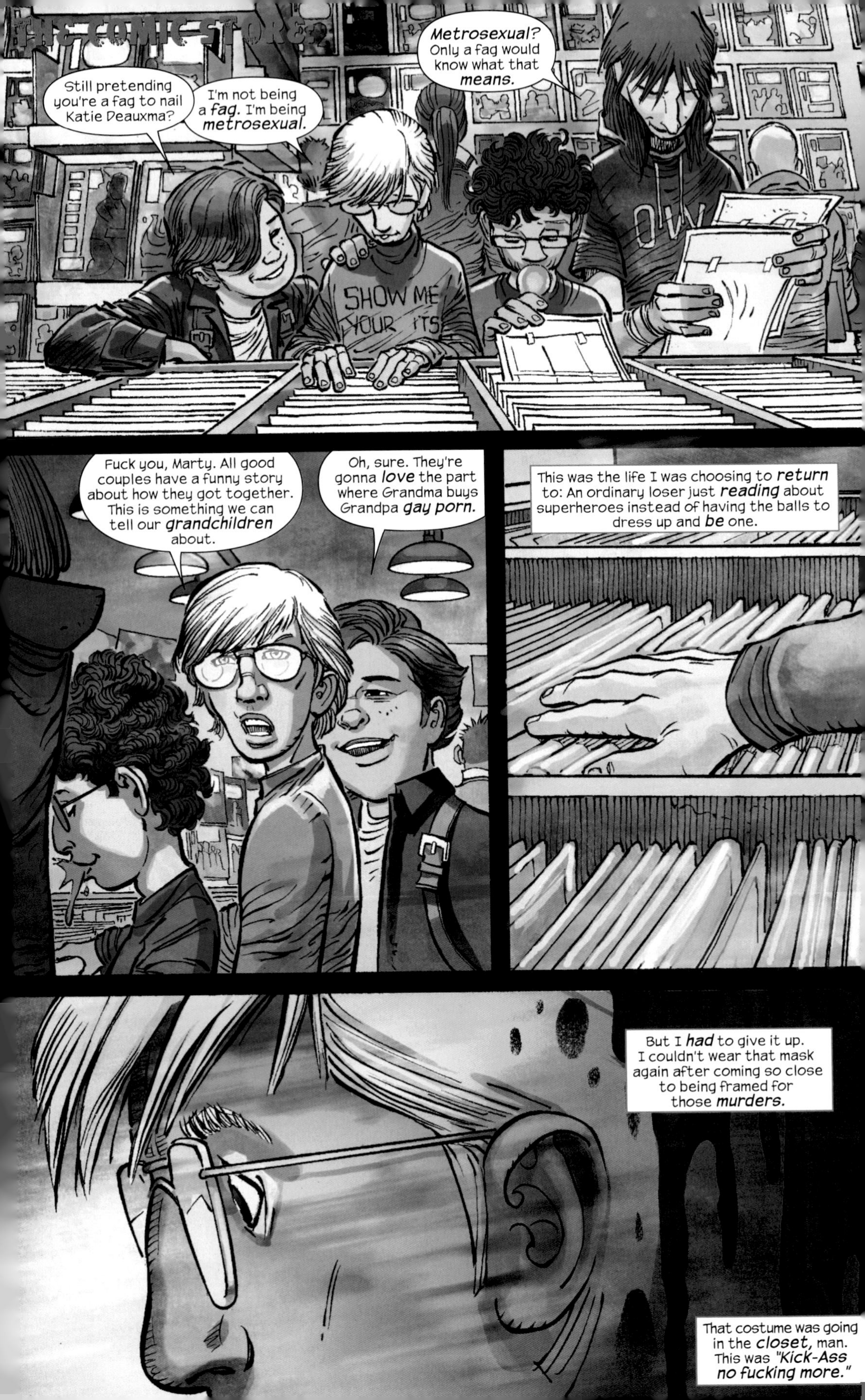
Still pretending you're a fag to nail Katie Deauxma?
I'm not being a fag. I'm being metrosexual.
Metrosexual? Only a fag would know what that means.
SHOW ME YOUR TITS
Fuck you, Marty. All good couples have a funny story about how they got together. This is something we can tell our grandchildren about.
Oh, sure. They're gonna love the part where Grandma buys Grandpa gay porn.
This was the life I was choosing to return to: An ordinary loser just reading about superheroes instead of having the balls to dress up and be one.
But I had to give it up. I couldn't wear that mask again after coming so close to being framed for those murders.
That costume was going in the closet, man. This was "Kick-Ass no fucking more."

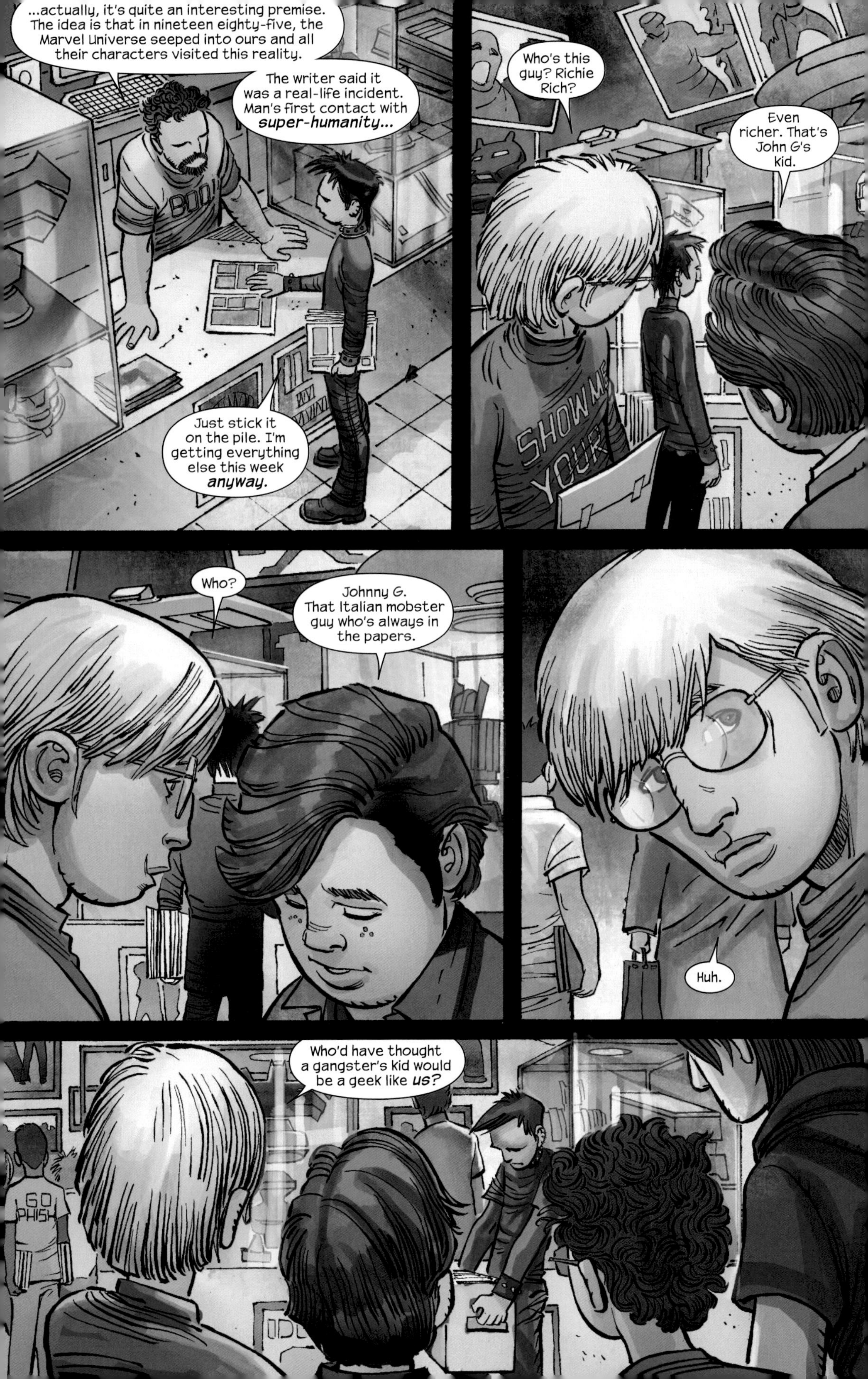
...actually, it's quite an interesting premise. The idea is that in nineteen eighty-five, the Marvel Universe seeped into ours and all their characters visited this reality.
The writer said it was a real-life incident. Man's first contact with *super-humanity...*
BOO!
Just stick it on the pile. I'm getting everything else this week *anyway.*
Who's this guy? Richie Rich?
Even richer. That's John G's kid.
SHOW ME YOUR
Who?
Johnny G. That Italian mobster guy who's always in the papers.
Huh.
Who'd have thought a gangster's kid would be a geek like *us?*
GO PHISH

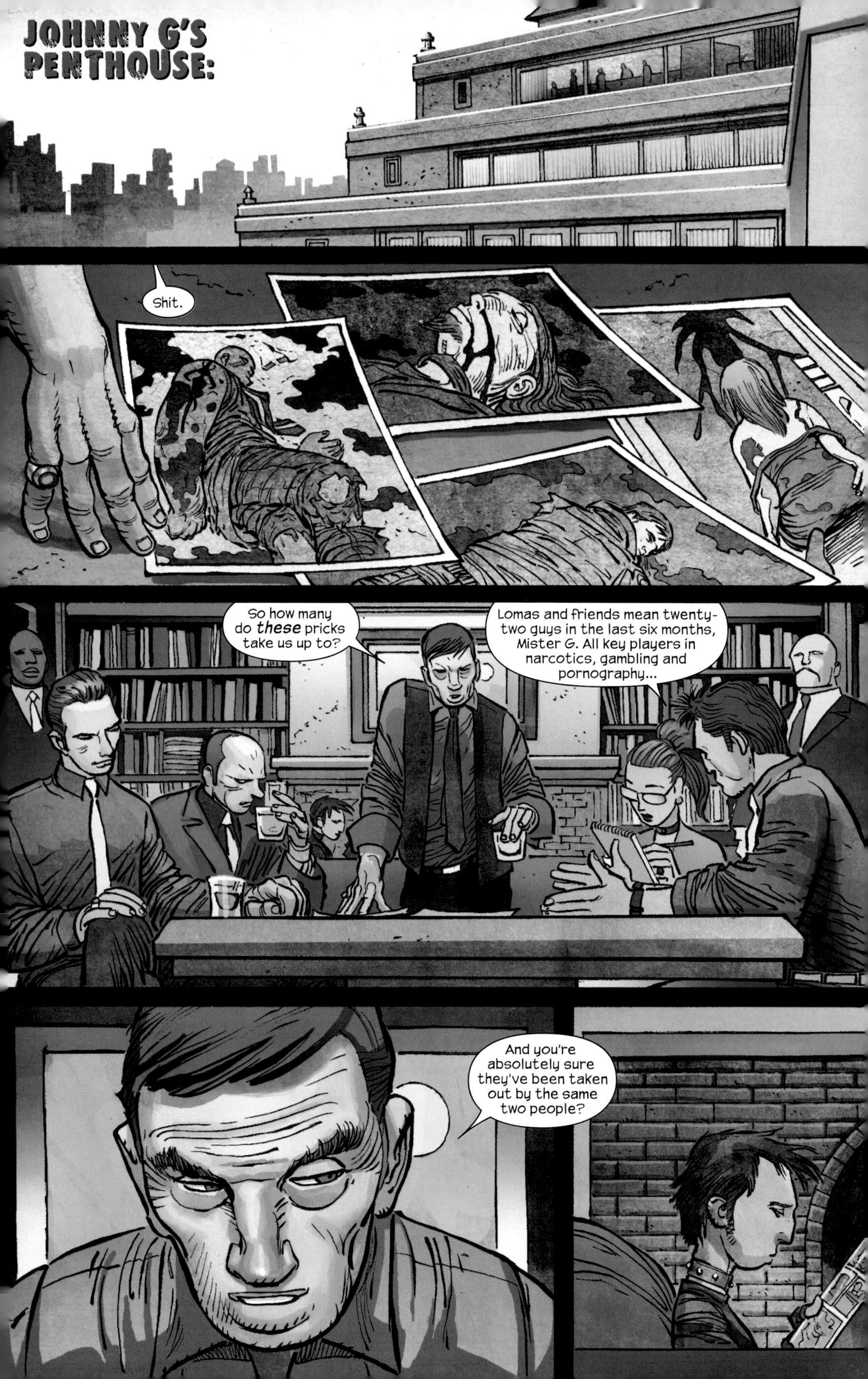
JOHNNY G'S PENTHOUSE:
Shit.
So how many do *these* pricks take us up to?
Lomas and friends mean twenty-two guys in the last six months, Mister G. All key players in narcotics, gambling and pornography...
And you're absolutely sure they've been taken out by the same two people?

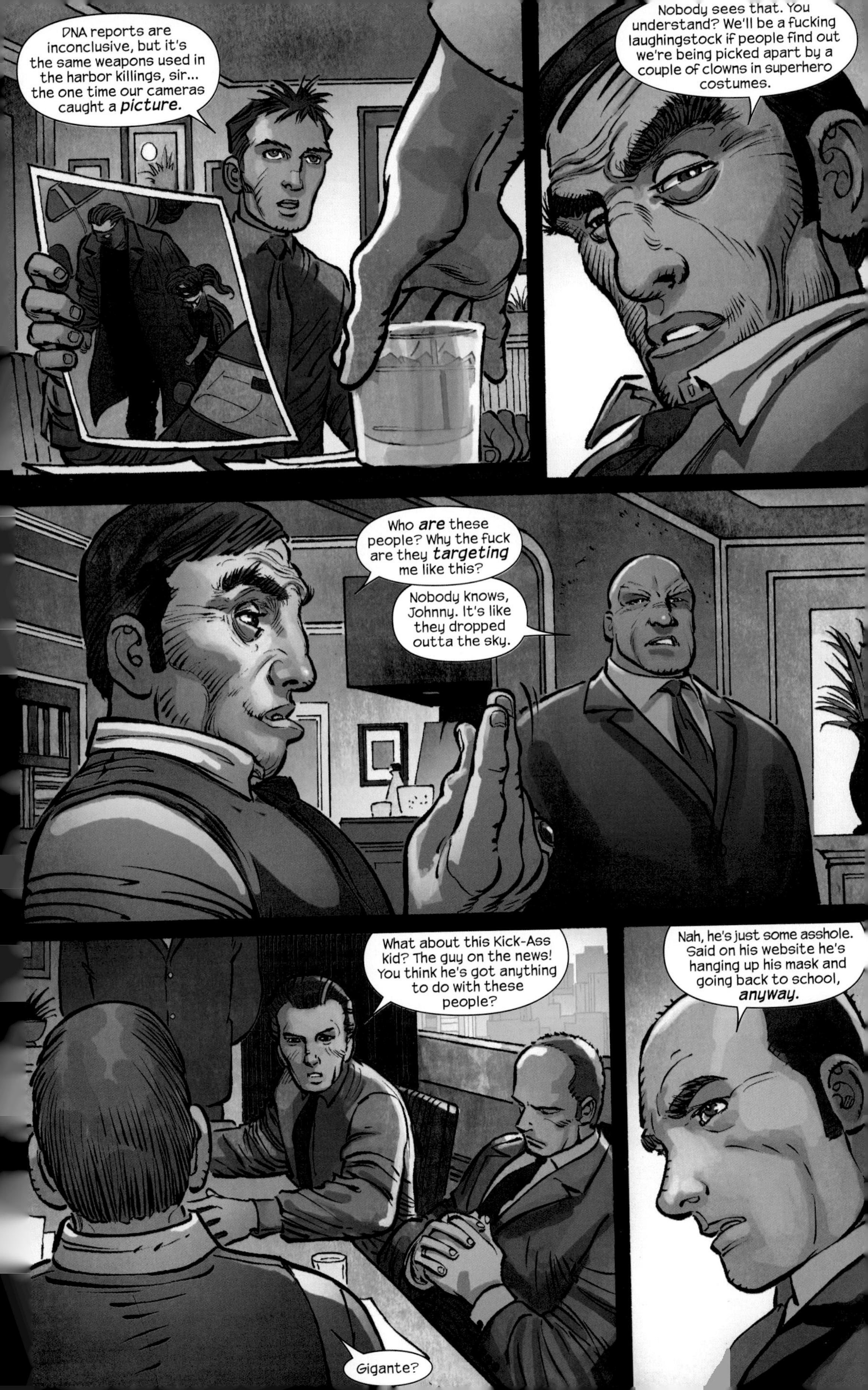
DNA reports are inconclusive, but it's the same weapons used in the harbor killings, sir... the one time our cameras caught a *picture.*
Nobody sees that. You understand? We'll be a fucking laughingstock if people find out we're being picked apart by a couple of clowns in superhero costumes.
Who *are* these people? Why the fuck are they *targeting* me like this?
Nobody knows, Johnny. It's like they dropped outta the sky.
What about this Kick-Ass kid? The guy on the news! You think he's got anything to do with these people?
Gigante?
Nah, he's just some asshole. Said on his website he's hanging up his mask and going back to school, *anyway.*

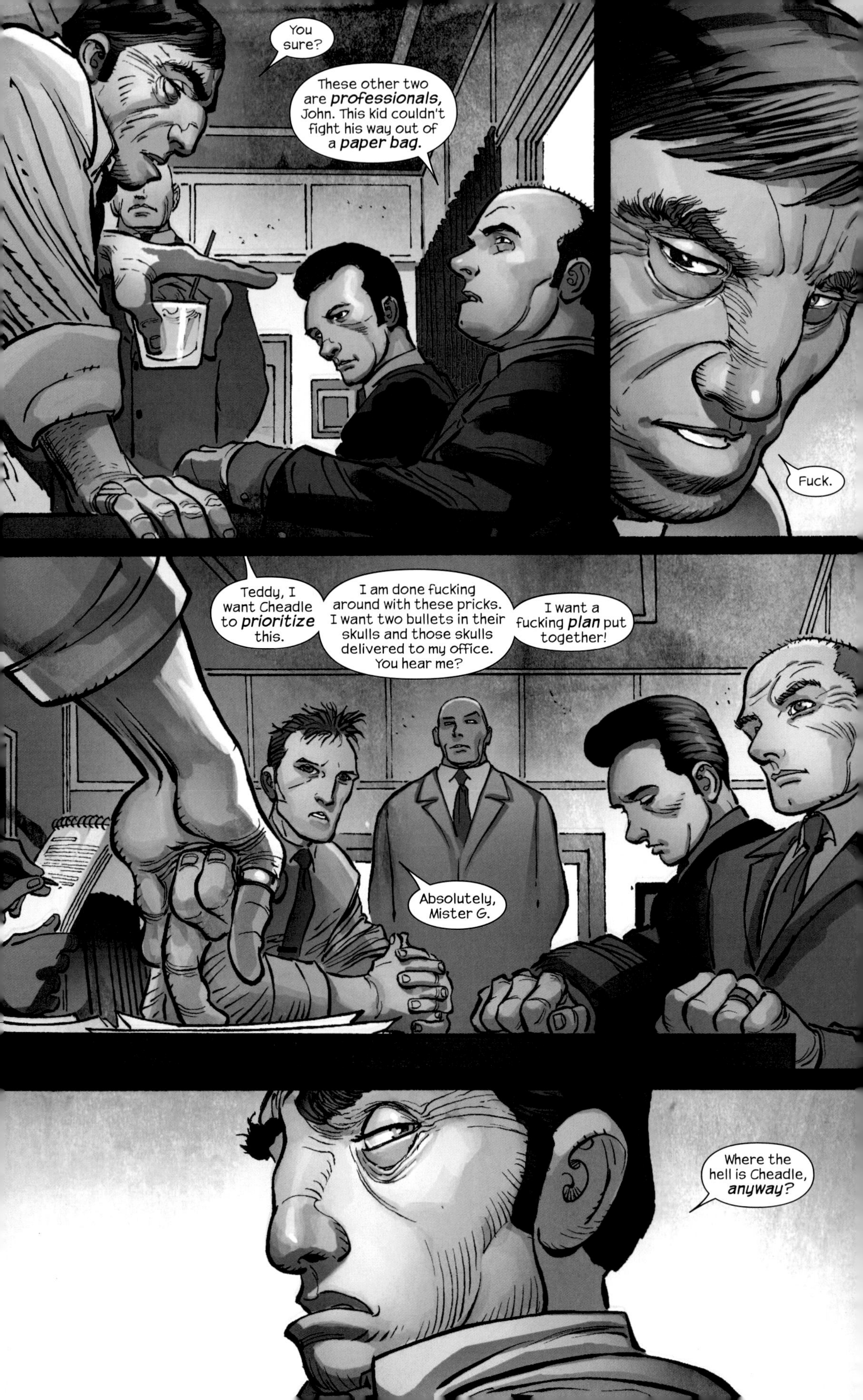
You sure?
These other two are professionals, John. This kid couldn't fight his way out of a paper bag.
Fuck.
Teddy, I want Cheadle to prioritize this.
I am done fucking around with these pricks. I want two bullets in their skulls and those skulls delivered to my office. You hear me?
I want a fucking plan put together!
Absolutely, Mister G.
Where the hell is Cheadle, anyway?

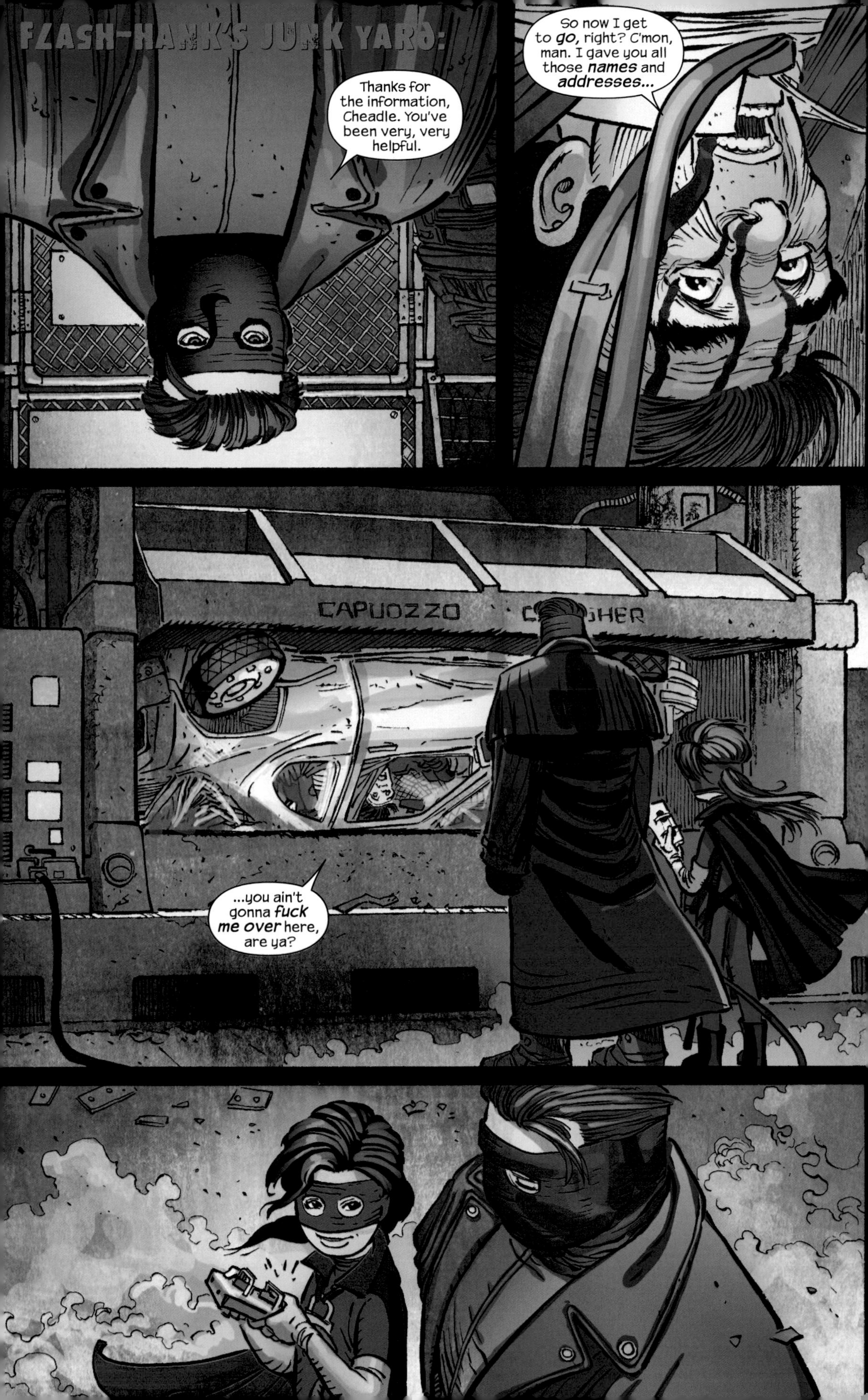
FLASH-HANK'S JUNK YARD:
Thanks for the information, Cheadle. You've been very, very helpful.
So now I get to go, right? C'mon, man. I gave you all those names and addresses...
CAPUOZZO
...you ain't gonna fuck me over here, are ya?

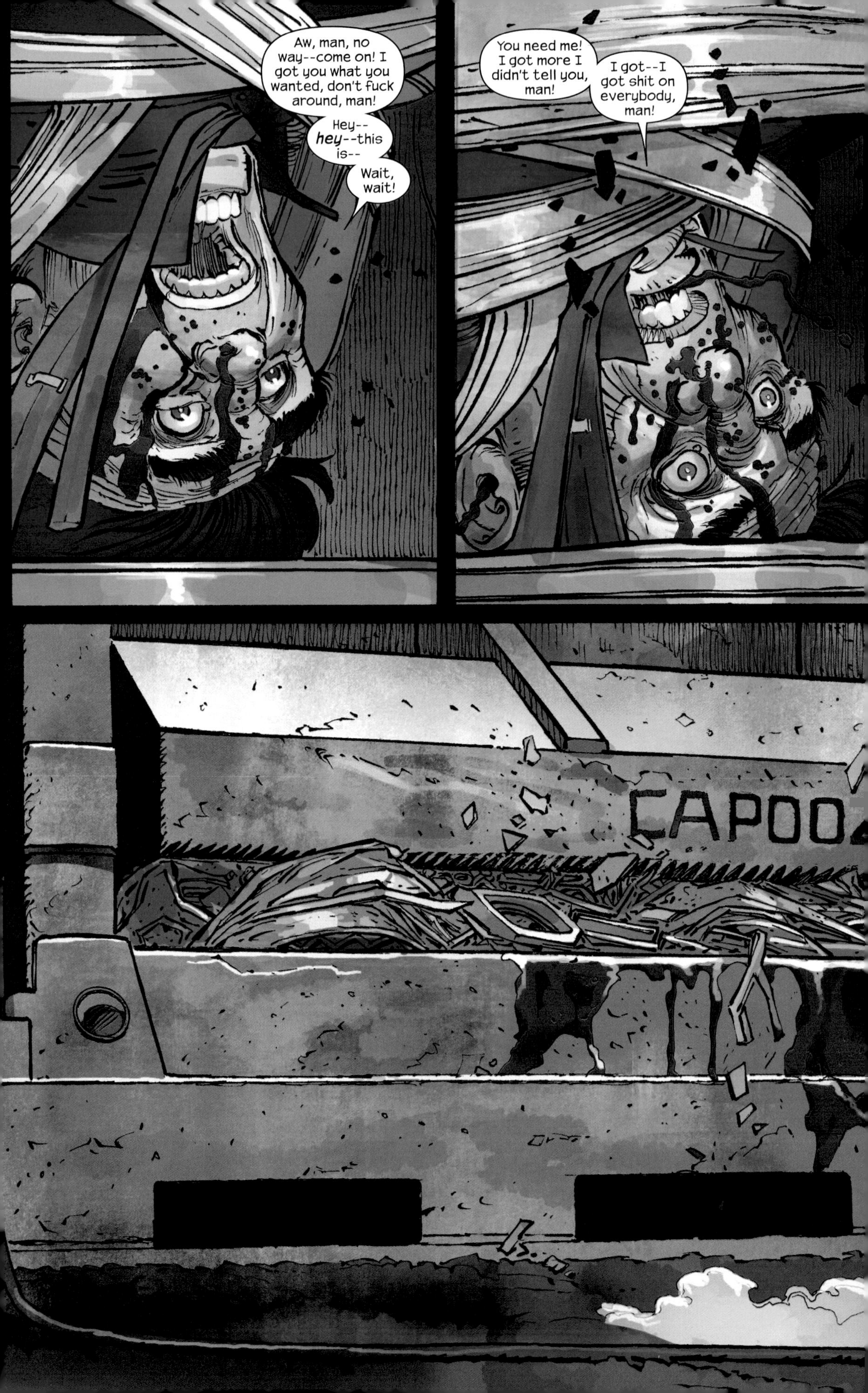
Aw, man, no way--come on! I got you what you wanted, don't fuck around, man!
Hey-- hey--this is--
Wait, wait!
You need me! I got more I didn't tell you, man!
I got--I got shit on everybody, man!
CAPOO

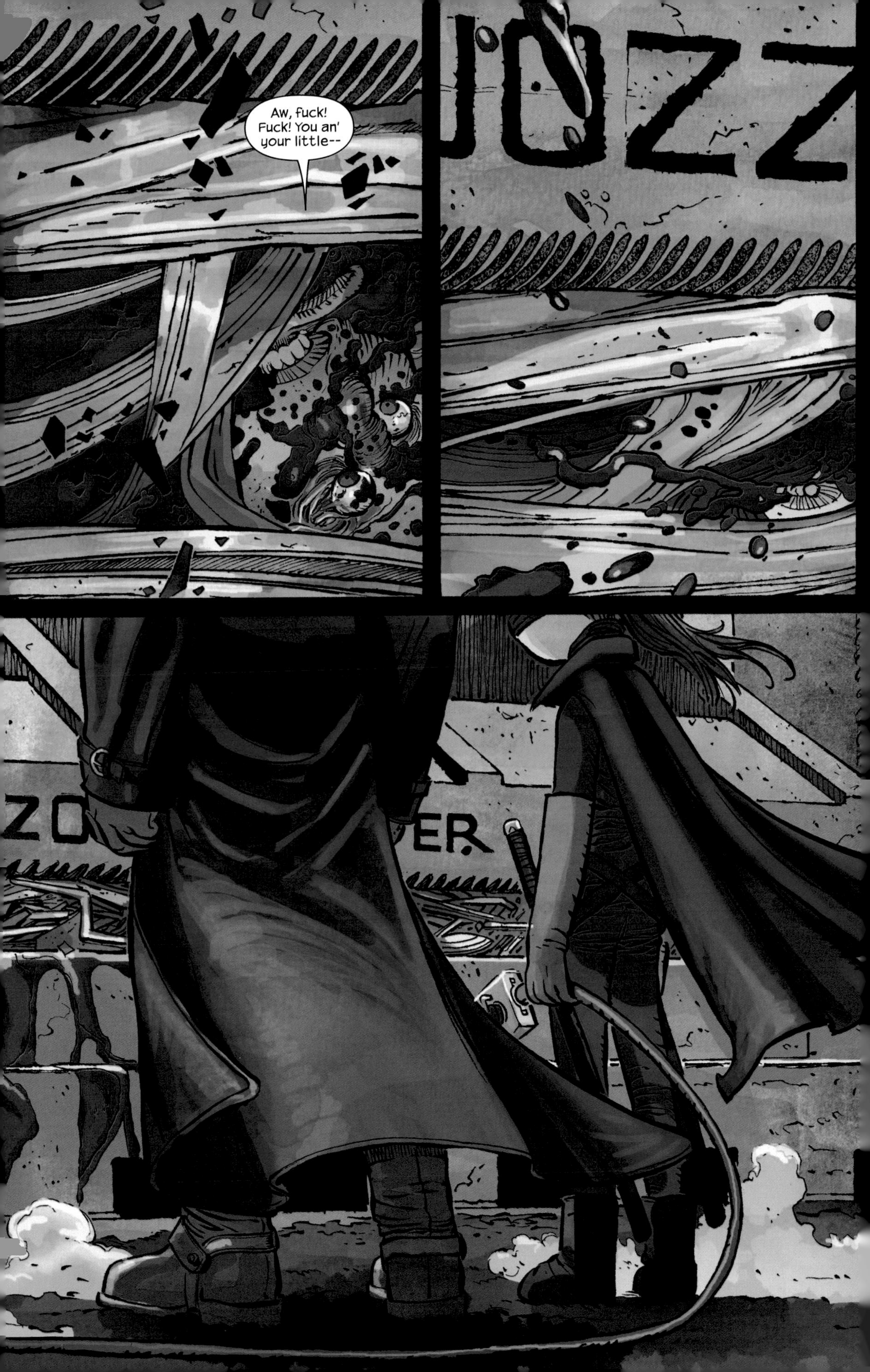
Aw, fuck! Fuck! You an' your little--

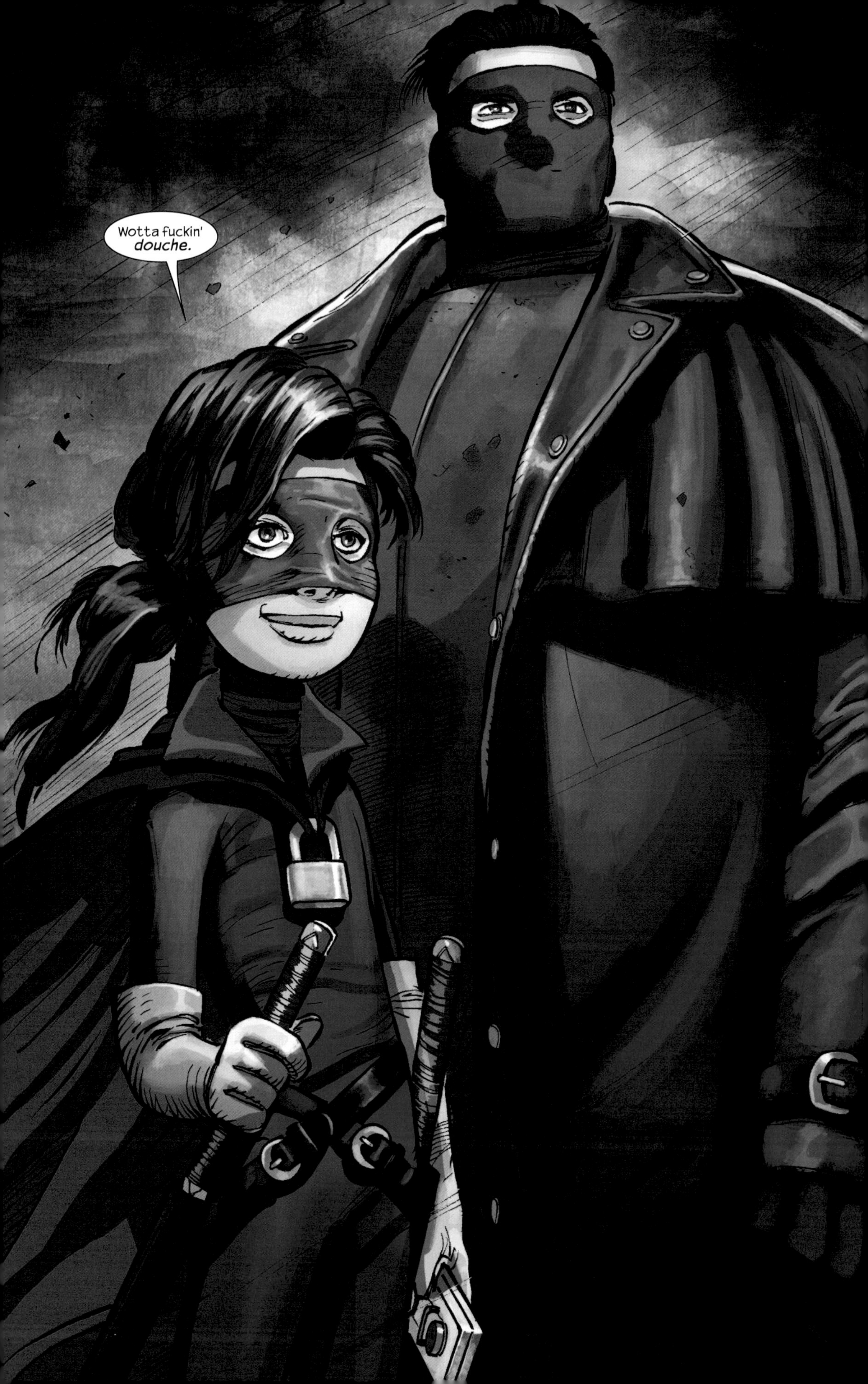
Wotta fuckin' *douche.*

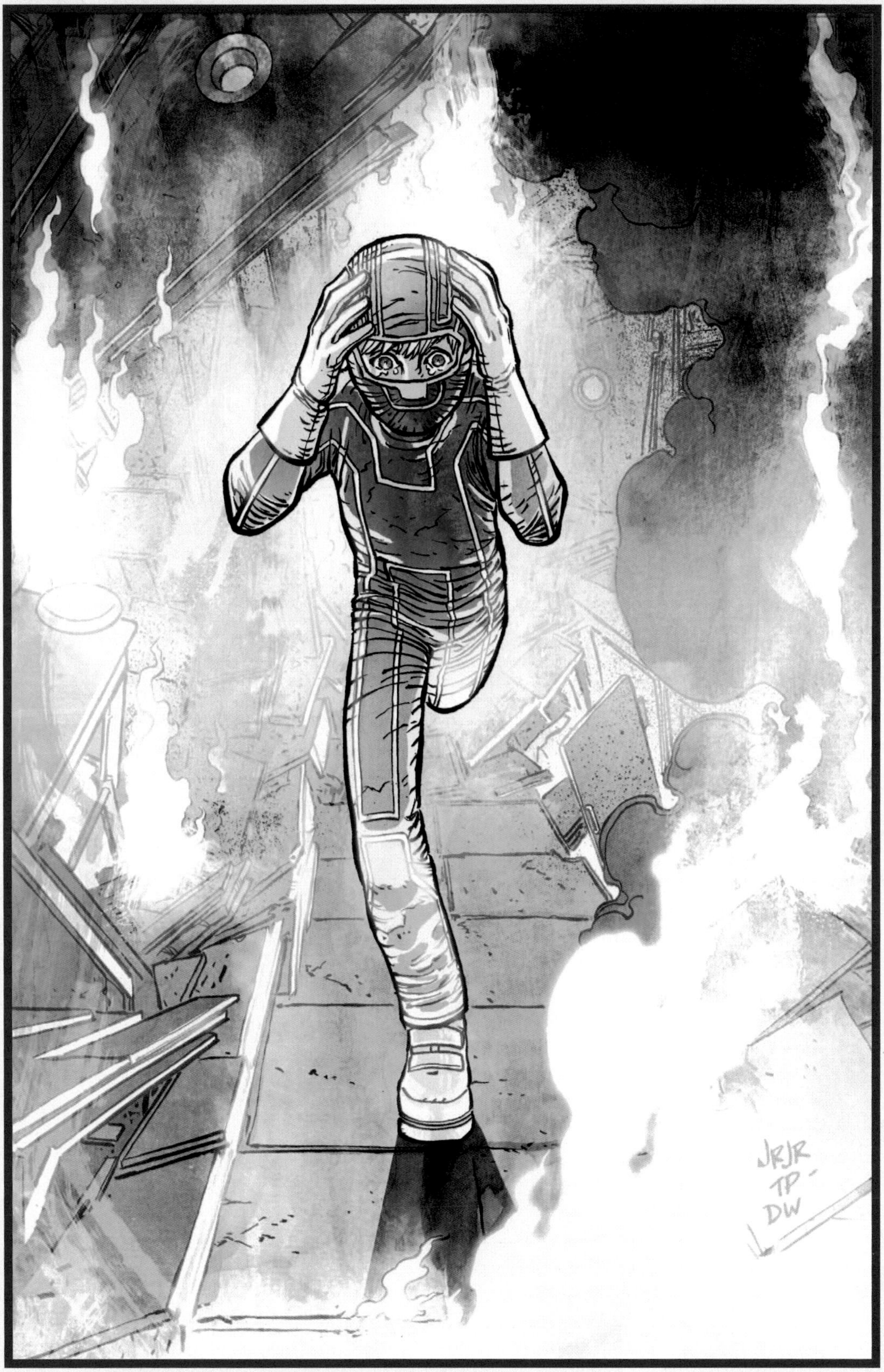
JRJR
TP
DW

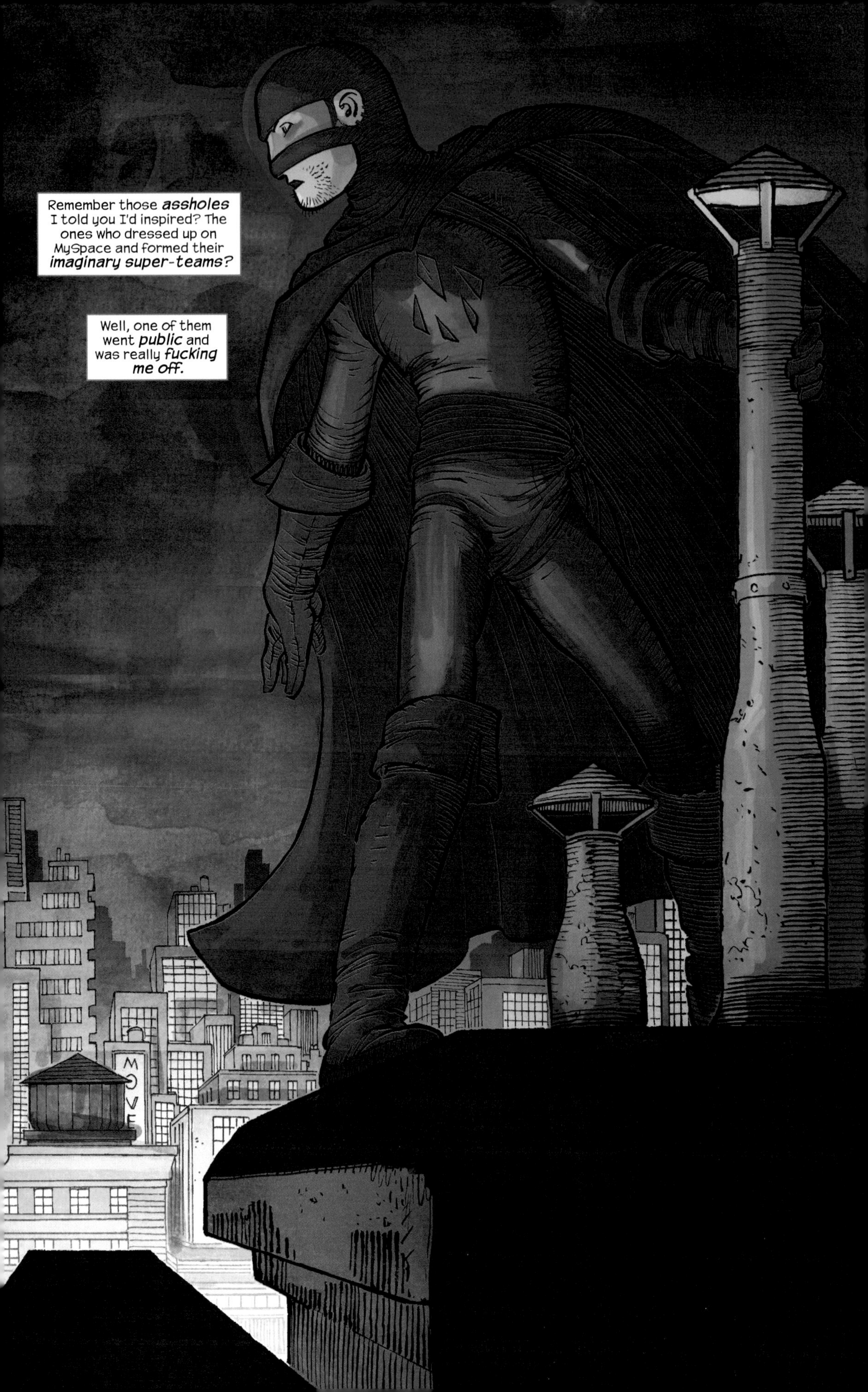
Remember those assholes I told you I'd inspired? The ones who dressed up on MySpace and formed their imaginary super-teams?
Well, one of them went public and was really fucking me off.
MOVE

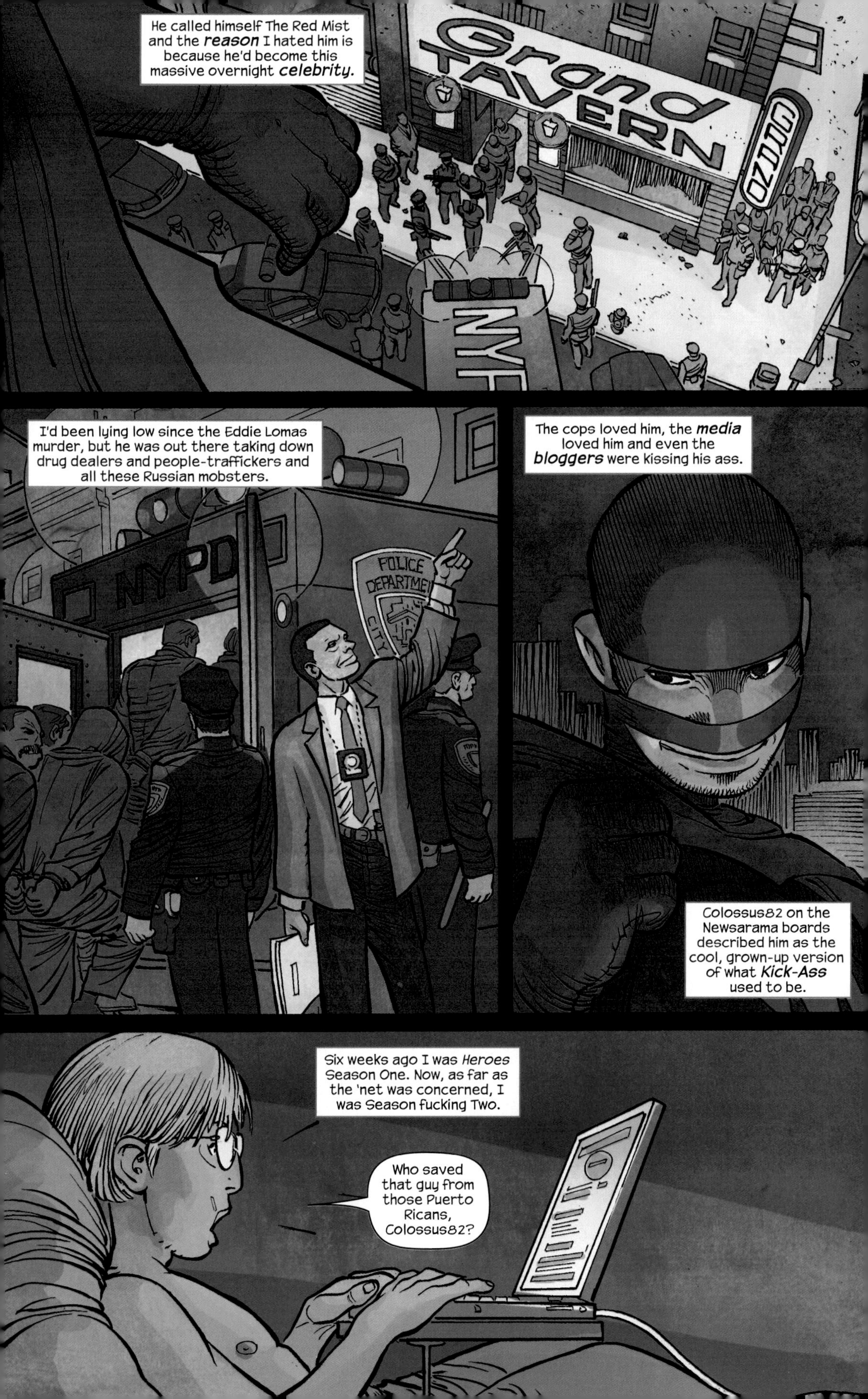
He called himself The Red Mist and the *reason* I hated him is because he'd become this massive overnight *celebrity.*
Grand TAVERN
NYPD
I'd been lying low since the Eddie Lomas murder, but he was out there taking down drug dealers and people-traffickers and all these Russian mobsters.
NYPD
POLICE DEPARTMENT CITY
The cops loved him, the *media* loved him and even the *bloggers* were kissing his ass.
Colossus82 on the Newsarama boards described him as the cool, grown-up version of what *Kick-Ass* used to be.
Six weeks ago I was *Heroes* Season One. Now, as far as the 'net was concerned, I was Season fucking Two.
Who saved that guy from those Puerto Ricans, Colossus82?

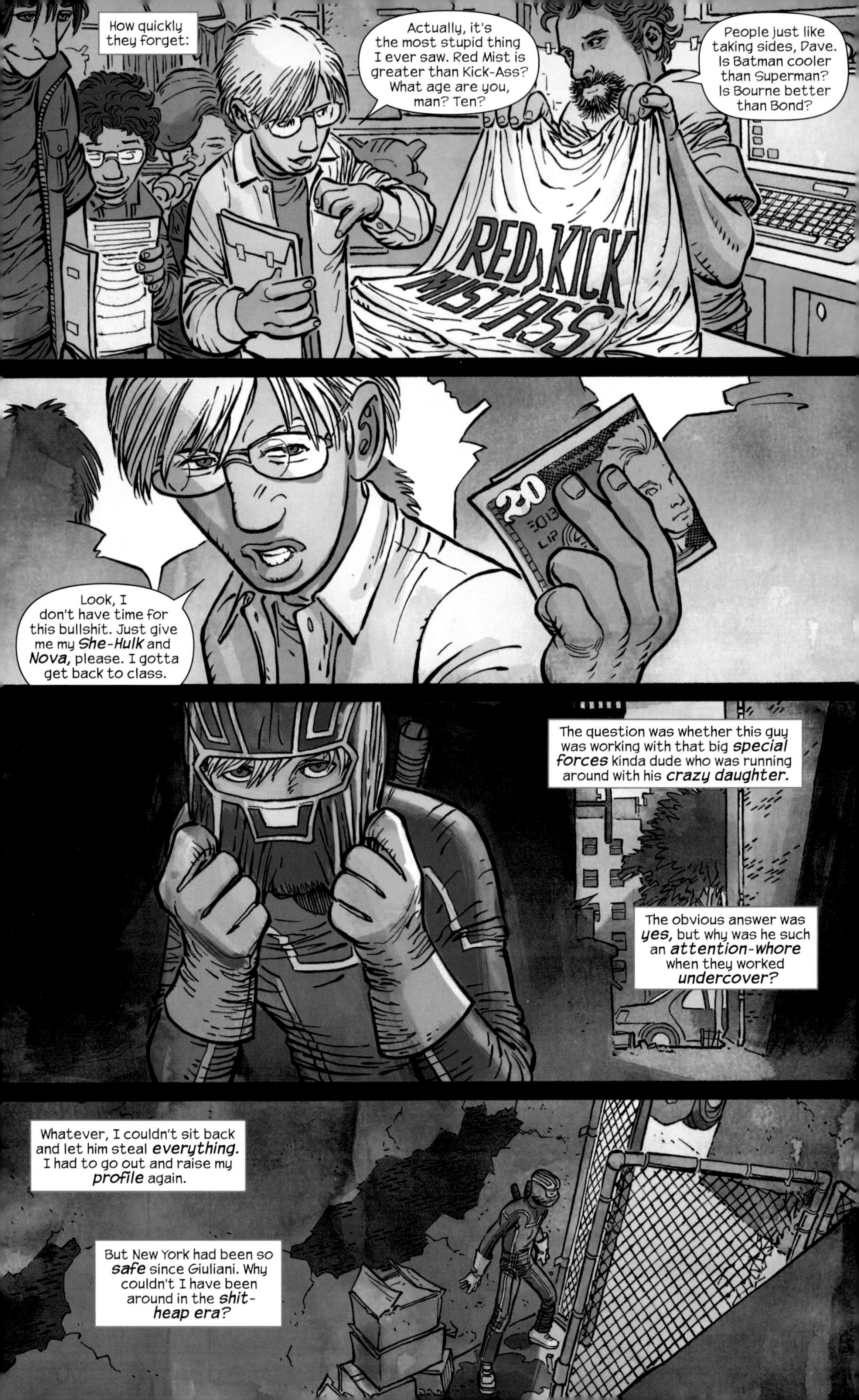
How quickly they forget:
Actually, it's the most stupid thing I ever saw. Red Mist is greater than Kick-Ass? What age are you, man? Ten?
People just like taking sides, Dave. Is Batman cooler than Superman? Is Bourne better than Bond?
RED MIST KICK ASS
Look, I don't have time for this bullshit. Just give me my *She-Hulk* and *Nova,* please. I gotta get back to class.
The question was whether this guy was working with that big *special forces* kinda dude who was running around with his *crazy daughter.*
The obvious answer was *yes,* but why was he such an *attention-whore* when they worked *undercover?*
Whatever, I couldn't sit back and let him steal *everything.* I had to go out and raise my *profile* again.
But New York had been so *safe* since Giuliani. Why couldn't I have been around in the *shit-heap era?*

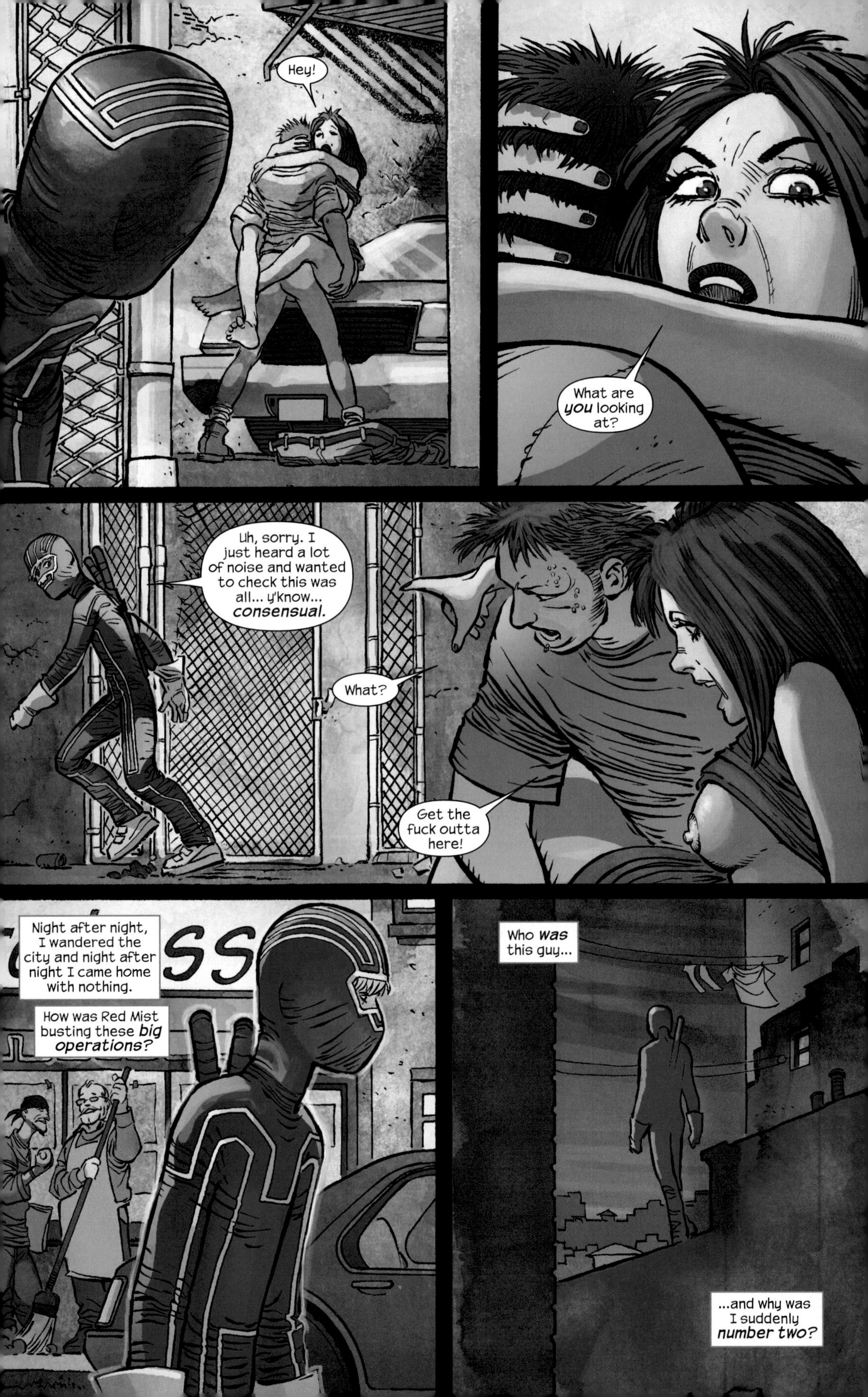
Hey!
What are you looking at?
Uh, sorry. I just heard a lot of noise and wanted to check this was all... y'know... consensual.
What?
Get the fuck outta here!
Night after night, I wandered the city and night after night I came home with nothing.
How was Red Mist busting these big operations?
Who was this guy...
...and why was I suddenly number two?

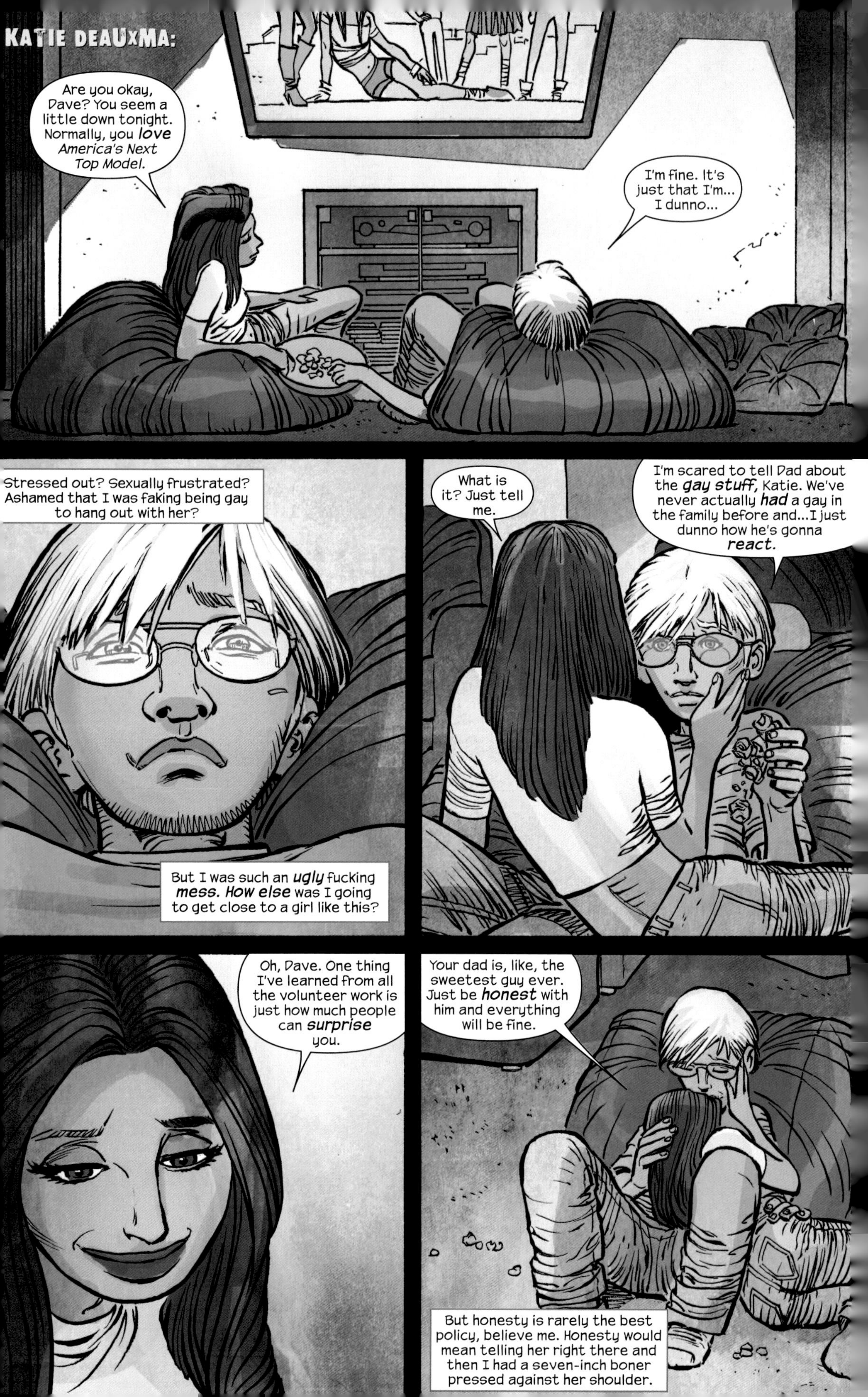
KATIE DEAUXMA:
Are you okay, Dave? You seem a little down tonight. Normally, you *love* *America's Next Top Model.*
I'm fine. It's just that I'm... I dunno...
Stressed out? Sexually frustrated? Ashamed that I was faking being gay to hang out with her?
But I was such an *ugly* fucking *mess. How else* was I going to get close to a girl like this?
What is it? Just tell me.
I'm scared to tell Dad about the *gay stuff*, Katie. We've never actually *had* a gay in the family before and...I just dunno how he's gonna *react.*
Oh, Dave. One thing I've learned from all the volunteer work is just how much people can *surprise* you.
Your dad is, like, the sweetest guy ever. Just be *honest* with him and everything will be fine.
But honesty is rarely the best policy, believe me. Honesty would mean telling her right there and then I had a seven-inch boner pressed against her shoulder.

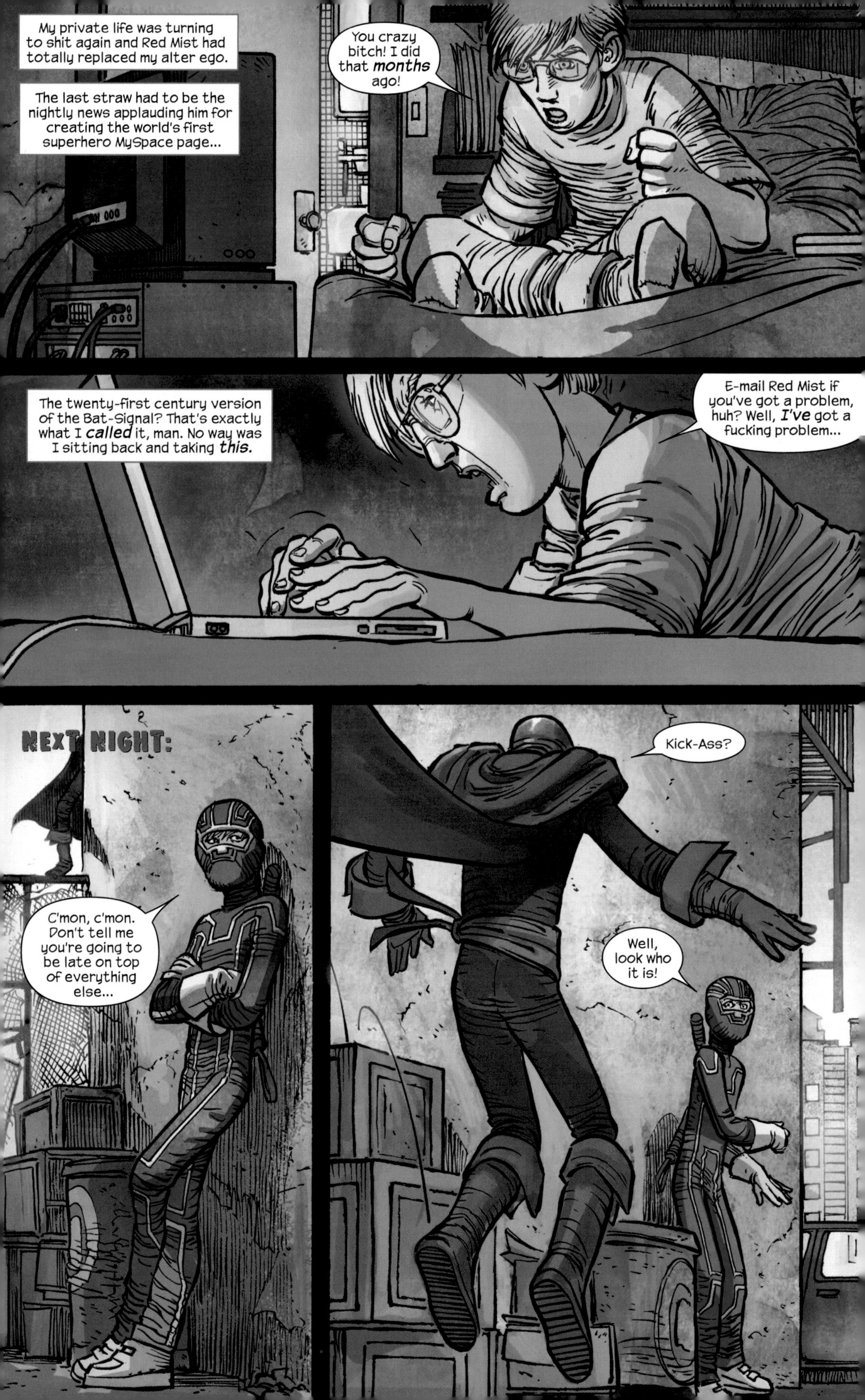
My private life was turning to shit again and Red Mist had totally replaced my alter ego.
The last straw had to be the nightly news applauding him for creating the world's first superhero MySpace page...
You crazy bitch! I did that *months* ago!
The twenty-first century version of the Bat-Signal? That's exactly what I *called* it, man. No way was I sitting back and taking *this.*
E-mail Red Mist if you've got a problem, huh? Well, *I've* got a fucking problem...
NEXT NIGHT:
C'mon, c'mon. Don't tell me you're going to be late on top of everything else...
Kick-Ass?
Well, look who it is!

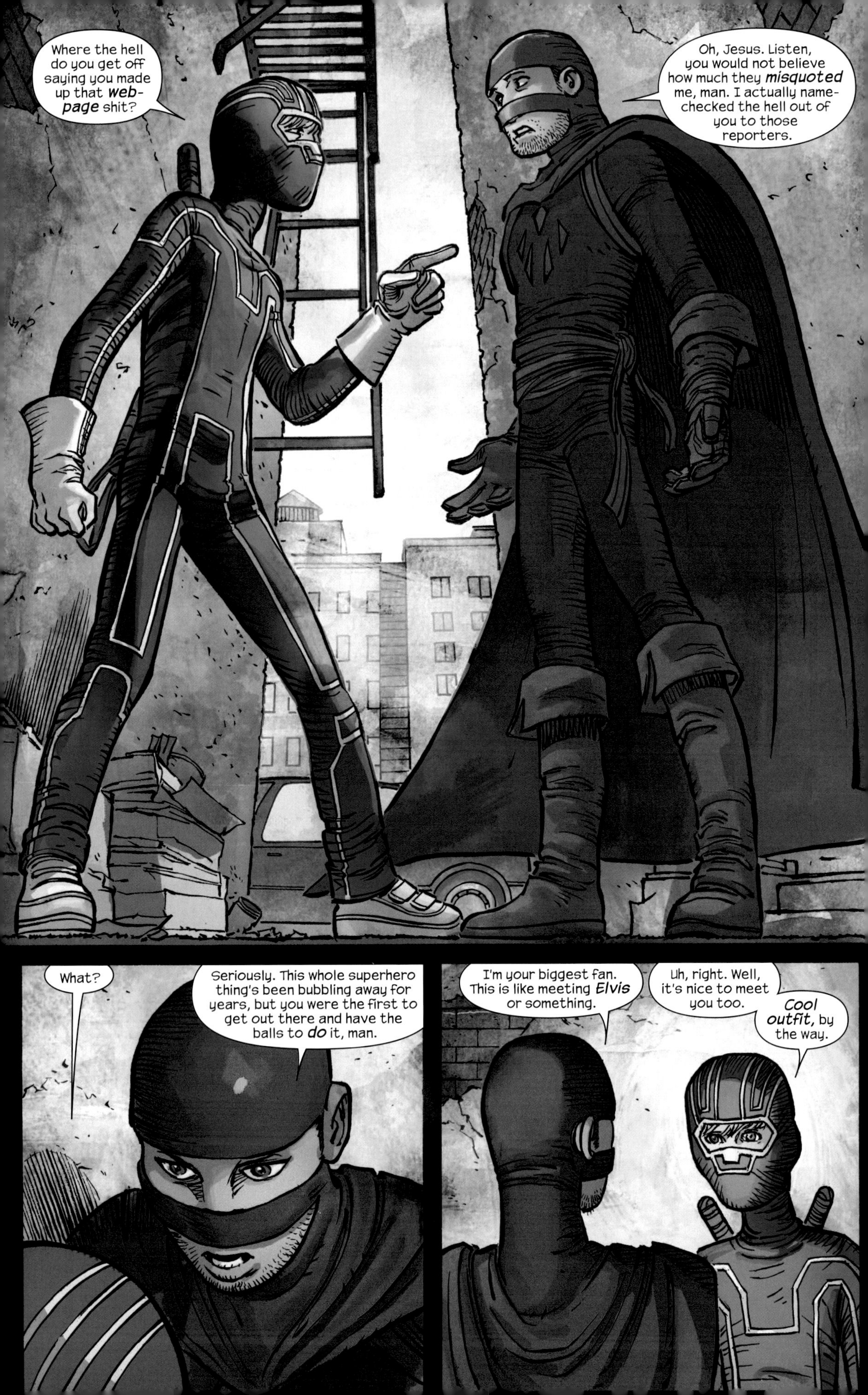
Where the hell do you get off saying you made up that web-page shit?
Oh, Jesus. Listen, you would not believe how much they misquoted me, man. I actually name-checked the hell out of you to those reporters.
What?
Seriously. This whole superhero thing's been bubbling away for years, but you were the first to get out there and have the balls to do it, man.
I'm your biggest fan. This is like meeting Elvis or something.
Uh, right. Well, it's nice to meet you too.
Cool outfit, by the way.

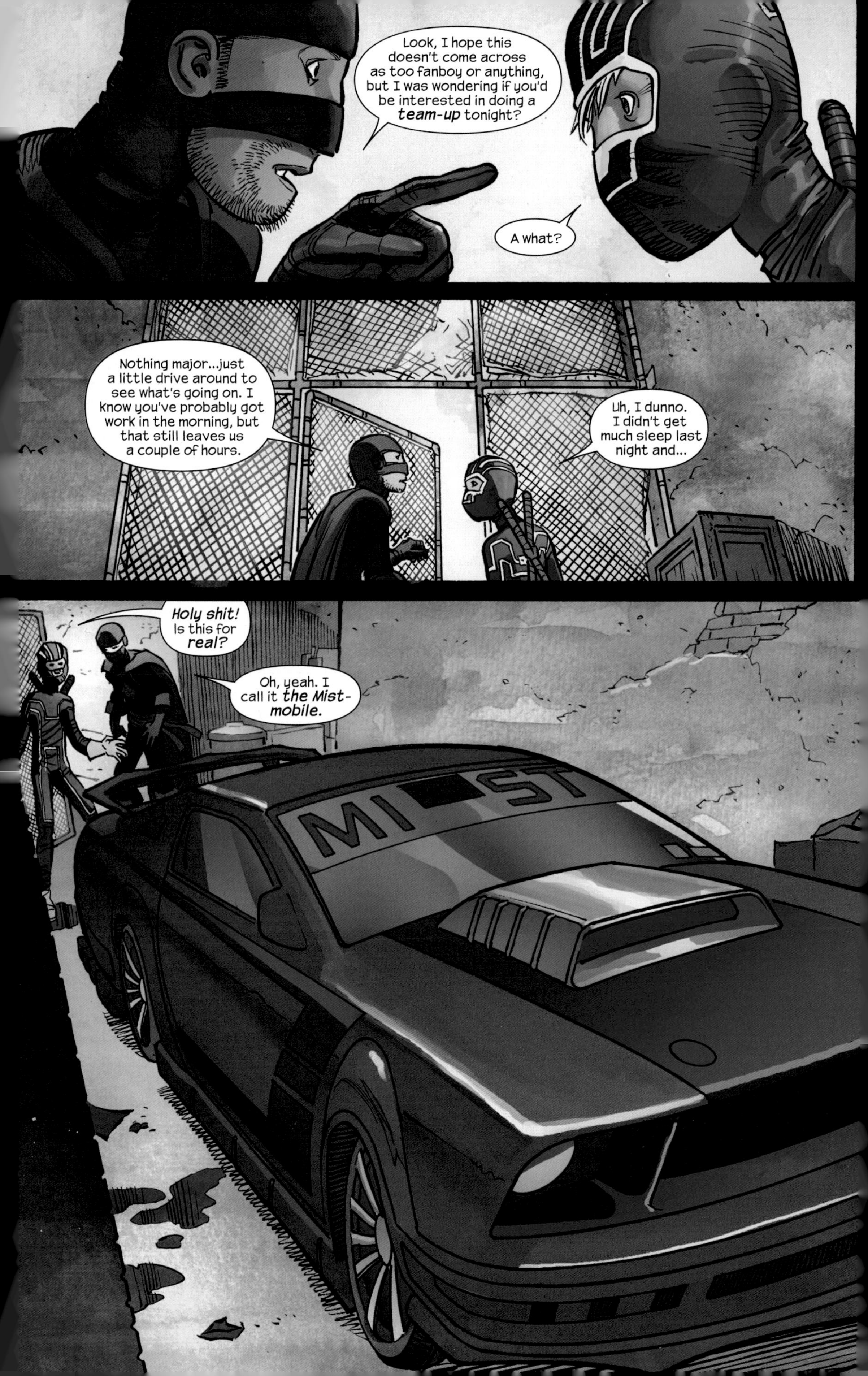

Look, I hope this doesn't come across as too fanboy or anything, but I was wondering if you'd be interested in doing a **team-up** tonight?
A what?
Nothing major...just a little drive around to see what's going on. I know you've probably got work in the morning, but that still leaves us a couple of hours.
Uh, I dunno. I didn't get much sleep last night and...
Holy shit! Is this for *real?*
Oh, yeah. I call it *the Mist-mobile.*

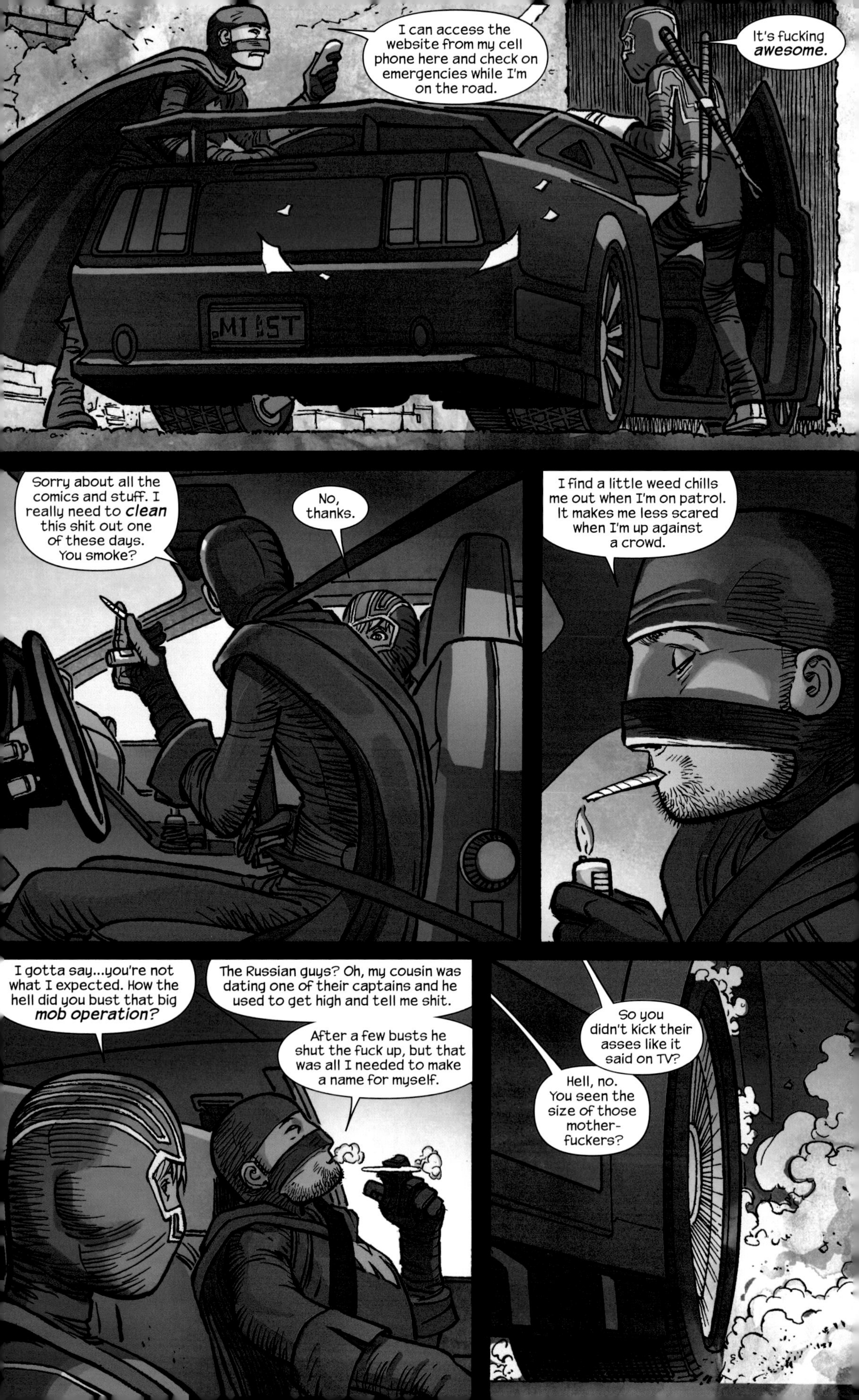
I can access the website from my cell phone here and check on emergencies while I'm on the road.
It's fucking *awesome.*
MI 5ST
Sorry about all the comics and stuff. I really need to *clean* this shit out one of these days. You smoke?
No, thanks.
I find a little weed chills me out when I'm on patrol. It makes me less scared when I'm up against a crowd.
I gotta say...you're not what I expected. How the hell did you bust that big *mob operation?*
The Russian guys? Oh, my cousin was dating one of their captains and he used to get high and tell me shit.
After a few busts he shut the fuck up, but that was all I needed to make a name for myself.
So you didn't kick their asses like it said on TV?
Hell, no. You seen the size of those mother-fuckers?

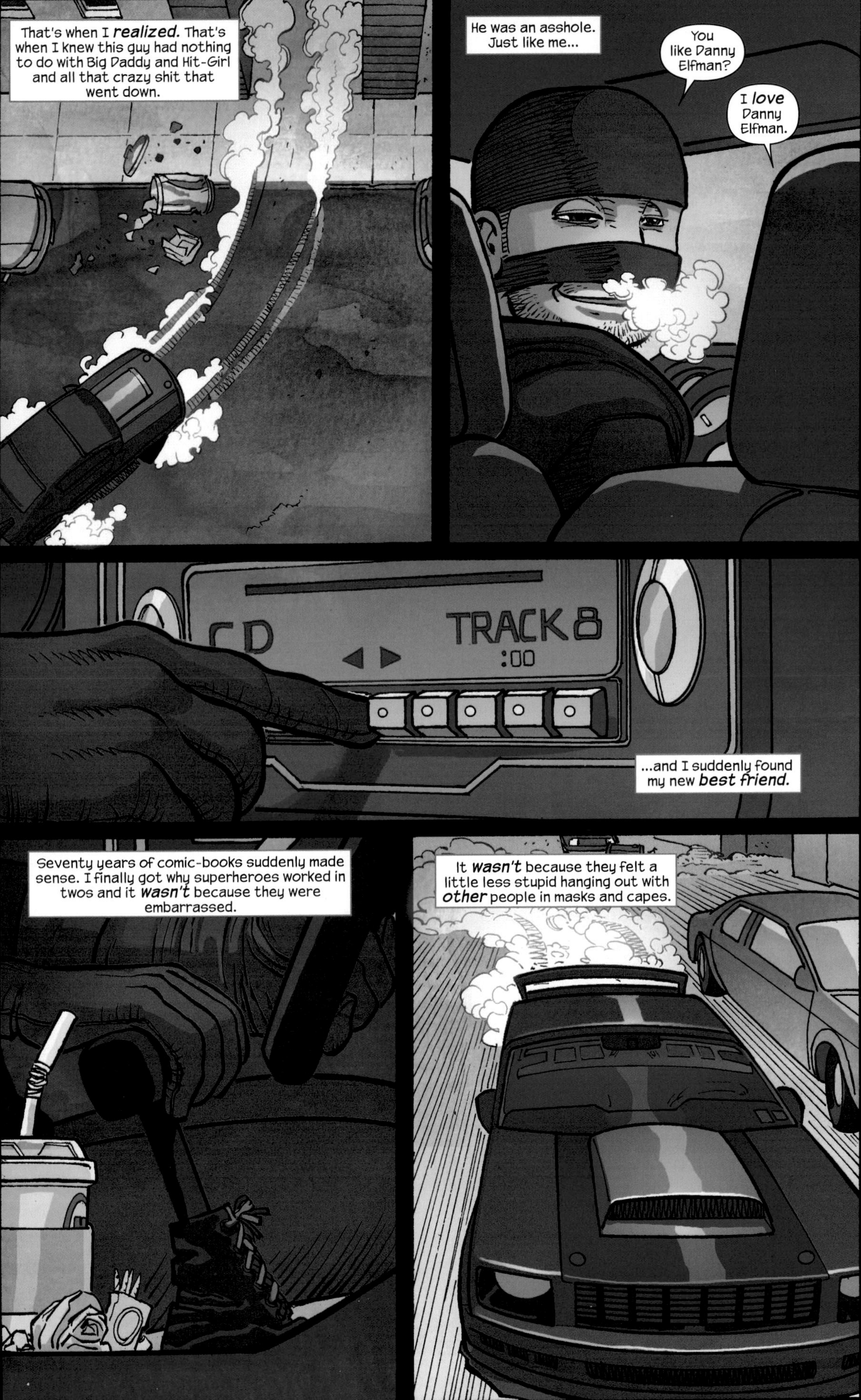
That's when I **realized.** That's when I knew this guy had nothing to do with Big Daddy and Hit-Girl and all that crazy shit that went down.
He was an asshole. Just like me...
You like Danny Elfman?
I **love** Danny Elfman.
CD
TRACK 8
:00
...and I suddenly found my new **best friend.**
Seventy years of comic-books suddenly made sense. I finally got why superheroes worked in twos and it **wasn't** because they were embarrassed.
It **wasn't** because they felt a little less stupid hanging out with **other** people in masks and capes.

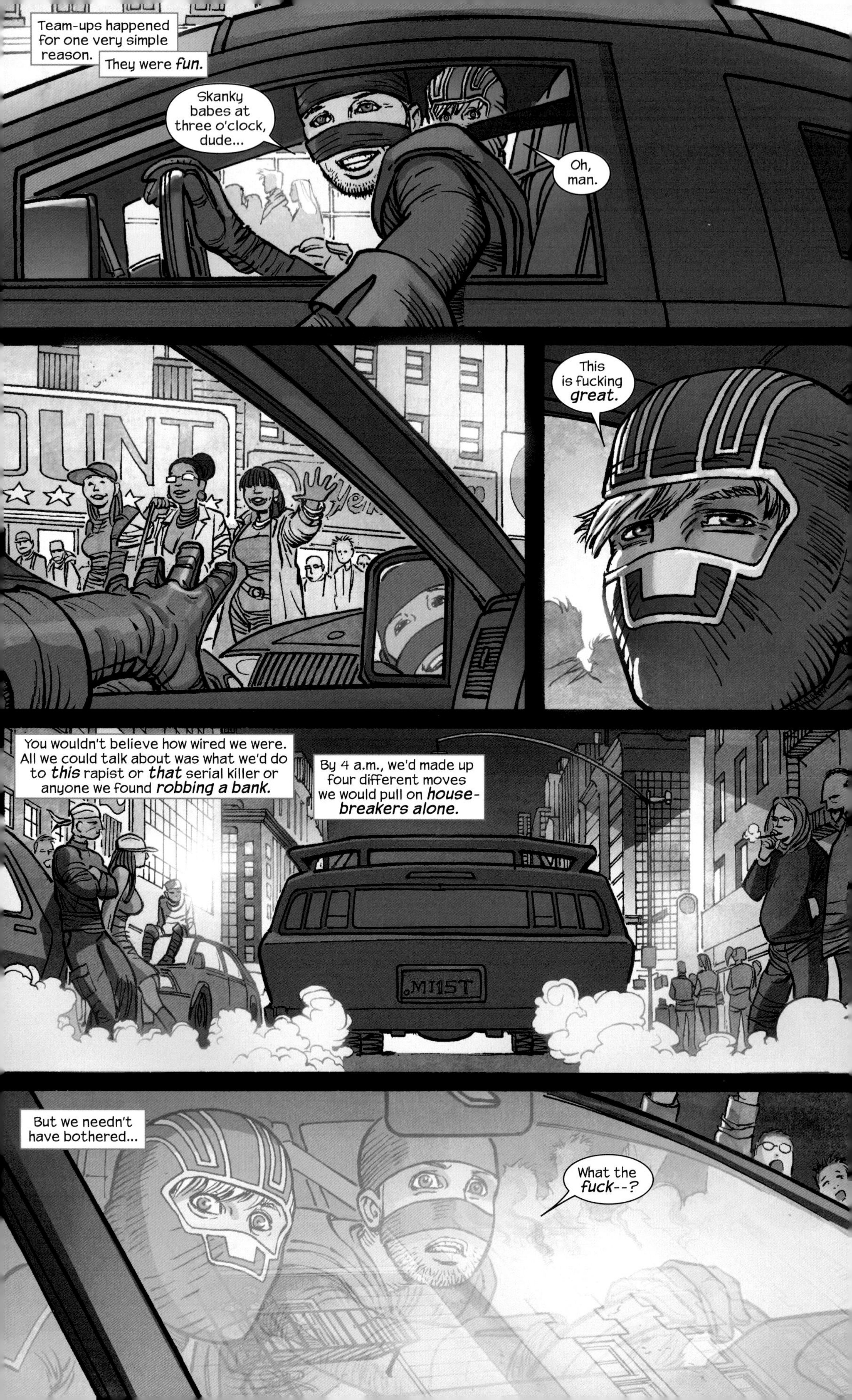
Team-ups happened for one very simple reason.
They were *fun.*
Skanky babes at three o'clock, dude...
Oh, man.
This is fucking *great.*
You wouldn't believe how wired we were. All we could talk about was what we'd do to *this* rapist or *that* serial killer or anyone we found *robbing a bank.*
By 4 a.m., we'd made up four different moves we would pull on *house-breakers alone.*
MI15T
But we needn't have bothered...
What the *fuck*--?

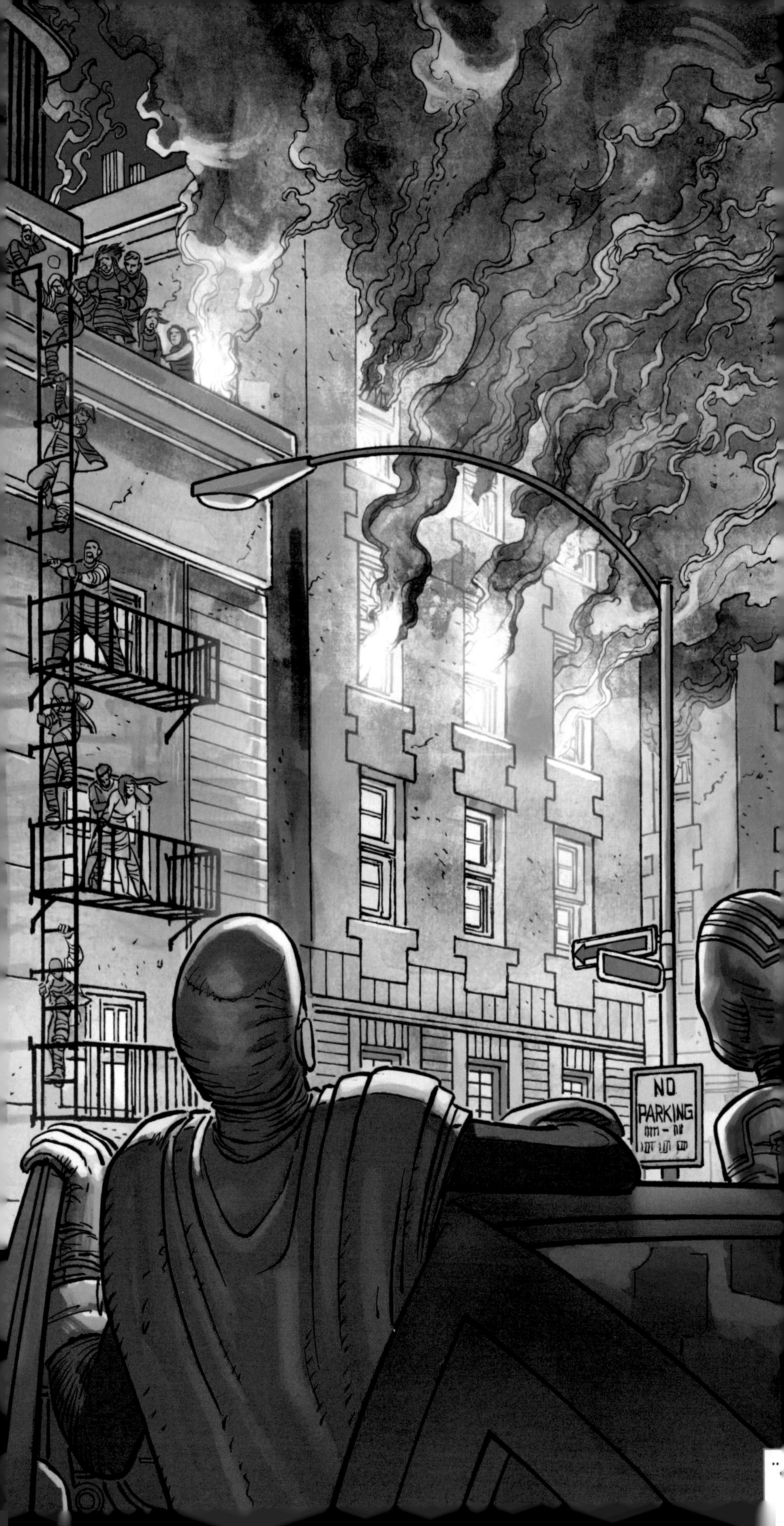
NO
PARKING

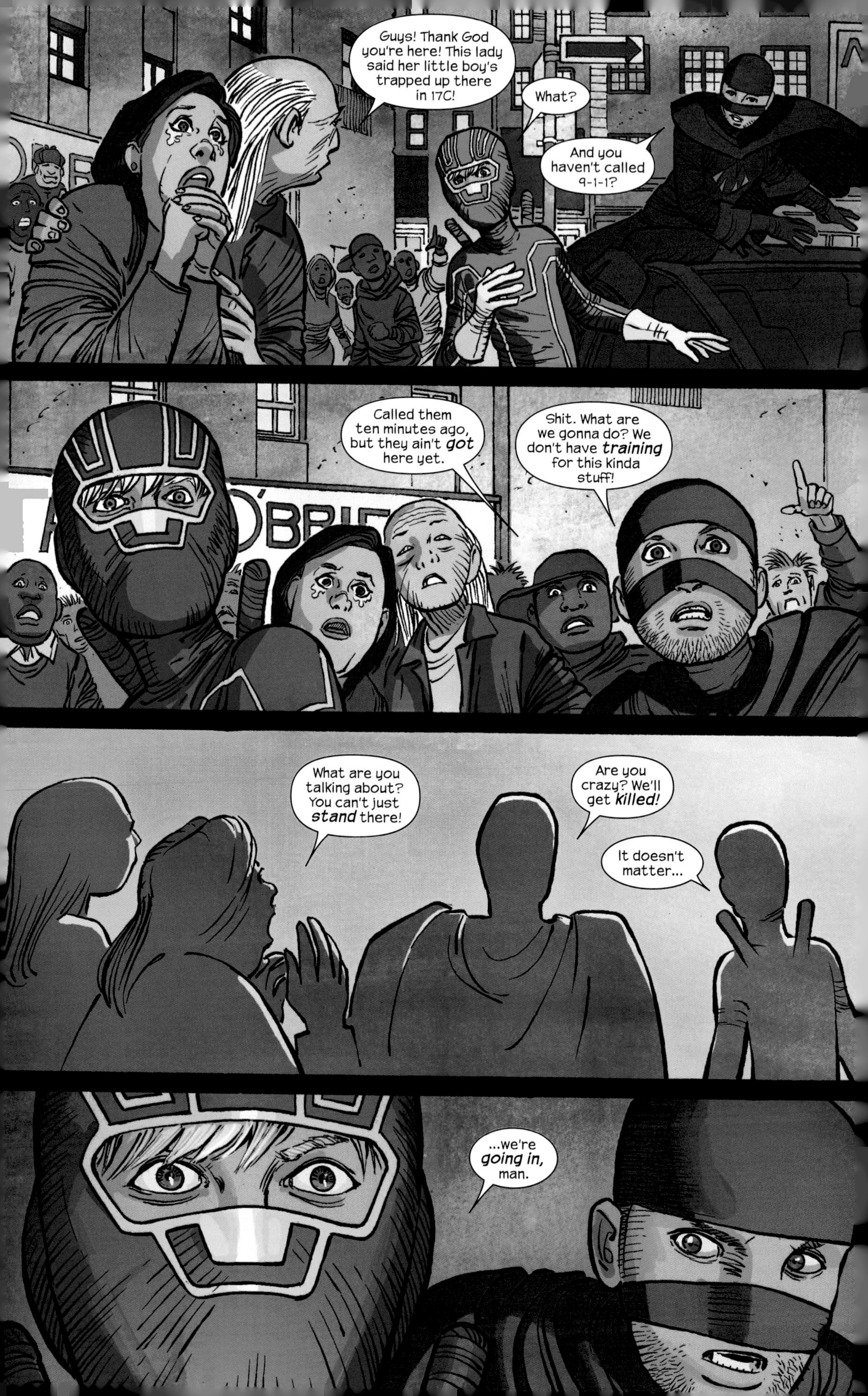
Guys! Thank God you're here! This lady said her little boy's trapped up there in 17C!
What?
And you haven't called 9-1-1?
Called them ten minutes ago, but they ain't *got* here yet.
Shit. What are we gonna do? We don't have *training* for this kinda stuff!
What are you talking about? You can't just *stand* there!
Are you crazy? We'll get *killed!*
It doesn't matter...
...we're *going in,* man.

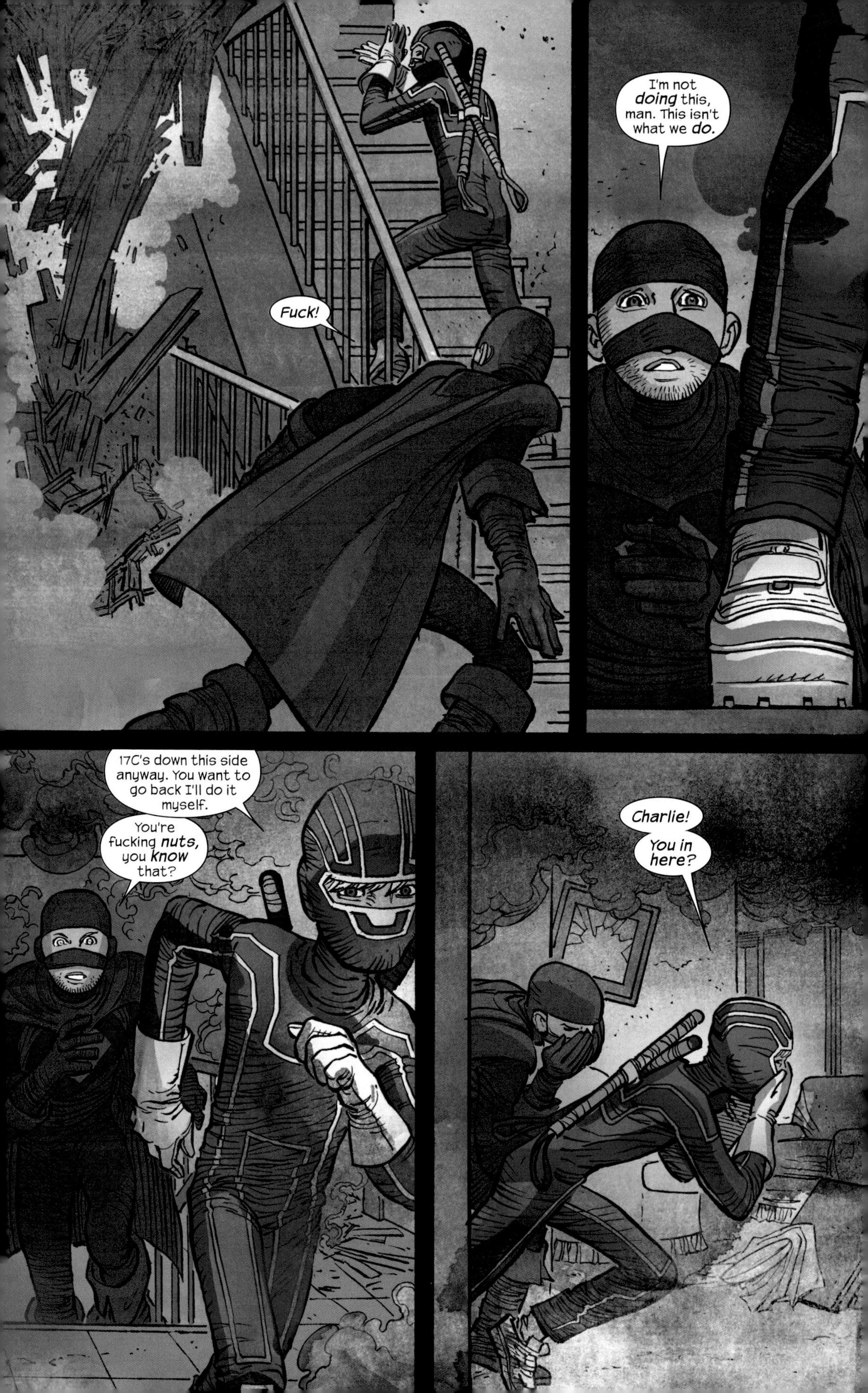
Fuck!
I'm not doing this, man. This isn't what we do.
17C's down this side anyway. You want to go back I'll do it myself.
You're fucking nuts, you know that?
Charlie!
You in here?

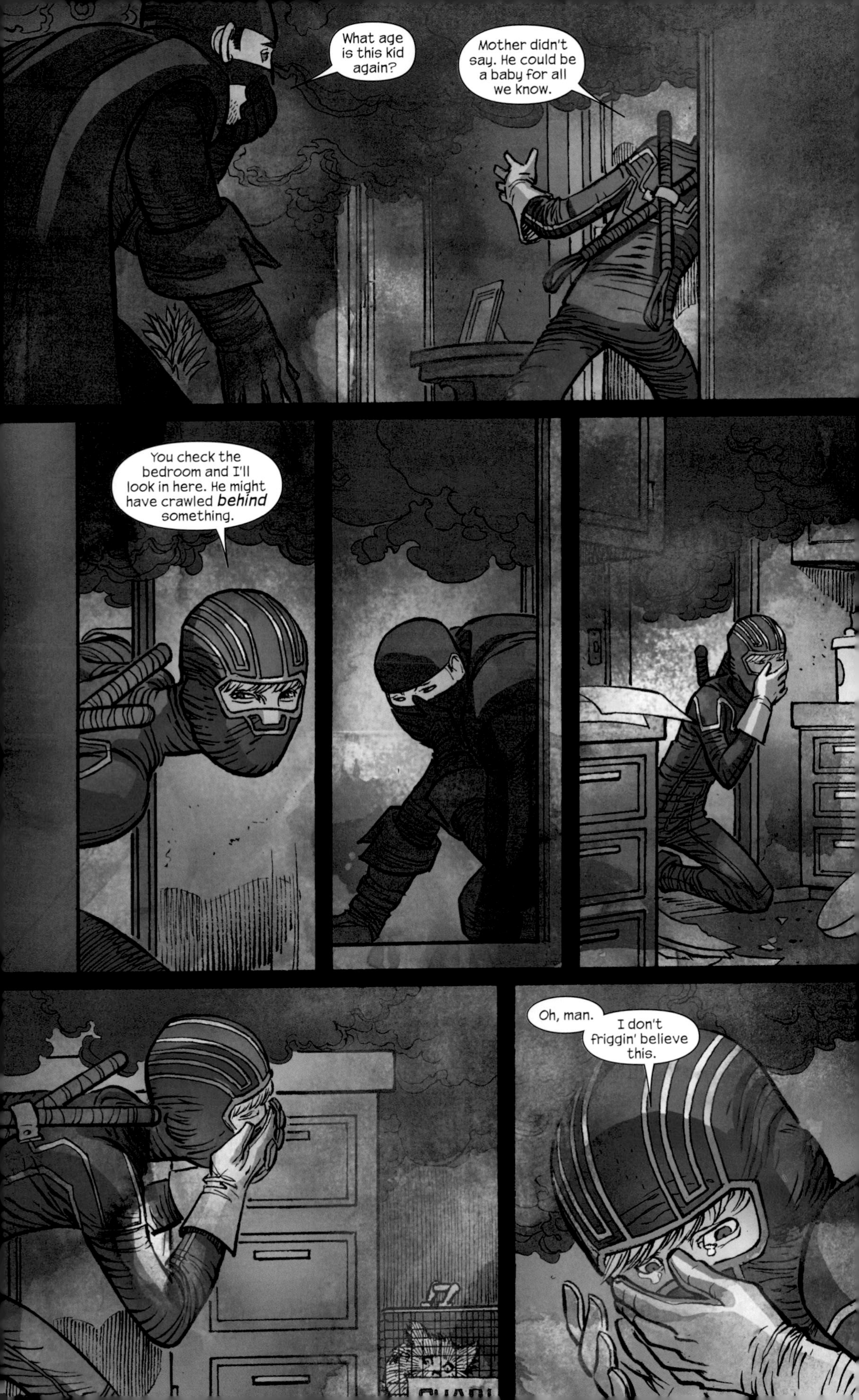
What age is this kid again?
Mother didn't say. He could be a baby for all we know.
You check the bedroom and I'll look in here. He might have crawled **behind** something.
Oh, man.
I don't friggin' believe this.

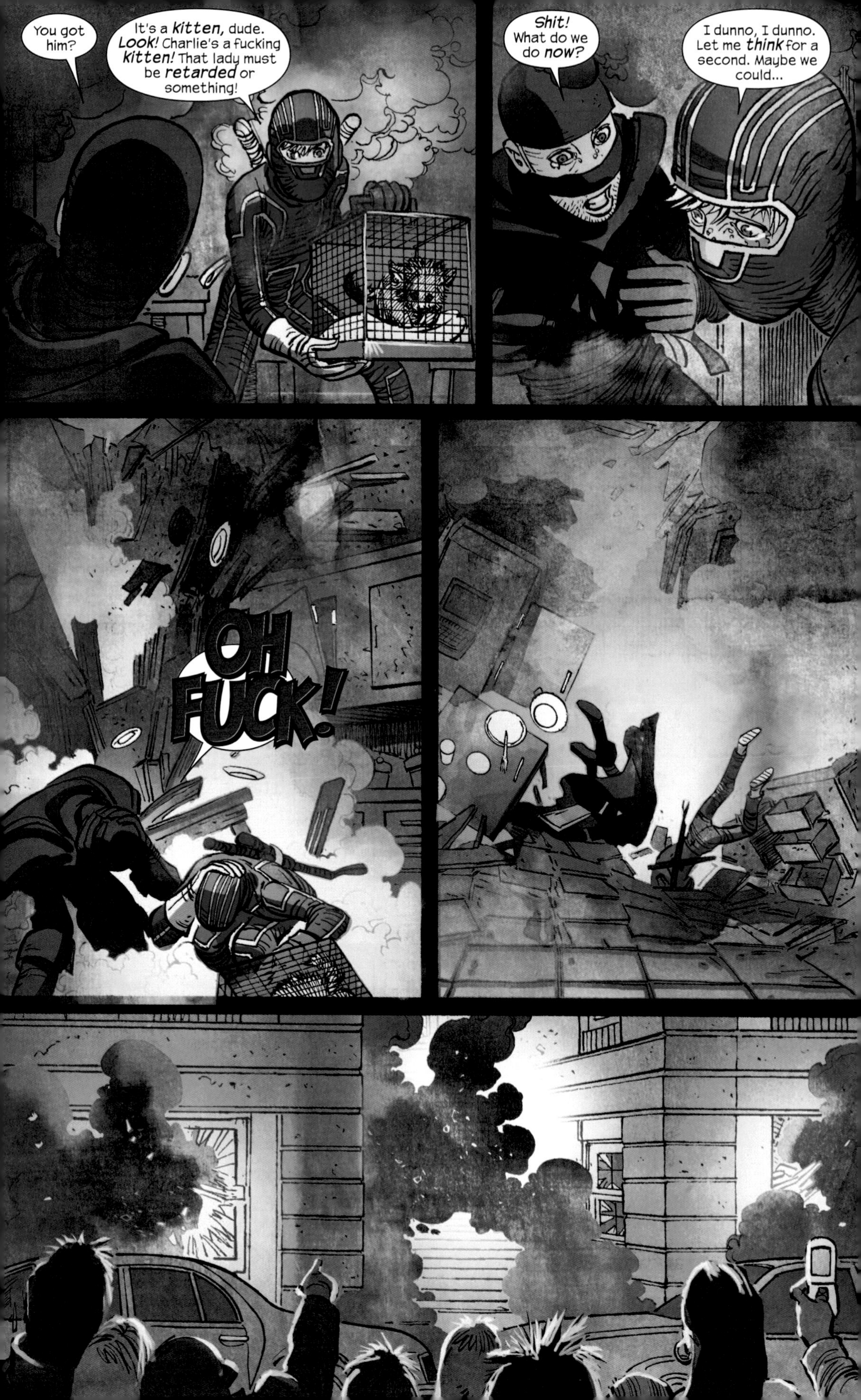
You got him?
It's a *kitten,* dude. *Look!* Charlie's a fucking *kitten!* That lady must be *retarded* or something!
Shit! What do we do *now?*
I dunno, I dunno. Let me *think* for a second. Maybe we could...
OH FUCK!

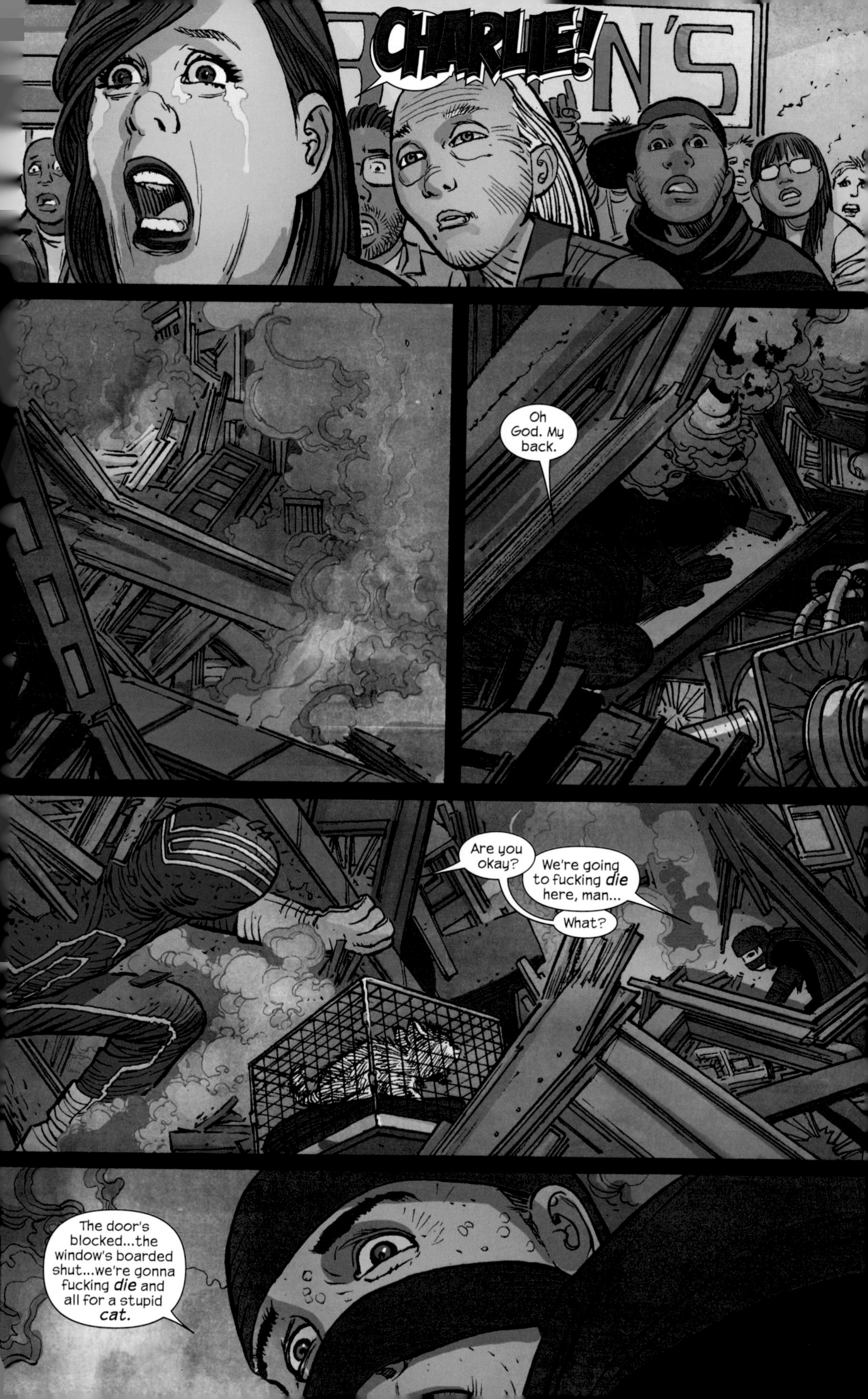
CHARLIE!
Oh God. My back.
Are you okay?
We're going to fucking *die* here, man...
What?
The door's blocked...the window's boarded shut...we're gonna fucking *die* and all for a stupid *cat*.

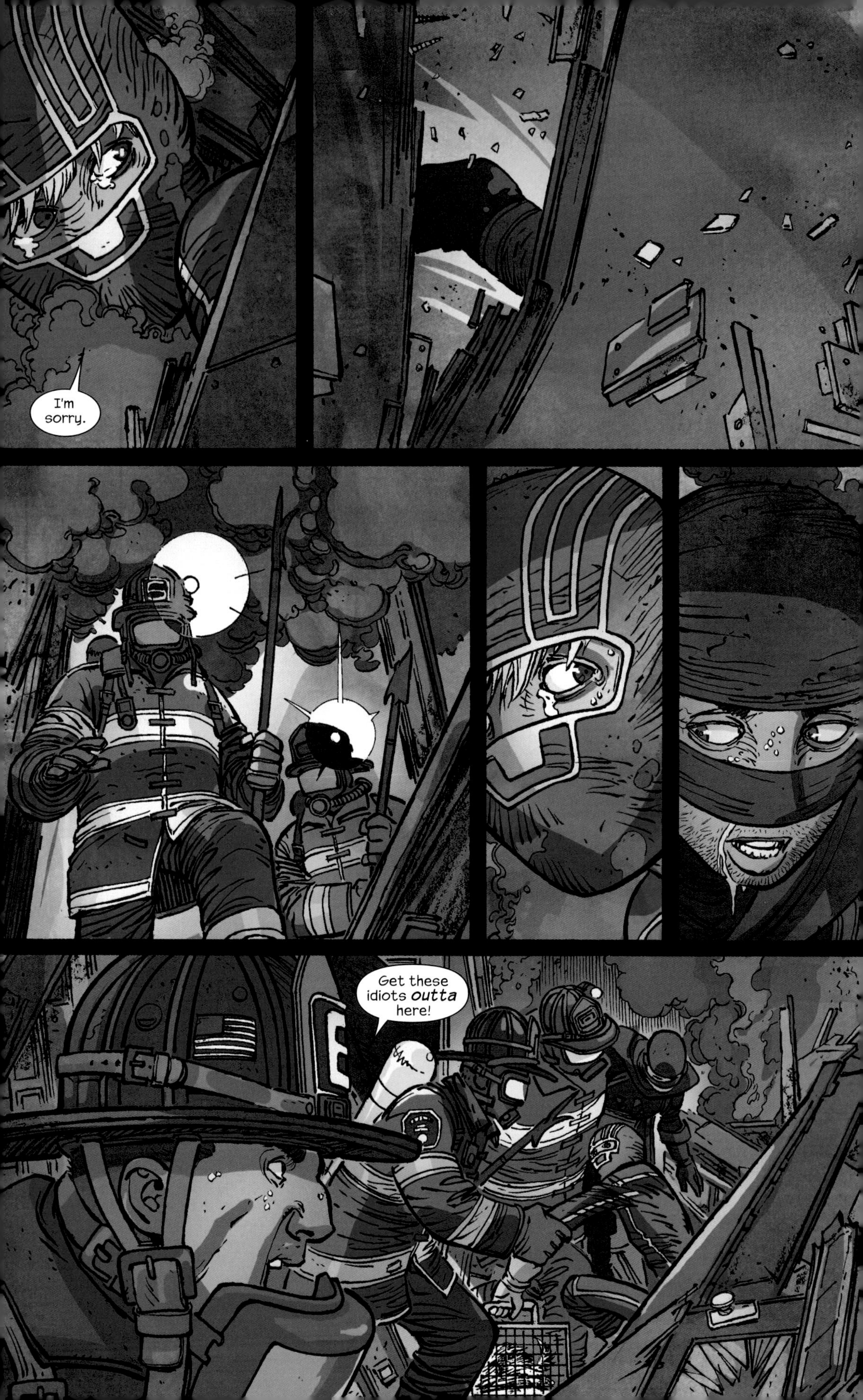
I'm sorry.
Get these idiots *outta* here!

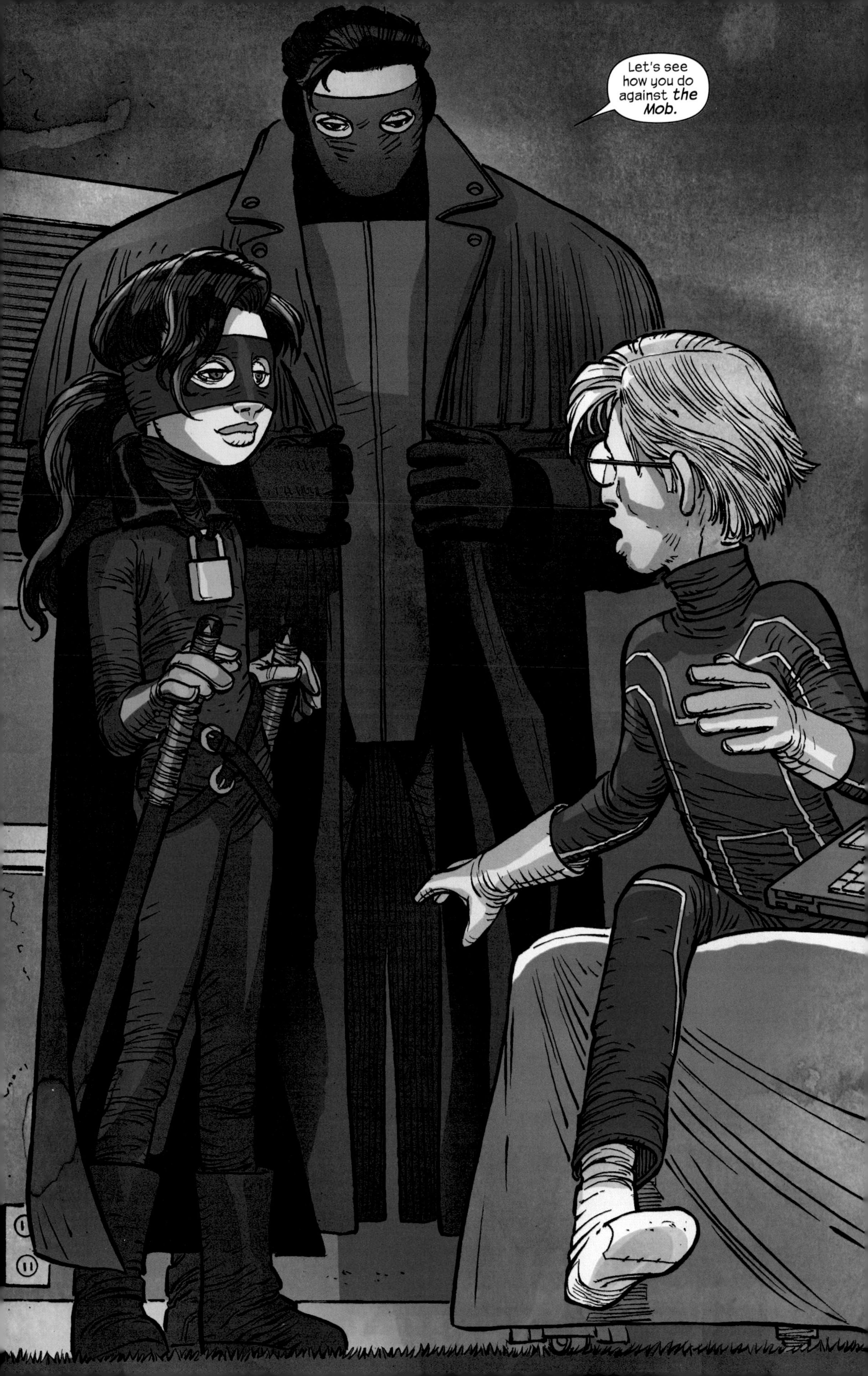
Let's see how you do against *the Mob.*

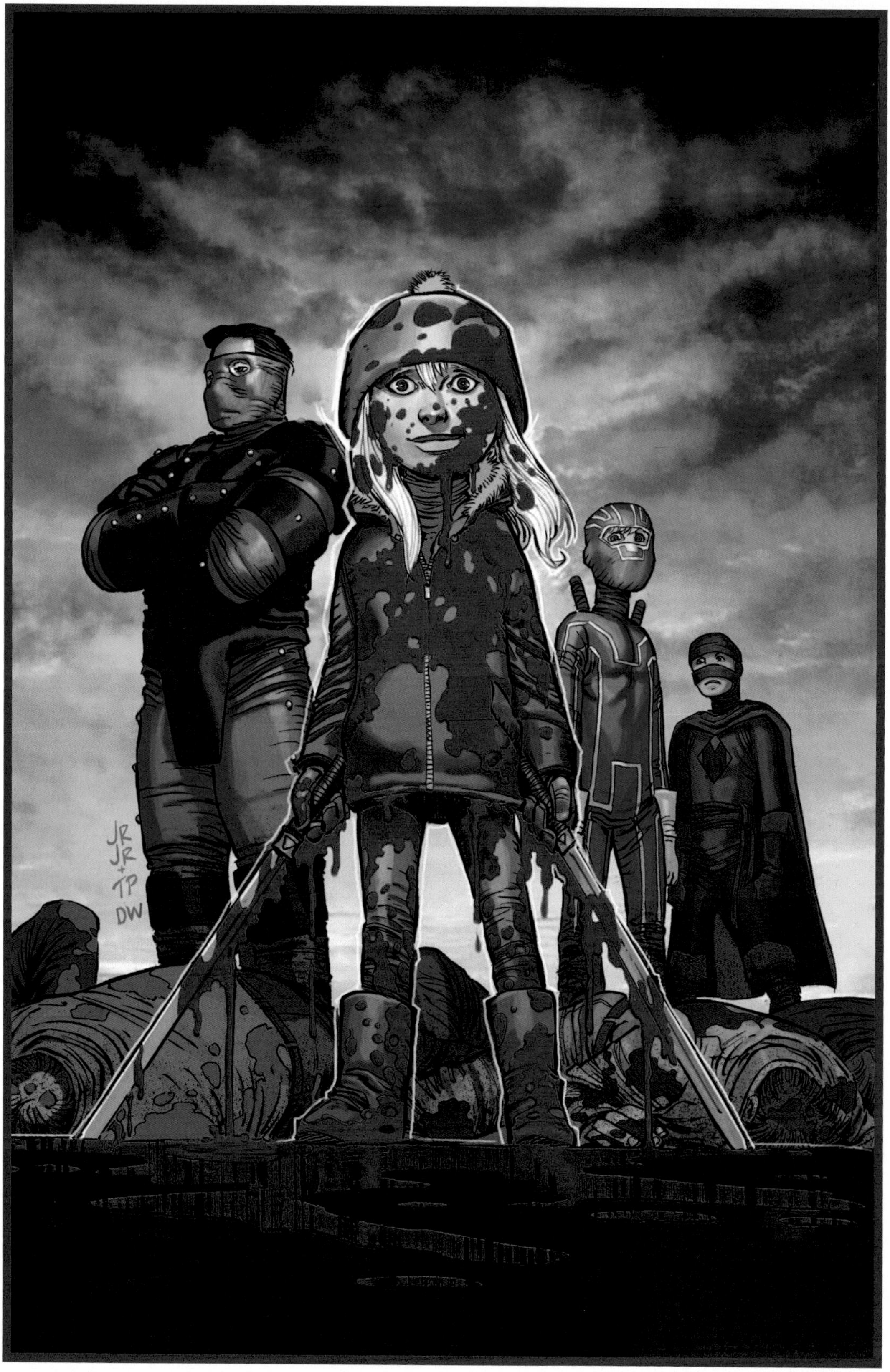
JR JR + TP DW

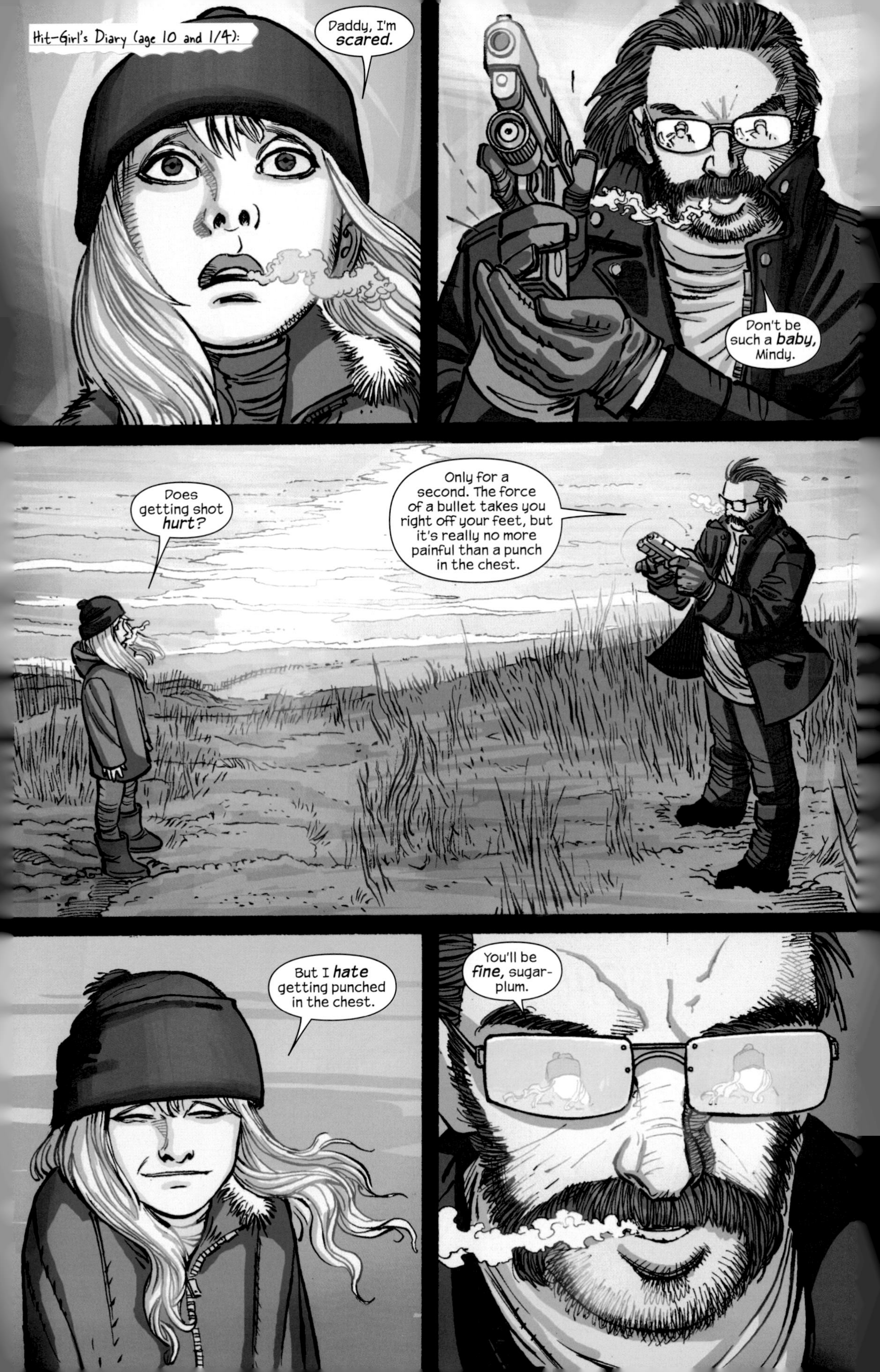

Hit-Girl's Diary (age 10 and 1/4):
Daddy, I'm *scared.*
Don't be such a *baby,* Mindy.
Does getting shot *hurt?*
Only for a second. The force of a bullet takes you right off your feet, but it's really no more painful than a punch in the chest.
But I *hate* getting punched in the chest.
You'll be *fine,* sugar-plum.

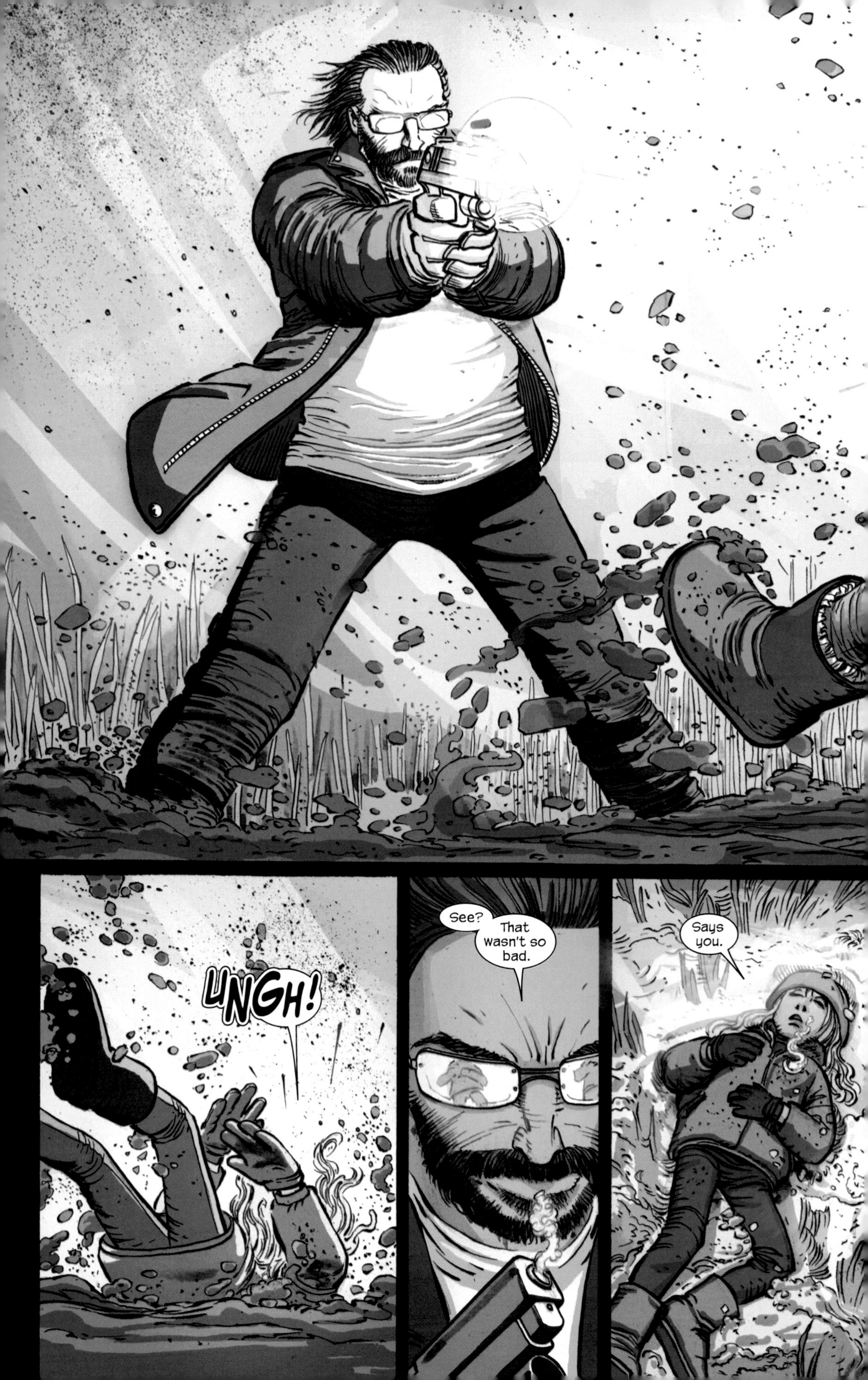
UNGH!
See?
That wasn't so bad.
Says you.

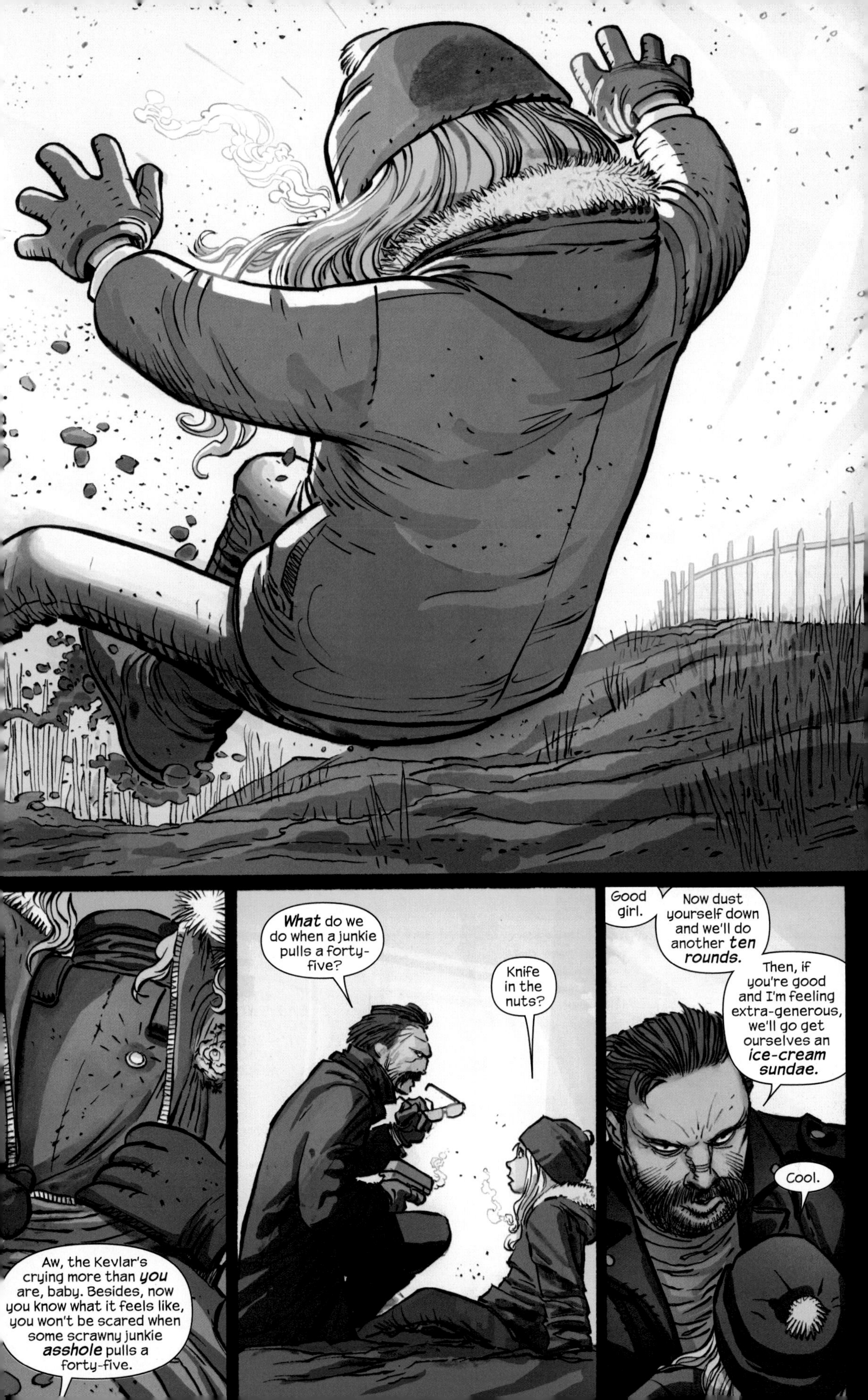

Aw, the Kevlar's crying more than *you* are, baby. Besides, now you know what it feels like, you won't be scared when some scrawny junkie *asshole* pulls a forty-five.
What do we do when a junkie pulls a forty-five?
Knife in the nuts?
Good girl.
Now dust yourself down and we'll do another *ten rounds.*
Then, if you're good and I'm feeling extra-generous, we'll go get ourselves an *ice-cream sundae.*
Cool.

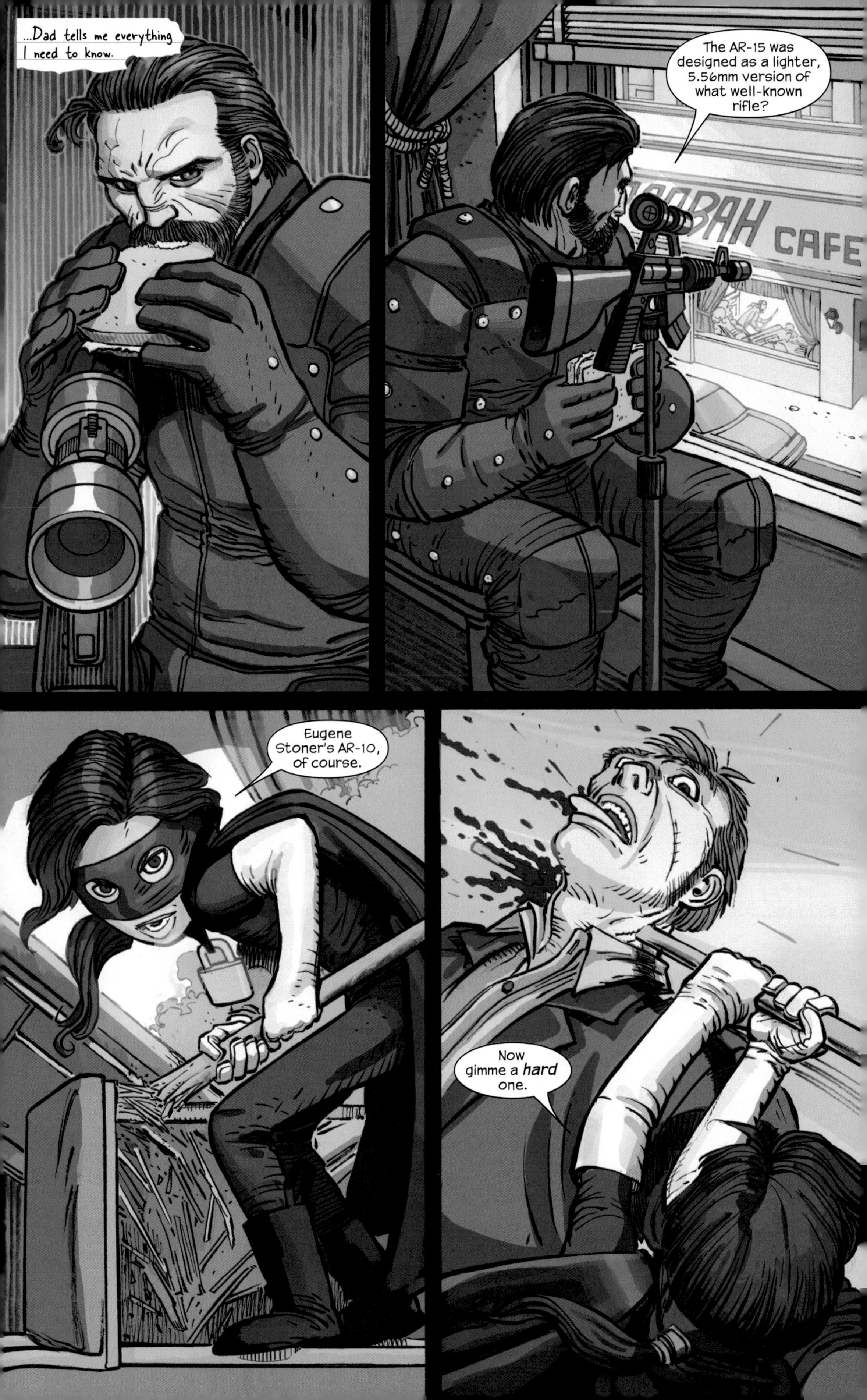
...Dad tells me everything I need to know.
The AR-15 was designed as a lighter, 5.56mm version of what well-known rifle?
BAH CAFE
Eugene Stoner's AR-10, of course.
Now gimme a *hard* one.

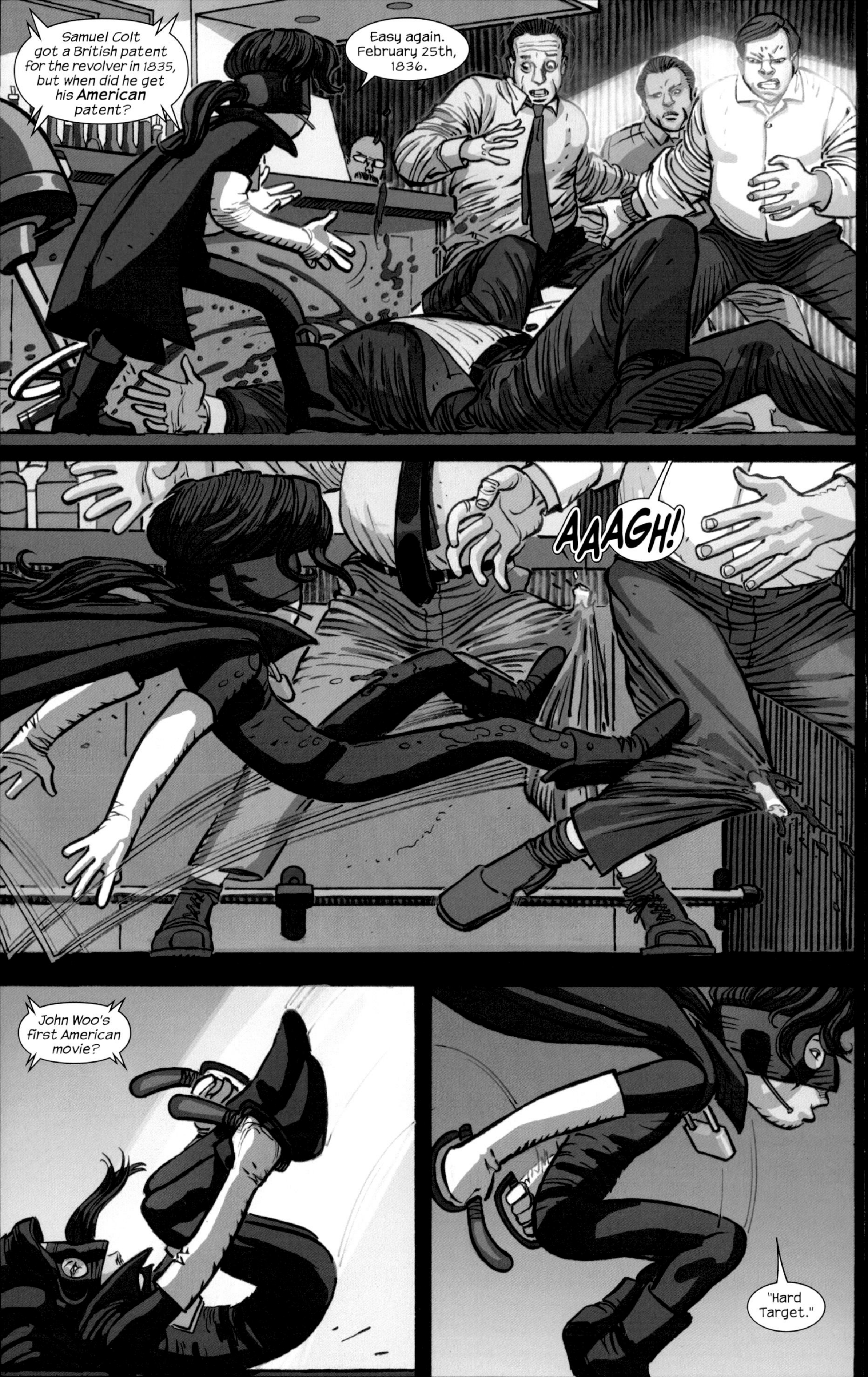
Samuel Colt got a British patent for the revolver in 1835, but when did he get his **American** patent?
Easy again. February 25th, 1836.
AAAGH!
John Woo's first American movie?
"Hard Target."

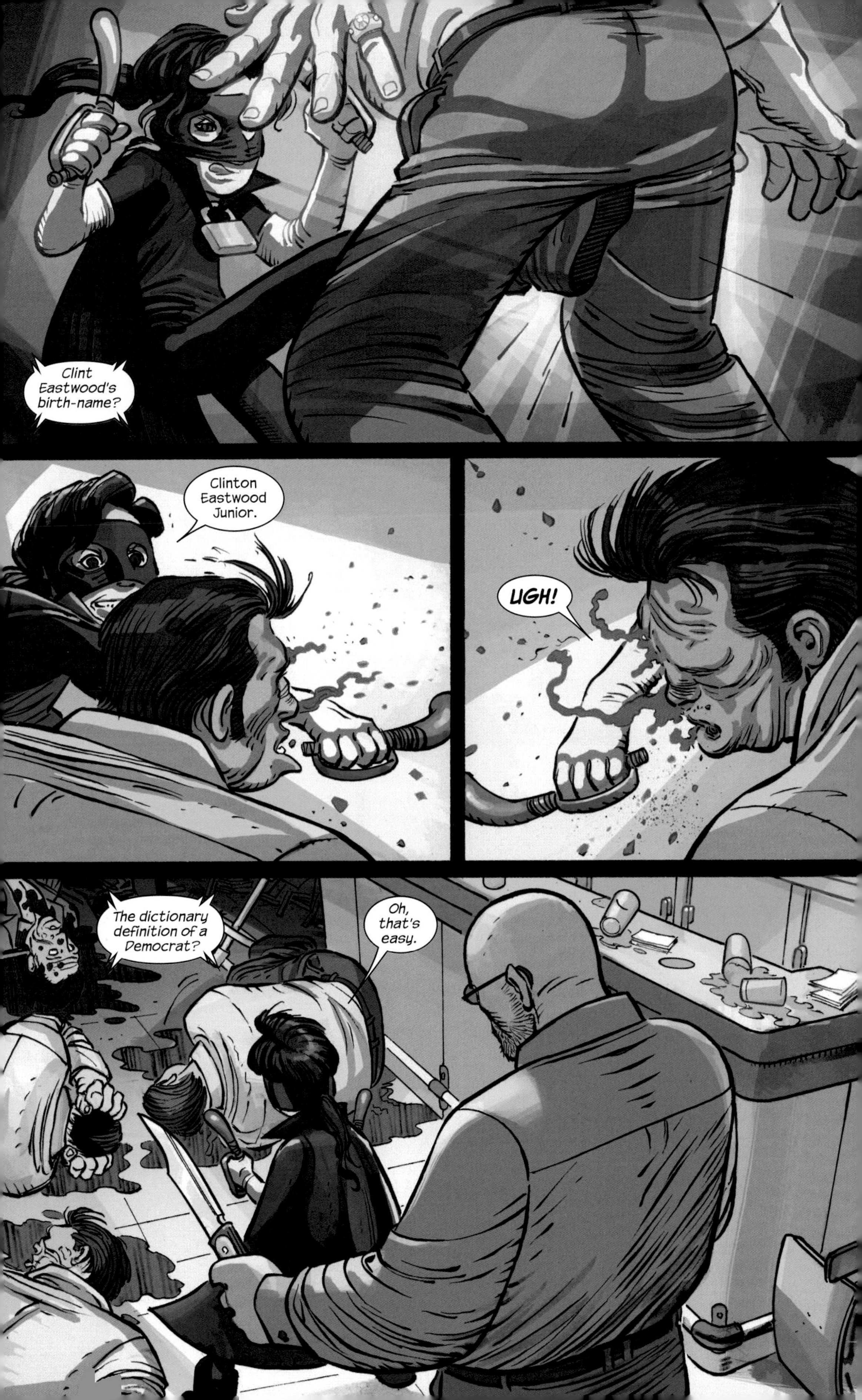
Clint Eastwood's birth-name?
Clinton Eastwood Junior.
UGH!
The dictionary definition of a Democrat?
Oh, that's easy.

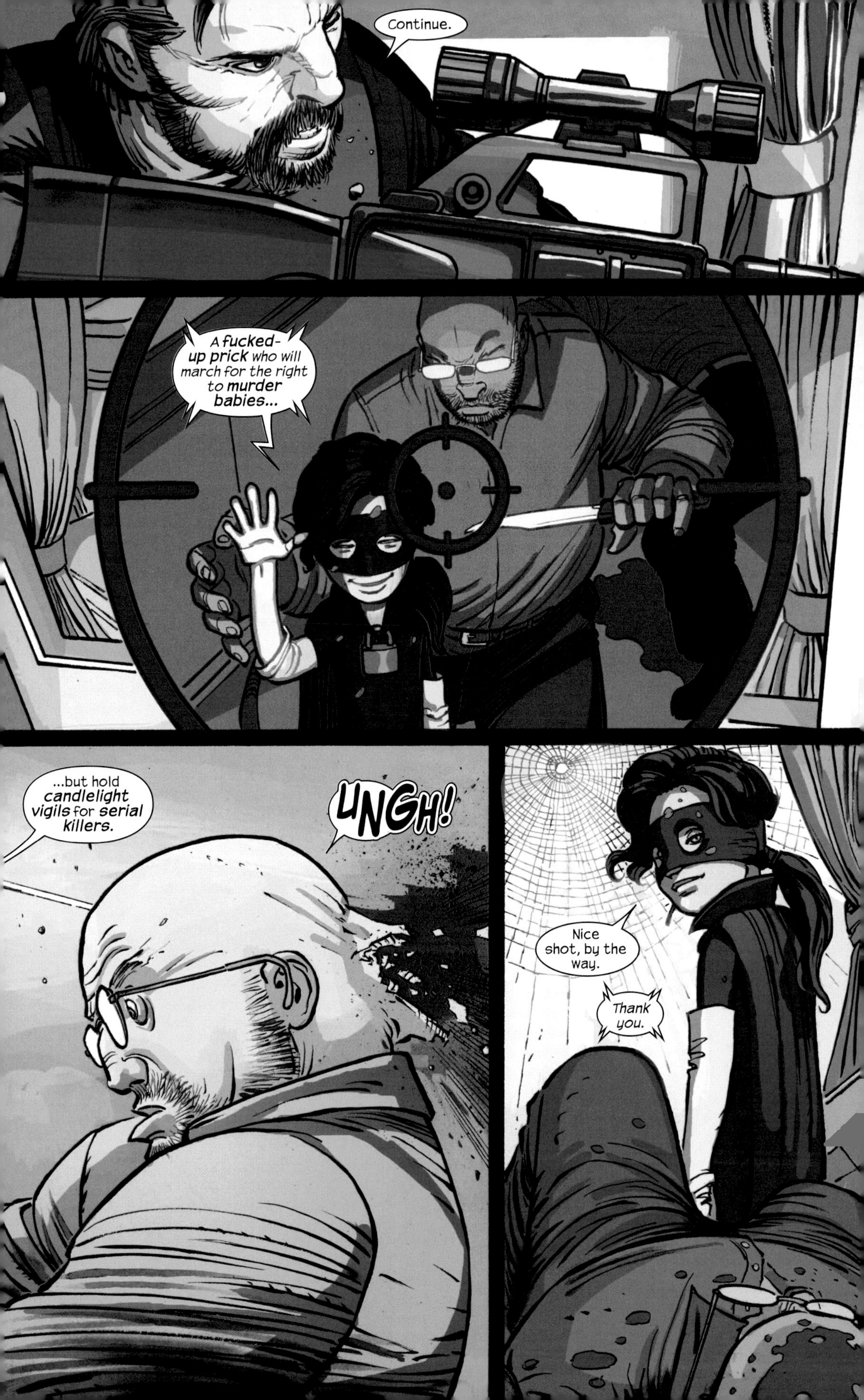
Continue.
A fucked-up prick who will march for the right to murder babies...
...but hold candlelight vigils for serial killers.
UNGH!
Nice shot, by the way.
Thank you.

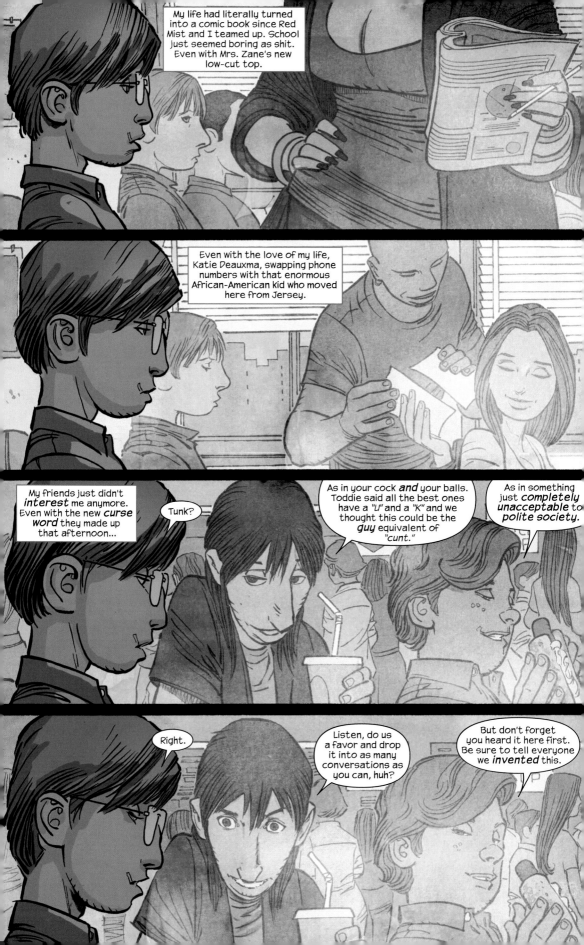

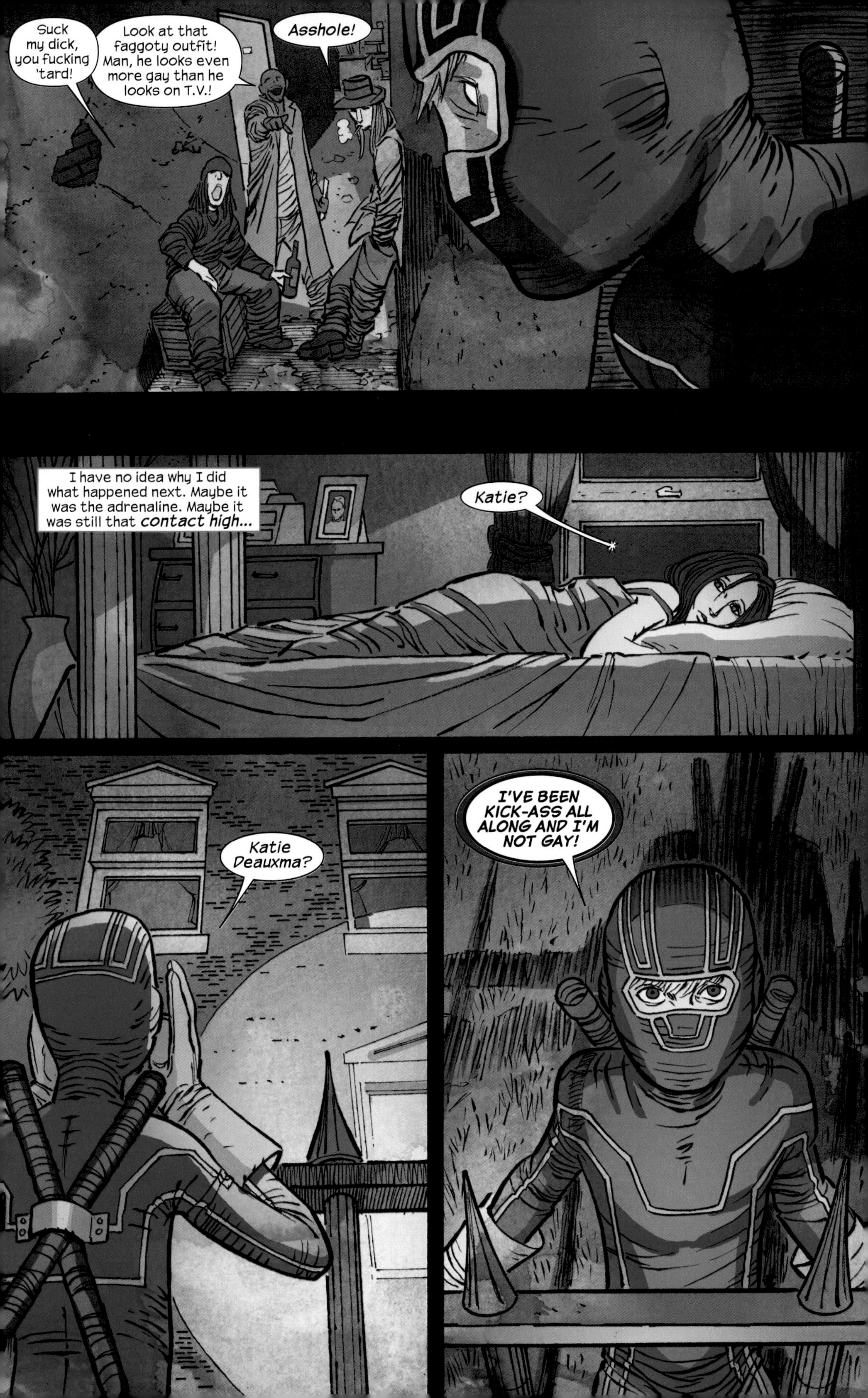
Suck my dick, you fucking 'tard!
Look at that faggoty outfit! Man, he looks even more gay than he looks on T.V.!
Asshole!
I have no idea why I did what happened next. Maybe it was the adrenaline. Maybe it was still that contact high...
Katie?
Katie Deauxma?
I'VE BEEN KICK-ASS ALL ALONG AND I'M NOT GAY!

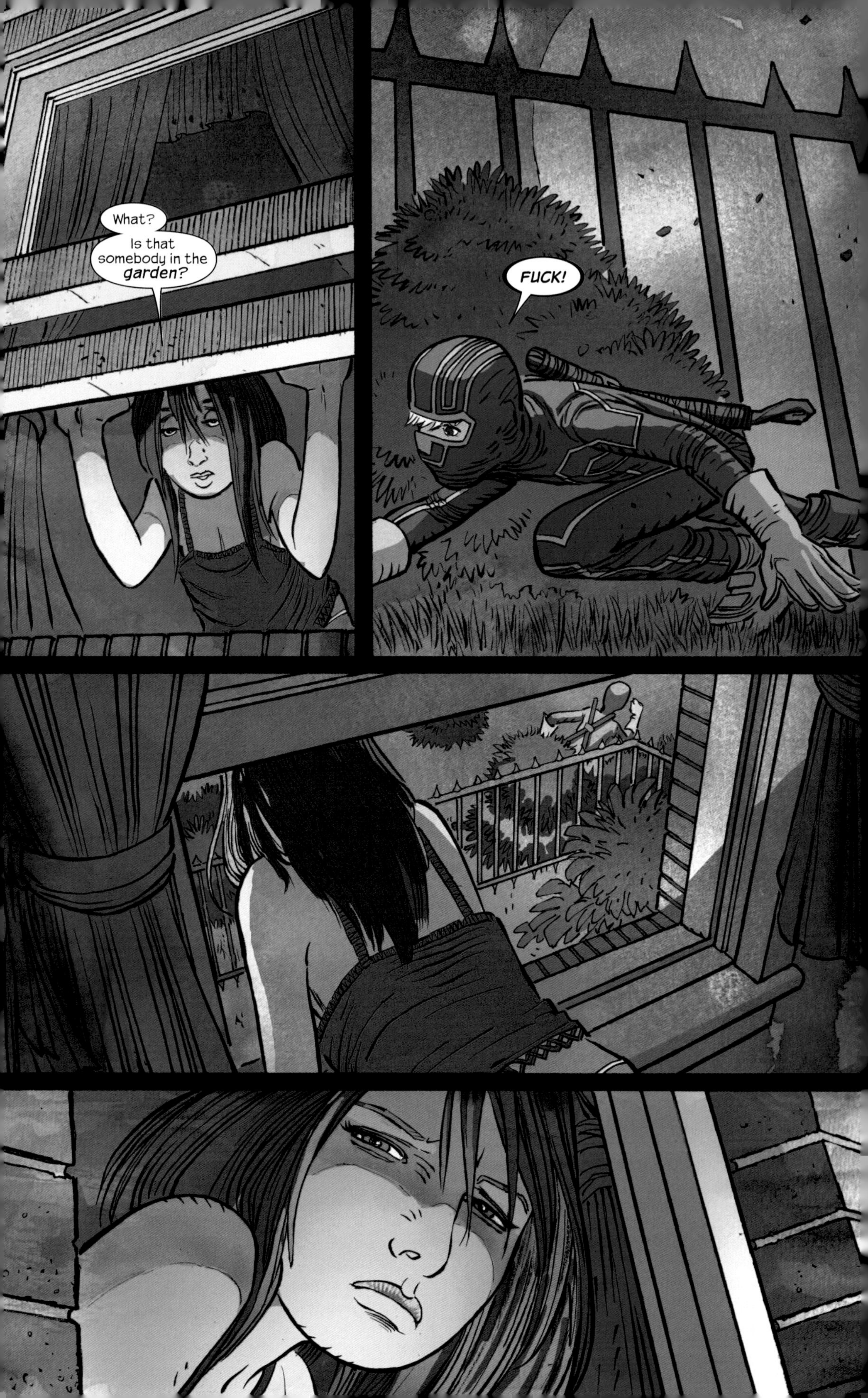
What?
Is that somebody in the garden?
FUCK!

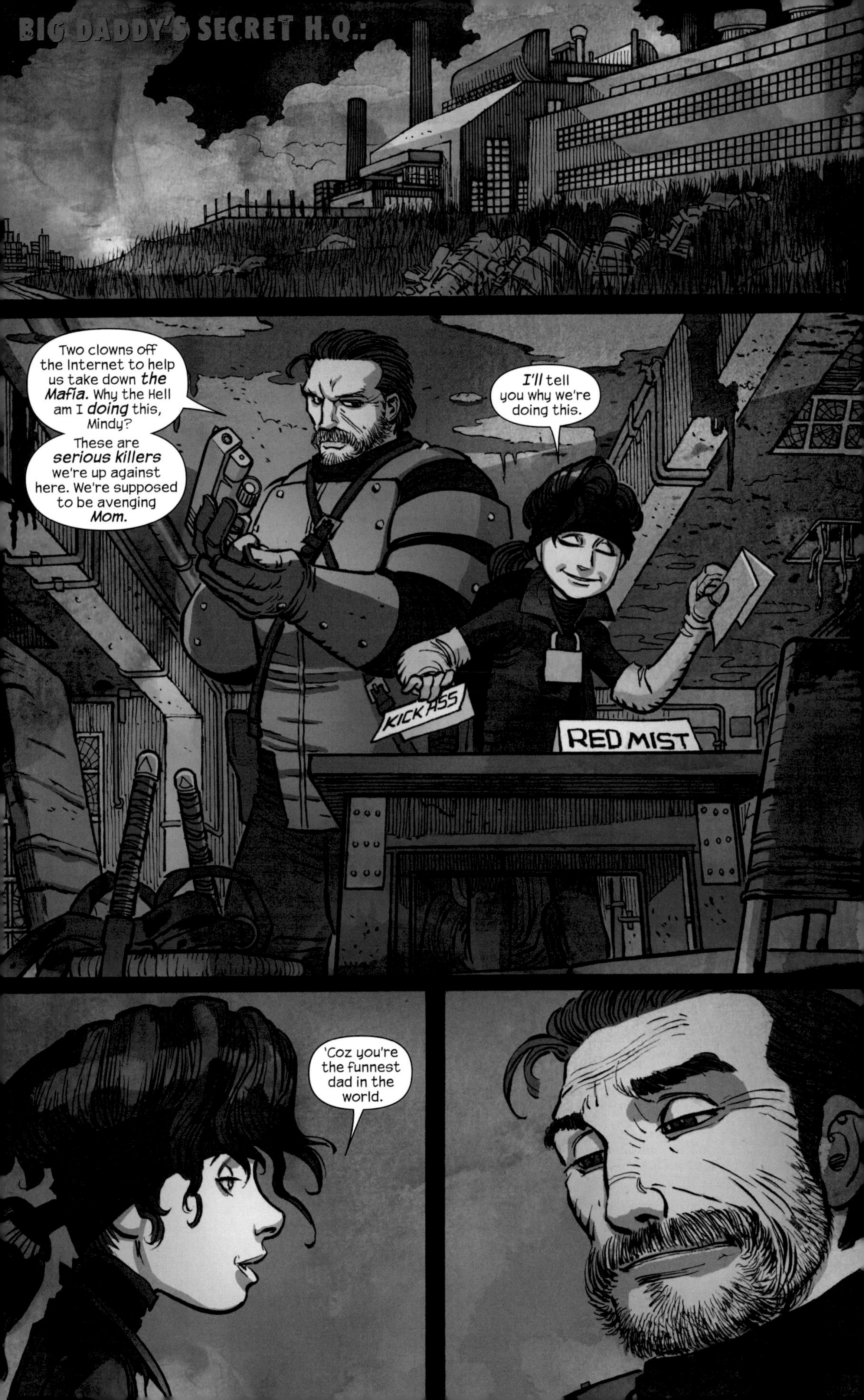
BIG DADDY'S SECRET H.Q.:
Two clowns off the Internet to help us take down *the Mafia.* Why the Hell am I *doing* this, Mindy?
These are ***serious killers*** we're up against here. We're supposed to be avenging ***Mom.***
I'll tell you why we're doing this.
KICK ASS
RED MIST
'Coz you're the funnest dad in the world.

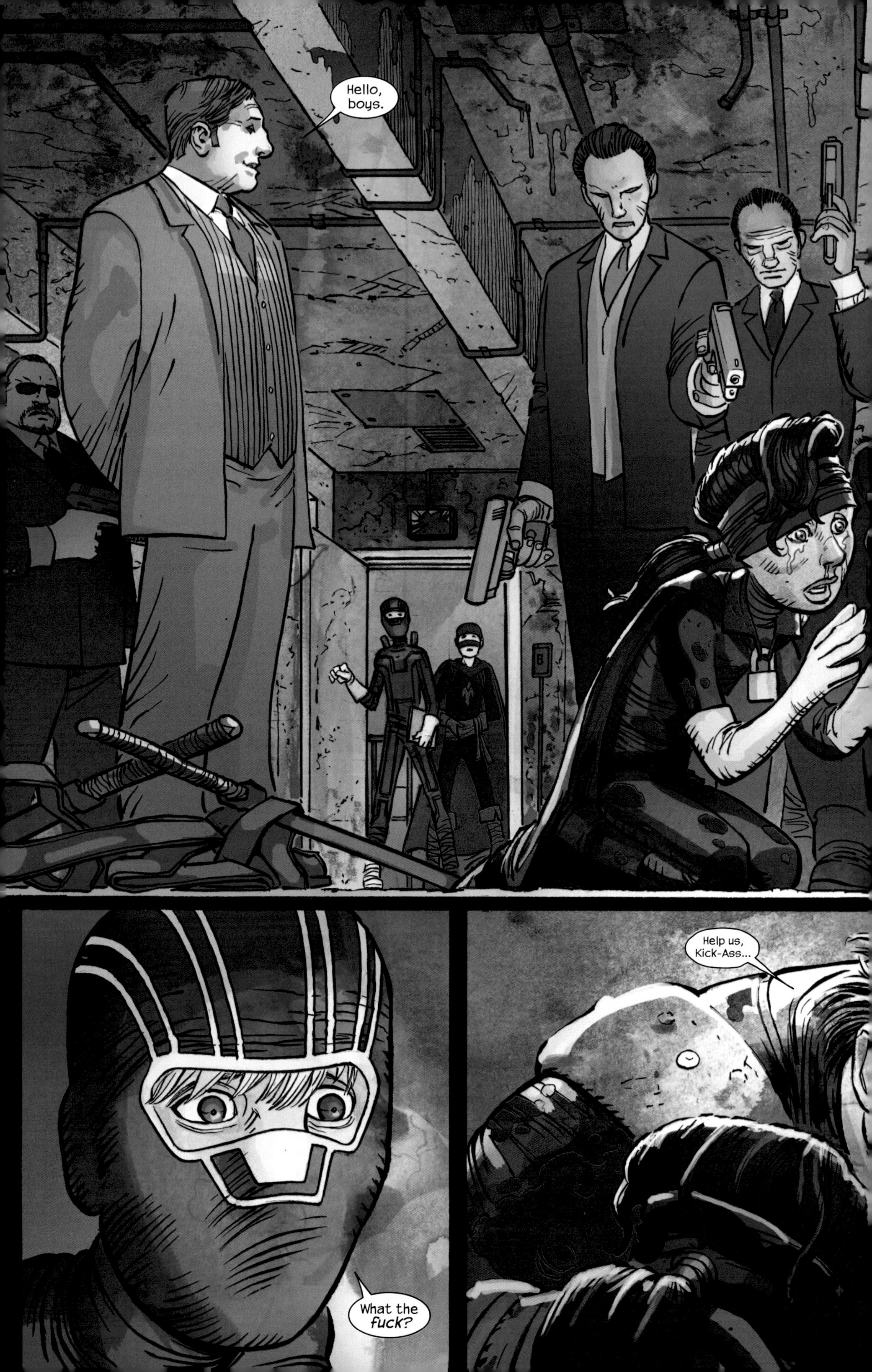
Hello, boys.
What the *fuck*?
Help us, Kick-Ass...

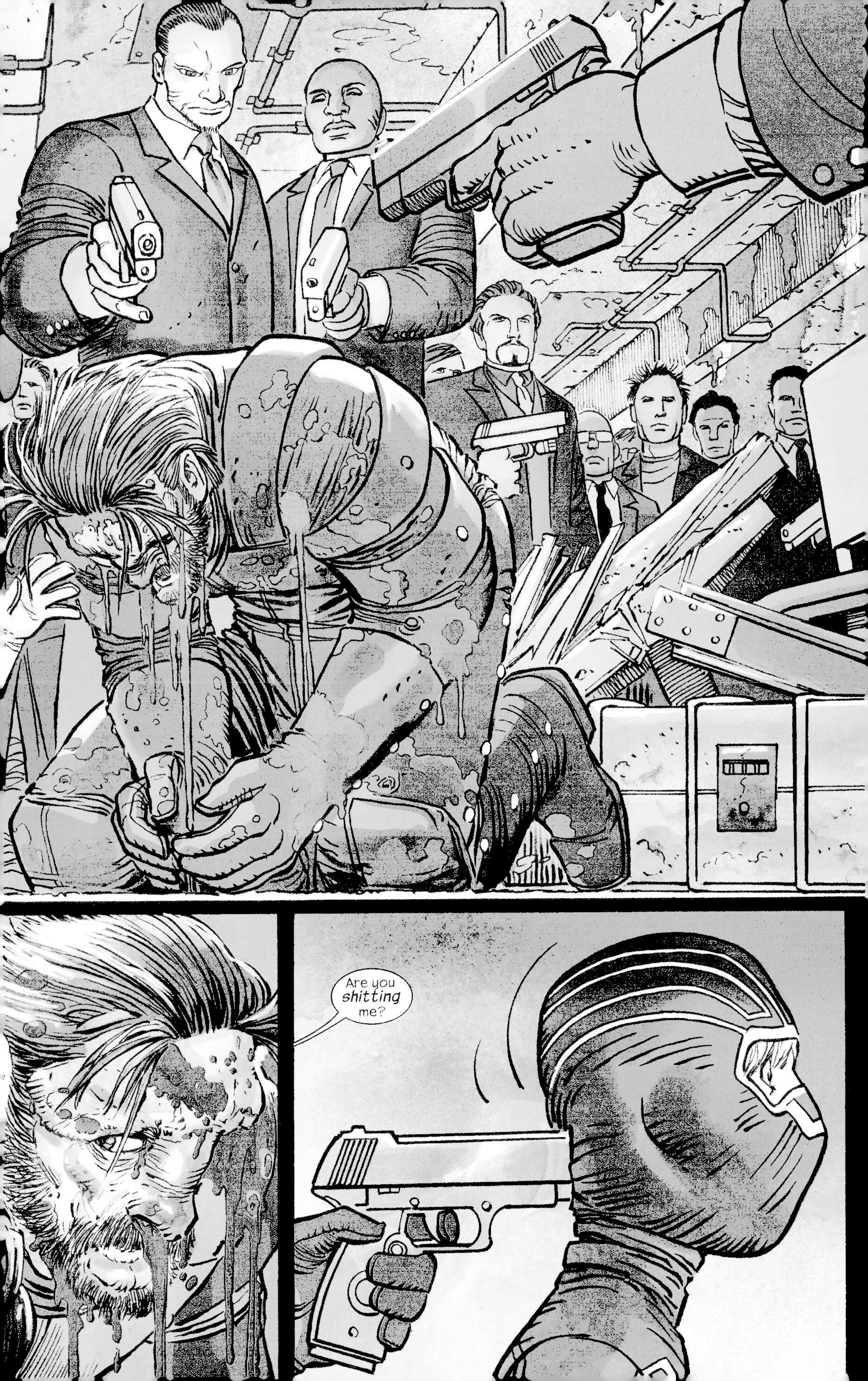
Are you
shitting
me?

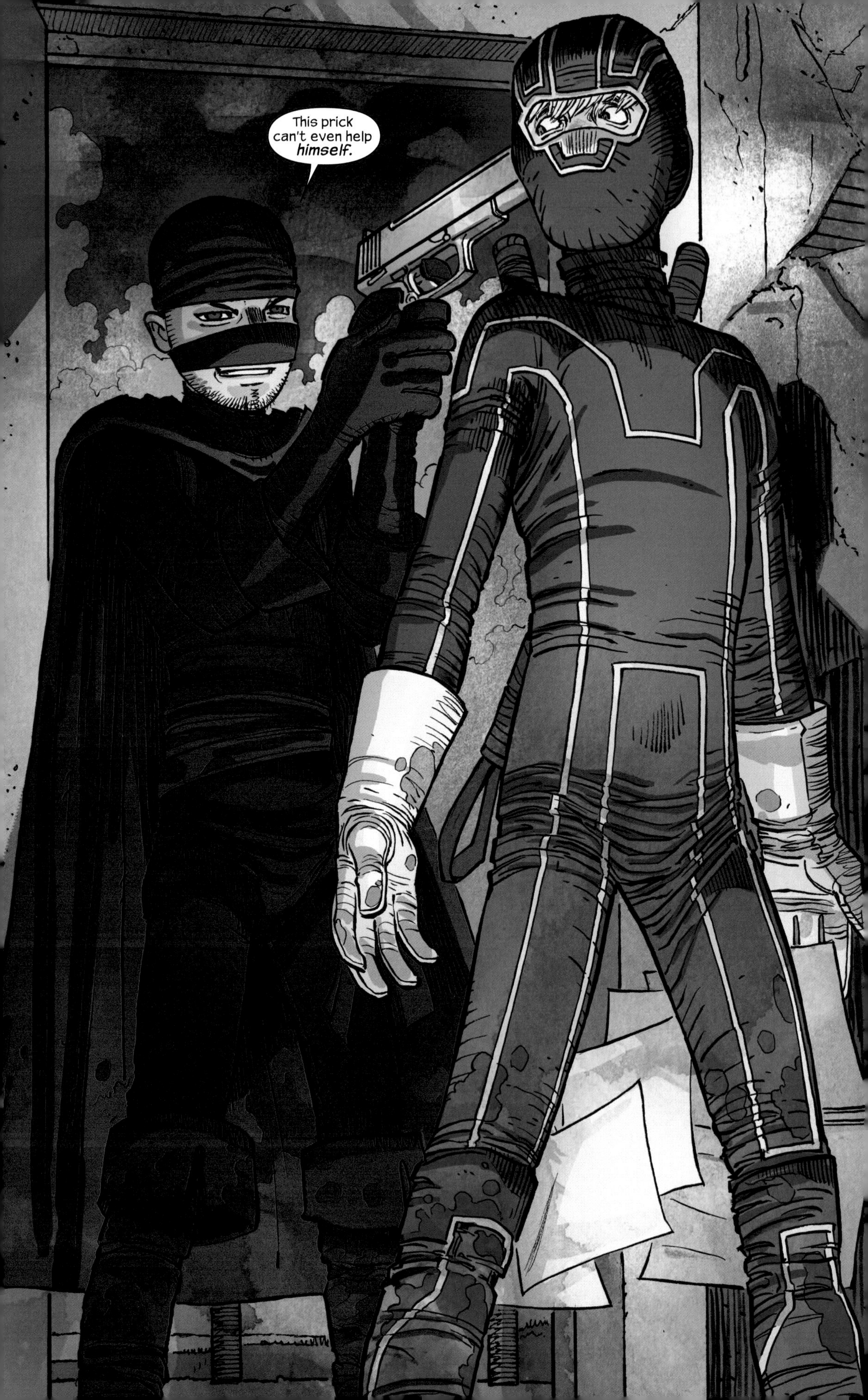
This prick can't even help *himself.*

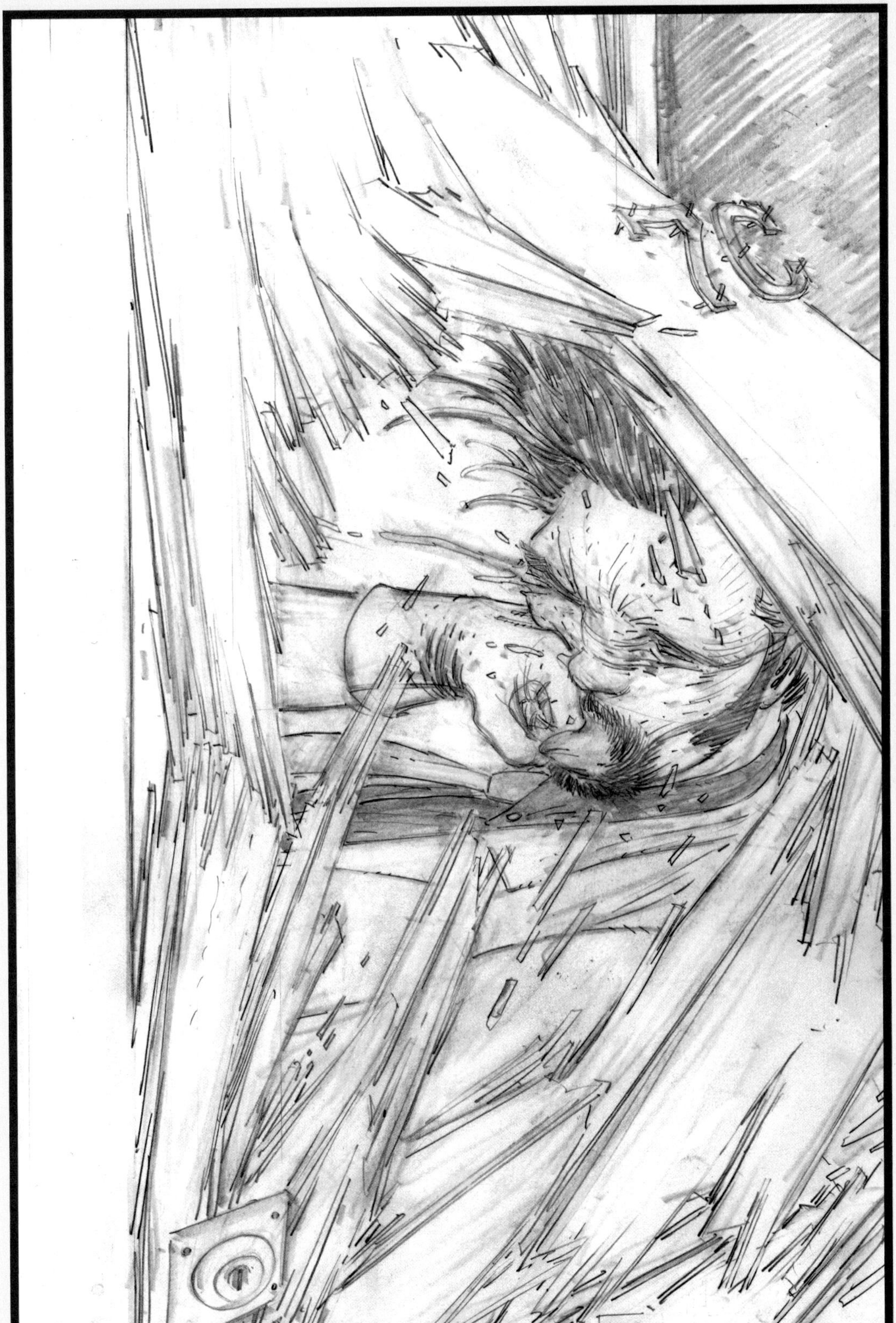
JRJR+

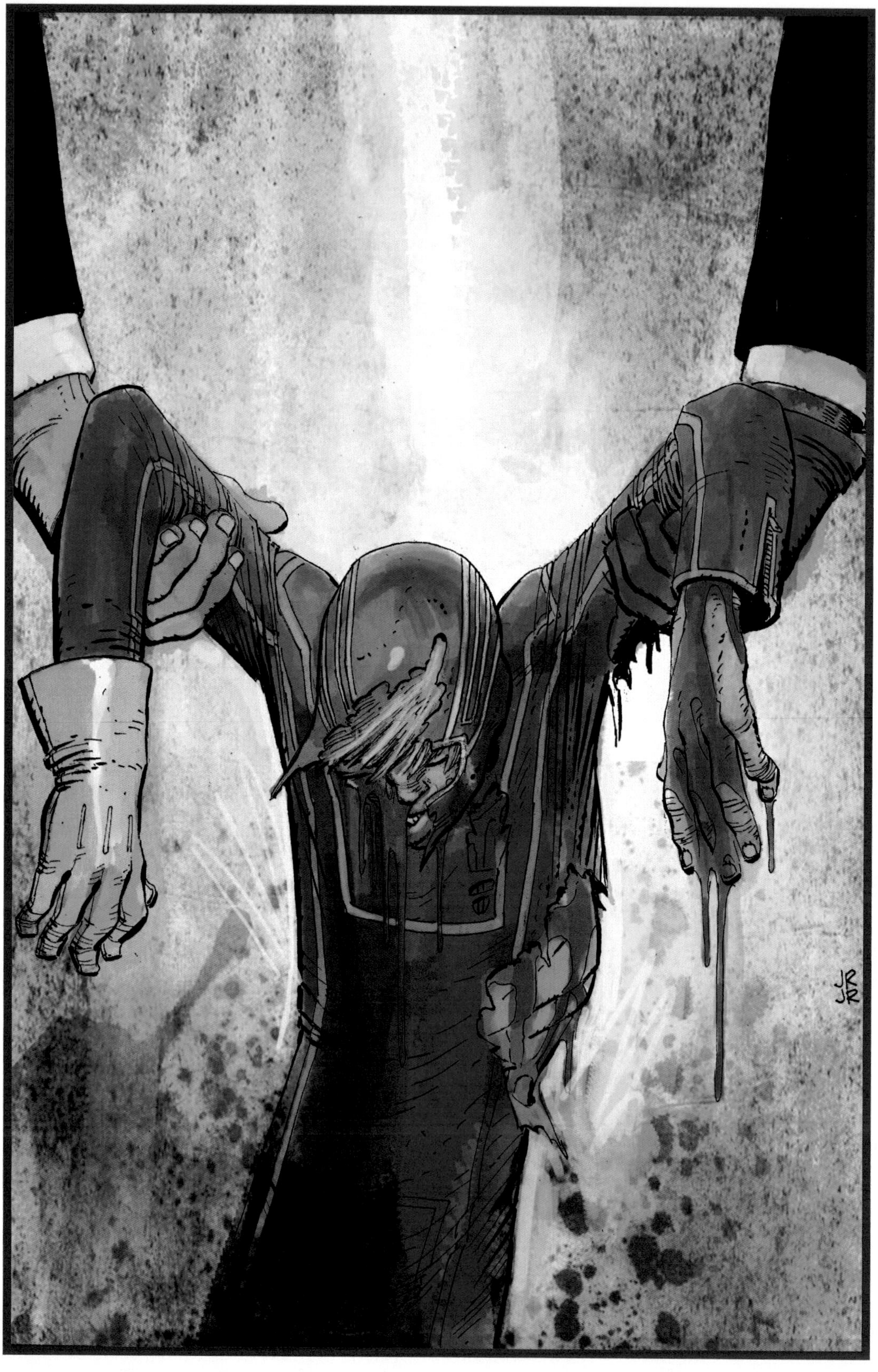
JR
JR

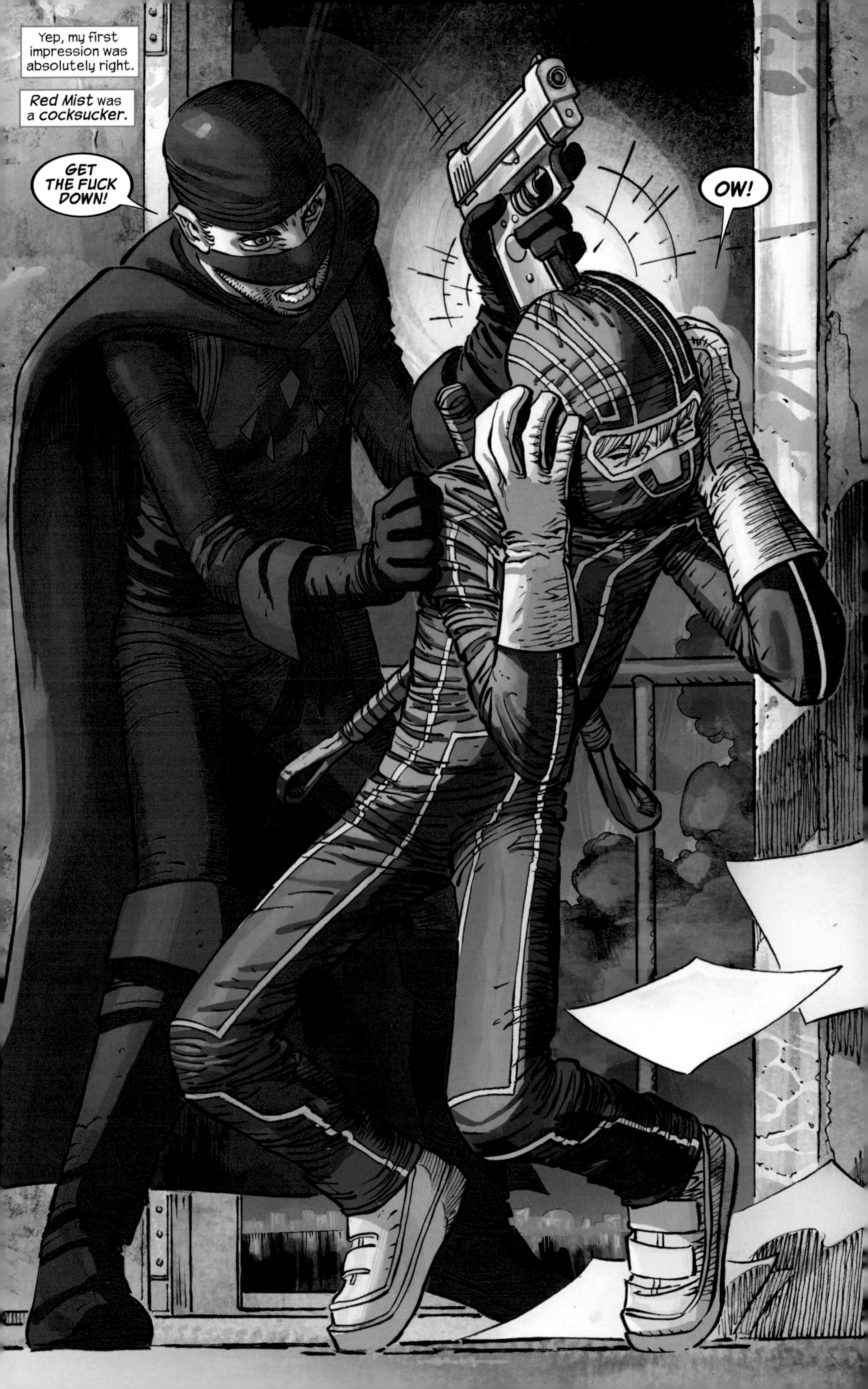
Yep, my first impression was absolutely right.
Red Mist was a *cocksucker*.
GET THE FUCK DOWN!
OW!

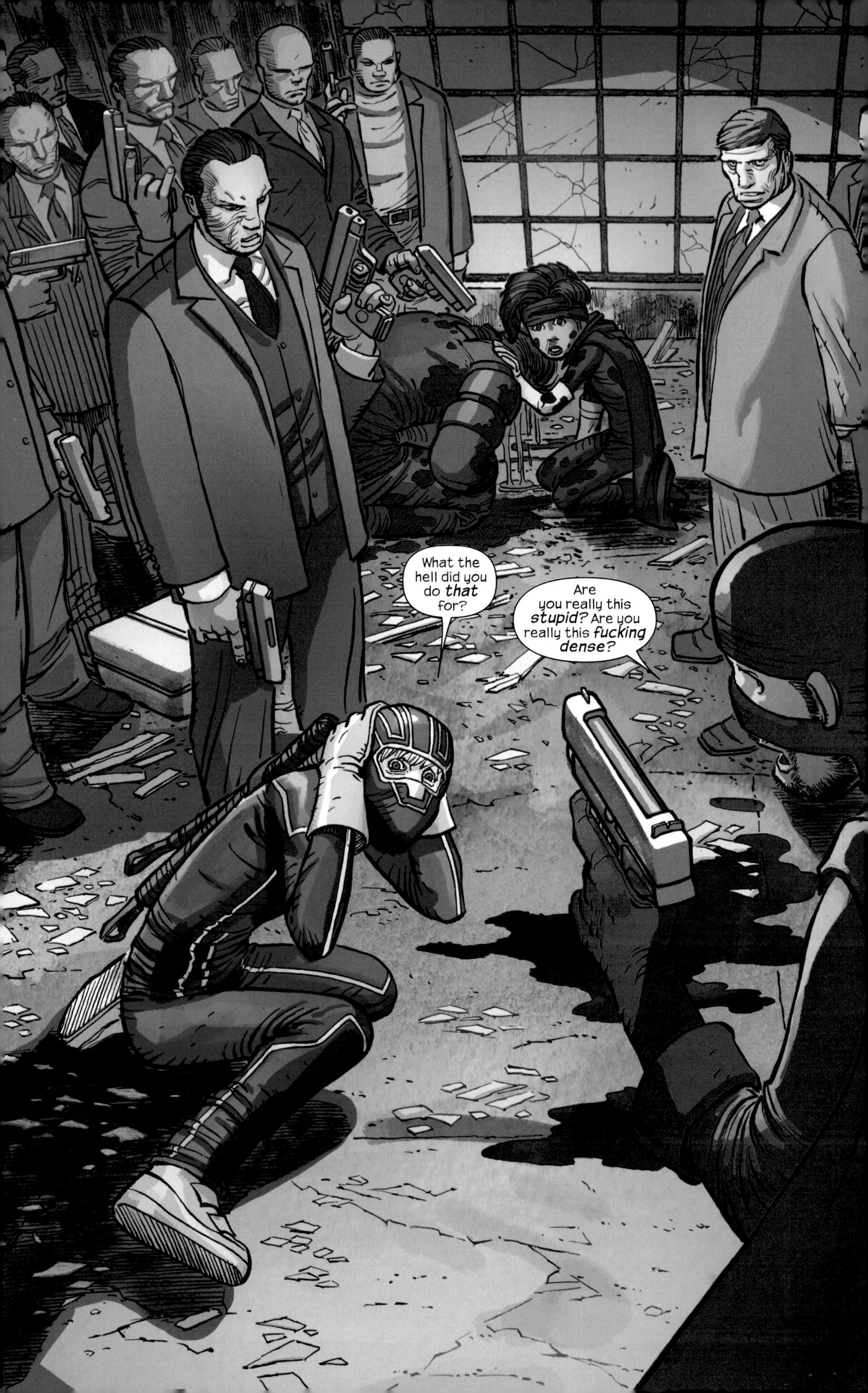
What the hell did you do *that* for?
Are you really this *stupid?* Are you really this *fucking dense?*

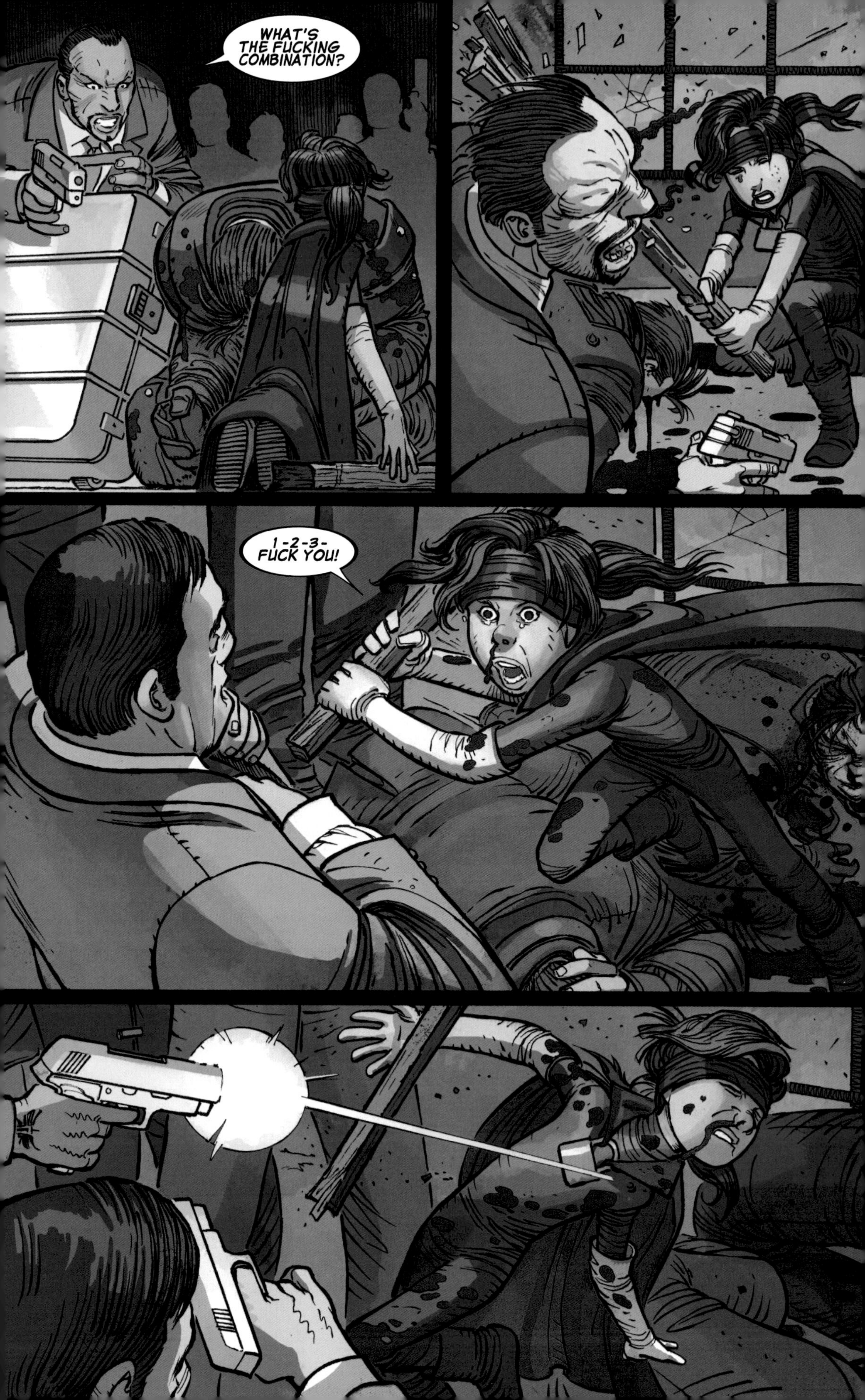
WHAT'S THE FUCKING COMBINATION?
1-2-3- FUCK YOU!

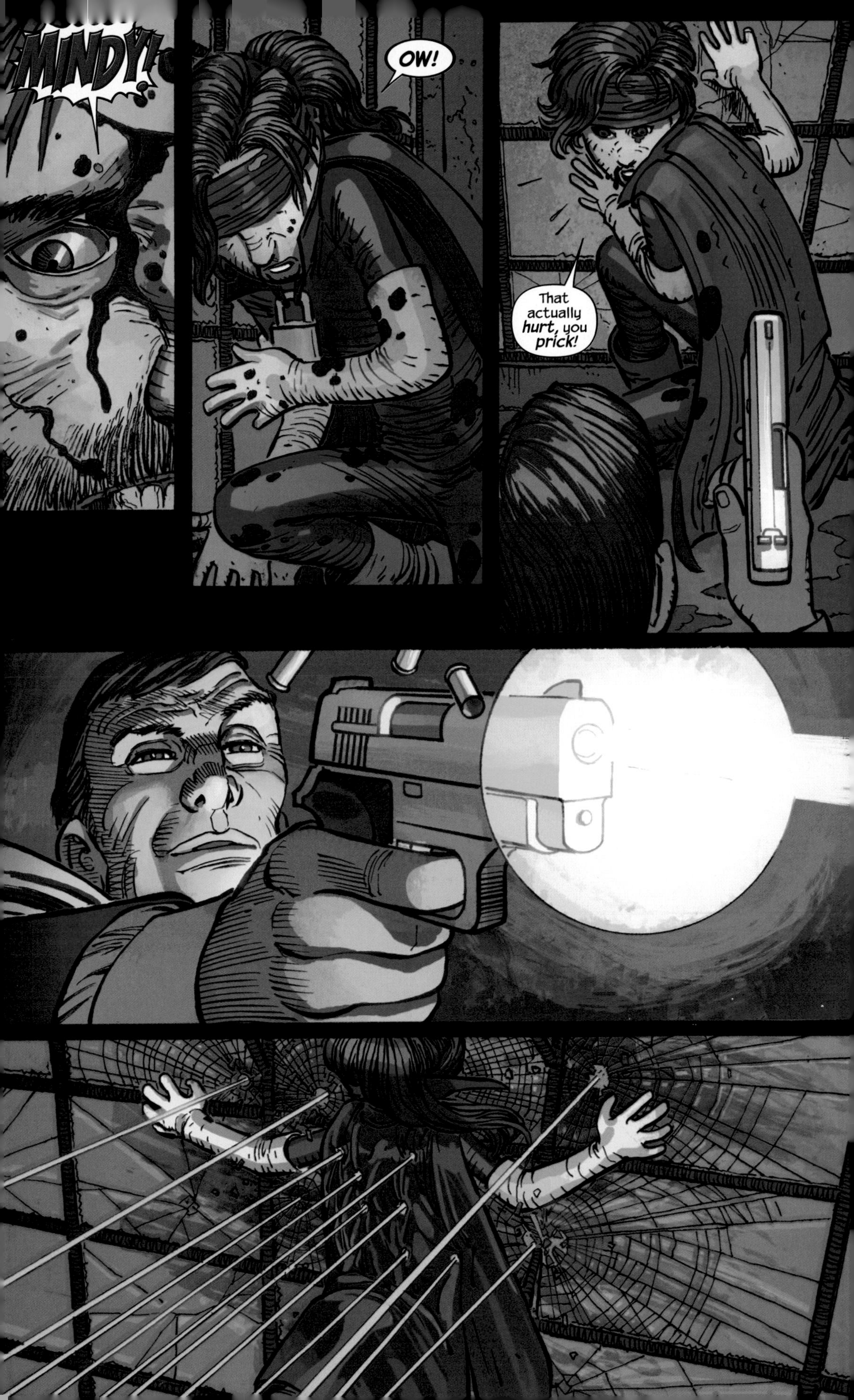
MINDY!
OW!
That actually *hurt*, you prick!

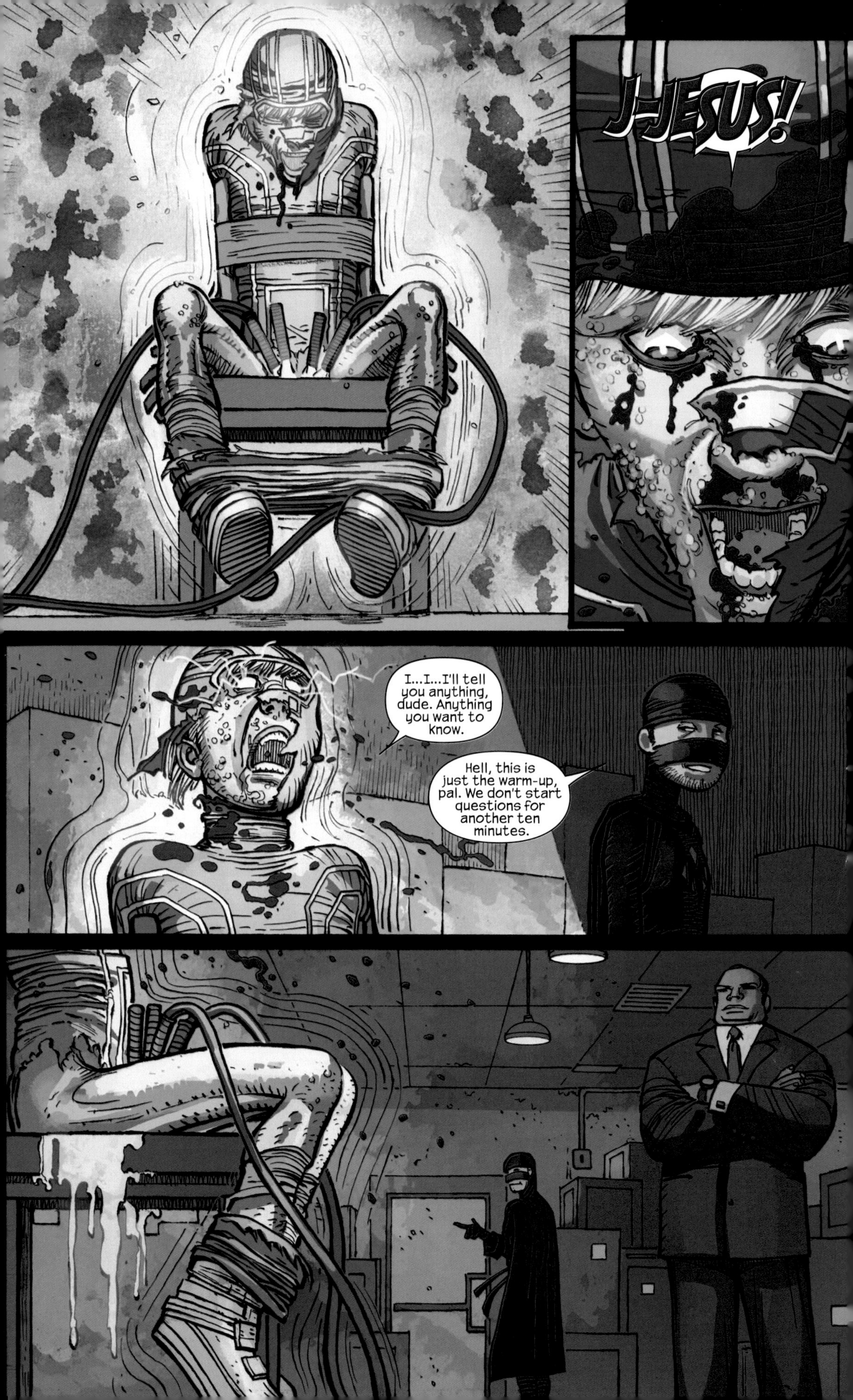
J-JESUS!
I...I...I'll tell you anything, dude. Anything you want to know.
Hell, this is just the warm-up, pal. We don't start questions for another ten minutes.

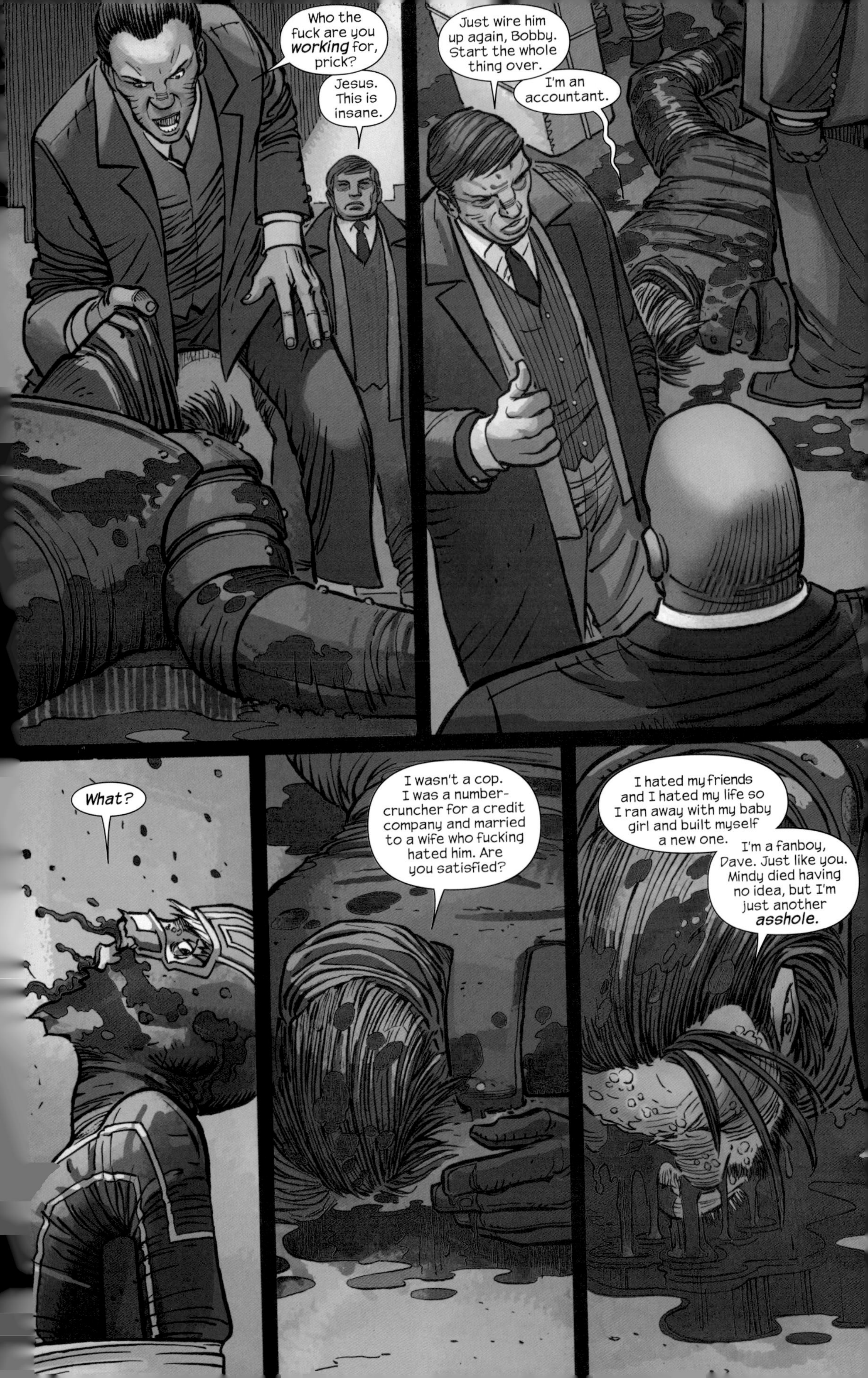

Who the fuck are you *working* for, prick?
Jesus. This is insane.
Just wire him up again, Bobby. Start the whole thing over.
I'm an accountant.
What?
I wasn't a cop. I was a number-cruncher for a credit company and married to a wife who fucking hated him. Are you satisfied?
I hated my friends and I hated my life so I ran away with my baby girl and built myself a new one.
I'm a fanboy, Dave. Just like you. Mindy died having no idea, but I'm just another *asshole.*

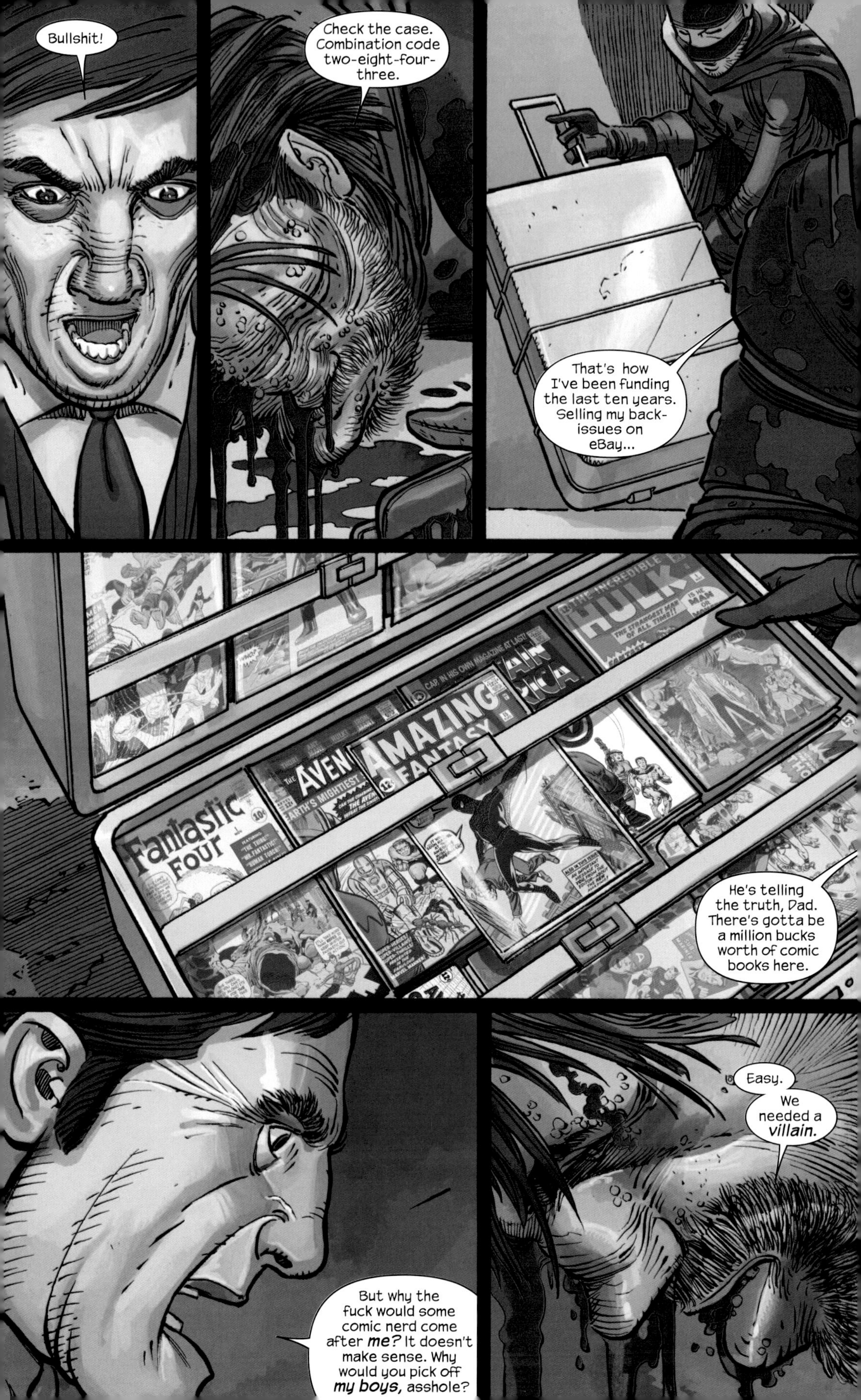
Bullshit!
Check the case. Combination code two-eight-four-three.
That's how I've been funding the last ten years. Selling my back-issues on eBay...
He's telling the truth, Dad. There's gotta be a million bucks worth of comic books here.
But why the fuck would some comic nerd come after *me?* It doesn't make sense. Why would you pick off *my boys,* asshole?
Easy.
We needed a *villain.*

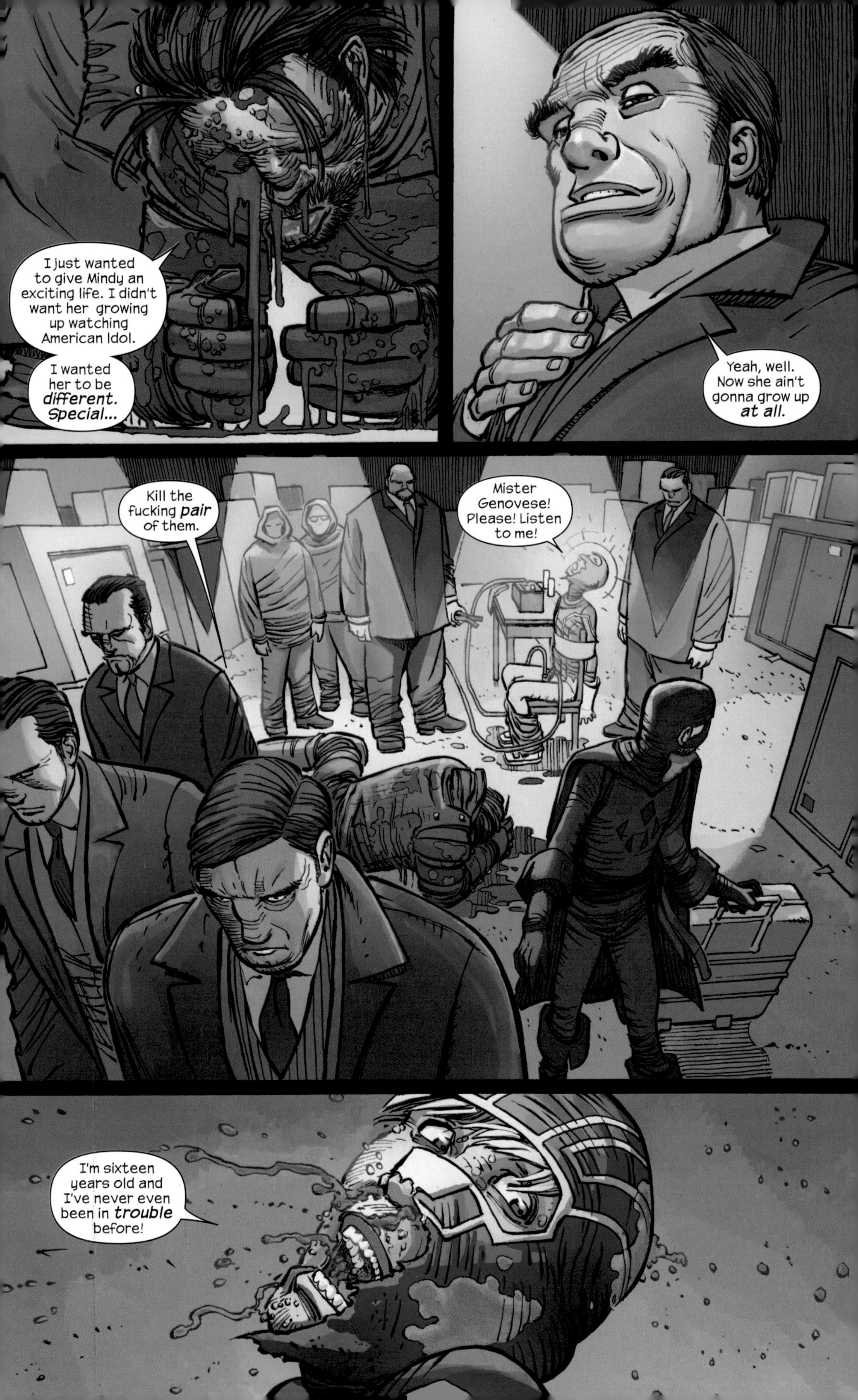
I just wanted to give Mindy an exciting life. I didn't want her growing up watching American Idol.
I wanted her to be *different. Special...*
Yeah, well. Now she ain't gonna grow up *at all.*
Kill the fucking *pair* of them.
Mister Genovese! Please! Listen to me!
I'm sixteen years old and I've never even been in *trouble* before!

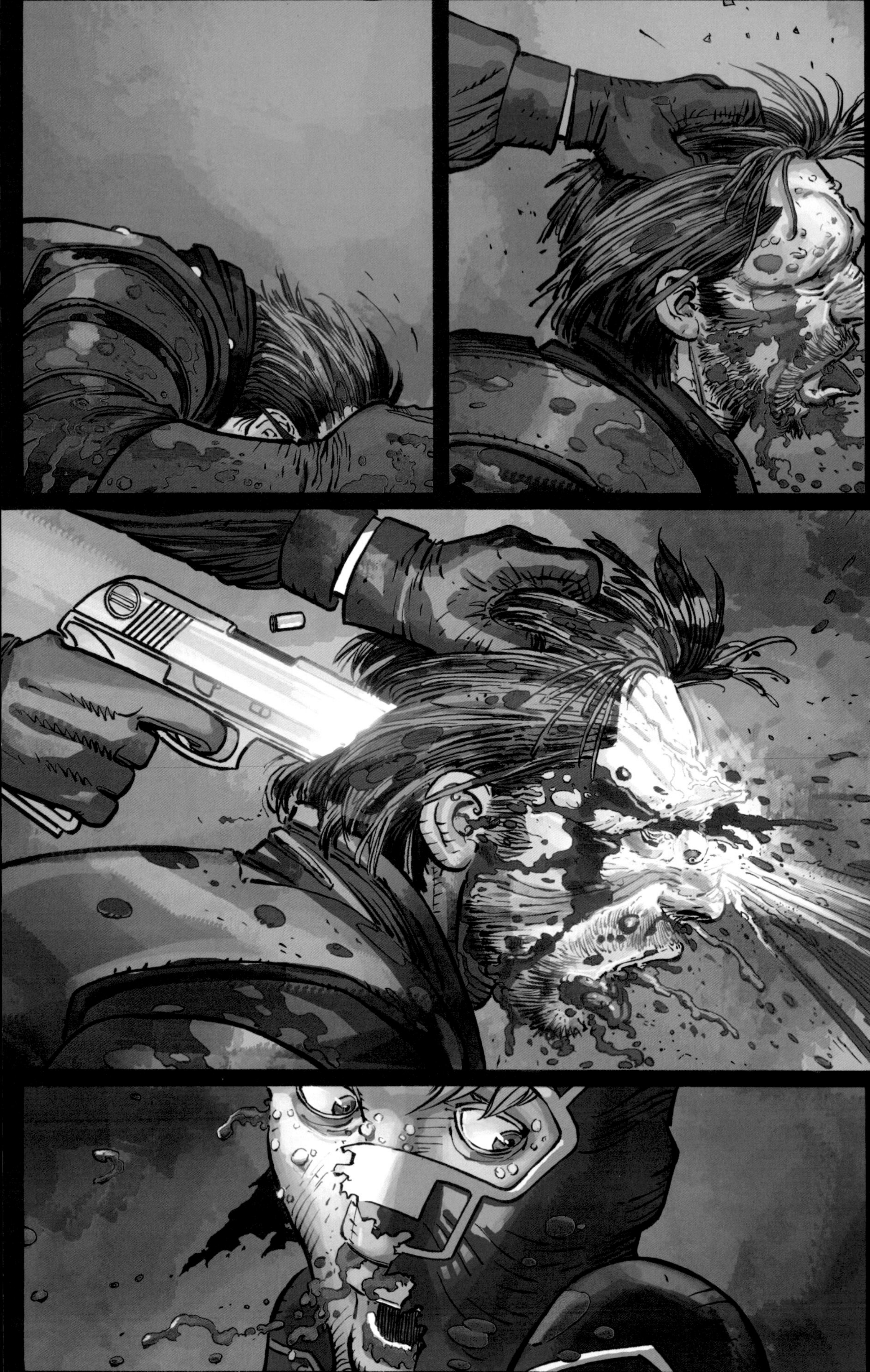

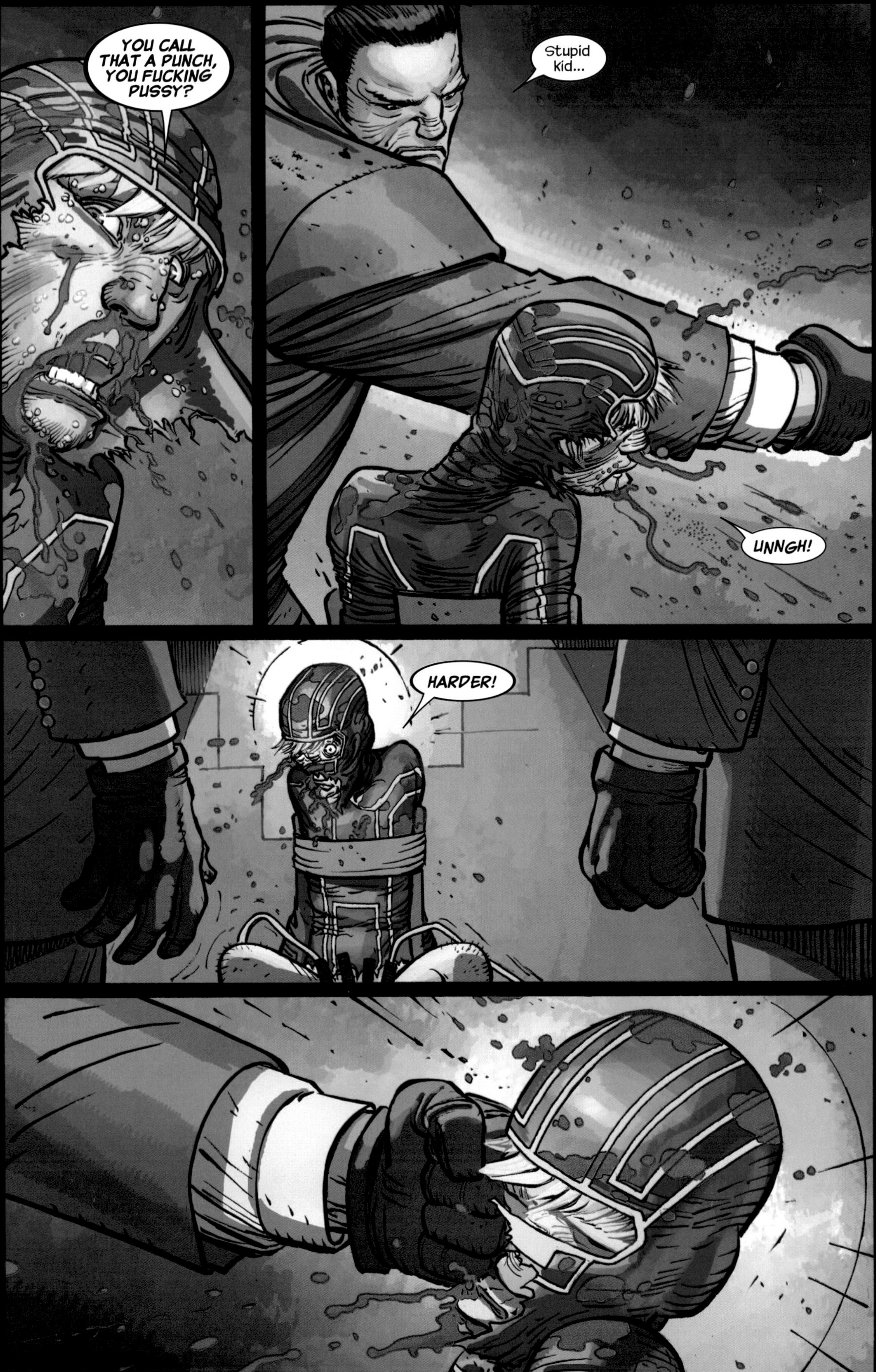
YOU CALL THAT A PUNCH, YOU FUCKING PUSSY?
Stupid kid...
UNNGH!
HARDER!

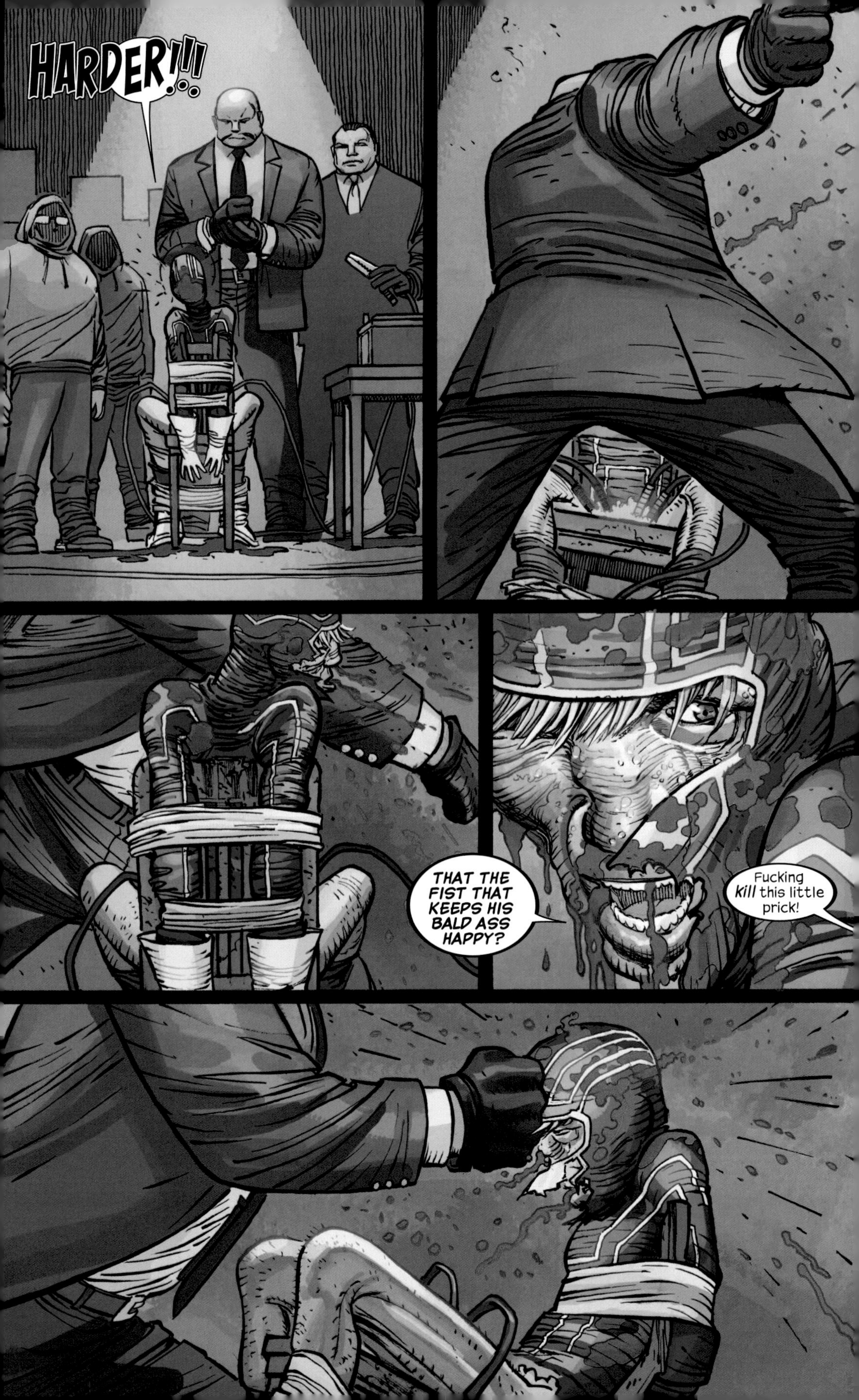
HARDER!!!
THAT THE FIST THAT KEEPS HIS BALD ASS HAPPY?
Fucking *kill* this little prick!

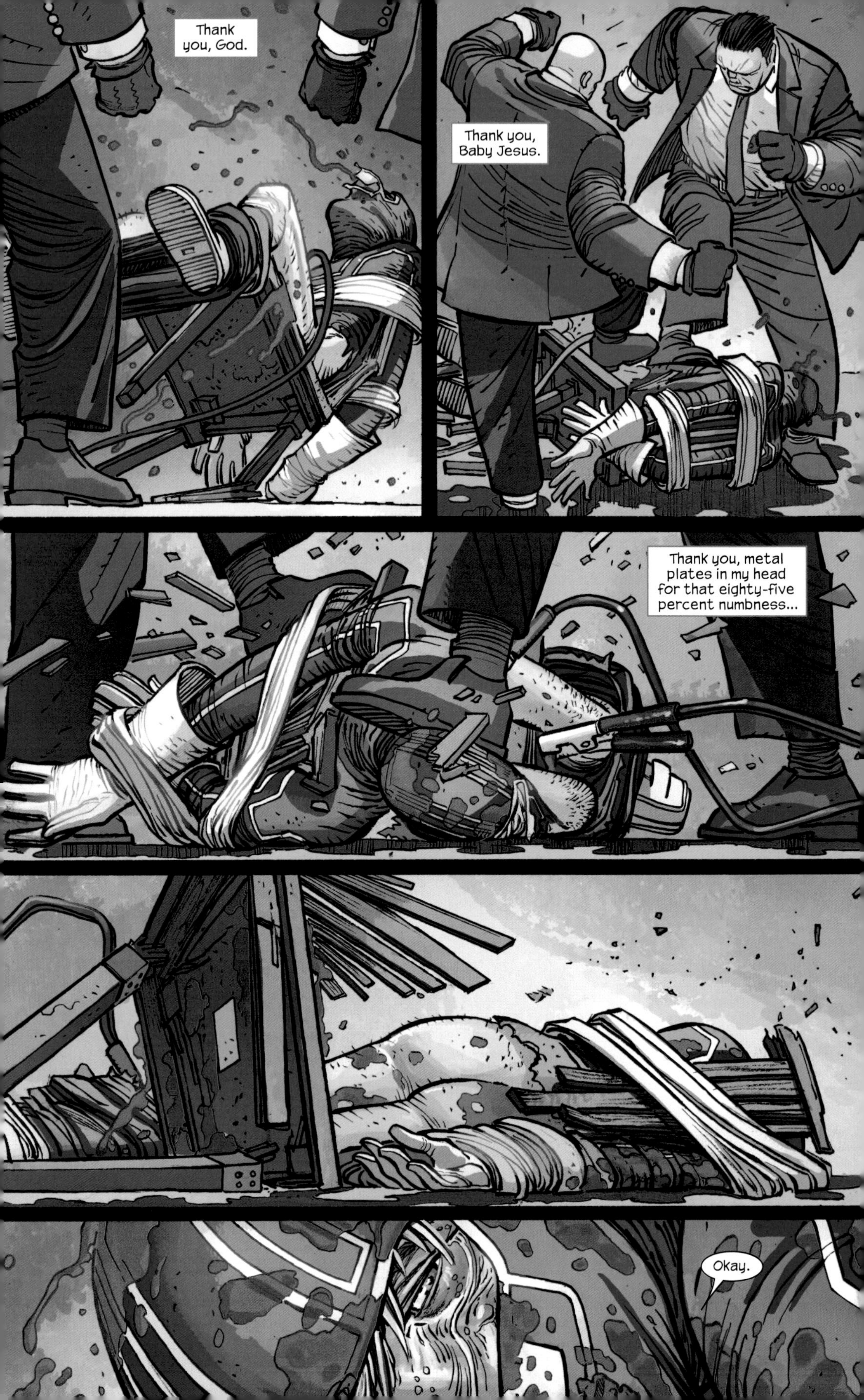
Thank you, God.
Thank you, Baby Jesus.
Thank you, metal plates in my head for that eighty-five percent numbness...
Okay.

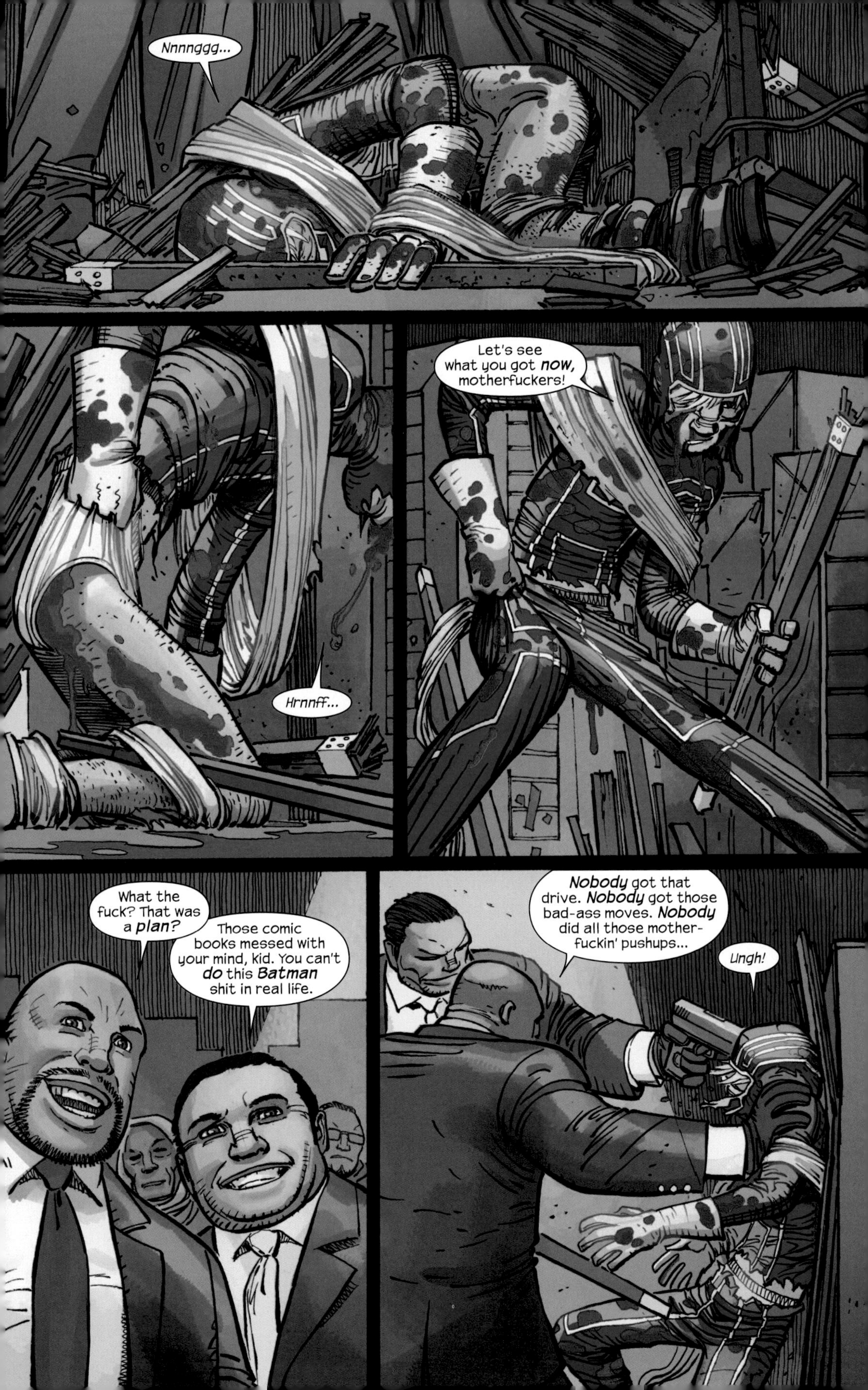
Nnnnggg...
Hrnnff...
Let's see what you got *now,* motherfuckers!
What the fuck? That was a *plan?*
Those comic books messed with your mind, kid. You can't *do* this *Batman* shit in real life.
Nobody got that drive. *Nobody* got those bad-ass moves. *Nobody* did all those mother-fuckin' pushups...
Ungh!

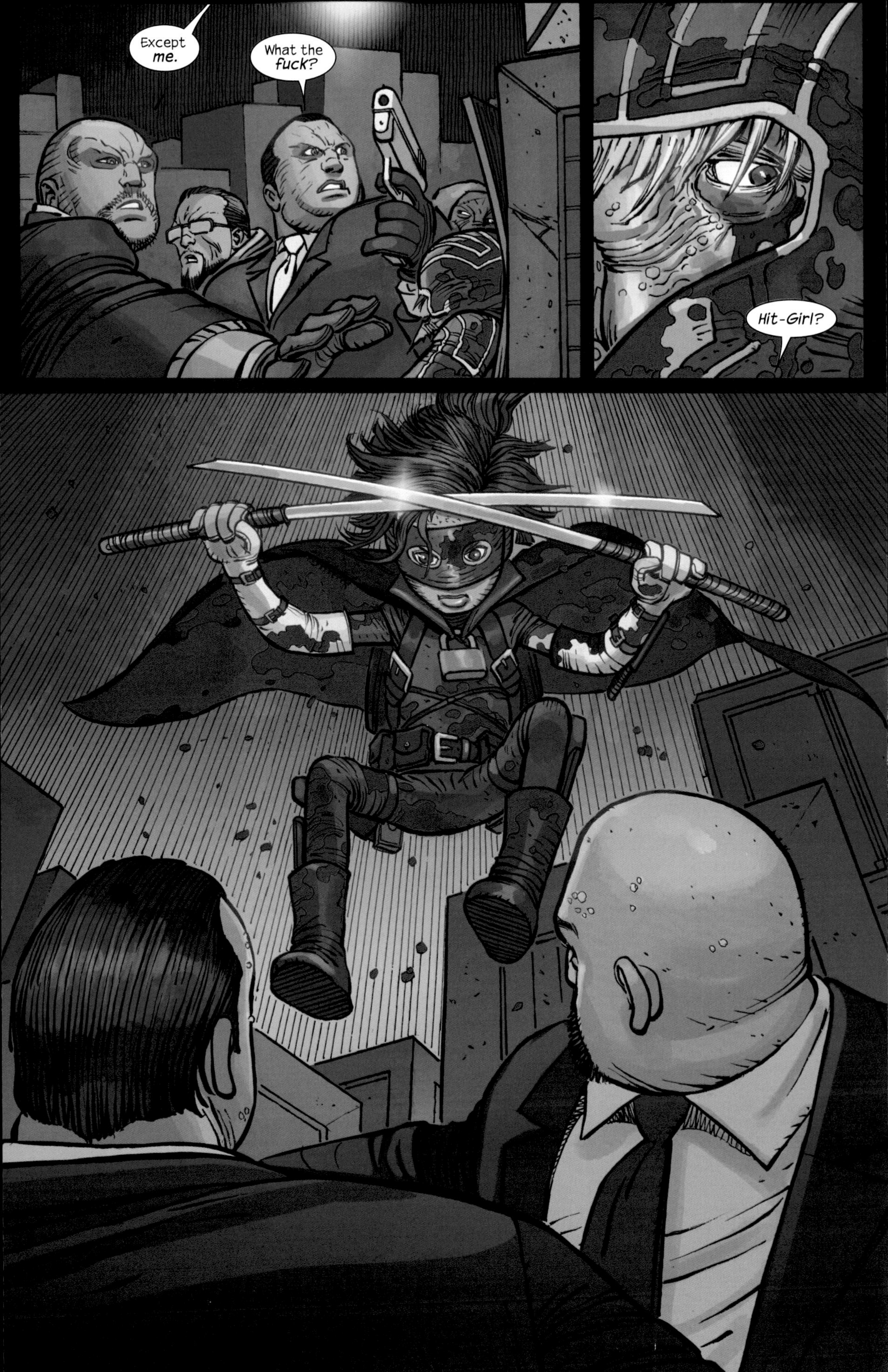
Except me.
What the fuck?
Hit-Girl?

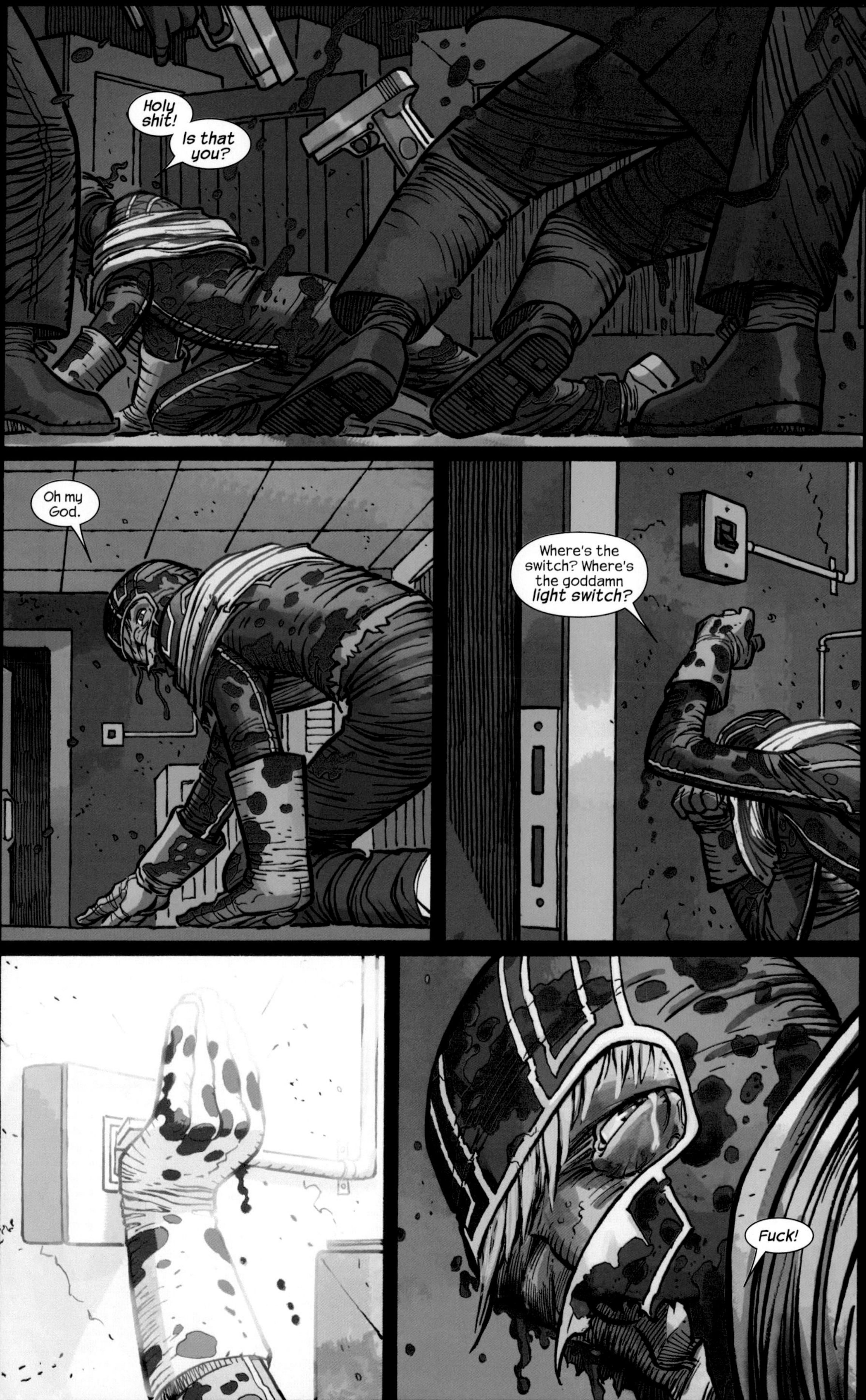
Holy shit!
Is that you?
Oh my God.
Where's the switch? Where's the goddamn *light switch*?
Fuck!

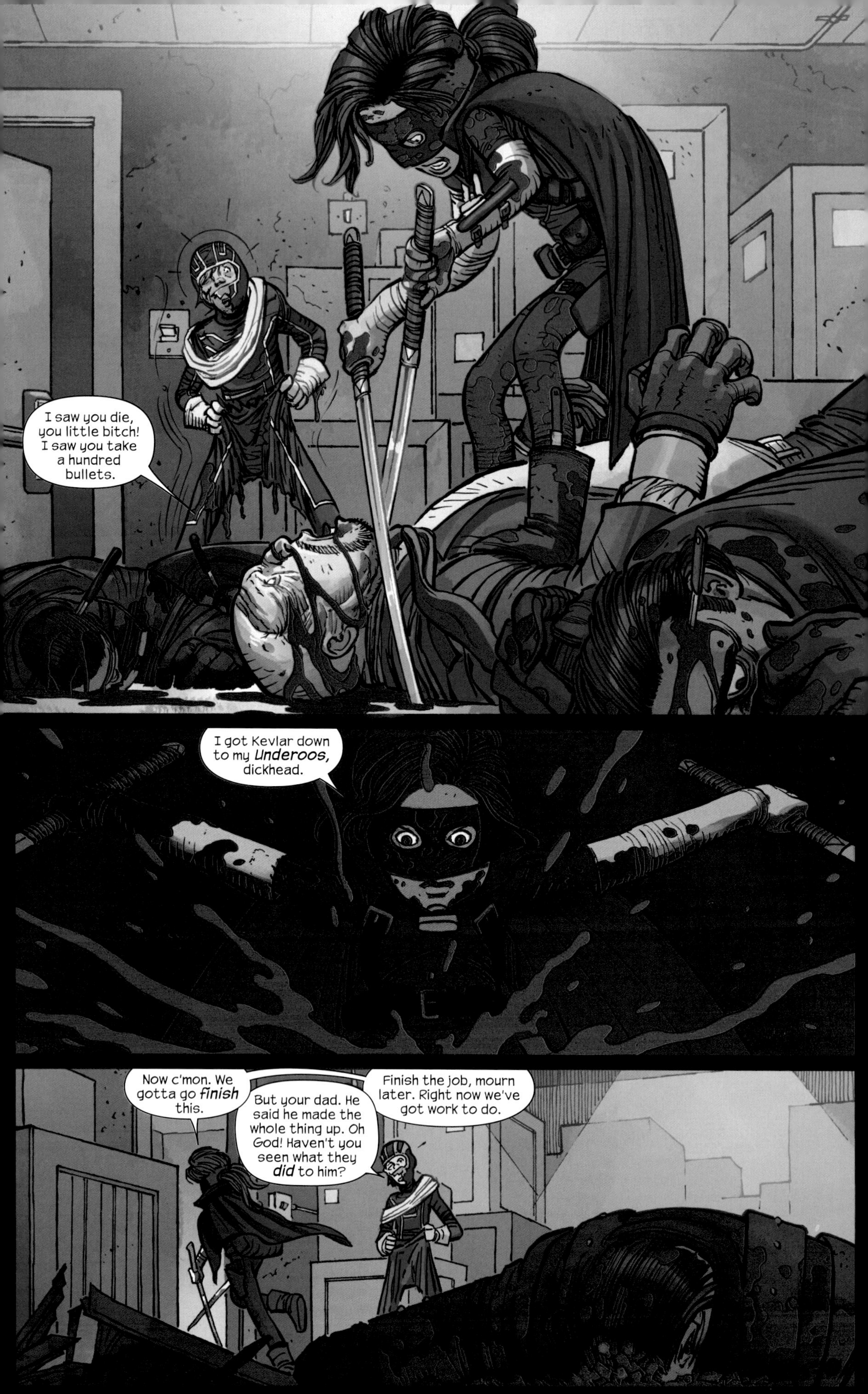
I saw you die, you little bitch! I saw you take a hundred bullets.
I got Kevlar down to my *Underoos,* dickhead.
Now c'mon. We gotta go *finish* this.
But your dad. He said he made the whole thing up. Oh God! Haven't you seen what they *did* to him?
Finish the job, mourn later. Right now we've got work to do.

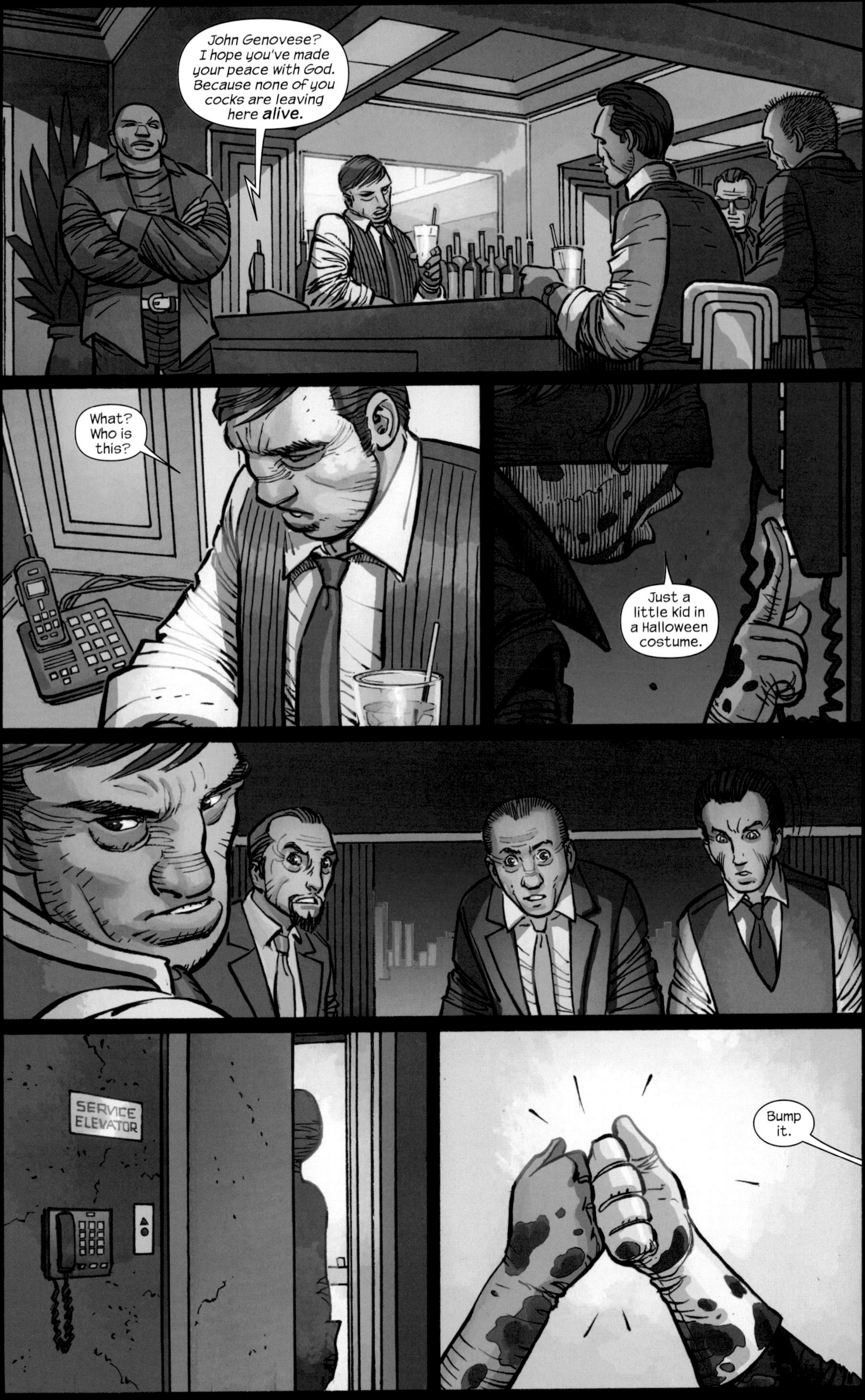
John Genovese? I hope you've made your peace with God. Because none of you cocks are leaving here **alive.**
What? Who is this?
Just a little kid in a Halloween costume.
SERVICE ELEVATOR
Bump it.

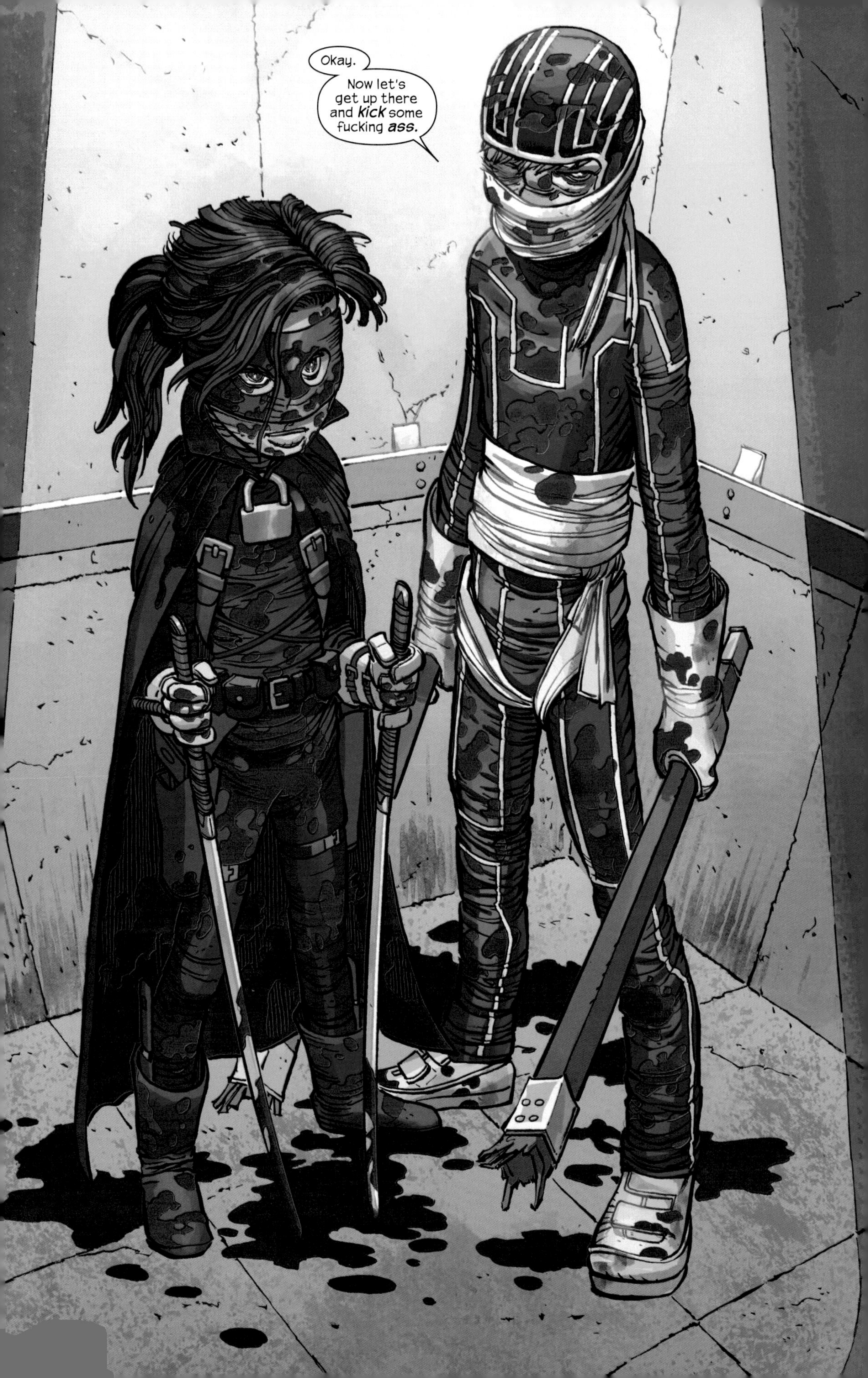
Okay.
Now let's get up there and kick some fucking ass.

EIGHT

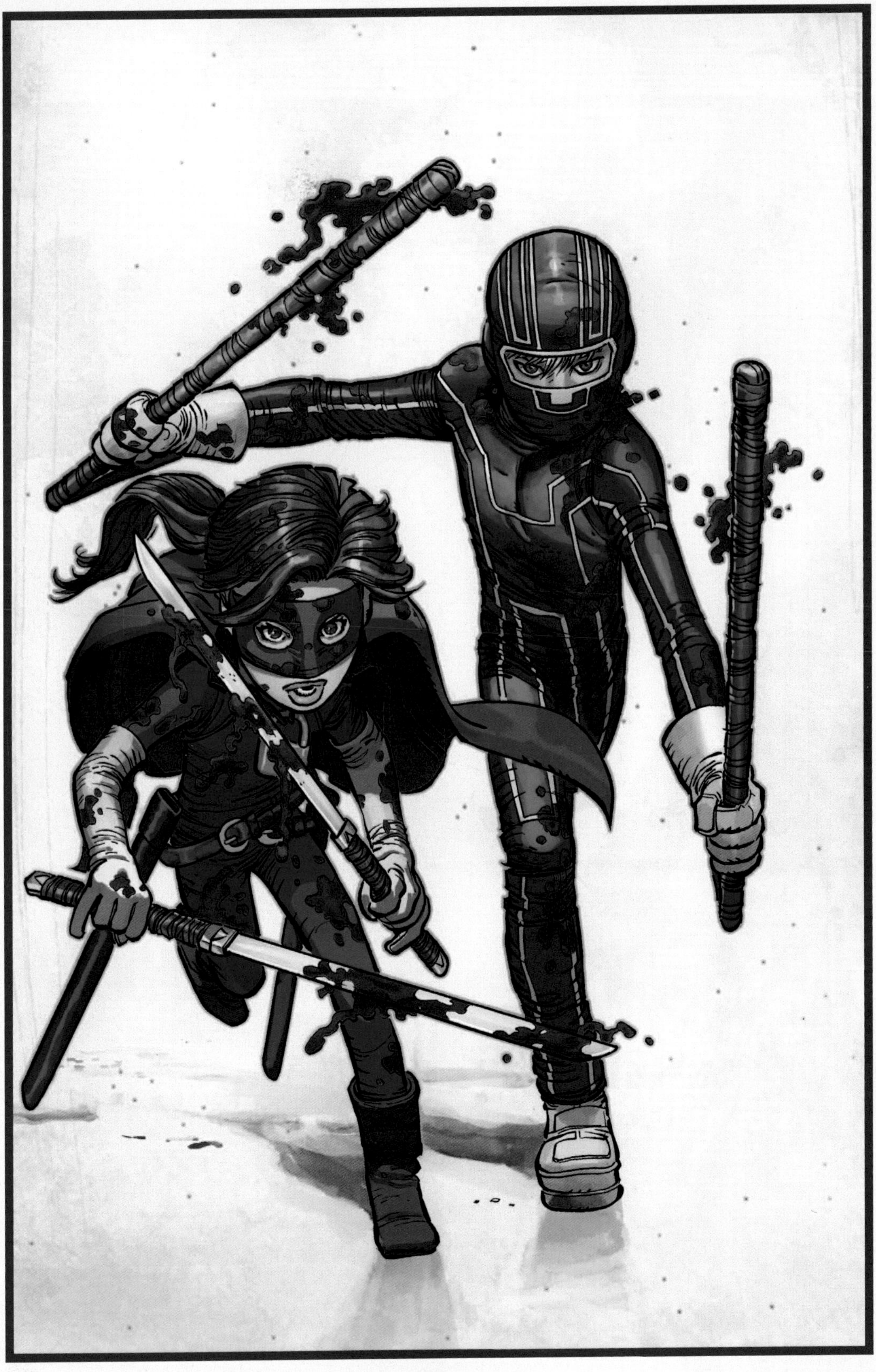

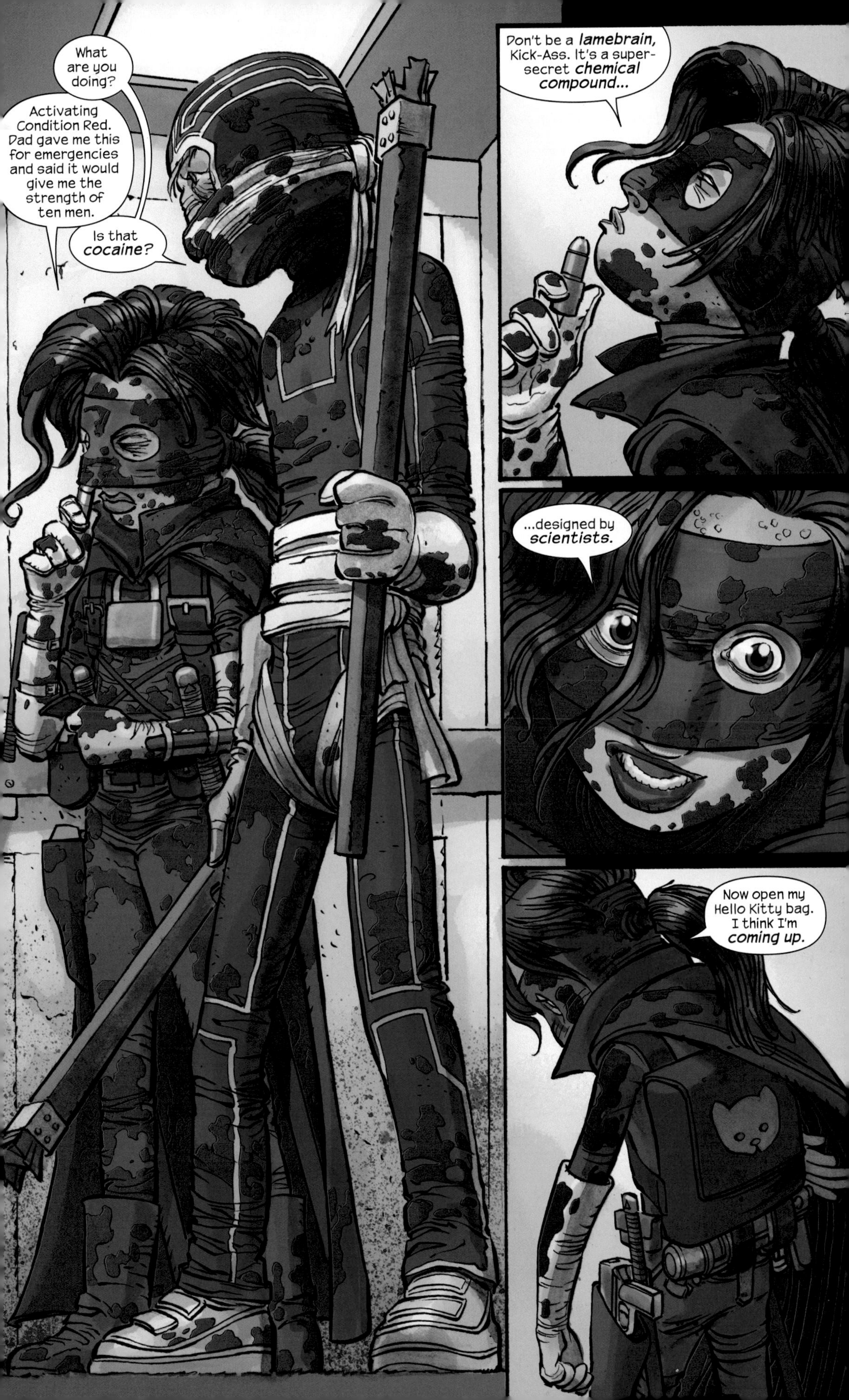
What are you doing?
Activating Condition Red. Dad gave me this for emergencies and said it would give me the strength of ten men.
Is that cocaine?
Don't be a lamebrain, Kick-Ass. It's a super-secret chemical compound...
...designed by scientists.
Now open my Hello Kitty bag. I think I'm coming up.

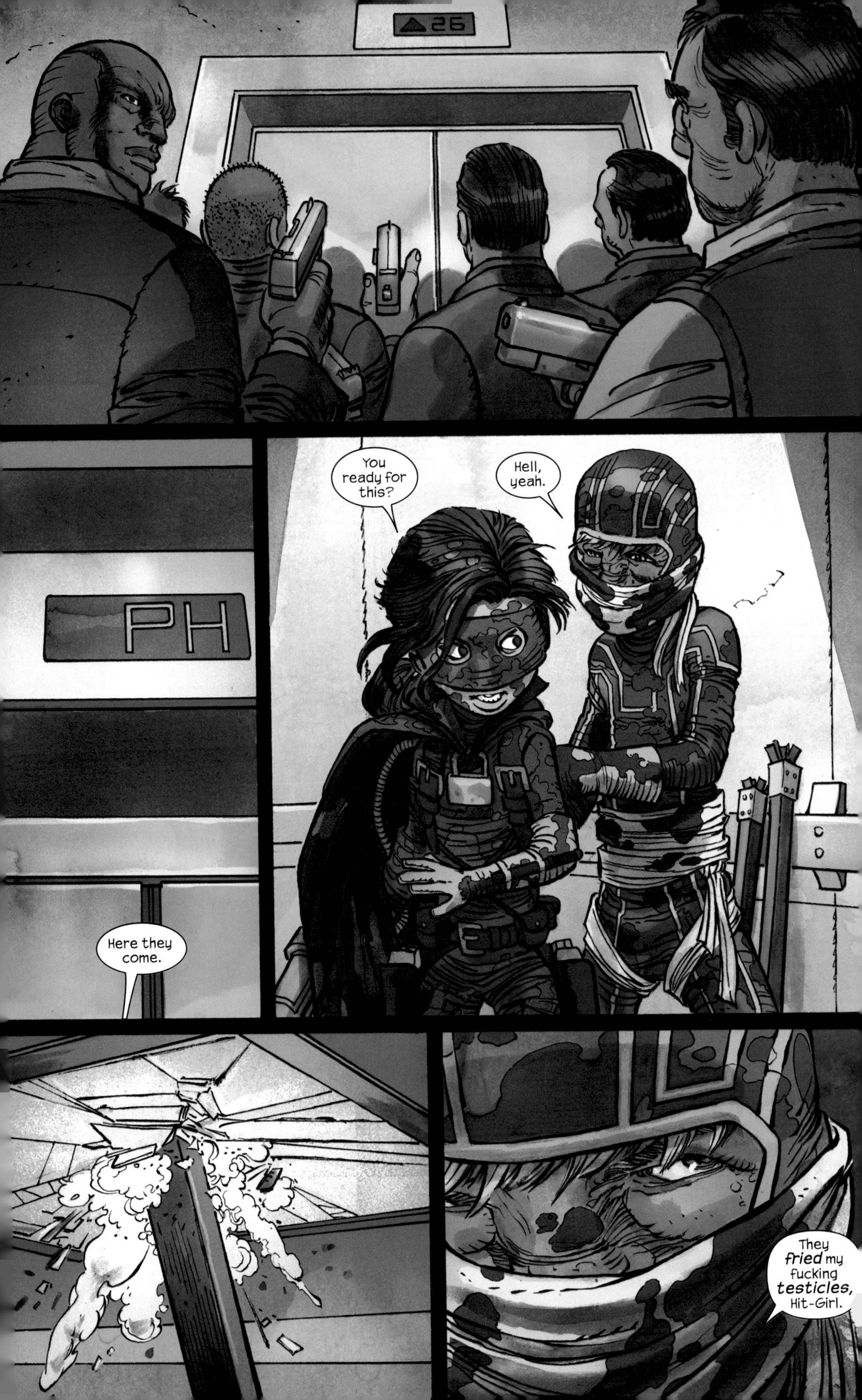
26
PH
Here they come.
You ready for this?
Hell, yeah.
They fried my fucking testicles, Hit-Girl.

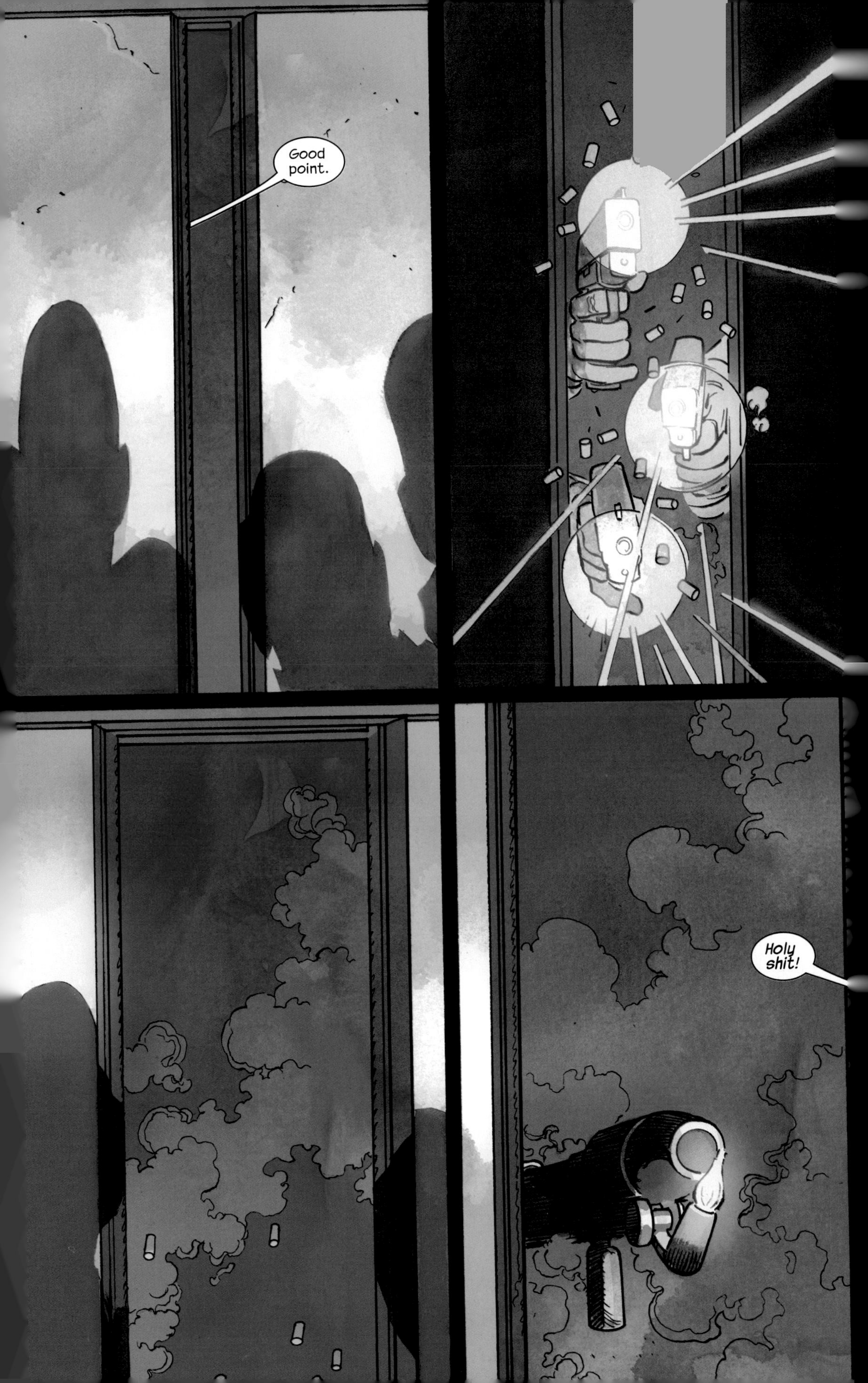
Good point.
Holy shit!

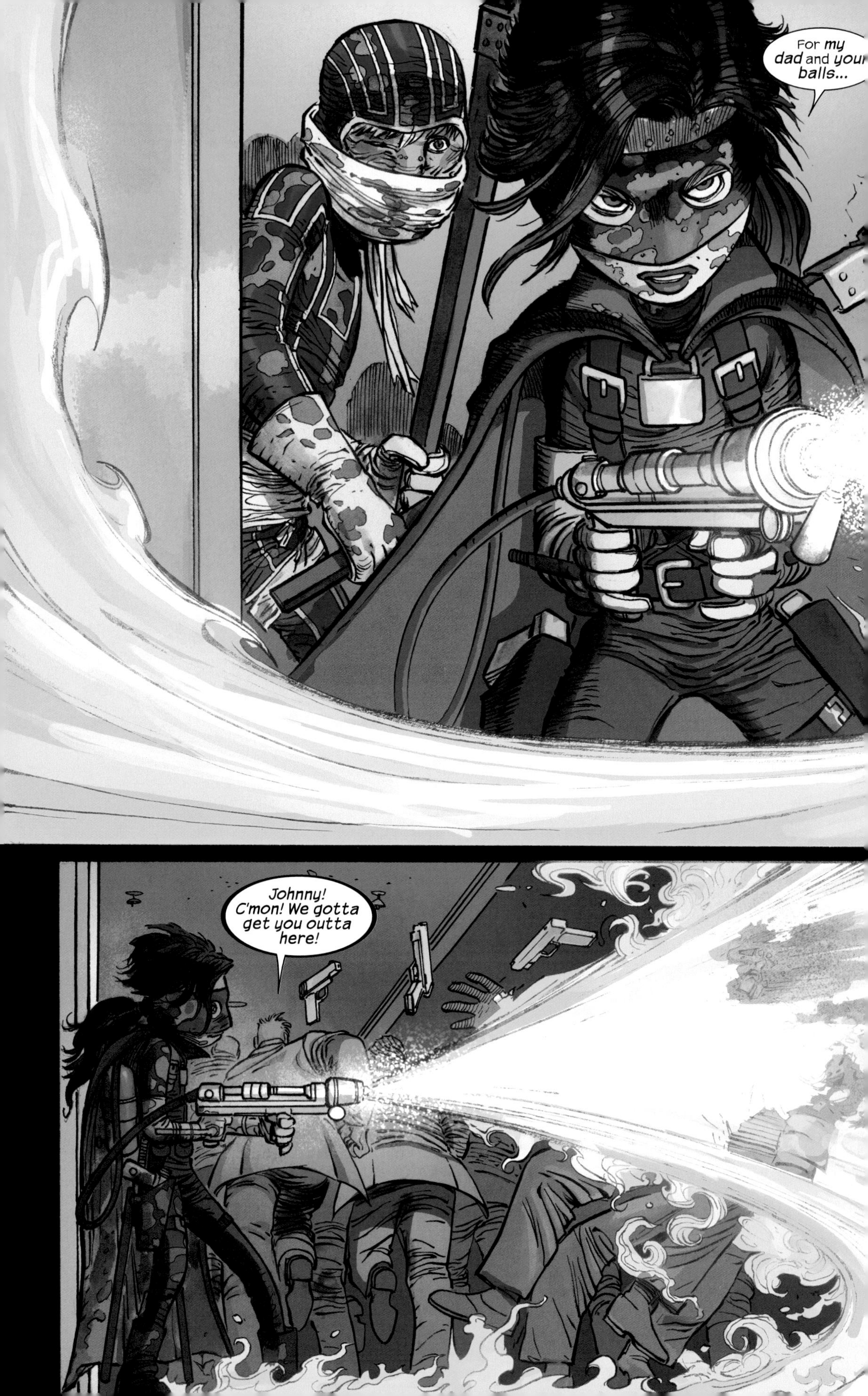
For my dad and your balls...
Johnny! C'mon! We gotta get you outta here!

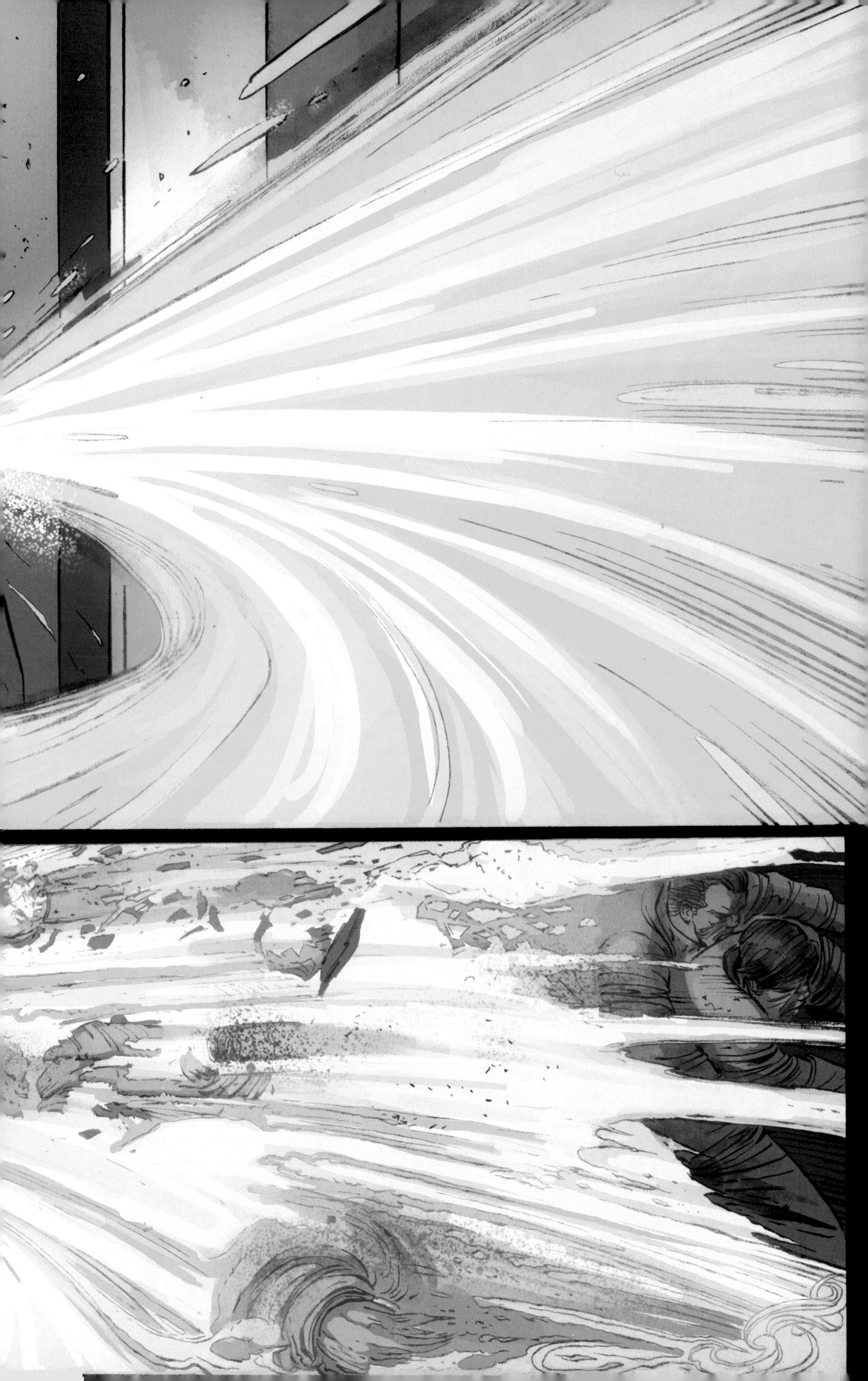

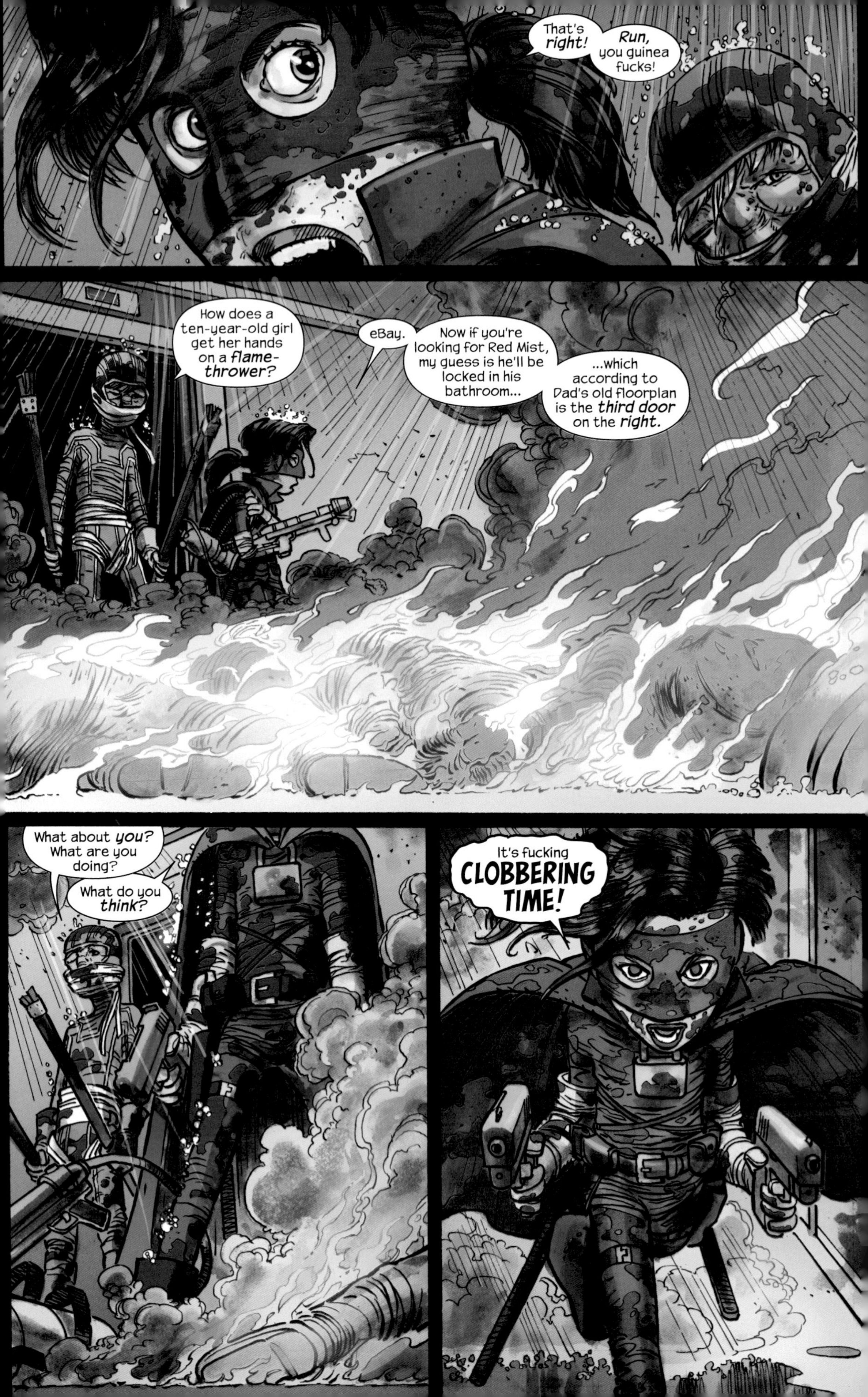

That's *right!*
Run, you guinea fucks!
How does a ten-year-old girl get her hands on a *flame-thrower?*
eBay.
Now if you're looking for Red Mist, my guess is he'll be locked in his bathroom...
...which according to Dad's old floorplan is the *third door* on the *right.*
What about *you?* What are you doing?
What do you *think?*
It's fucking **CLOBBERING TIME!**

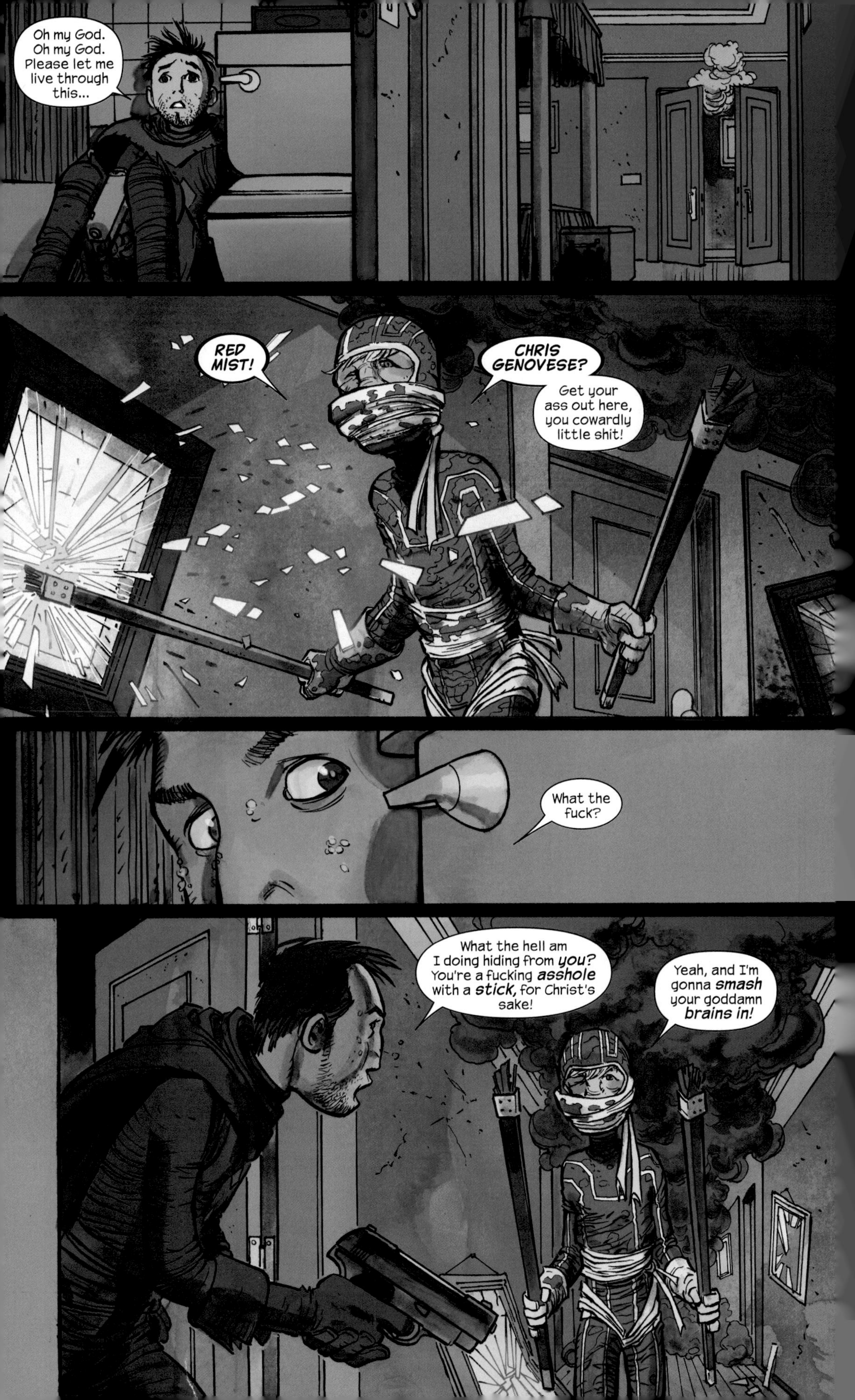
Oh my God. Oh my God. Please let me live through this...
RED MIST!
CHRIS GENOVESE?
Get your ass out here, you cowardly little shit!
What the fuck?
What the hell am I doing hiding from *you*? You're a fucking *asshole* with a *stick*, for Christ's sake!
Yeah, and I'm gonna *smash* your goddamn *brains in!*

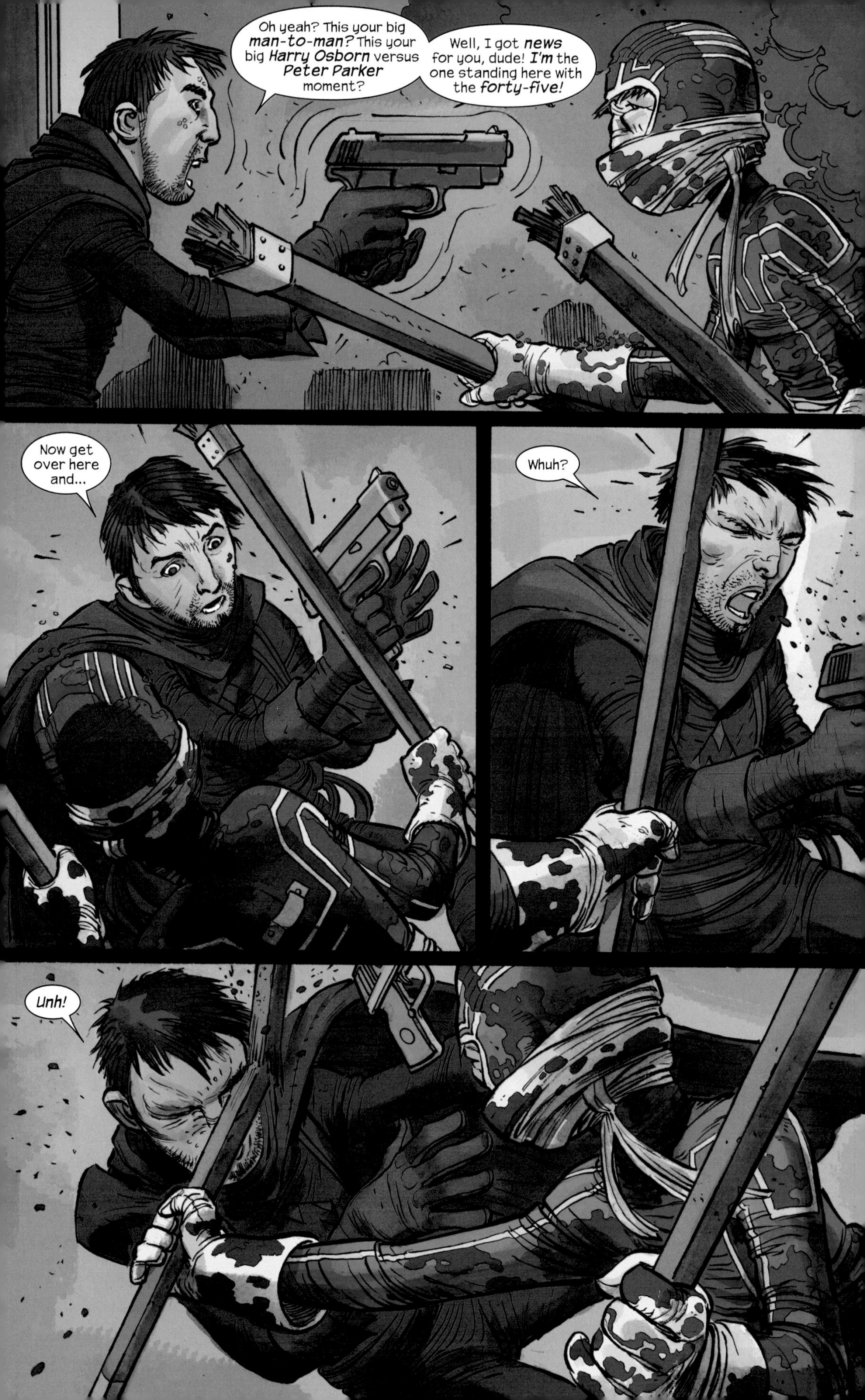
Oh yeah? This your big man-to-man? This your big Harry Osborn versus Peter Parker moment?
Well, I got news for you, dude! I'm the one standing here with the forty-five!
Now get over here and...
Whuh?
Unh!

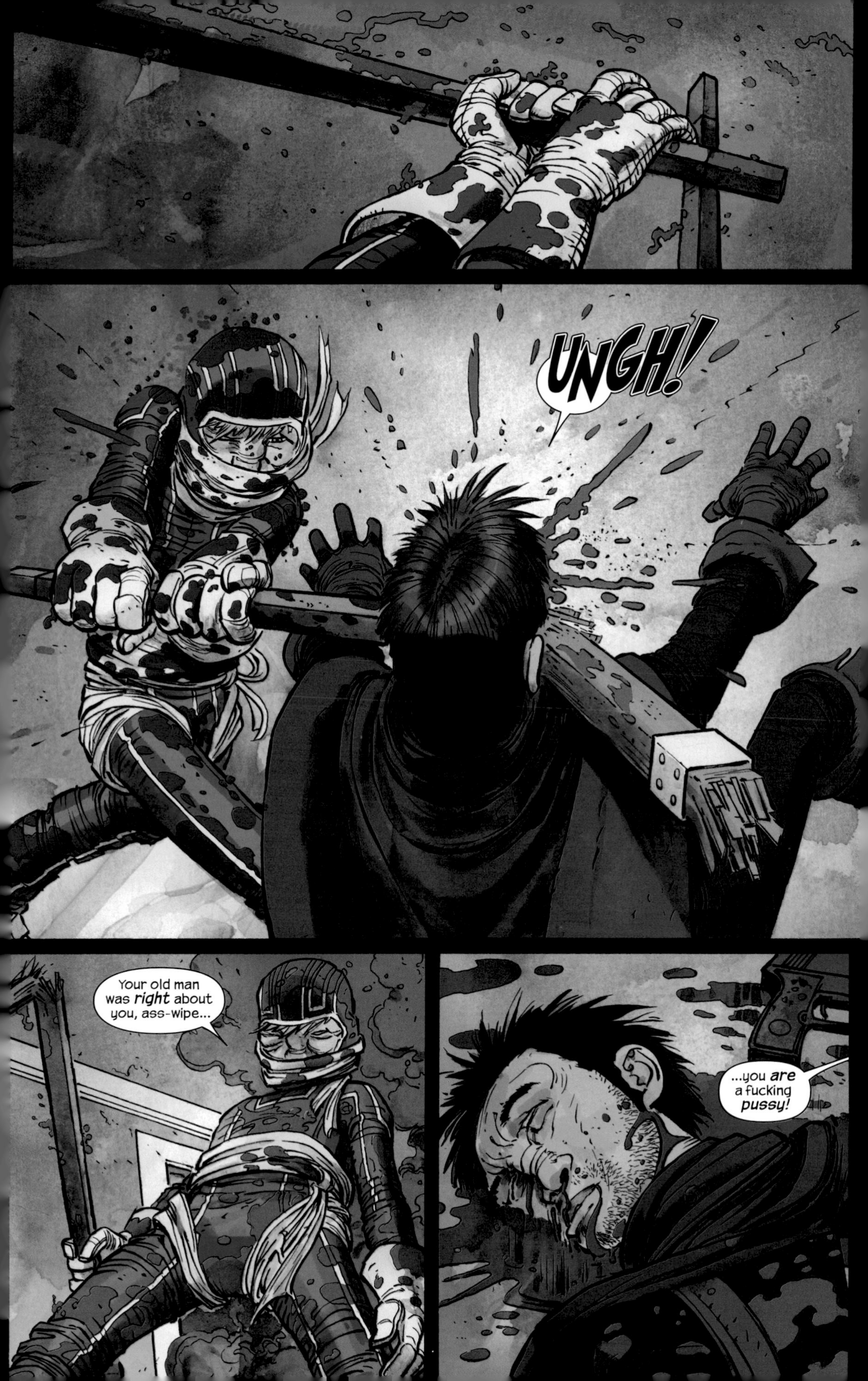
UNGH!
Your old man was right about you, ass-wipe...
...you are a fucking pussy!

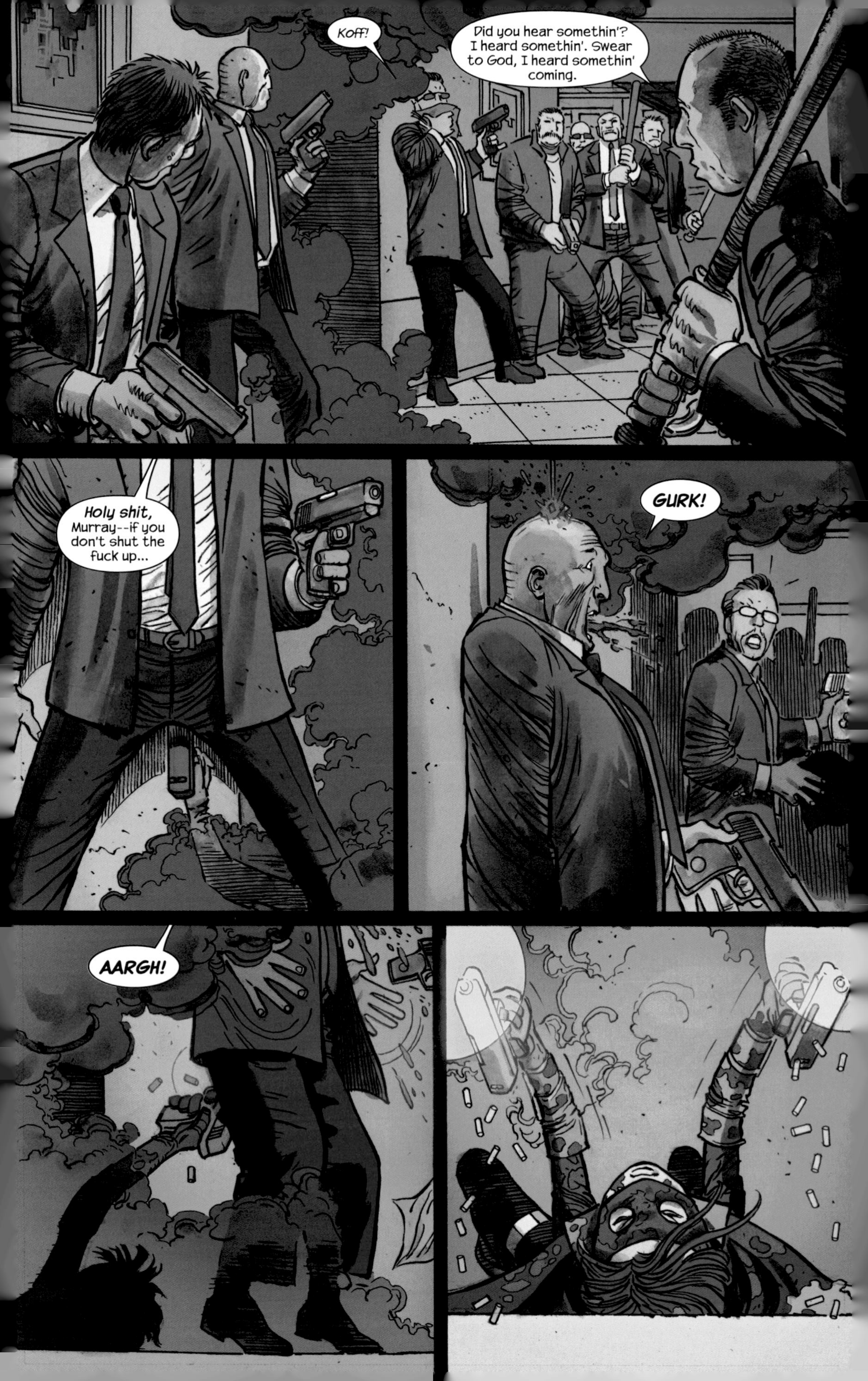
Koff!
Did you hear somethin'? I heard somethin'. Swear to God, I heard somethin' coming.
Holy shit, Murray--if you don't shut the fuck up...
GURK!
AARGH!

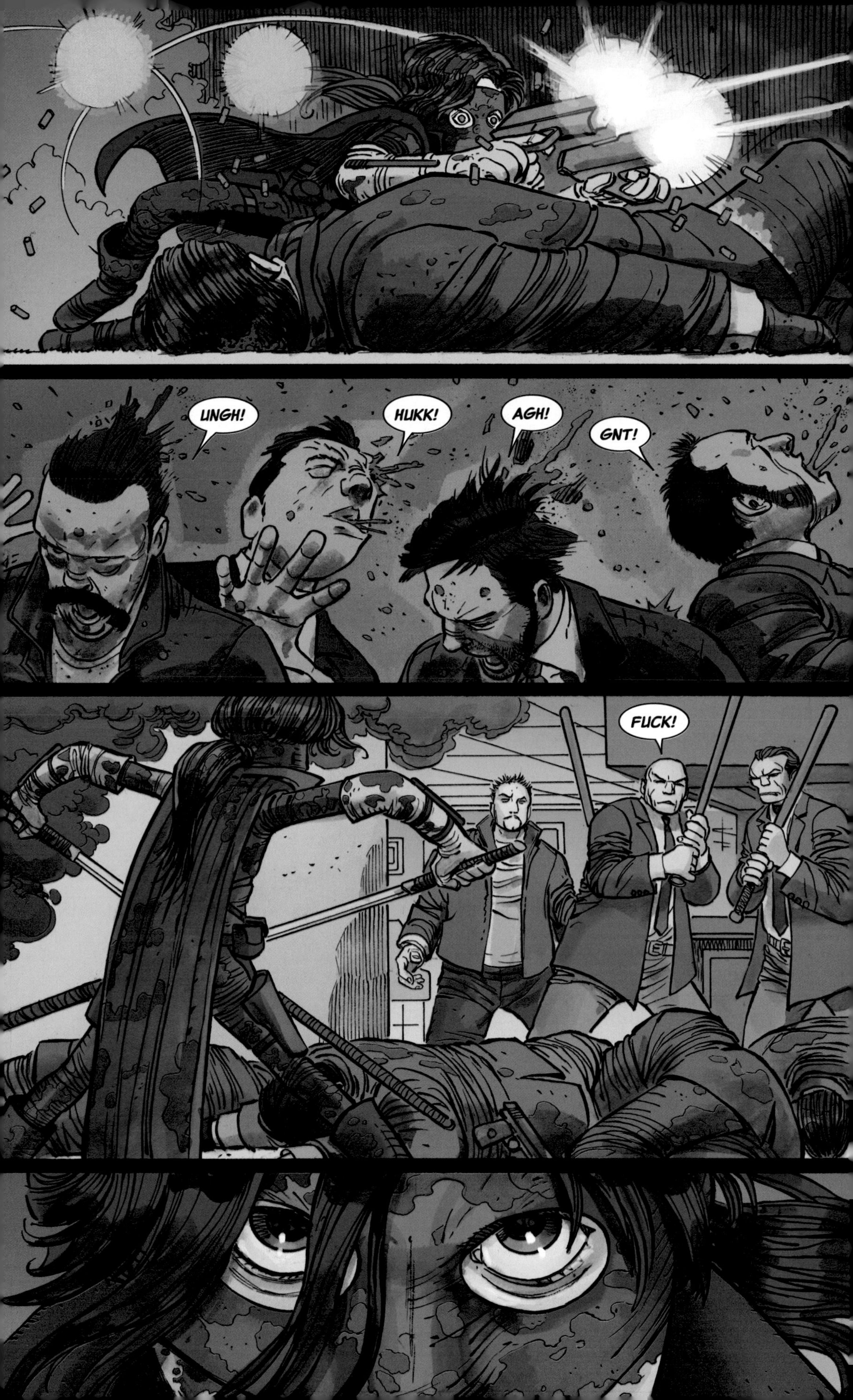
UNGH!
HUKK!
AGH!
GNT!
FUCK!

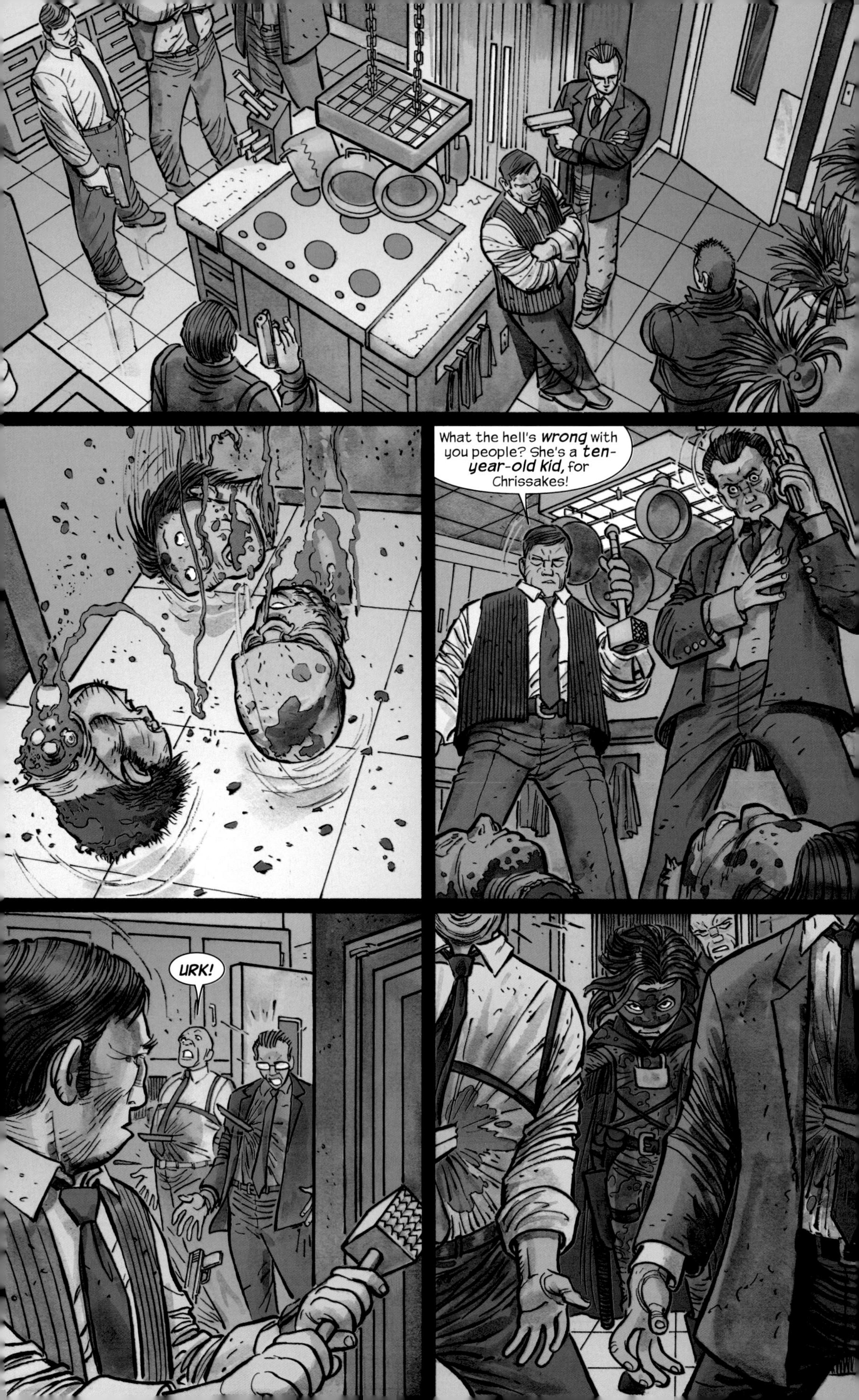
What the hell's *wrong* with you people? She's a *ten-year-old kid,* for Chrissakes!
URK!

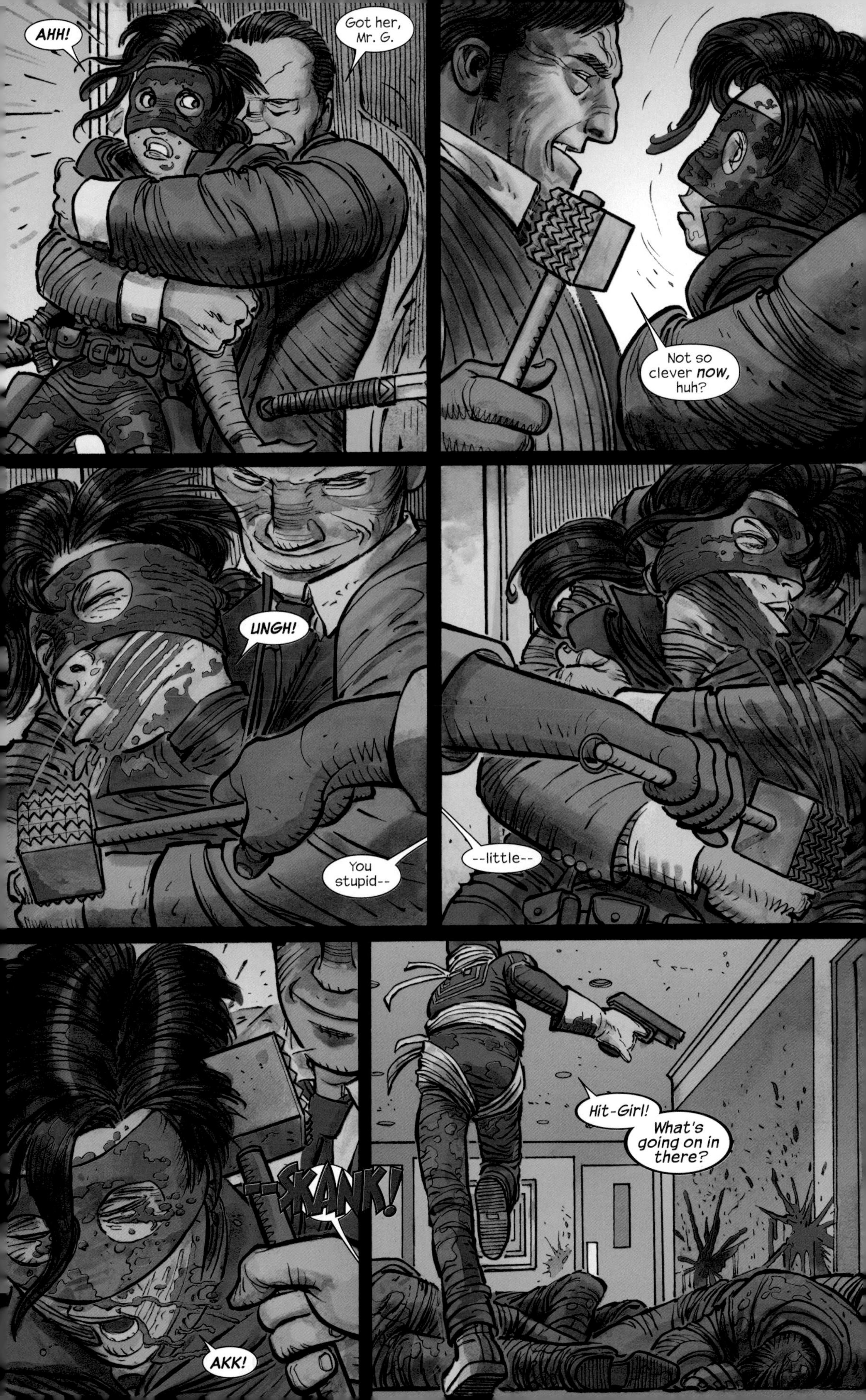
AHH!
Got her, Mr. G.
Not so clever NOW, huh?
UNGH!
You stupid--
--little--
--SKANK!
AKK!
Hit-Girl!
What's going on in there?

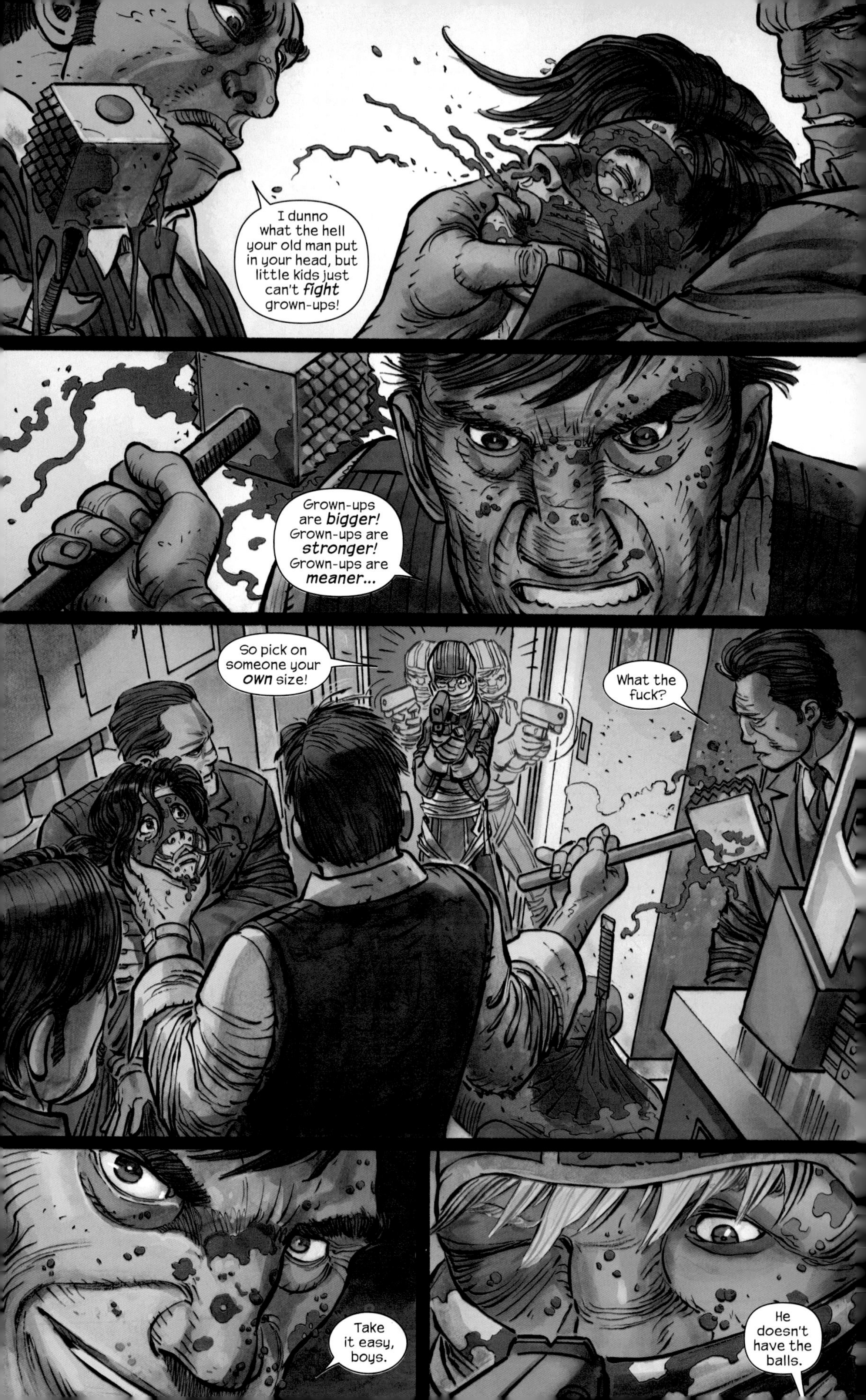
I dunno what the hell your old man put in your head, but little kids just can't *fight* grown-ups!
Grown-ups are *bigger!* Grown-ups are *stronger!* Grown-ups are *meaner...*
So pick on someone your *own* size!
What the fuck?
Take it easy, boys.
He doesn't have the balls.

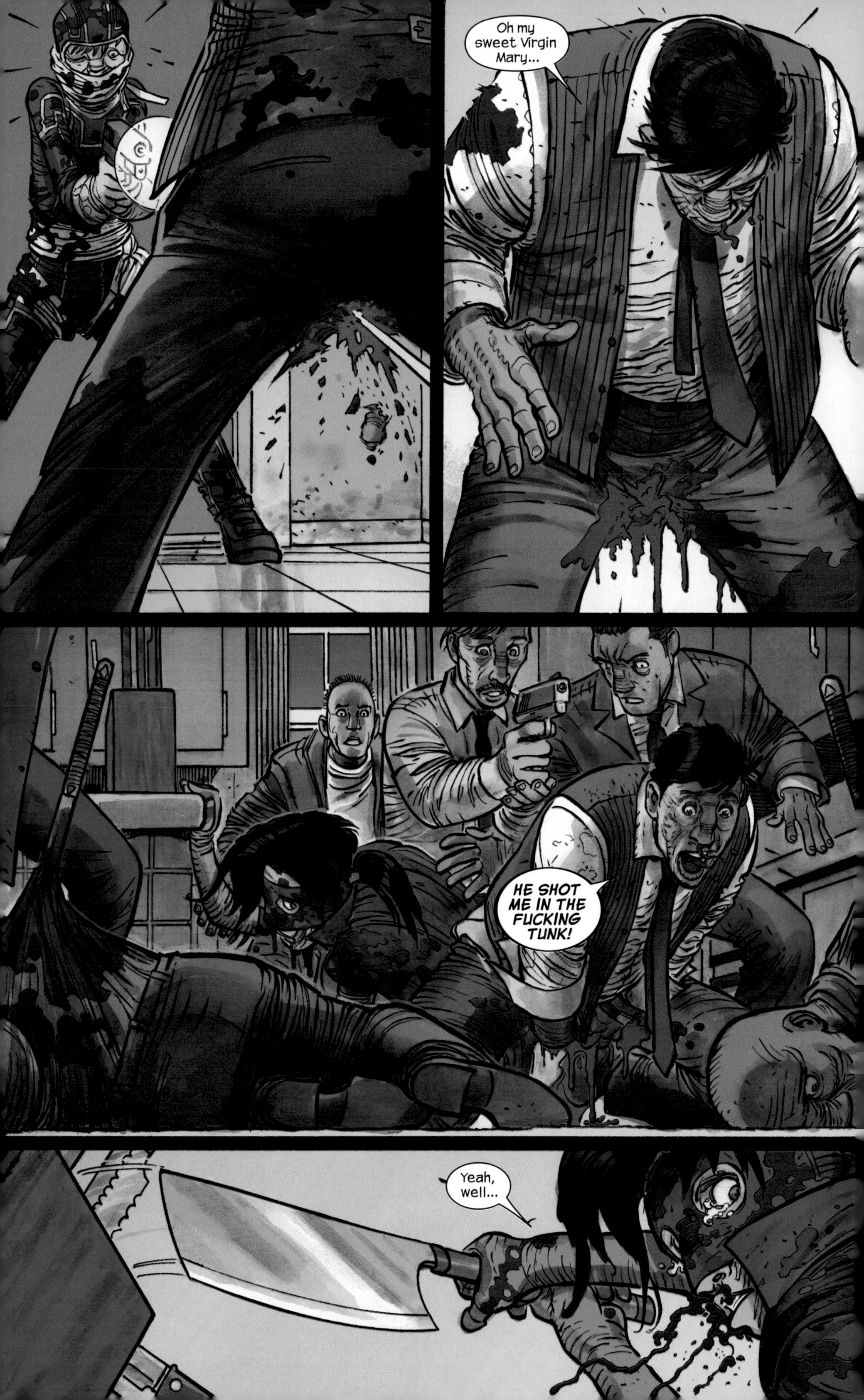
Oh my sweet Virgin Mary...
HE SHOT ME IN THE FUCKING TUNK!
Yeah, well...

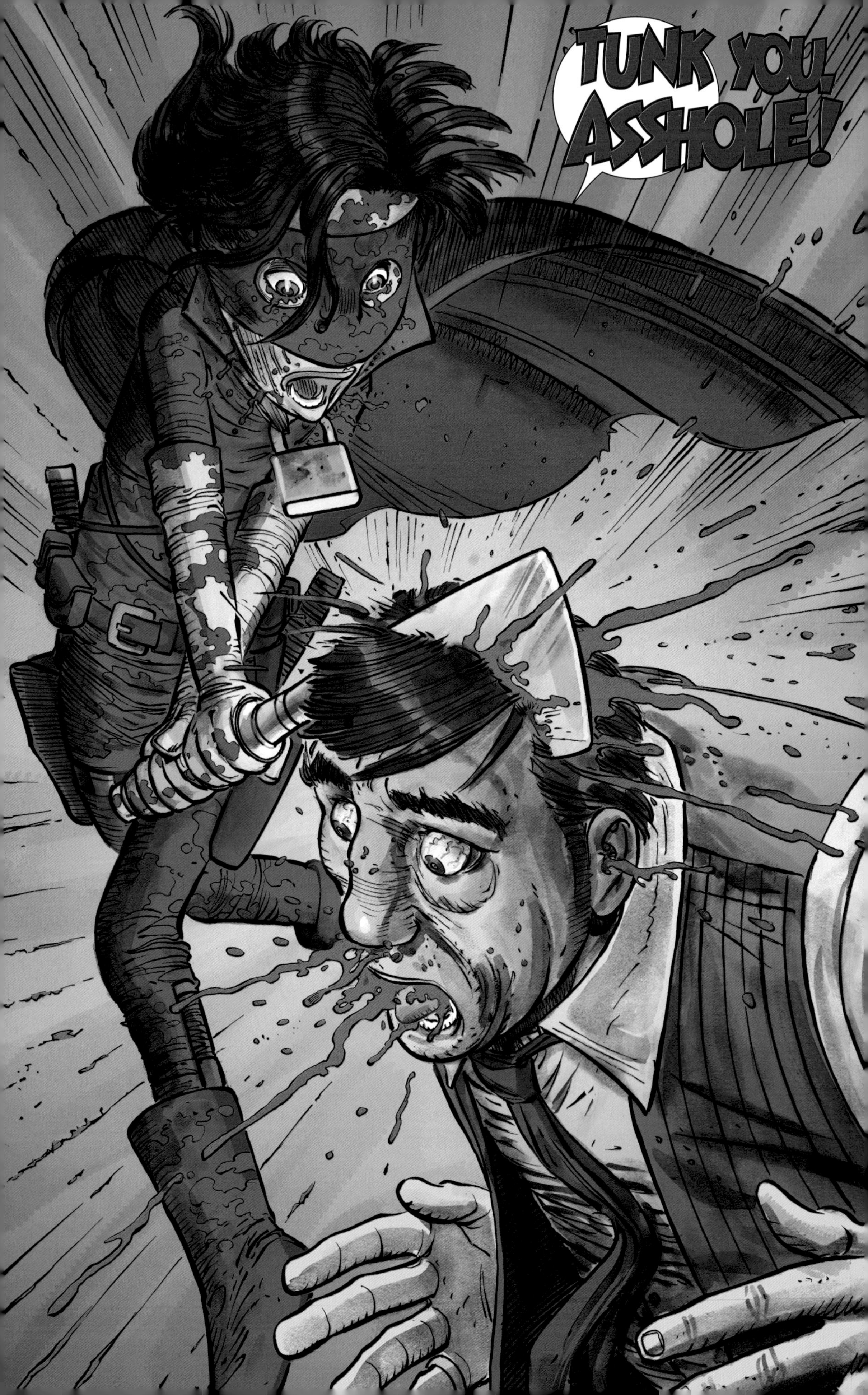
TUNK YOU, ASSHOLE!

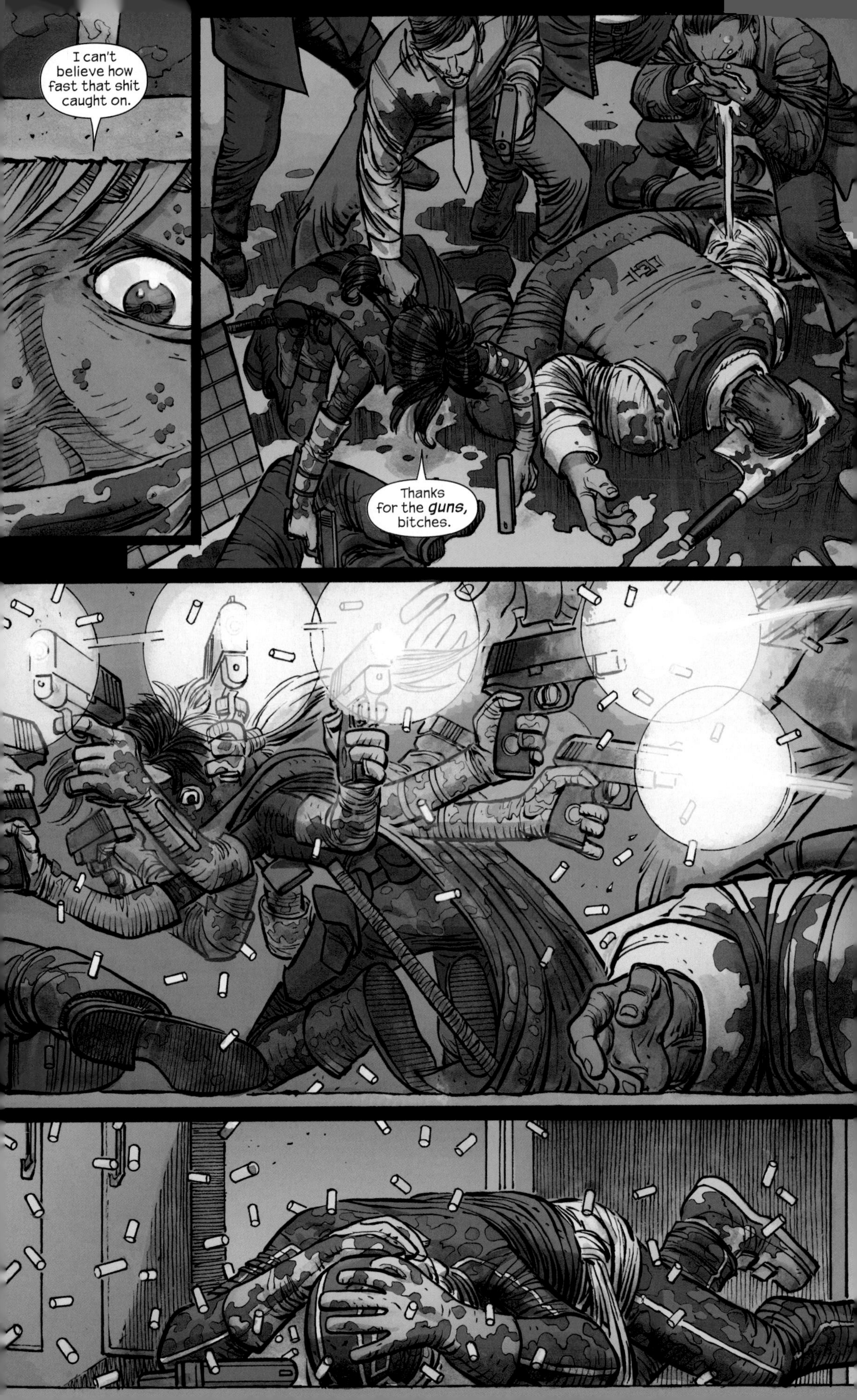
I can't believe how fast that shit caught on.
Thanks for the guns, bitches.

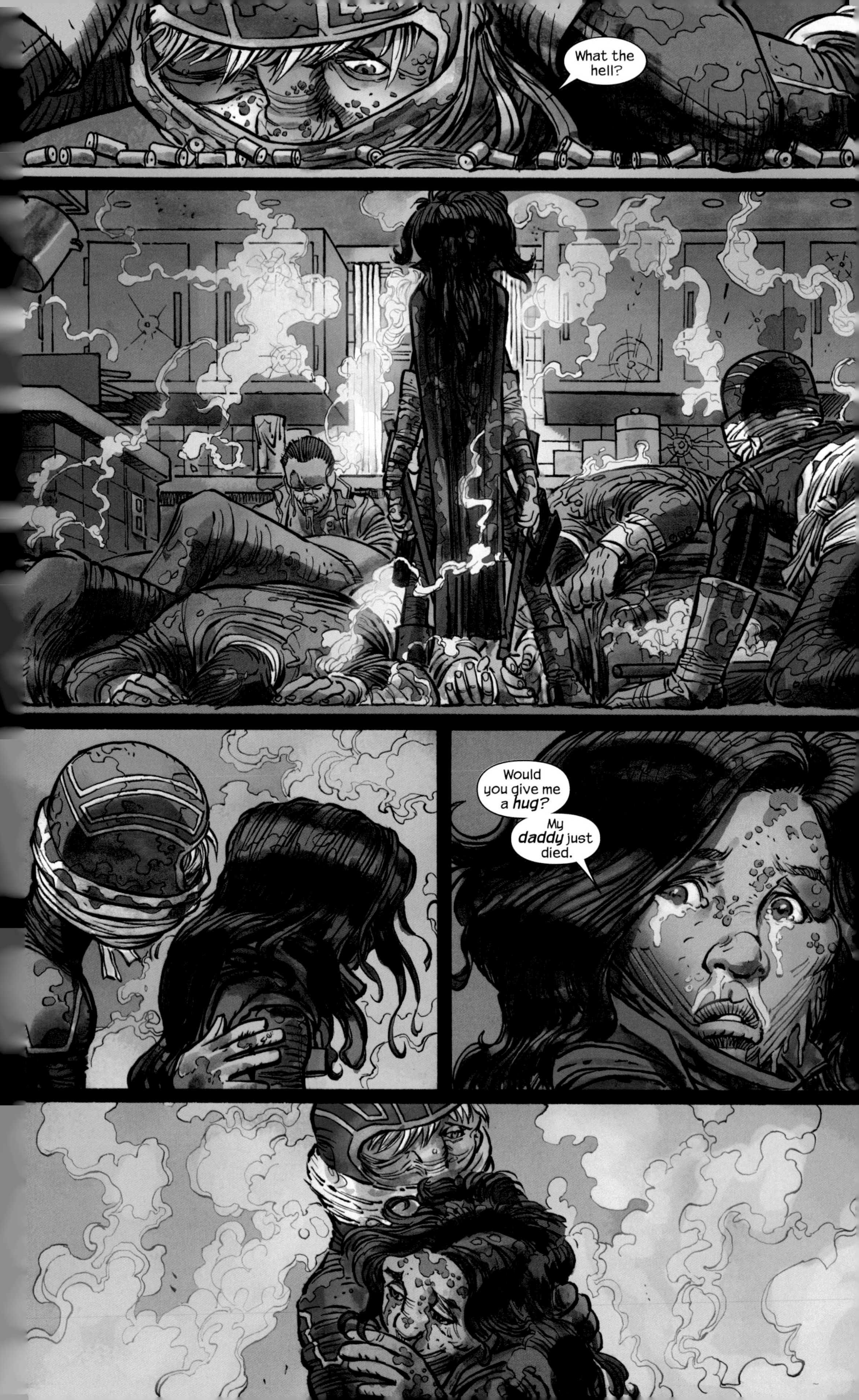
What the hell?
Would you give me a *hug*?
My *daddy* just died.

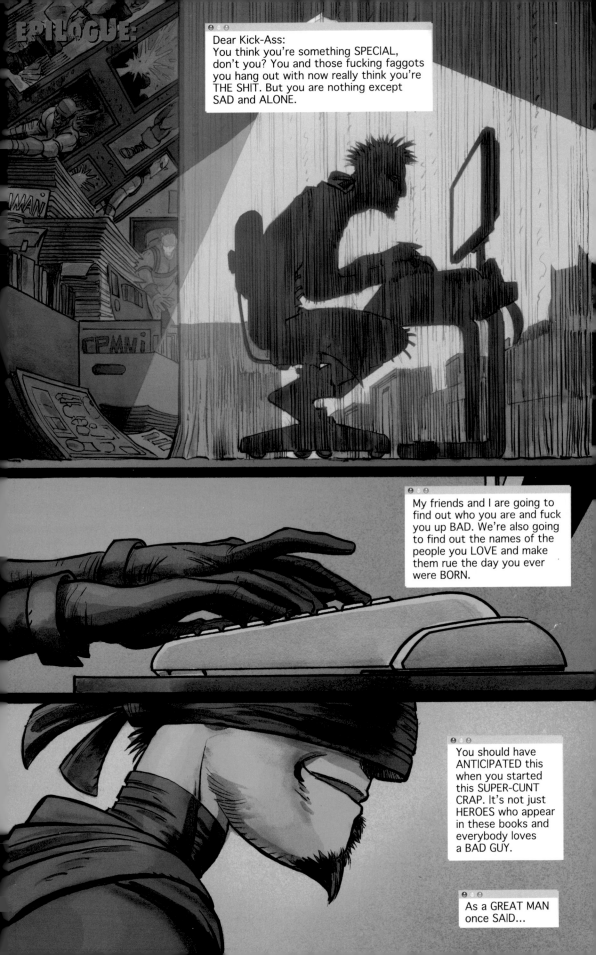

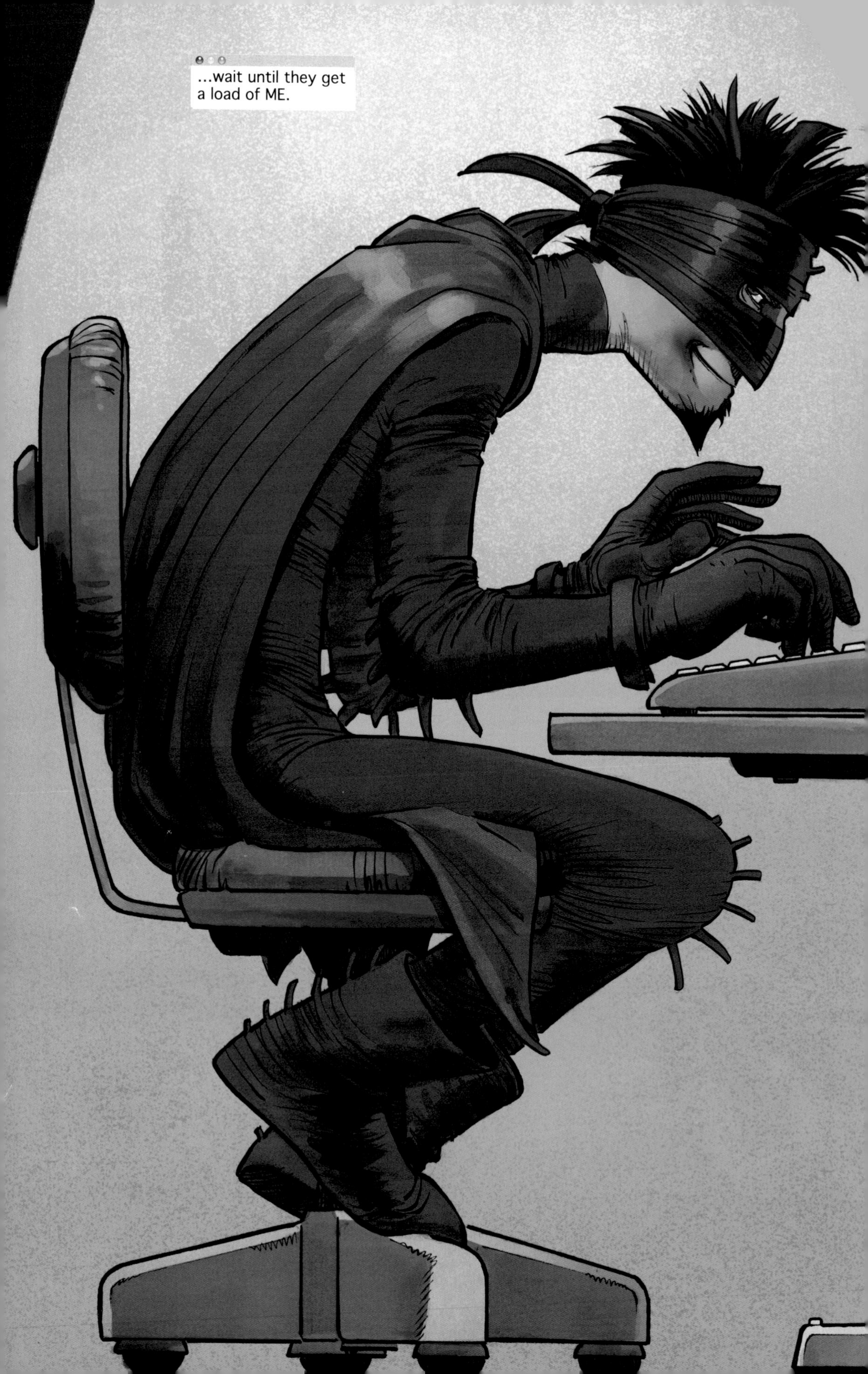
...wait until they get a load of ME.

END OF BOOK ONE

MARK MILLAR has been one of the key writers for Marvel Comics in the 21st century. Millar's first major contribution to Marvel was *Ultimate X-Men*, which achieved great creative and commercial success throughout his two-year run. Working with artist Bryan Hitch on *The Ultimates*, Millar surpassed his own success with that commercial and critical darling. Next, joining up with some of the industry's top creative talent, the Scottish writer took on two of Marvel's most iconic characters: Spider-Man and Wolverine. While working on creator-owned books like *Wanted*, turned into a Hollywood blockbuster staring Angelina Jolie, he penned *Civil War*, the epic miniseries that definitively reshaped the landscape of Marvel's heroes. More recently, Millar has reunited with Hitch on *Fantastic Four* and with *Civil War* artist Steve McNiven in both the pages of *Wolverine* and the upcoming *Nemesis*, as well as returning to the Ultimate Universe with *Ultimate Avengers*.

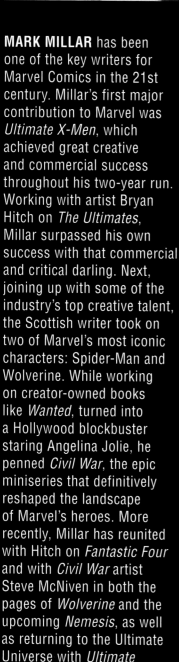

JOHN ROMITA JR. is a modern-day comic-art legend. A loyal Marvel artist since the late '70s, he has followed in his father's footsteps and helped keep the Romita name on the list of top-shelf talent. Timeless runs on *Iron Man*, *Uncanny X-Men*, *Amazing Spider-Man*, and *Daredevil* helped establish him as his own man artistically, and his art on *Wolverine* is arguably the decade's most explosive comic art—trumped perhaps only by his own work on the massive summer blockbuster event *World War Hulk*. JRJR has also paired with renowned writer Neil Gaiman for *The Eternals*, their reworking of the classic Marvel Comics characters, and has recently returned to *Amazing Spider-Man*; he will follow that up with another high-profile Marvel series.

TOM PALMER has worked as an illustrator in the advertising and editorial fields, but he has spent the majority of his career in comic books. His first assignment, fresh out of art school, was on *Doctor Strange*, and he has gone on to lend his inking talents to many of Marvel's top titles, including *X-Men, The Avengers, Tomb of Dracula*, and more recently *Punisher, Hulk,* and *Ghost Rider.* He lives and works in New Jersey.

DEAN WHITE is one of the comic industry's best and most sought-after color artists. Well-known for his work on titles such as *The Amazing Spider-Man, Punisher, Dark Avengers, Captain America, Black Panther, Wolverine* and countless more, Dean's envelope-pushing rendering and color palette bring a sense of urgency and power to every page he touches.

CHRIS ELIOPOULOS is a multiple award-winner for his lettering, having worked on dozens of books during the twenty years he's been in the industry—including Erik Larsen's *Savage Dragon*, for which he hand-lettered the first 100 issues. Along with his success as a letterer, he also publishes his own strip *Misery Loves Sherman*, wrote and illustrated the popular *Franklin Richards: Son of a Genius* one-shots, and writes Marvel's *Lockjaw and the Pet Avengers* series.

MICHAEL HORWITZ's student thesis (a five minute documentary about the private lives of cabbages) was met with resounding indifference by NYU, forcing the Virginia native to realize a career in experimental film wasn't in the cards. With a résumé padded to the extreme (and omitting a regrettable excursion into the world of go-go dancing), Michael somehow fooled Marvel Comics into hiring him, where he now edits such titles as Laurell K. Hamilton's *Anita Blake* and Stephen King's *The Dark Tower*.

JOHN BARBER self-published his own comics before joining the world of webcomics, and later co-wrote a book called *Webcomics*, with Steven Withrow. In 2003, Barber joined the Marvel Comics editorial team and became editor of the Wolverine franchise, before leaving to pursue a freelance career— including a return to comics on the web (webcomicsnation. com/thejohnbarber). He stuck around on *Kick-Ass*, though, which is a hell of a way to go out, editorially speaking.

KICK-ASS'S GREATEST HITS

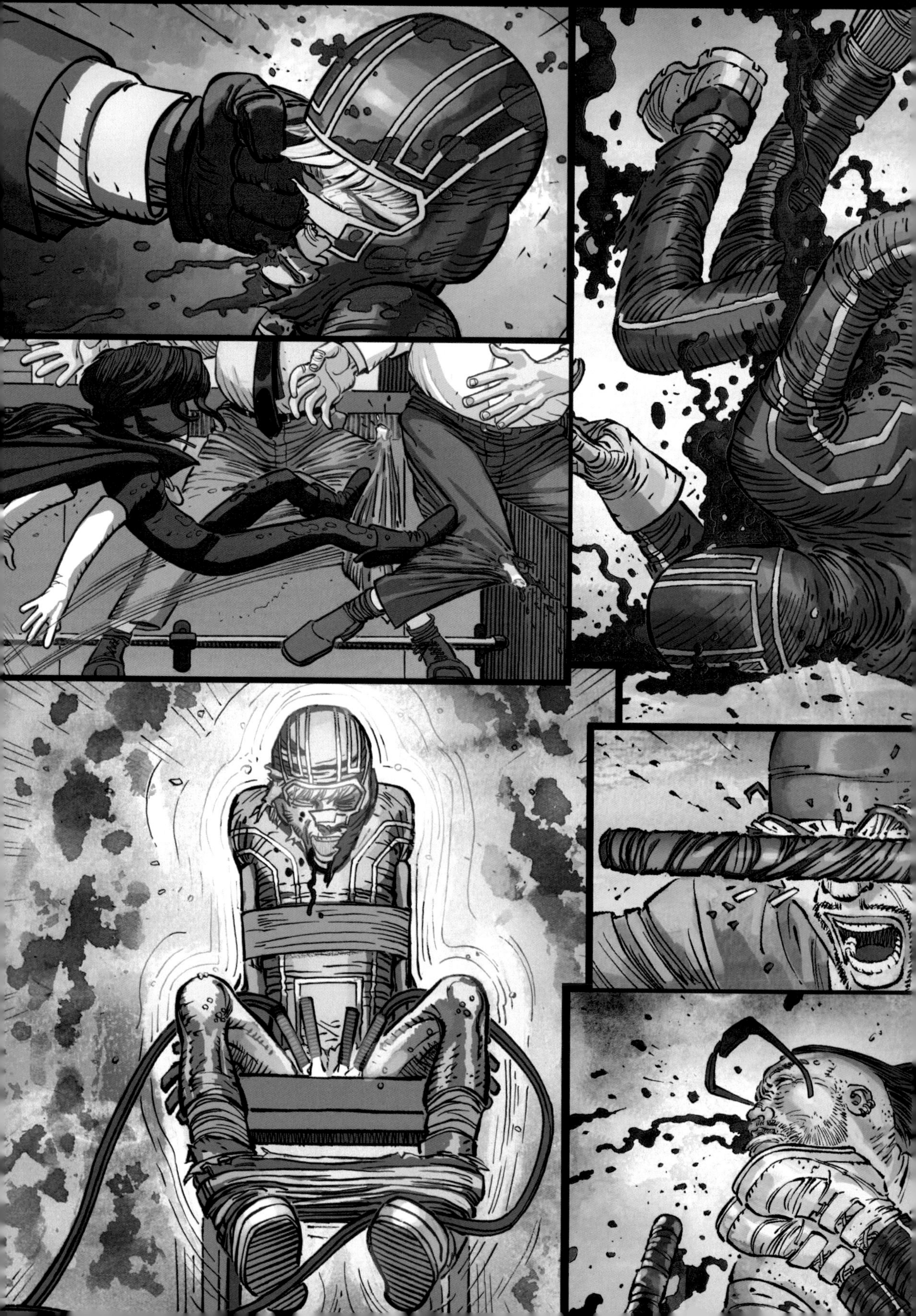

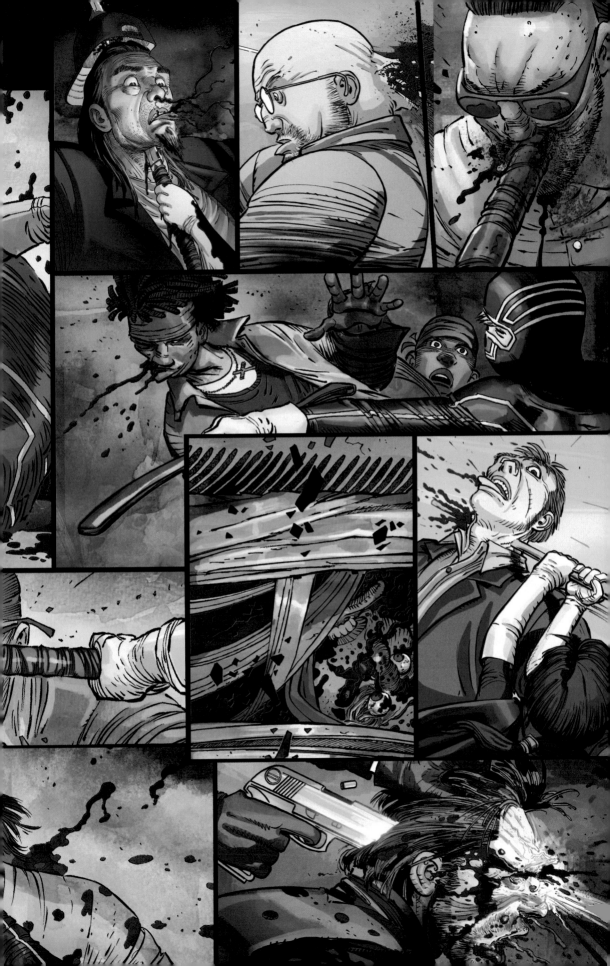

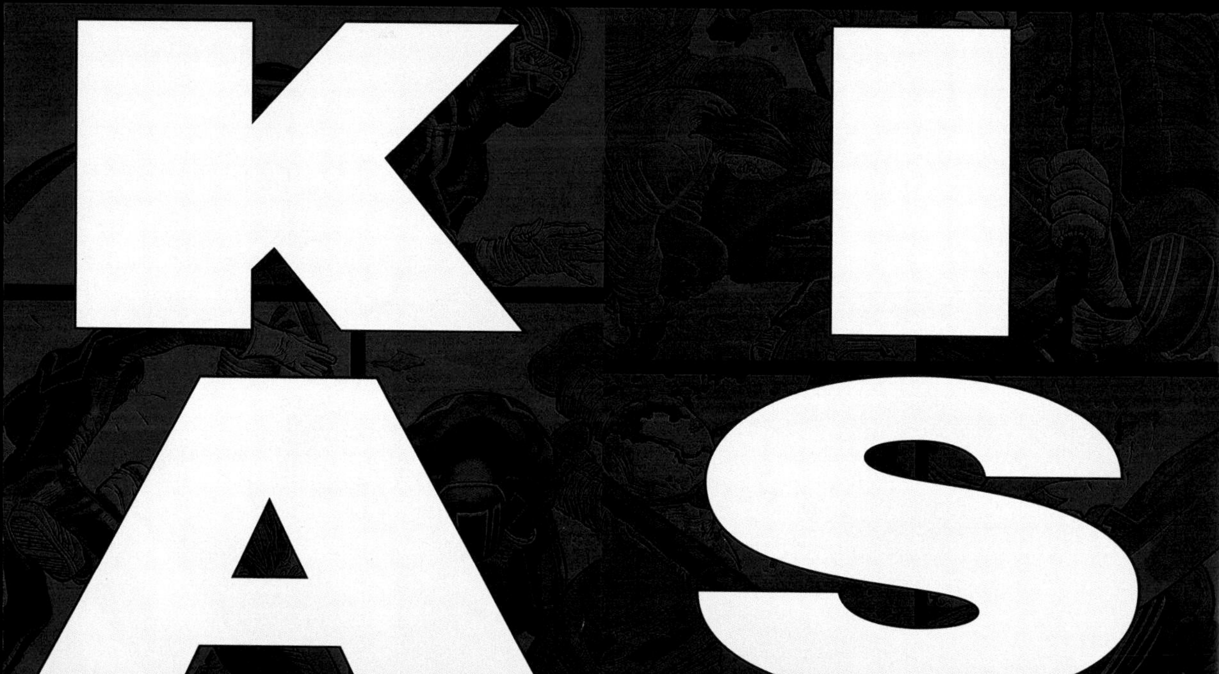
KI
AS

COMBINED COVERS FOR ISSUE #1 6TH PRINTING, #2 4TH PRINTING, #3 4TH PRINTING AND #4 3RD PRINTING

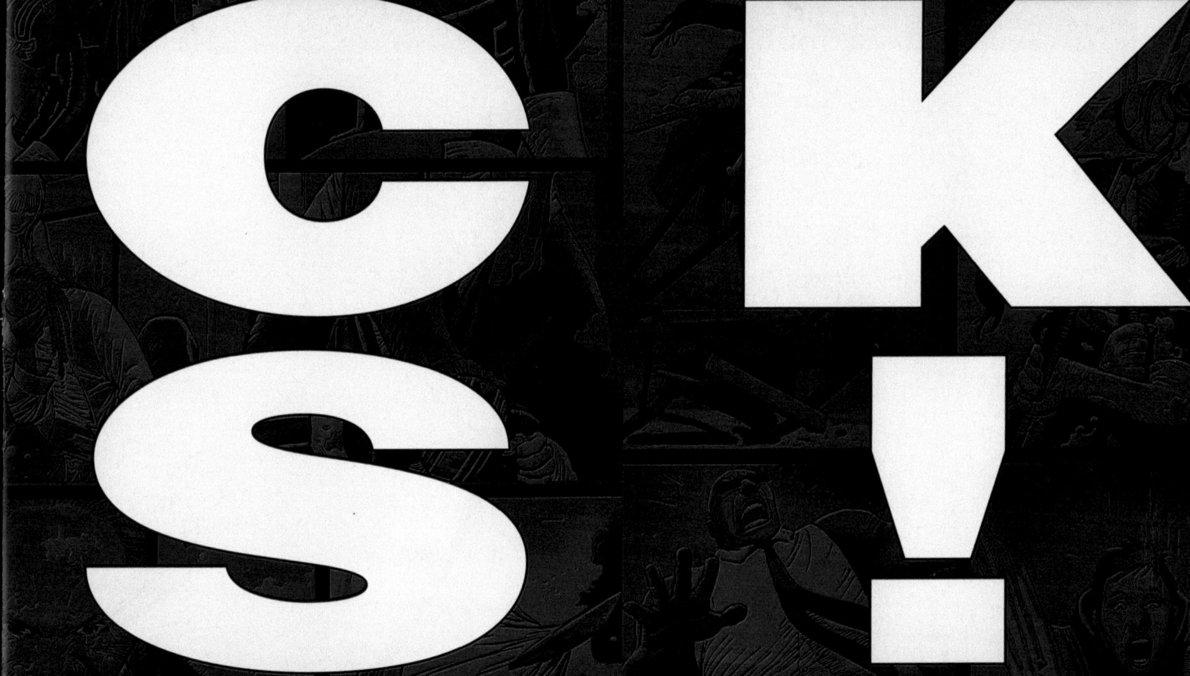
CK
S!

ONE (VARIANT BY MCNIVEN)

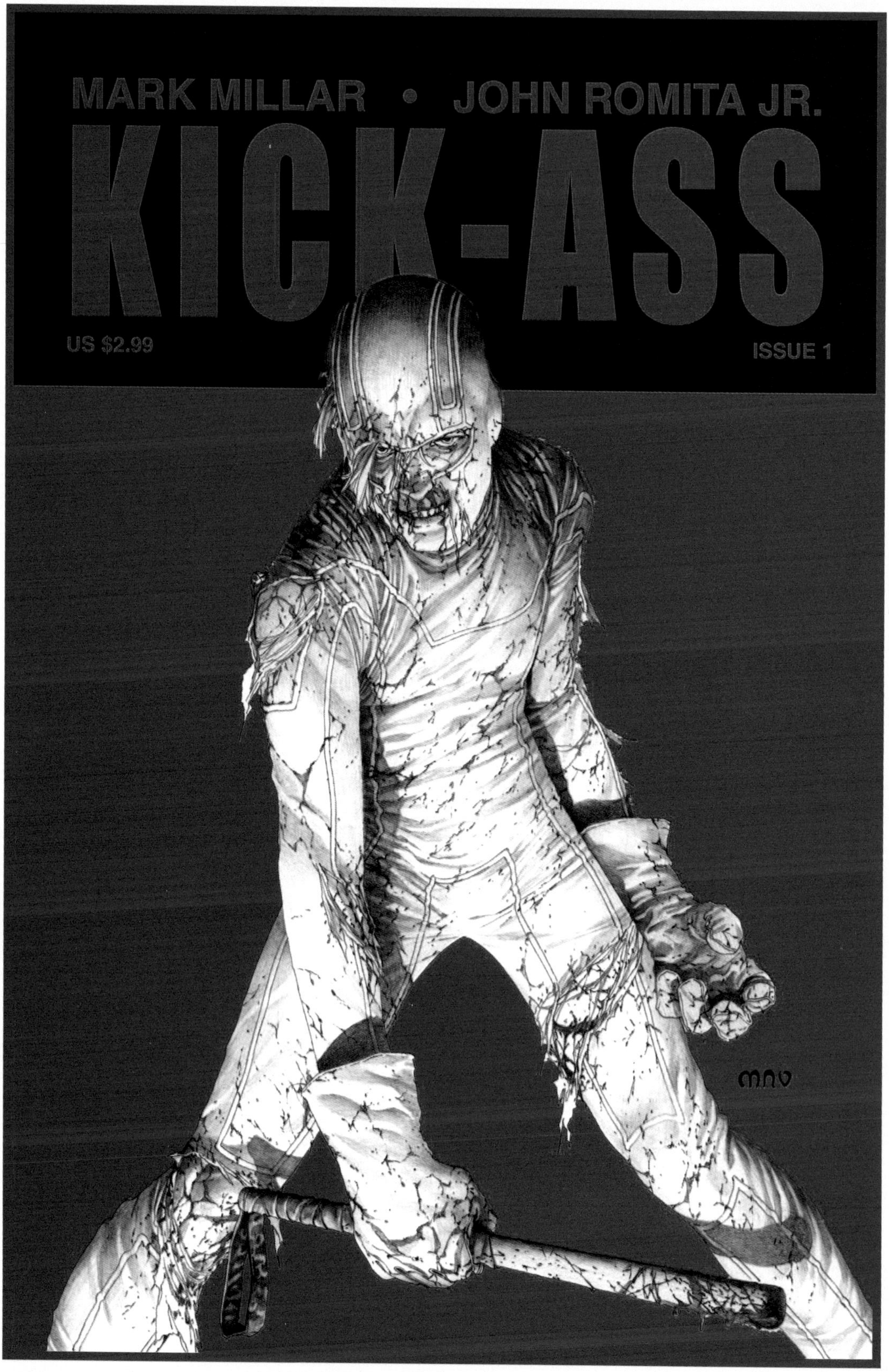
MARK MILLAR • JOHN ROMITA JR.
KICK-ASS
US $2.99
ISSUE 1
mnv

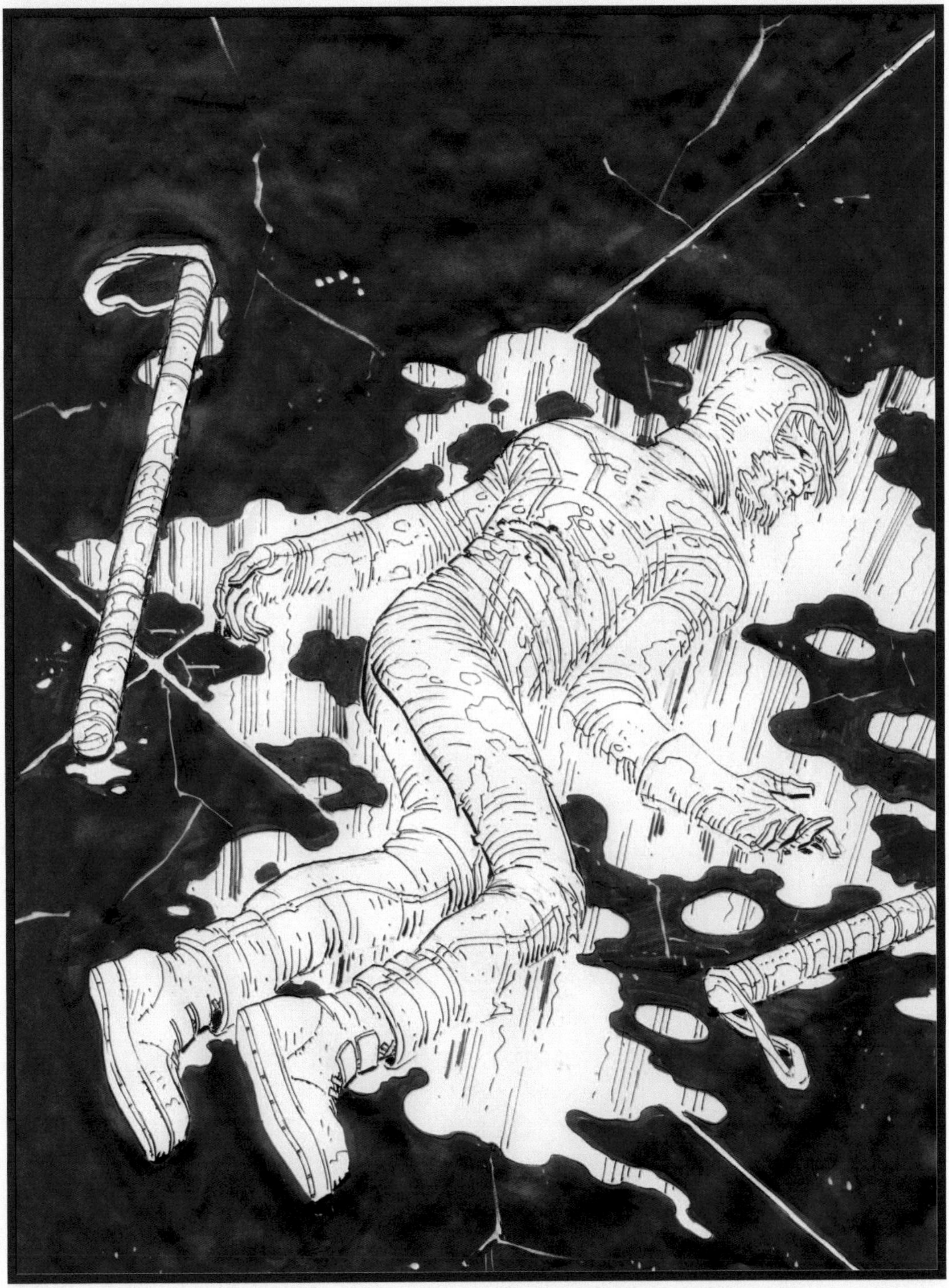

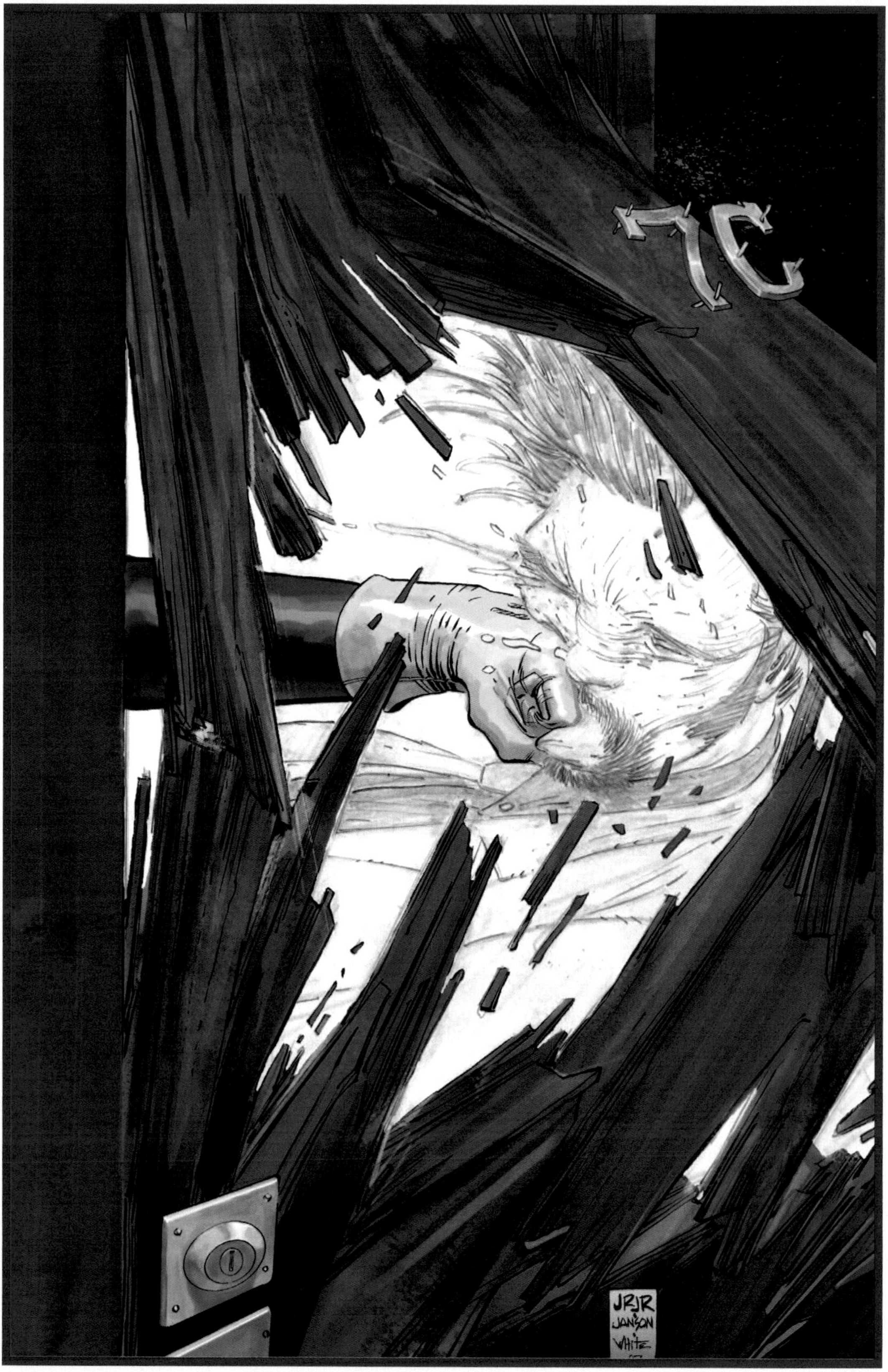
JRJR
JANSON
WHITE

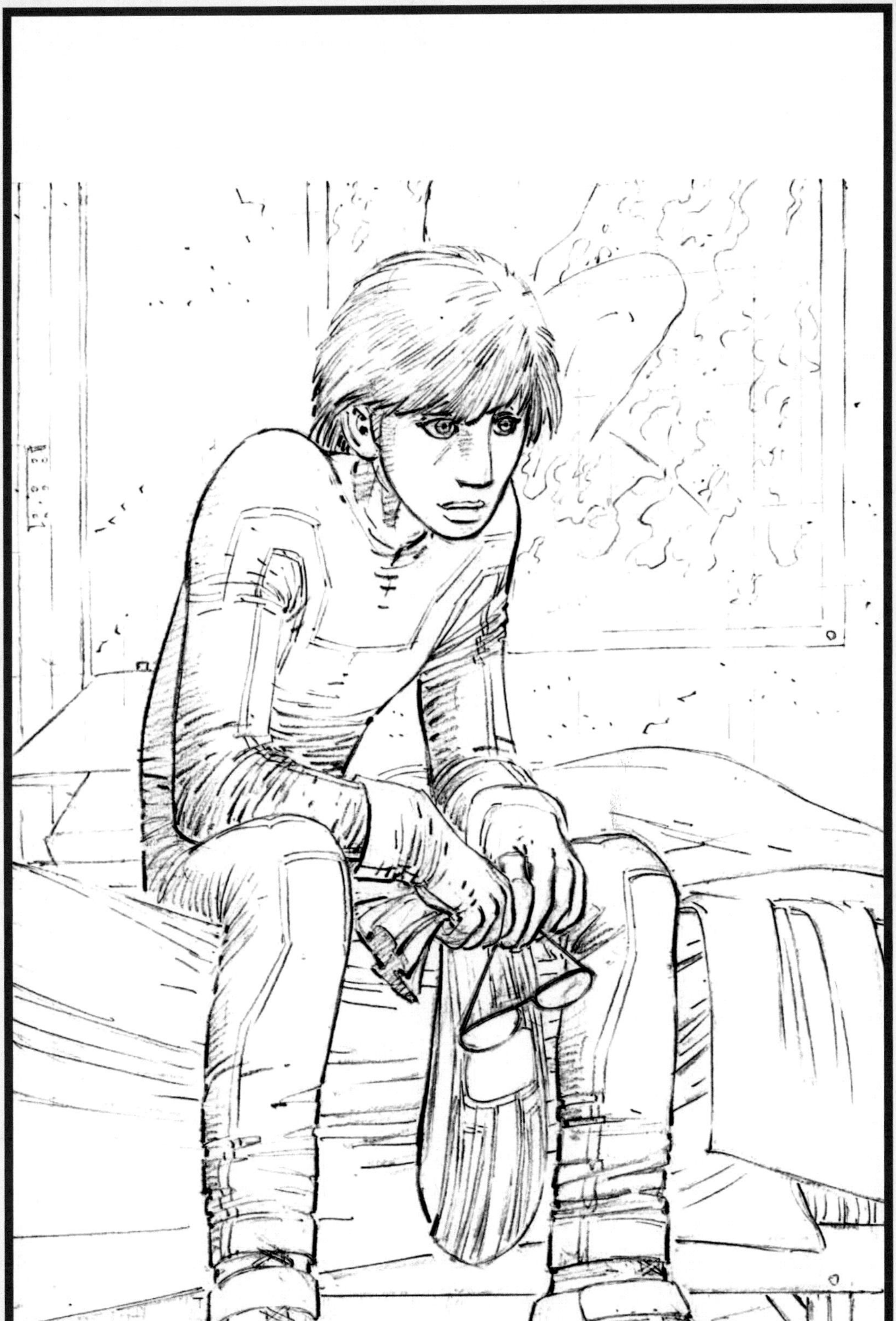

KICK-ASS

THE MOVIE

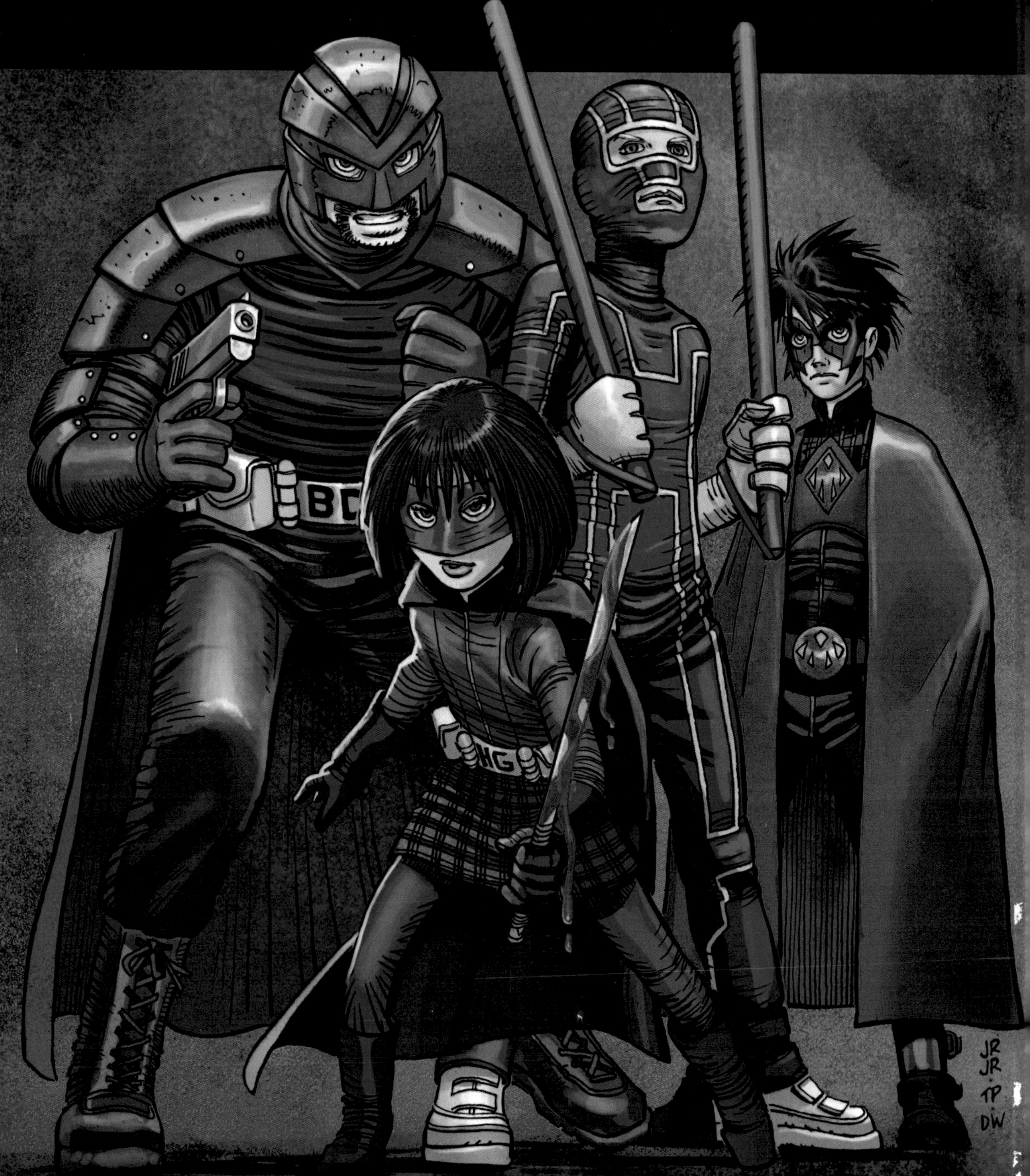

BD
HG
JR JR TP DW

COMING SOON